William Henry Fremantle

The World As the Subject of Redemption

Being an attempt to set forth the functions of the Church as designed to embrace the whole race of mankind. Eight lectures

William Henry Fremantle

The World As the Subject of Redemption
Being an attempt to set forth the functions of the Church as designed to embrace the whole race of mankind. Eight lectures

ISBN/EAN: 9783337000042

Printed in Europe, USA, Canada, Australia, Japan

Cover: Foto ©Lupo / pixelio.de

More available books at **www.hansebooks.com**

THE WORLD

AS

THE SUBJECT OF REDEMPTION

THE WORLD

AS THE

SUBJECT OF REDEMPTION

BEING

AN ATTEMPT TO SET FORTH THE FUNCTIONS OF THE CHURCH
AS DESIGNED TO EMBRACE THE WHOLE RACE
OF MANKIND

EIGHT LECTURES DELIVERED BEFORE THE UNIVERSITY
OF OXFORD IN THE YEAR 1883

ON THE FOUNDATION OF THE LATE REV. JOHN BAMPTON, M.A.
CANON OF SALISBURY

BY THE HON. AND REV.

W. H. FREMANTLE, M.A.

CANON OF CANTERBURY
AND FELLOW OF BALLIOL COLLEGE, OXFORD

RIVINGTONS
WATERLOO PLACE, LONDON

M DCCC LXXXV

Oxford
PRINTED BY HORACE HART, PRINTER TO THE UNIVERSITY

EXTRACT

FROM THE LAST WILL AND TESTAMENT

OF THE LATE

REV. JOHN BAMPTON,

CANON OF SALISBURY.

—— "I GIVE and bequeath my Lands and Estates to the
" Chancellor, Masters, and Scholars of the University of
" Oxford for ever, to have and to hold all and singular the
" said Lands or Estates upon trust, and to the intents and
" purposes hereinafter mentioned; that is to say, I will and
" appoint that the Vice-Chancellor of the University of Ox-
" ford for the time being shall take and receive all the rents,
" issues, and profits thereof, and (after all taxes, reparations,
" and necessary deductions made) that he pay all the re-
" mainder to the endowment of eight Divinity Lecture Ser-
" mons, to be established for ever in the said University, and
" to be performed in the manner following:

" I direct and appoint, that, upon the first Tuesday in
" Easter Term, a Lecturer be yearly chosen by the Heads
" of Colleges only, and by no others, in the room adjoining
" to the Printing-House, between the hours of ten in the
" morning and two in the afternoon, to preach eight Divinity
" Lecture Sermons, the year following, at St. Mary's in Ox-
" ford, between the commencement of the last month in Lent
" Term, and the end of the third week in Act Term.

Extract from Canon Bampton's Will.

"Also I direct and appoint, that the eight Divinity Lecture
"Sermons shall be preached on either of the following Sub-
"jects—to confirm and establish the Christian Faith, and to
"confute all heretics and schismatics—upon the divine au-
"thority of the holy Scriptures—upon the authority of the
"writings of the primitive Fathers, as to the faith and prac-
"tice of the primitive Church—upon the Divinity of our Lord
"and Saviour Jesus Christ—upon the Divinity of the Holy
"Ghost—upon the Articles of the Christian Faith, as compre-
"hended in the Apostles' and Nicene Creeds.

"Also I direct, that thirty copies of the eight Divinity Lec-
"ture Sermons shall be always printed, within two months
"after they are preached; and one copy shall be given to the
"Chancellor of the University, and one copy to the Head of
"every College, and one copy to the Mayor of the city of
"Oxford, and one copy to be put into the Bodleian Library;
"and the expense of printing them shall be paid out of the
"revenue of the Land or Estates given for establishing the
"Divinity Lecture Sermons; and the Preacher shall not be
"paid, nor be entitled to the revenue, before they are
"printed.

"Also I direct and appoint, that no person shall be quali-
"fied to preach the Divinity Lecture Sermons, unless he hath
"taken the degree of Master of Arts at least, in one of the
"two Universities of Oxford or Cambridge; and that the
"same person shall never preach the Divinity Lecture Ser-
"mons twice."

PREFACE.

THE publication of these Lectures has been delayed through my having to take up new work at Canterbury and at Oxford immediately after their delivery. I do not think it right to delay it longer; but I am conscious that the Lectures still bear in some respects the marks of insufficient care.

In a work which takes in so large a range of history it is hardly possible that there should not be some mistakes of fact or inference, which will be noticed as blemishes by those who have made special periods their study, or who have been able to devote more time to historical pursuits than has been possible to me. But I have endeavoured to verify each statement which I have made, and to give references to the facts and to the books in which they may be found.

In the formation of the views which I have set forth in the Lectures I have received considerable help from the works of Dr. Arnold, and the Theological Ethics of Richard Rothe. There are points, however, in which I differ from the conclusions of those great teachers, and I have indicated my dissent from one main position of Rothe's (p. 333, and Appendix, Note XX). Having formed my views on the subject of these Lectures early in life, I have been able to test them, not only by reading various authors who have touched upon the subject, but by constantly endeavouring to apply my views to the discussions of the last thirty years, and above all to the conduct of active parochial work during nearly the whole of that period. I commend them therefore to my readers, not merely as a plausible theory, but as the expression of convictions which have stood the test of experience.

W. H. FREMANTLE.

BALLIOL COLLEGE, OXFORD,
January, 1885.

ANALYTICAL TABLE OF CONTENTS.

LECTURE I.

UNIVERSAL REDEMPTION. THE WORLD AS A WHOLE.

	PAGE
The Christian Church is designed, not to save individuals out of the world, but to save the world itself	1
To exhibit this is the best Apology for Christianity	2
Two questions answered. I. What is the World? It is the universal organism of which mankind is the head; not evil in itself, but, though fallen into an evil state through human selfishness, capable of restoration	4
Views of the Protestant and the Catholic theology on this, compared with the view maintained here	7
II. What is the Church? It is the portion of Human Society which partakes of Redemption—ultimately the World Redeemed	9
The Church, therefore, is in process of formation	11
This is verified (1) from Scripture	12
Two passages being selected as examples, (a) the introduction to St. John's Gospel	13
and (b) the Epistle to the Ephesians	15
These allow for the idea of the immanence of God	17
(2) from Human History	18
Views of writers on the Philosophy of History	19
(3) from the doctrine of evolution	20
Two cognate truths are involved in this:—	
(1) That all goodness is essentially Christian	23
(2) That independent study of morals must further the cause of true Christianity	27
Nevertheless the world needs redemption, as Israel did	28
The study of comparative religion shows this	30
The process of restoration is by the principle of election	31
Human progress is identical with the influence of the spirit of Christianity ...	33
Each association of men demands for its perfection the Christian spirit	33

Analytical Table of Contents.

	PAGE
As seen in the family	35
in the associations for the pursuit of knowledge and art	36
in trading associations	37
and in social and political life	38
Christianity and Culture ultimately coincide	39
Culture for its expansion requires a spiritual bond	40
Which is supplied by Christianity	41
The Christian ideal of life comprehends and vivifies the others	42
But Christianity takes form in an organized community	44
This community is ultimately the world transfigured by the spirit of Christ	44
The Lectures will show this worked out as follows :—	
Lect. II. in the Jewish polity	45
Lect. III. in the Church of the New Testament	45
Lects. IV, V, VI, in the attempts at a Christian Society made by the Imperial and Mediæval Church, the Reformation, and the English Commonwealth	46
Lects. VII. and VIII. will show the spiritual basis needed for human Societies, and the path which leads from the present state of the world to its redeemed state	46
A sound theory of Christian progress conduces to hope and energy	47

LECTURE II.

THE HEBREW THEOCRACY. THE TRAINING IN NATIONAL RIGHTEOUSNESS.

Religion consists in right relations of men with God and with one another	48
True historical study is the study of these relations	49
Hebrew history discloses these relations in a rudimentary form	50
The laws of Israel reflect the higher mind of the nation	51
Hebrew poetry shows the attachment of the people to the law	55
Their religious value for the land tended to peace and industry	56
The Laws prescribing social relations and care for the poor, endeared the law to the common people	58
Polygamy and slavery were modified	59
The Alien law was exceptionally mild	60
The brotherly character of the law prepared the way for the teaching of Christian love	61
The law is the centre of (1) the Constitution of the Nation, (2) its Theology, (3) its History, (4) its Literature	62
1. The Constitution. The duty of the Judges, both ordinary and special, was to enforce the law of just relations	62

Analytical Table of Contents. xi

	PAGE
The Monarchy and the national Centre ministered in another way to unity and brotherhood	65
The organization is important as being not municipal but national	66
2. The Theology. The Theocracy was the rule not of priests, but of the Divine law of just relations	67
The ceremonial law kept before the people the idea of holiness ...	69
Through the law Jehovah Himself dwells in the nation	70
The Judges and Kings are gods	72
The assertion of a peculiar relation of Israel to God is justified ...	72
We can trace a growth in the conceptions of God as a Moral Being	73
The struggle against idolatry was a struggle against injustice and immorality	75
3. The History. Prosperity came through keeping the law	77
The law gave strength for the uprising of the nation after oppression	78
The beneficence of the law palliates the conquests	79
The prophets, as statesmen, sought to maintain the law of just relations as the true source of national prosperity	80
4. The Literature in its three divisions shows also the supremacy of the Law	83
We can trace the supreme influence of the Law of just relations—	
(1) in the Pentateuch	84
(2) the Historical books and Prophets	85
(3) the Hagiographa and Psalms	85
and also in the æsthetic development	87
The religion of Israel was national, but yet expansive	88
The Ideal of Israel was righteousness	89
The religious and political value of the Old Testament is permanent	91

LECTURE III.

THE NEW TESTAMENT CHURCH. BEGINNINGS OF THE UNIVERSAL SOCIETY.

The New Testament expands the idea of a Theocracy	94
The theocracy of Christendom is the Righteous God abiding in mankind ...	96
Christ is the Saviour of Society	96
His first effort was to impart the consciousness of the Fatherhood of God ...	97
But He looked forward to the changes which His teaching would eventually cause	98
He gave little more than hints as to the organization of the body of His followers	100

Analytical Table of Contents.

	PAGE
The first hope was that the Jewish commonwealth might be converted	101
As this fails a new departure may be discerned	102
The teaching becomes more positive	103
The Twelve are ordained as a nucleus of the new kingdom	104
The Kingdom gradually passes over from the old to the new body	106
The Kingdom is misunderstood by those who look for selfish advantage, but also by those who ignore its political results	108
Christ's Kingdom is not of this world, but only in the sense that it is not worldly and selfish	108
It is a spiritual society in that its object is faith and goodness which in their deepest influence are beyond human law	110
But all spiritual life works itself out in actual life	111
Its effort is to make the kingdoms of the world into kingdoms which are not of *this* world	112
Christ's words reveal the spiritual character of true government	113
From Him as the centre the divine spirit flows into all human relations	114
The renunciation of self for the society is the first and absolute requirement	114
The Society is governed by principles which, however, pass into laws	116
The social capacity of the Church was restrained at first by the need of instruction	118
Yet there was even during our Lord's life a rudimentary organization	119
The organization becomes a matter of necessity after Pentecost	121
The primitive Church sought to supply all the needs of its members	122
The Jews' rejection of Christianity hastened the organization of the Church	123
The Societies founded by St. Paul aimed at a complete social life	125
This follows both from their Jewish and their Gentile antecedents	126–7
Their organization was freely adapted to their needs, as is shown by the growth and functions of the offices of Deacon and Presbyter	128
This organization was chiefly for purposes of government	130
Teaching and prayer were free, subject only to the rule of decency and order	131
The Pastoral Epistles show great activity in the functions of government	132
A body of rules was formed by a natural growth	133
Through these a new world was gradually being formed	135
This new world is the object of the apocalyptic hopes	136
In the Christian family was first realized the Kingdom of Christ	137
But it was seen to be the type of an universal Christian Society	138
The change of the world into the Kingdom of Christ is gradual and hard to gauge	139
Our duty is to strive for the purification of the Kingdom and its expansion	140

LECTURE IV.

THE IMPERIAL AND MEDIÆVAL CHURCH. UNITED CHRISTENDOM ATTEMPTED.

	PAGE
The Church at the end of the first century had all that was needed for its spiritual conquest	142
Its first object was to impress on the conscience of mankind the ideal of the life of Christ	143
Both the ordinances and doctrines were designed to do this	144
This ideal assimilated the current ideas and motives of goodness	145
But it harmonized them and inspired them with hope	148
Moral ideas spread through many channels	148
Christianity gave also a new stimulus to the pursuit of goodness	150
The form taken by the Christian ideal has varied in different ages	151
Its constant factors have been love, faith, and beneficence	154
The causes of its winning upon mankind as given by Gibbon are true, but need expansion	155
The last cause named by him is the discipline of the Churches	158
This involves the attempt to become a sovereign society	159
Which enforces its will by punishments and rewards	160
This discipline should, however, be limited by the rights of the individual conscience	162
From Constantine onwards attempts have been made to make Christendom an organic whole	162
We must try to see the faults through which these attempts have failed	163
The fault in the era of Constantine lay in not acknowledging the Imperial rule as a function of the Church	164
The Church had acquired the habits of a sect	165
This was caused by the doctrinal controversies	166
And by the ascetic tendency and the transfer of men's interests from this world to the next	167
The Church leaders had no public spirit	169
And the clergy became separate from the laity	170
The rise of the Papacy and the False Decretals augmented this separation	171
Hence sprung the strife of the Clerical and Imperial powers	173
The real contrasts introduced by spiritual religion were not in question	174
The theory of Mediæval Society was that of unity, not of separation	176
Charles and the great Emperors and Kings ruled in the name of God	177
The Papacy might have exercised a sanctifying and harmonizing influence	180
But the Popes aspired to, and for a time acquired, an external domination	181
Their domination bequeathed many great benefits to Europe	184
But it failed because it divided instead of harmonizing human life	186

And because the supremacy of the clergy perverted the Christian ideal ... 187
But the true ideal of the Middle Ages survives 188
It presided over a vast religious and social progress, and thus prepared for the better era 189-91

LECTURE V.

THE CHURCHES OF THE REFORMATION. EFFORTS FOR A CHRISTIANIZED SOCIETY.

The Mediæval Church though it had failed, had left the idea of a social system inspired by the Christian spirit 192
The Churches of the Reformation had to aim at the same results separately 193
The Reformation is primarily a positive, incidentally a negative, movement 194
    as is seen in matters of doctrine and of general enlightenment ... 195
    as also in the uprising of the laity and the national spirit ... 196-7
The liberty it claimed was a free course for truth and goodness 198
    and was the spring of political liberty 199
Its public action was upon separate nations and cities 200
Among preparatory instances we may recall the politico-religious work of Arnold of Brescia (1142-55) 201
And of Savonarola (1490-8) 203-8
Among the efforts of the Reformation we may examine the organization of Geneva by Calvin (1536-64) 209-12
    the Jesuit counterwork which was designed as a social restoration 213-217
    the Church-State system of Zwingli, Wolfgang, and Erastus 217-222
    the system established by the Scottish National Covenant (1581) 222-226
    and the Puritan Settlements in New England early in the 17th century 227-235
The hope presented by these efforts is that of a society leavened by the spirit of Christ 236-7

LECTURE VI.

THE ENGLISH CHURCH AND COMMONWEALTH. CHRISTIAN NATIONALISM.

England presents the best study of the attempt to Christianize Society ... 238
In Saxon times the Nation was both Church and State 239
From the Conquest onwards the Sovereign still asserted the national supremacy over the clerical system 240
The English Reformation, therefore, was necessarily both religious and political 241

Analytical Table of Contents.

	PAGE
The struggle with the Papacy was the assertion of national righteousness against an interloping and unjust system	242-4
The fear of a similar non-national system at home led to the Submission of the Clergy and the Acts of Supremacy	244-6
The Supremacy of the Crown is that of the Nation over all its parts	246
and especially of the lay power over the ministry of public worship	247
This Settlement was the expression of a national faith	249
which showed itself also in the Prayer Book and Articles of Religion	249
It was approved by the leading men of the period	249
and by the religious Reformers, especially William Tyndale	250
The grounds of the Settlement, and of the attempts made to alter it	252
It is said that religion to be pure must be separate. But religion languishes when separated from the general life	255
Also that clerical separation is required for liberty of conscience. But the demand is really not for liberty but domination	256
The truth aimed at is that public worship is one of several spheres with which the central government should interfere but little	257
It must, however, ensure the harmonious working of the system	259
The Supremacy has passed rightly from the Sovereign to the Parliament and the Prime Minister	262
This system of Christian Nationalism was maintained in the reigns of Henry VIII and Edward VI	263
Elizabeth failed to recognize that the ecclesiastical power of the Crown must be shared by Parliament	265
Hooker gave formal expression to the system, but failed to see the danger of the rising clericalism	266
The people believed that the religion of the Bible was Puritanism	269
The counter claim of clerical supremacy was urged by violence	270
Puritanism would have yielded to reason and constitutional action	272
The Puritan ideal was noble, but was driven into narrowness and tyranny	273
Puritanism, though conquered, regained its political influence, and the supremacy of the Commons is permanent	275
The Toleration Act did not constitute separate churches, but gave freedom of worship to the Christian community	276
The religious traditions of the 17th century lasted through the 18th	277
Driven from the field of worship it influenced the national legislation and the progress of science, art, and general expansion	279
The recognition of the whole national life as the sphere of religion should not blunt, but quicken the sense of sin and of the need of redemption	282
The Church must breathe the Christian spirit into the spheres most destitute of it	283
and build up the community in justice and the fear of God	284

LECTURE VII.

THE CHRISTIAN BASIS OF HUMAN SOCIETIES.

	PAGE
Religion must be connected with the general life	285
Its purpose is to unite mankind in an organized Christian brotherhood	286
All men are affected by it. Besides its stage of conviction, Christianity has its proleptic and unconscious stages	287
and it must be identified with moral goodness	289
It works by the principle of Election in the whole and in each part	289
We must deal with the elect portion while keeping the whole in view	291
It works also by a Sacramental system, using outward things for spiritual purposes	293
and in doing this it forms a universal priesthood	294
The Church includes many separate organisms, each of the same character as the whole	295
The individual as the subject of redemption is a Microcosm	296
and seeks, in union with others, to exert a redemptive power upon the world	297
This work is gradual and multiform	297
but all circles of human life are capable of inspiration and redemption	298
There are seven such circles within the Universal Humanity, which is the eighth	299
1. *The organization for public worship* is not itself the Church	300
but it joins in the redemptive process when it ministers to universality	301
by means of its prayers, Sacraments, instruction, and beneficence	302–6
Its leaders must form the most open of all orders	306
2. *Family life* is naturally Christian	306
It is a microcosm and must inspire itself with the Spirit of the Universal Church	307–9
3. *The associations for the pursuit of knowledge* are in their true nature religious	309
All true knowledge is universal	309
and essentially moral	310
The votaries of knowledge form a branch of the universal church	311
4. *Art* is also a religious pursuit	312
It is the expression of feeling: it is creative and aspires to excellence	312–14
The fellowship in Art becomes a branch of the universal church	314
5. *Social Intercourse*, as ministering to mutual knowledge, interest, affection, and discipline, becomes religious; and affects the nation and the world	315–17

6. *Trade and professional life*, as ministering to the universal needs of men and drawing them together, also join in the redemptive process 317-20
7. *The Nation* is at present the highest form of the Church, being most complete ... 320-1
   A constitutional state especially forms a Christian brotherhood ... 321
   The true ruler is a minister of God and a Pastor of the people ... 322
8. *The Universal Church* is as yet unorganized ... 324
   The union of the nations, attempted in the Middle Ages, must be re-attempted ... 325
   Its function is to maintain peace and the spirit of Christ among all its branches ... 327
Two conclusions follow :—
   (1) The branches of the Church are permanent and help one another ... 328
   (2) The organization for public worship, if fulfilling its purpose aright, will maintain its preeminence ... 329

LECTURE VIII.

STEPS TOWARDS REALIZING THE IDEAL OF A CHRISTIAN WORLD.

We can only indicate the direction, not describe the process, of restoration 330
1. *Public Worship* must not be a separate cult, but seek to raise the tone of the general life ... 331
   Its point of contact with the general life is the Parochial system ... 334
   The question, so-called, of Church and State, is really the question whether the Church or Christian Nation should maintain a system of public worship ... 335 7
   This must depend on the attitude of the clergy ... 337
2. *Family Life*, especially in England, is on the way to perfection ... 338
   There are, however, two dangers—(1) The tendency in France and America to limit the duty of parentage ... 338
   and (2) The Social evil ... 340
   The general elevation of the Church by the spirit of Christian unselfishness is alone capable of surmounting these evils ... 341
3. *Knowledge* needs co-ordination; especially the harmonizing of the Humane with the physical branches of knowledge ... 341-3
4. *Art* needs popularizing and the realization of its mission to elevate and gladden the life of mankind ... 343-4
5. *Society* must acknowledge a stewardship of its privileges, and a missionary character in its intercourse ... 344-8
6. *Trade* must cultivate rectitude and trustfulness ... 346
   It must reconcile capital with labour by co-operation ... 347

b

The part which the Nation can take in trade depends on the prevalence of the higher and unselfish motives ... 348
7. *In the Nation* the constitutional system is a product of the Christian spirit ... 349
It requires constant readjustment in the relations of the whole and the parts ... 350
It must direct its legislation and administration to the elevation of the weaker classes ... 352
8. *The Universal Church* must promote European peace by such means as Arbitration ... 353
It must apply Christian principles to the intercourse of nations ... 356
This is the object of International Law ... 357
The task is gigantic, but not beyond the powers of the Church ... 357/

The subject of these Lectures is at one with the purposes of individual piety 358
The democratic movements of our day are favourable to Christian influences 359
 if Christianity be understood to be not of a stationary, but of a missionary character ... 360
There are four conditions in which Christianity may thus work upon the World ... 361
 (1) It must be confident that this is its destined task ... 361
 (2) It must be a life, not a system ... 362
 (3) It must abandon clericalism ... 364
 (4) It must induce men to regard their common duties as Christian ministries ... 365
To show that this may be done is the best confirmation of the Christian Faith, which is the object of the Bampton Lecture ... 366
Scepticism arises mainly from the narrowing of the idea of the Church ... 367
When men see its capacity to further the Redemption of the World they will rally to it ... 368
We may thus restore the element of hope ... 370
This hope brings the heavenly spirit into the World and makes the World a preparation for heaven ... 370-3

LIST OF NOTES IN APPENDIX.

	Page in Appendix.	Corresponding page in Lectures.
I. Passages in the New Testament, in which αἰών is used rather than κόσμος to designate this World	377	5
II. Extracts from the Papal Encyclical and Syllabus of Errors issued Dec. 8, 1864	378	6
III. Analysis of St. Augustine's De Civitate Dei, with extracts showing that it is not an anticipation of a Christian Commonwealth	380	8, 169
IV. Extract from 'La Mission Actuelle des Souverains,' showing the proper use of the words Religion, Worship, Church and Churches	385	9
V. Extracts from Aristotle showing the use in Greek Philosophy of the words importing Priority of Being	385	15
VI. A short account of M. Comte's anticipations of the future of Political Society in Europe	386	20
VII. Extracts from Professor Tyndall's Address to the British Association at Belfast, Aug. 19, 1874	389	21
VIII. Extract from Professor Huxley's 'Man's Place in Nature'	391	21
IX. The relation of the doctrine of Evolution to that of Free Will	392	22
X. Illustrations of the contrast between the Eastern and Western Church-teachers in their estimate of the virtues of the Heathen	393	25
XI. Expressions of Aristotle confessing the practical impotence of his Moral Philosophy	394	30
XII. Extracts from Leaders of Modern Thought on the relation of Knowledge to Morality and Religion	394	36
XIII. The influence of Greek Philosophy and Roman Law on Christian Theology, from Sir H. Mayne's Ancient Law	397	43
XIV. Keshub Chunder Sen on Christianity for Europe and Asia	398	43
XV. Extract from Mill's Logic on the use of Hypothesis in Scientific Investigation	399	47
XVI. An Excursus on the Books of the Old Testament as a basis for History	400	51
XVII. Customary Law, as described by Sir H. Mayne	407	52

xx   *List of Notes in Appendix.*

	Page in Appendix.	Corresponding page in Lectures.
XVIII. (1) Extracts from Baron Bunsen, showing the working of Absolutism in the Church in Germany	409	221
(2) Explanation of the reformed Prussian Church Law	411	221
XIX. Hooker on the making of Ecclesiastical Laws and the Royal Supremacy	412	261
XX. Richard Rothe on the Church	415	300, 333
XXI. Extract from 'Ecce Homo.' The Law of Edification	417	305
XXII. Religion and Art. Extract from an Address of Sir F. Leighton to the Students of the Royal Academy	418	312, 314
XXIII. Extracts from 'A Fragment on the Church,' by Dr. Arnold	421	112, 161, 322
XXIV. The Views of International Jurists as to a Tribunal of Arbitration as a substitute for War	426	326, 327, 357
XXV. The Parish as a Church. Extracts from a Pastoral Address	428	335
XXVI. The Maison Leclaire at Paris, an example of successful co-operative industry	433	347
XXVII. St. Augustine's Confession of Agnosticism, extracted from his work De Doctrinâ Christianâ	436	363

LECTURE I.

UNIVERSAL REDEMPTION. THE WORLD AS A WHOLE.

St. John iii. 17. God sent not His Son into the world to condemn the world, but that the world through Him might be saved.

THE purpose of this course of Lectures is to restore the idea of the Christian Church as a moral and social power, present, universal, capable of transforming the whole life of mankind, and destined to accomplish this transformation. The Church has often been presented to men as if it had no object but public worship and teaching, with some few accidental adjuncts of beneficent action. It is regarded as a society, but a society of which public prayer and preaching are the supreme, if not exclusive, ratio essendi. If a further object is assigned, it is to prepare men for another world. In contrast to this limited view of its functions, the Church will be here presented as the Social State in which the Spirit of Christ reigns; as embracing the general life and society of men, and identifying itself with these as much as possible; as having for its object to imbue all human relations with the spirit of Christ's self-renouncing love, and thus to change the world into a kingdom of God. It is proposed to show that this, and no narrower purpose, was contemplated from the beginning; that it is to this that all natural indications point as the destination of a spiritual society; that it is this which, in spite of the fundamental misconception which has been noticed, has been in the main the aim of the Church. The attempts which have been made thus to *save the world* will be reviewed, and an estimate formed of their success or failure. It will be shown, further, how the Church principle, that is, the principle of Christian love working in organized bodies of men, would operate if society were brought fully under its dominion. And, lastly, the present state of society will be examined, and suggestions made as to the practical means by which our social state may, in all its circles and relations, become fully Christian, and capable of the indwelling of God.

Such a presentation of the Christian Church, if it can be successfully drawn out, will serve, it is hoped, to turn the attention of men away from the controversies engendered by an exclusive interest in worship and dogma to the more fruitful field of a practical influence on the national and universal life. It will tend to show the complete identity of Christianity with goodness in its widest sense. It will exhibit the unity of the various spheres of moral and intellectual life. It will also present a point of hope to all who long and strive for the general good of mankind, and give a direction to their energies; while, in reference to the special and apologetic object of the Bampton Lecture, it will rally men to the Christian standard by a renewal of the hope which in the early days inspired the army of believers.

Apologetics have often been no more than a vindication of the original guarantees of Christianity, and of the documents in which it was at first enshrined. But, partly because the thing to be defended was vague, partly because the argument seemed after all inconclusive, they rarely kindled enthusiasm. They often failed even to attract the attention of those to whom they were addressed. It was not certain whether by Christianity was meant the Roman Catholic or the Anglican, the Presbyterian or Independent system of worship or church government, the Calvinist or Arminian system of doctrine, the clerical or the liberal view of the Christian life; and whether, therefore, its acceptance might require a man to adopt any of these systems, or to engage in controversies about them. It was not certain whether by the Church were not meant some exclusive body having little to do with the actual life of mankind, perhaps even drifting into hostility to the convictions of men engaged in secular callings, and to the progressive tendencies of modern societies. Moreover, it is not enough that religion should be merely capable of defence. It must inspire and lead, or else it dies. We must show that it is capable of influencing, stimulating and guiding the progress of humanity; and, further, that the world itself demands the Christian religion as alone capable of sustaining its hope and its energy. This is what these Lectures will attempt.

Let us begin by asking two questions,—1st. What is the world, the salvation of which was designed by

Christ and His apostles? 2nd. What is the Church through which its salvation is to be wrought out?

I. What is the world which Christ came to save, and which is to be changed into His Church? We mean by the world the organized constitution of things in which we live, including the material universe so far as we apprehend it, but chiefly humanity, which (taking the world as known to us) is its crown. The world is the universe as conceived of and wrought upon by men. It partakes, therefore, of man's rise and fall; for, if man be degraded, outer nature becomes evil to him, and through him the source of evil to others; whereas, when man rises to his true position, all outer nature is first viewed as serving the spiritual good of mankind, and then is actually used for this purpose. The world thus conceived is a harmony. But the harmony is broken through when man is driven helplessly by the physical powers by which he is surrounded; when he reckons them above instead of below him, as idolaters do, and he thus becomes *impotens sui*, resigning his rightful supremacy; or when he drifts on without a perception of the Moral Order; or, again, when he uses nature and his fellow-men wilfully or selfishly, instead of seeking that they and he should serve the highest spiritual purpose. The harmony is restored when the spiritual aim is understood and embraced. Then men are at one through their common pursuit of justice and love, and outer nature is subservient to this pursuit. This harmony is also properly divine; the world thus conceived is a manifestation of God. He who perceives and acts upon this harmony is a believer in God, whether he name the sacred name or not. He who through moral indifference does not recognize it, at least as 'the purpose of the ages,' and he alone, may properly be called an atheist. But he who with mind and heart embraces this harmony, embraces the thought and purpose of God Himself. We may say more. Since God dwells in the world as thus conceived, since He is the justice and the love which gives it its character, he who thus conceives it takes in the divine nature, or rather is taken into it, and he thus becomes an agent of God's will and of His purpose—a member and a minister of Him who fills all in all.

When the world is under the dominion of selfishness, then it becomes an evil thing. As such it is constantly spoken of in Scripture, where sometimes the unreal and transitional character of this stage is marked by the expression '*This* world.' 'The Prince of *this* world cometh [1];' 'the rulers of the darkness of *this* world [2];' and the word αἰών rather than κόσμος is used to denote this transitional state [3]. It is also thus that we commonly speak of 'the world,' or 'worldly people.' But at this point is apt to arise a fatal confusion of thought. Christians have very commonly believed that the order of things in which we live is permanently, necessarily, incurably corrupt. For many ages, by a fatal dualism, they looked on the material fabric of the world, and their own bodies, as evil; and then Christianity became asceticism. And even now the impression on many minds is that human society at least will never be delivered from the bonds of corruption. This causes

[1] John xiv. 30.   [2] Eph. vi. 12.   [3] See Note I.

them, not only to hold aloof from the pleasures of life
even when they are innocent, but to look on many of
its most serious interests, such as science or politics,
as secular and profane. In consequence of this, Christianity has been deprived of a large part of its proper
influence. It has been assumed that human society must
be left to run out its selfish and doomed career, and
that it is at best a scaffolding, inside of which another
society, the Church or kingdom of God, is to grow up,
while the existing society, instead of being transformed,
must eventually dwindle and be destroyed. And,
further, the conflict of the Church and the world,
which was real at first, has been prolonged when there
is no further reason for it. It has seemed quite natural
that the Church should neglect the general interests of
society; for why should it busy itself about anything
so transient? And more, when movements of a liberal
character, movements which are often essentially Christian in their tendency, sometimes even in their origination, arise in society, instead of looking at these as
the work of the Divine Spirit, the official representatives of the Church have looked askance at them and
misjudged them. Even in Protestant communities the
whole reforming tendency of the last hundred years
has often been opposed by those who are held to
represent the Church; while in the Roman Catholic
community the Syllabus of the Pope[1] all but binds the
believer to an irreconcileable war with modern civilization; and the tone commonly attributed to the Church
in doctrinal writings is that of a despised and perse-

[1] See Note II, Quotations from the Papal Encyclical and Syllabus of Errors.

cuted woman, rather than that of a strong man with an arm to succour and a heart to comfort, engaged, with manly hope, in restoring to society its true principle of life, and forwarding its progress towards a state of perfect justice and love.

We must admit, with both Scripture and experience, that the world is very imperfect and, in many of its arrangements, unjust; and that its condition consequently, at any given time, is liable to the condemnation that it has 'fallen short of the glory of God,' or even that it 'lies in wickedness.' But its whole structure bears witness to a higher destiny; and we equally follow Scripture and experience in conceiving of it as painfully undergoing a deliverance into a state of spiritual liberty.

Another result of the misconception which sees no hope of deliverance for the world is, that salvation is looked upon merely as the deliverance of individuals. The idea of the salvation of society has been ignored, though it stands out prominently in both the Old and the New Testament[1]. The Protestant theology, which centres in the doctrine of justification by faith, has perhaps contributed to this, by insisting too exclusively on the relation of the individual soul to God. It has narrowed the notion of faith, so as to take no notice of that half-conscious or embryo faith which operates very widely, as a general and national sentiment, and consequently has not attended to the influence which

---

[1] This is fully shown in the Second and Third Lectures, which point out the evolution of the social and political idea of religion in the Old and New Testament respectively.

faithful men ought to exert on the organization of social life as a direct part of the Christian scheme; nor, again, to the influence which Society, if imbued with the Christian spirit, may exercise on all its members. It has not dared to think of a saved and living Society, even as an object of hope; but has conceived of the surrounding social state merely as hindering the individual, more or less, according to its greater or less corruption. The Catholic theology, on the other hand, which has in some sense maintained the idea of the Christian community, has yet never set itself to realize a Christian state of society generally as the object of the Church's endeavour. It was observed, indeed, by Mr. Ripley, the translator of Jouffroy's Essays [1], that the ordinary Catechisms teach a philosophy of history. 'If you ask a Catholic child whence came the human race, he knows; if you ask him what it is engaged in, whither it is going, he knows.' But this is more than can be truly asserted. No doubt the common Church teaching has this element of greatness, that it conceives of the human race as one; but that it teaches a sound doctrine as to the true aims and hopes of the race is more than questionable. It has, like St. Augustine in the *De Civitate Dei* [2], drawn out the contrast between the worldly and the heavenly cities, and has represented the heavenly society as using the earthly, only as a stranger might use an inn, on its way to a better land. The existing

---

[1] Introductory notice to Jouffroy's Essays, pp. 23, 24, quoted in Flint's Philosophy of History, p. 4.
[2] See Note III, in which the true scope of the *De Civ. Dei* is shown.

society appears in this theology, not as the object of the redemptive efforts of Christ's servants, but as withering away under their scorn. Or, again, it has attempted to overlay the existing society with Christian forms, and to place it under the dominion of the clergy. It has never frankly fallen in with human progress, and sought to inspire it with Christian principle. The Church, as represented in the Catholic theology, has always been a separate organization and a cause of division in human life. The truer theology would partly combine the Protestant and the Catholic, partly supersede them both. It would acknowledge with the Protestant the paramount importance of individual conviction, while it would maintain with the Catholic that the full development of the redemptive work is to be seen only in an organized society. But it would assert that this organized society must ultimately be coextensive with the world[1]; and therefore that the main object of Christian effort is not to be found either in the saving of individuals out of a ruined world, or in the organizing of a separate society destined always to hold aloof from the world, but in the saving of the world itself.

II. What then, we may ask, secondly, in view of this purpose of God to save the world, is the Christian Church? It can be nothing else than that portion of human society which is renewed by the Christian spirit, a portion which must grow till it becomes the whole. This ideal, or destination, of the Church, is that of the vision drawn out in the 4th and 5th

---

[1] See Note IV, a quotation from 'La Mission Actuelle des Souverains.'

chapters of the Apocalypse[1]. In the centre is the slain Lamb, that is, God made known to us through the self-renouncing love expressed in the Cross of Christ. Round this central figure are ranged first the elders, representing the redeemed humanity; then the four living beings who represent the animate creation: and, beyond these, partaking in a more distant manner of the common redemption, every creature in heaven and earth is heard joining in adoration. We must take this vision as representing, not a world removed from our own, but this world itself, in its ideal state and in its destined renewal: and this renewal, not as a sudden transformation after a vast cataclysm, but as wrought out gradually through the Christian centuries by the operation of the divine judgments and the expansion of the Christian Church. When men are brought into living contact with the redemptive love of God and of Christ, the effect of this is not only upon the first-formed brotherhood which consciously realizes it, but upon the whole course of society and of nature: first upon the social condition of men and the institutions under which they live, then upon the animals who are their fellow-creatures and fellow-servants, then upon inanimate nature, upon the fields they cultivate and the earth which it was their original mission to subdue; till, out of the chaos which selfishness has made, there arises a new harmony of creative love. This also is expressed in the Apocalypse by the visions[2] in which for

---

[1] This vision is embodied, in idea though not in detail, in Van Eyk's magnificent picture, the worship of the Immaculate Lamb.   [2] Rev. xix. and xx.

the Babylonian world-power is substituted, after a long vista of judgment and conflict, the heavenly city, the bride and the abode of God.

It is of the greatest importance to us to restore this wide, universal idea of the Church: for nothing short of this can satisfy those who have entered into the divine thought which is the substratum of the universe. But we must look upon this Church-idea, not as fully realized, but as that towards which human society is working, under the direction of divine providence. The Church is in process of formation, it is never complete. It constitutes an aspiration, not a full possession. It begins necessarily with a little society of those who can trust one another, with special forms of speech and action; but it opens itself out to the society in which it lives. The law of its life is assimilation. Its work is the hallowing of all social conditions. And, as one by one the various circles in which men's natural needs have bound them together own the higher principle of Christian love, they realize and express the Church-idea. The Church thus clothes itself with the various forms of the society into which it passes. It was at first a Jewish sect, then a Roman Hetæria. It touched, and quickened, though hardly with a conscious aim, the various spheres of Roman life. It grew till it seemed to lay its hand upon the empire. But the task was too great, and had to be begun again with the fragments of the broken unity. It worked again throughout the Middle Ages to combine Western Europe into a kingdom of God; but again the task proved too great, and had to be begun once more after the Reformation, with the separate fragments. If we try to define it in its transitional state, we must say that it is that portion of organized humanity in which the Spirit of Christ is practically recognized as supreme. It is now mainly represented by a brotherhood of Christian nations, and the various circles of moral life which they include. But it tends to universality, to the union of Christendom, to the incorporation and training of the weaker races. It can never be perfect, never fully constituted, until it includes every individual of the human race, and till they all sustain true relations, relations of which love is the central word, towards God, towards one another, and towards the universe of which they form a part. This establishment and maintenance of true relations between spiritual beings in the universal community is that which we may set down as the purpose of God, the goal of human development.

This conception of the Church as synonymous with the world redeemed must be verified by reference, (1) to Scripture, (2) to history, (3) to the modern doctrine of development.

(1) Scripture begins with the presentation of the world as a harmonious whole springing up under the hand of God, rank above rank, and culminating in man, who is intellectually and morally supreme within it. It gives us the idea of what the world would be were man really subject to God, and the universe to man as made in God's image. It presents to us, next, the marring of this ideal through man's mistrust and selfishness; then the rise of the typical or normal religion

and its gradual purification in the history of Israel, until the fulness of moral light shines forth in the life of our Lord; and, lastly, the explanation of this great fact, and its influence upon mankind and the world.

I will select two passages, one from the writings of St. John, the other from those of St. Paul, in which this explanation and this influence are described.

1. I take the opening paragraph of St. John's Gospel, which describes the universal significance of the appearance of Christ. The Word, he says, (I represent the meaning by a paraphrase), the Word, which is none other than God, was present in the whole process of creation; that is, the moral and spiritual purpose is the central fact to be traced in the universe. All things are made with reference to it, nothing is apart from it. This Word is the universal light which enlightens every man, the moral and spiritual centre of universal humanity; and this is true, although it was a light shining in darkness, playing upon a social state which did not comprehend it, although even the race of Israel, who were its own, who were specially adapted to receive it, did not receive it fully. But those who did receive it, that is, the faithful in Israel, and, generally, in all ages and countries, became children of God; their minds and hearts reflected the thought of God, they saw and felt truly. At length the Word found its adequate expression in the person of Jesus Christ. This was the culmination of the process; and the exhibition of Christ as the complete expression of the divine word forms the subject of

the Gospel according to St. John. Yet in the discourses at the close of St. John's Gospel it is recognised that the appearance of Christ is the beginning of a long process, and that from the central spring there opened the Spirit is to flow forth upon the world [1]. This diffusion of the Spirit of Christ through the world, which is the work of the Church, is recognised as being a greater work than that of Christ Himself [2], inasmuch as the full development is greater than the first implanting of the germ.

If we dwell on the assertion here made, that, apart from the Word which took human form in Christ, nothing in the whole world came into being, we have in this the strongest assertion of the unity of the world, and of its moral order and purpose. The material creation culminates in humanity, humanity culminates in Jesus Christ; and this process we must take as present in the divine mind from the beginning. Just as an architect first conceives the purpose which is to be served by the building before he has commenced the designs, and this purpose is present in every line which he draws and presides over the whole execution; so the ideal of manhood which stood forth at last in the person of Christ must be conceived of as present to the Creator from the beginning of the process by which the world came into being; and it must have been by and through this, as the mental instrument, that the whole

---

[1] John xvi. 7, 8: If I go not away, the Comforter will not come unto you; but if I depart, I will send Him unto you. And when He is come, He will convict the world.

[2] John xiv. 12: He that believeth on Me, the works that I do shall he do also; and greater works than these shall he do.

was conceived and executed. As Aristotle says—πρῶτον τῇ φύσει ἔσχατον τῇ γενέσει [1].

But we see also that this implies the connexion of every individual of the whole race of mankind with the Word of God as the source of that moral and spiritual life, of which all are susceptible, and to which some in every age open their hearts. And the same may be said of every division of the race, of families, and nations, and great aggregates of men. None of them is formed without the Word of God. But this is, apart from the knowledge of Christ, potential rather than actual. The manifestation of the Word in the person of Christ had for its purpose to make this potentiality actual, so that the children of God, those who had already received the light but were scattered abroad, should be drawn to one centre [2], and that through their agency the world itself should be brought back to God.

2. The passage which I select from the writings of St. Paul is the first chapter of the Epistle to the Ephesians, in which the human race is spoken of as chosen in Christ before the foundation of the world [3], to be the adopted children of God. Those who form the first fruits of this process [4] are described as quickened by the divine spirit shown forth in the life of Christ; and then the mystery is disclosed that this process of quickening is destined to be universal: the barrier between Jews and Gentiles is broken down; the Gentiles are to be fellow-heirs in the Church [5], which is the body of Christ,

---

[1] See the philosophical expressions from the Metaphysics and the Politics quoted in Note V.
[2] John xi. 52; cf. x. 16.   [3] Ver. 4, 5.   [4] Ver. 11-13.   [5] Eph. iii. 6.

the fulness of Him that filleth all in all[1]. And, further on in the Epistle[2], this process is traced out as one by which all spiritual forces and combinations, all powers and principalities, all organizations of spiritual beings, are to be influenced. 'That to the principalities and powers in heavenly places might be made known by the Church the manifold wisdom of God.' And, still more, the purpose of God is absolutely universal[3]: 'That in the dispensation of the fulness of time, he might gather together in one all things in Christ, both which are in heaven and which are in earth.' Whether, then, we use the old language of theology, and say that these are inspired words which reveal God's purpose, or whether we take them as the impression made on one of deep spiritual insight by the moral grandeur of the life of Christ, and by the recognition of its redemptive power and its necessary effect upon mankind, in either case they disclose, as the purpose of God and the task of the Church, a spiritual unity which is absolutely universal, in which all men everywhere, and all the creation of which man is the centre, are destined to be partakers.

These passages do not stand alone. We might support them by citing the views expressed in St. Paul's speech at Athens, or the claim of universal dominion ascribed to our Lord in the close of St. Matthew's gospel, or the assertion of that claim by the Apostles in such passages as the second chapter of St. Paul to the Philippians; or, again, the hope expressed in St. Peter's epistle of a new world in which dwelleth righteousness;

[1] Eph. i. 23.   [2] Eph. iii. 10.   [3] Eph. i. 10.

or, lastly, the vision of the Apocalypse already touched upon. They are all an expansion of the assurance expressed in the words—' The kingdoms of the world are become the kingdoms of our Lord and of His Christ.'

It may be right here to observe that such passages as these bring into prominence a view of the Divine nature which is specially important in the present day— that of the immanence of God in nature and in man. God may be conceived of as transcendental, that is, as transcending all the visible and cognizable universe, as existing apart from it, and working upon it from without; or as immanent, dwelling within it as its moral and spiritual centre, its guiding force. The two ideas are by no means incompatible, they are both of them expressed in Scripture; and it would probably be a great spiritual loss so to dwell upon one of them as to exclude the other. But it is certain that the thought of a transcendental God dealing with the world *ab extra* has been dwelt upon in the past in such a way as to exclude the thought of an immanent God working upon the world from within. It is certain also that this idea of a transcendental God is one which, by seeming to imply continual interference with the regular course of the world, is peculiarly difficult to grasp in a scientific age. And equally is it certain that the idea of God as the Word and the Spirit is that to which both Scripture and experience point as specially suitable to our age. The theologian, however little he follows out his thought, owns this, when he says that this is the dispensation of the Spirit. And it is evident that what we have to do, as believers in God, is not to speculate upon His abstract nature, or to think of realms altogether beyond the range of human experience, but to trace the course of nature and history as moving under the divine impulse ; to make ourselves conscious of the constraining moral force of the life of Christ, which, as the crown of the development, fully represents the divine power within, and of the Spirit which has flowed from this life throughout the Christian ages ; to estimate and to associate ourselves with the intention which may be traced in the development of the world ; and to follow it out with all our energy to its furthest results, as organs of the Divine Spirit, and as fellow-workers with God.

(2) Does then the course of human history support the view which has been taken ? Does it point to a moral and spiritual order destined to reign throughout the universe ? It may be confidently said that this is the result to which all the enlarged study of history points. No one is now content to study one corner of the field of history by itself after the manner of a mere chronicle. The student of history conceives of mankind necessarily as a whole, or, at least, as tending to unity; and of history as an orderly progress of which the moral and spiritual training of mankind is the connecting thread. The physical conditions of life, though they may check, yet ensure the progress towards unity. Contiguity of dwelling, the expansion of population, the growing needs which can only be supplied by commercial intercourse, constrain men in the same direction. Religion, in its larger sense, the recog-

nition of God and of the moral order, necessarily tends to universality, whether in the East or the West, within or without the sphere of the Hebraic and Christian revelation. The political development may also be traced out as a progress towards unity and the organization of moral relations. And all these elements, material, religious, political, combine in the comprehensive unity of Christendom. The human race is being drawn powerfully together; ideas circulate with constantly increasing rapidity; and the sense of fellowship which is thus engendered, and a certain body of common moral sentiments, are, we may believe, preparing the advent of a fuller unity and more brotherly relations throughout the world.

It may be remarked that the philosophy of history is a study of recent growth. The facts were there, but they were not presented in a harmonious and articulated form. Yet human history is evidently not without a purpose. That which strikes us again and again is that individuals and nations have pressed on towards a predestined goal, often in complete unconsciousness of what they were doing[1]. And this fact we denote by speaking of the purpose of God and the universal destination of the Church. We have to trace the intimations of history and the half-conscious prophecies of which it is full, so as to clear the path of future progress.

Those who have written on the Philosophy of History[2]

[1] See Guizot's Eur. Civ., Lect. xi. p. 5.
[2] I take the account of these writers from Flint's Philosophy of History in France and Germany.

have usually been content to note the stream of tendency, but have shrunk from a definition of its goal such as would have presented a clear aim for human endeavour. The general hope of the prevalence of Christianity, or of a sound political constitution, and of the reign of peace, as drawn out by Kant or Jouffroy; the mental liberty and full development of the individual, as presented by Herder; the complete sociality and civilization described by Guizot, are all of them somewhat vague. Those who have been more precise, like Comte[1], have usually suggested an Utopia. We may believe that in speaking of the establishment and maintenance of true relations throughout the whole body of a united and organized humanity, under the influence of the Christian spirit of righteousness and love[2], we are placing before ourselves, with as much precision as is possible, the destination of human society; and that in developing this ideal we shall evoke the energy and enthusiasm of mankind. History combines with Scripture in pointing to this destination.

(3) It may be affirmed that the modern doctrine of evolution points also in the same direction.

The thoughts of men in our day are unavoidably coloured by this doctrine, which, if it is not proved in the whole range which some of its advocates claim, and if it is subject to possible modifications, yet commends itself so largely to inquirers in all departments, that Christians naturally ask how, if its widest assertions

---

[1] See Note VI. A short account of M. Comte's anticipations as to the future of Political Society in Europe.

[2] I may refer the reader to the systematic working out of these ideas in the Lectures VII and VIII.

be true, it affects Christian teaching and institutions. It may be answered that with such a view of Christianity and of the Church as we are now presenting it is in almost entire accord. It might appear to be only another name for that process of the Divine Spirit which we have been describing. It is applicable universally; there is no particle of matter, and no moral phenomenon, with which it has not to do. It traces a single principle of life, working throughout the whole range of things known, and maintains that this existed potentially and in the germ in the original atoms of which the world is made[1]; so that the barriers fall away which seemed to separate organic from inorganic matter, or species from species, or animal from man, or, to carry the thought in its fullest result, ordinary men from Christ[2]. There is nothing in this theory which would require a denial of the pre-eminence in the order of nature of the human mind and heart[3], nor which would prevent our recognising the absolute moral supremacy of our Lord in human nature[4]; nor, again, is it at all incompatible with the belief in a living God and the sense of His design or purpose in

---

[1] See Note VII. An extract from Professor Tyndall's address at Belfast.
[2] The boldest and most thorough appropriation of the doctrine of development by a Christian minister may be seen in 'A theologico-political Treatise' by the Rev. G. D'Oyly Snow (Trübner, 1874).
[3] See Note VIII. A passage from Professor Huxley's work 'Man's place in Nature.'
[4] This moral supremacy is only another form for the assertion of our Lord's divinity. If the idea of the Divine immanence be maintained, then Christ stands at the summit of the whole development in which God manifests Himself. 'The image of the invisible God, the first-born of all creation; for in Him were all things created ... all things have been created through Him and unto Him, and He is before all things, and in Him all things consist.' (Col. i. 15, 16. Rev. Version.)

the larger significance of these terms. The mechanical illustrations of design, such as that of the workman making a watch, are, no doubt, no longer valid to the Christian who accepts the doctrine of evolution; but his consciousness of unity, of harmony and of purpose in the development of the world and of mankind can hardly fail to be increased. Nor, lastly, is it repugnant to a sober assertion of freewill and independence, since even in the lowest forms of life it is individual origination and peculiarity on which depends the progress which it assumes[1]. If this be so, then it corresponds in a remarkable manner with that doctrine which we have traced in Scripture and in human history, the doctrine of the Spirit and the Word, working upwards from the beginning towards the complete form of human development. The world is the manifestation of a power[2] which is present and active in every part of it, harmonizing it, educing from it life and morality; a power, the first traces of which may be seen far back in the origin of things, but which tends to the fullest expansion of moral and spiritual relations. If so, then man as man, whatever his aberrations may be, is the organ of this power, and all human institutions are built up by it, and tend to higher life, higher morality, under its incessant impulse.

[1] See Note IX. Extracts from the writings of Darwin on the Relation of Evolution to Free Will.

[2] The Agnostic philosophy, as represented by Mr. Herbert Spencer, (see his article on Religion, Past and Future, in the Nineteenth Century for January, 1884), fully recognises this power: but it maintains that, beyond the fact that it exists, we can have no knowledge of it. And yet, how can we be said to be without knowledge of a power, the working of which forms the subject of all our knowledge?

Further, the subordinate doctrines of the struggle for life and the survival of the fittest, are applicable to spiritual as well as to natural life and fitness; and if the Christian ideal be, as it has hitherto shown itself, the highest and the fittest, these doctrines would point to its eventual supremacy. They are applicable also to the social organizations of mankind; and, if the idea of a universal society, inspired by Christian love, be that to which historical experience points, these doctrines will help us to believe that such a universal society will eventually supersede those formed on any other social ideal, and grow to its full expansion.

Thus biological no less than Christian and historical research leads up to the hope of a redeemed humanity, a universal Church. The effort of human society must be to inspire itself more and more with this hope, and to direct itself with a view to this final and complete organization.

We must here pause to emphasize two consequences or cognate truths which stand in close connexion with what is now being advanced.

The first of these is that all goodness is essentially one, and therefore essentially Christian. We are not to suppose that Christianity is an exotic plant introduced into a region to which it is strange, and meant to overlay the course of nature with a foreign and external application. It is, on the contrary, the crown of a long development. It had in spirit and aspiration been working in the constitution of human life from the beginning. We are accustomed to trace this in the history of the Hebrew race. But there was a

Praeparatio Evangelica of a similar kind going on in other nations also; they were, to use St. Paul's words, 'seeking the Lord, if haply they might feel after Him, and find Him.' There was an aspiration towards goodness and towards God, which we may trace out in various systems of religion and morality, most of all in the Greek philosophy, and which was a kind of faith in the good things that were to come. When the Brahman [1] declares God to be the One, the Beginning, the Middle, and the End, the goodness of all that is good; when Buddha teaches that 'to abhor and cease from sin, this is the greatest blessing;' when we read in Confucius the evangelical maxim, 'What you would that men should do to you, that do to them;' when we find in the Zend Avesta such praise of truthfulness as made that central virtue the basis of moral training to every Persian, and such teaching of the unity of God and of immortality as is believed to have recalled the Jews during the captivity to those primary principles of religion [2]; when Plato [3] argues that the test of righteousness is to act justly whether gods and man see it or not, and though crucifixion should be his reward; when Horace [4] speaks in words worthy to stand beside those of the 46th Psalm, of the just man standing firm though the world should go to ruin around him; when Marcus Aurelius closes

[1] These statements as to the Eastern religions are taken from *The Faiths of the World*, being Lectures at St. Giles' Church, Edinburgh, and from Bunsen's *God in History*.

[2] For the influence of Zoroastrianism on Judaism, see Stanley's *Jewish Church*, iii. 184, and a remarkable passage in Lessing's *Education of the Human Race*.

[3] *Republic*, Bk. ii. pp. 361-2, 366-7; Bk. x. p. 612.

[4] Od. iii. 3.

his Soliloquies[1] with the expression of resignation in death, 'Go in peace, for he that dismisses thee is at peace with thee;' we must recognize in such teaching, amid whatever faults of life or thought, the presence of the Spirit of God. And so it is now with all sincere moral life which does not as yet own the Christian name. Its virtues are not to be denied, still less to be represented, according to some of the Western (not the Eastern) fathers[2], as splendid vices, unless indeed they are contented and self-sufficient instead of progressive and aspiring. Wherever justice and love are to be found in all their various manifestations, the love of kindred and of country, the generous and courteous demeanour of man to man, valour, love of truth, obedience, self-discipline, purity; wherever there is anything that is lovely and of good report; there is that which is an adumbration of, an aspiring towards, the image of Christ. We sometimes hear it said that an action or a character is good, but not Christian. What is usually meant by this is that it does not accord with some partial ecclesiastical standard of goodness. If it were really possible that there should be any virtue which is excluded from the Christian ideal, the Christian ideal would cease to be supreme, and would, consequently, cease to be divine. The confession of the divinity of our Lord is the assertion that all the scattered rays of light which shine in the world are gathered up in Him and radiate from Him again. What sometimes appears

---

[1] Bk. xii. 36.
[2] See Note X. On the contrast between the Eastern and Western Fathers in their view of the virtues of the heathen.

to be non-Christian virtue is really a stunted, perhaps a perverted, form of Christian virtue. Take away its restrictions, bring it back to its original principle, give it its full development, and it will shine forth as at least an aspiration towards the Christian ideal. It is thus that lives such as those of Saul or of Samson, though exceedingly faulty if judged by a Christian standard, are yet included in the cycle of revelation, and find their place among the moral phenomena which represent the half-conscious longings of the darker ages towards the Redeemer who was to come. The same thing may be said of all the imperfect forms of goodness which we find growing up among the heathen whether in ancient or modern times, or in Europeans who have not accepted the received Christianity. The ideal of life presented by Sakyamouni, or by Mahomet, or, again, by Plato, or by Marcus Aurelius, or, in the later centuries, by Lorenzo de Medici, or by Goethe, must partly be made to combine with our present Christian morality, partly be purified by it, partly be allowed to amplify our idea of what is morally good and Christian. Nay, we may ask whether there is any system of professedly Christian morals which does not need, on account of its imperfection, to undergo a similar process. There are also aspirations which have lost their way, like some of the Utopias of modern revolutionists, but which yet contain an element of truth and self-renouncing love. They all have in them some germ of the spirit of Christ, which touches the springs of all that is good in human nature. From that spirit all sincere moral systems arise; towards the full development of that they converge; from that they gain their constant renewal, and by it are lifted out of pedantry, or narrowness, or self-sufficiency, into union with the divine and eternal goodness.

The other consequence of Christian universality which I wish to emphasize relates to the question of the mutual independence of morals and religion. It is loudly claimed by some that ethics must be free, by which is usually meant that they must be free from ecclesiastical ideas and control. It is as loudly denied, on the other side, that there can be any true ethics but those of Christianity. If what has been advanced here be true, the dispute falls to the ground. If the Word of God is the light of men everywhere, and that Word is to be identified with the spirit of the life of Christ, then it follows that all moral truth is essentially Christian truth, and all true goodness, Christian goodness. What, then, is needed in a moralist is simply that he should be truthful. Let him be as independent as he possibly can, provided that independence does not mean caprice, or prejudice, or breaking away from fact and the necessary conditions of the problem. No thought can be genuine unless it be independent and original. Let him refuse to be guided by any authority but such as commends itself to his mature convictions. We may be quite sure that if he is seeking moral truth he is really seeking Christian truth, and the result of his thoughts will be to set forth some aspect of the manifold wisdom of Christ.

These considerations will, it is hoped, be helpful to many minds, as replacing by a higher unity the dualism which has been supposed to exist, the enmity between

Christianity and ordinary morals, while yet maintaining the supremacy of Christ. But there will be those who will think that the view here advanced drags down Christianity from its exalted pedestal, that it is incompatible with the doctrine of redemption through the life and death of Christ. If the presence of the Divine Spirit be recognized everywhere, it may be objected, and if the world itself has a moral purpose apparent even in its actual constitution, where is there room for the work of redemption? The difficulty is not one which is suggested by any new view. The question might have been put to St. Paul, when he said of Christ, 'By Him all things consist (or stand fast):' If all things stand fast in Christ, where is the need of a special Gospel? Or again, when he quoted the saying of Aratus, 'We are also His offspring:' If all men are God's children, what is the need of the tremendous sacrifice of Calvary to make them God's children? The answer, perhaps, may best be given by recurring to the example of the prophets and faithful men of Israel, whom we acknowledge to have been partakers of the Spirit of Christ before Christ appeared in the world. We may speak of them in scriptural language, not only as distant recipients of salvation to come, but as being themselves saviours[1] of their people. We may also trace the Spirit of Christ in the laws and life of Israel. But we do not argue from this that Christ's appearance in the world was nugatory. The relation of the men of the former dispensation to Christ, as described in Scripture, may be represented

[1] 2 Kings xiii. 5; Neh. ix. 27.

as that of the component stones of the arch to the keystone. 'They without us could not be made perfect.'

In a similar way we may trace the working of the Divine Spirit much more widely. That which was said of Israel, 'The Lord his God is with him,' may be said of humanity generally in various degrees. But, as Israel needed a redeemer, so, and still more, did the rest of mankind. The manifestation of the Son of God had a power altogether different from the secret influences of the unmanifested Word. It gathered, like a magnet, the scattered atoms of goodness; it was the assurance that God dwells among men, as betokened by the name Immanuel; it was the clear, fierce light which 'blackened the blot' of selfishness upon the face of humanity, and showed that it was by death and abnegation alone that it could be removed; it was the beacon which gathered in one the children of God who were scattered abroad, the fire at which they might re-kindle their aspirations, and an ever-fresh starting-point for redemptive effort. We need not speculate upon this, for what we are saying is merely a record of the long experience to which in this nineteenth century we can appeal. History shows us two things: first, that every social state has a divine element working within it, so that if it could attain the ideal at which it aims, it would fulfil the divine purpose; but secondly, that every social state is in disorder, and therefore needs a redemptive process to restore it to harmony. It is Christ whose spirit alone can restore the broken altar of human life, and, by bringing back the world to its true constitution, change it into the kingdom of God.

We can estimate in the present age better than in any that have gone before the merits of other systems of religion and morality as compared with Christianity. We see their merits more clearly, and can frankly acknowledge them. But we see, also, more clearly their inadequacy for the redemption of the world. The study of the history of Israel, as the typical people, exhibits a longing rather than an attainment. 'Many prophets and kings have desired to see the things which ye see, and have not seen them.' The truth which was struggling needed its full expression in the life, and, still more, the death of Christ, to assure its dominion over men's hearts and consciences[1]. If that was true of Judaism, it is still more true of other systems of morality and religions. The best among the Greek philosophers confessed[2] their need of some new power to give practical effect to their theories; and who can say that the life of Greece was not greatly deteriorated in the second and third centuries of our era from what it had been in the days of Aristotle and Demosthenes? The ironical strength of Socrates had no redeeming force. The beautiful life of Marcus Aurelius gives the impression of resignation, not of hope. The excellent maxims of Con-

---

[1] The Jews of the present day practically interpret the law as Christ interpreted it, and acknowledge self-sacrifice and the universality of the Divine Love. They thus partake very largely of the benefits of a redemption the means of which they do not as yet recognize.

[2] See Note XI. Expressions in Aristotle confessing the practical impotence of his moral philosophy.

fucius at most bound fast the life of China in an iron law. Buddhism gave peace, but it was, at least as to the social and political life, the peace of resigned despair. Mahomet's grand iconoclasm spent itself almost in its first onset, and has failed to exhibit any new principle of vitality. But the cross of Christ is new in every age, and has changed the face of the world, and has been the spring of civilization and of an untiring progress. The nations among which it is acknowledged form the head of humanity, although it has hitherto asserted its influence over them very partially. We cannot doubt that it is capable of far greater results in the future than that which we can trace in the past; for we are only now beginning to recognize it as a social and political force which is able to do for commonwealths and great societies of men that which it has done for individuals, to uplift fallen nations, to breathe hope into the weaker classes and races of mankind, to give a human heart to systems of commerce and science and art which have seemed non-moral before, to abolish war, to blend the whole world into one.

If now we are convinced that the Christian spirit which flows from the cross of Christ, and which works in the Church, is capable of thus renewing the world, we must observe carefully the method by which this renewal is accomplished. The process is not uniform. Not every individual or every community receives the redemptive power equally or at the same time. The principle of election is always apparent. By this is not meant an arbitrary selection of individuals or of nations to be made happy or good, while the rest are excluded; but their call to pre-eminent service, often to pre-eminent suffering, with a view to the final inclusion of the rest. 'Salvation is of the Jews.' It is an undoubted fact that the true religion came to us through the chosen nation, and that we profit by their long and painful training in righteousness. In the world of the present day there are elect nations which are actually and professedly Christian, and also nations which are only potentially Christian: and so it is with individuals. And, further, in every circle of moral life there are those in whom the Christian spirit is vigorous, and those who only partially share it. It is the task of those who possess it most fully to communicate it to the rest. Through schools and churches, through Christian families, through uprightness in professions, through a noble self-abnegation in political life, through unselfish devotion to the pursuit of knowledge or of art, through a thousand channels in which self-renouncing love and noble aspiration may work, with infinite varieties of operation, now sudden and now gradual, the process of salvation goes on. Those who actively and consciously set their faces towards the goal of the complete salvation of mankind, form the actual Church which now exists; a body which, since it is growing, it is impossible to define. Those who are subject to the saving influence, or may become subject to it, but have not yet fully admitted its dominion, form the Church of the future. When the potential Church becomes the actual Church, the redemptive process will be complete—the salvation of the world will be effected.

It may be thought that, in this exposition of our subject, we have assumed too much, that we have started with the belief that the world requires such a power as that of Christian faith, which is rather the thing that needs to be demonstrated. Indeed, when the progress of mankind through the Christian centuries is described, it is sometimes asked whether it is indeed Christianity which has been the cause of good, and not rather some power inherent in the race itself, and the natural development of mankind[1]. If, however, the views we have endeavoured to set forth be true, we need not draw this contrast, since the spirit of Christ is the true spirit of humanity, and moral progress is necessarily Christian progress. We need not think of Christ's influence as exercised mainly from without, and operating upon the world as a separate power, but rather as a spiritual process going on within, though witnessed by striking outward events, and especially by the life of our Lord Himself. But what it is important to show is that every human society demands for its proper completion that spirit of which the life and death of Christ are the fullest expression—the spirit of self-renouncing love. Let us put aside theology for the moment. We arrive equally at our result when we deal with social ideas in themselves and ask what it is that society requires in order to reach its proper development.

Every association of men requires for its maintenance

[1] See for instance the book entitled 'Gesta Christi; or, a History of Humane Progress under Christianity,' by Mr. C. Loring Brace (Hodder and Stoughton), and the review of it in the *Times* of Feb. 13th, 1883, in which this question is raised.

the spiritual principle of self-renouncing love, and requires it the more the more solid and intense its life becomes. Without this society cannot reach its ideal, but falls to pieces. What gravitation is to the physical universe, that Christian love is to the moral world and to each of the moral microcosms contained within the whole body of humanity. In whatever association men unite, the fact that they live together demands some abatement of animality and selfishness, some confession of mutual dependence, some bond of just relations. Even in its lowest stages we must reckon these moral dispositions as forms of the spirit of Christ; but, as men advance in refinement, in organization, in the power to apprehend humanity as a whole, the fuller righteousness becomes a necessary condition of their social life. We may trace the rudiments of just relations even in the lower creatures. In mankind we trace them more distinctly, even in the most backward stages of development; not even savages can exist together without some tenderness of family relations, some moralizing laws; and in these love and public spirit are evoked. But when the higher culture is attained, and civilization becomes more complex, there is a demand for a deeper spiritual affection; the moral ideas and customs which sufficed before suffice no longer. At last, the Christian ideal of righteousness becomes an absolute necessity. And the case is similar if we trace the progress of men from a state of lonely thought to complete sociality. In thought and in the pursuit of knowledge men seem most independent; in these spheres moral considerations seem hardly to have any place, and the mind is left alone with its object. But it is not really so. The very condition of thought is sympathy. In all branches of knowledge, even in those which seem most remote from human life, we are sustained by our consciousness of the bearing of our thought on mankind, and by the spiritual presence of those who have worked in the same field before us, and of those now working at our side. We are quickened by discussion, and incited by a wish to communicate our thought to others; and this implies some form of moral affection. But the isolated thinker is not the typical man. The social life is man's proper sphere, that round which all thought circles, and in which the results of thought are tested, harmonized, and made fruitful. In this the need of the Christian spirit for the sustenance and working out of true relations becomes more fully apparent. All the branches of human life, the family, the associations of men for the pursuit of knowledge or of art, their commercial and political associations, the more general relations of the races and nations to each other, demand the Christian spirit to complete their proper development [1].

How can family life, that most necessary of social states, be conducted without unselfish affection? The family has, through Christian influence, come to be no longer, as it once was, the abode of selfish indulgence and of tyranny, but the training-place of mutual

---

[1] I have worked out these thoughts more fully in Lect. VII, on 'The Christian Basis of Human Societies.' But it seemed desirable to give a preliminary sketch here of what is implied in the redemption of *the World*.

respect and subordination. It is a spiritual, not a material bond, which unites its members; and the support of this spiritual bond, by the cultivation of the Christian spirit, must be the chief concern of all who wish family life to increase its beneficent influence, and not to succumb to the dangers which threaten it. Can education go on without the spiritual principle? If education is in its fullest form the training of character, it demands the exercise by the educator and pupil alike of the highest spiritual feelings.

Is the advance of knowledge, then, apart from the spiritual life? On the contrary, it must be, if genuine and comprehensive, identical with the advance of spirituality [1]; for a thing known is a thing incorporated into the human personality and made spiritual; and if we consider humanity as the spiritual centre of the world, and Christ as the crown of humanity, we shall be least willing to say that 'science and Christ have nothing to do with each other;' but rather shall think of Christ as the highest object of knowledge. And still more, when men combine for the pursuit and co-ordination of knowledge in schools, and universities, and learned societies, the bonds, both objective and subjective, which hold them to their work and to one another, must be those of the Christian spirit, which is at once the highest object of knowledge, and the greatest incentive to its pursuit.

If we turn to the sphere of art, the demand for the Christian spirit is no less evident. The purpose of art

[1] See Note XII. Extracts from Carlyle, Lubbock, and Darwin on the relation of knowledge to morality and religion.

is to make life lovely; its degradation comes from dulness and conventionalism and the mercenary spirit, and it needs an elevation and a refreshment which must come from the spiritual region. How can art gladden us unless it is inspired by hope? How can the world sustain itself as worthy of the grace which art sheds over it, except through those nobler feelings which we identify with Christianity? If we say that art should be childlike, not reflective, this only draws it into closer connexion with the childlike spirit which Christ commended. But further, not only is the poet, whose art is the highest, justly recognized as a prophet through the longings and yearnings which he evokes in us; but the painter or sculptor who makes nature and the human form more loveable, and the musician who carries us out of the reach of care into 'realms where the air we breathe is love,' is a revealer to us of the nature of God. But to fulfil this function he must have his mind open to the ideal and the divine. Even good taste, which governs artistic performance, lies mainly in the perception of harmony, in the *esprit d'ensemble*, which is almost identical with religion. To maintain this spirit, it must be in contact with the channels by which Christian universalism diffuses itself through the world.

If we turn to the sphere of commerce, is it not clear that the soul of the nobler relations in trade is honesty and trustfulness; and also that it is the witness of the unity of the race, the bond of amity between nations? But to preserve this higher spirit, to prevent trade from sinking into mere materialism and becoming the handmaid of selfishness and the parent of violence, it must cultivate the spiritual perception, the unselfish spirit which aims constantly at justice and the general good.

Pass on to the political and social life; these are, in their highest state, the very home of justice and of love. A bad state of society is one which is dull or frivolous, tasteless or immoral; what social life needs is the breath, the spirit, which is divine, first in its purity and truth, and then in its bright living character, which makes it, like the salt, a preservative from insipidity and corruption. Similarly, what political life needs is disinterestedness, and magnanimity, and largeness of view, all of which are pre-eminently a part of the Christian mind. Extend the ideal of society and politics to international affairs, and you have the need of the Christian spirit in the most eminent degree. That spirit is one of love, which is expansive and universal; and it is this which is specially needed in international relations; it is this which is incessantly demanded by those who are striving for universal peace. If nations are ever to cease from the fanatic dislike which has its aliment in difference of customs, or language, or race, or national traditions; if ever the horror of vast standing armies is to cease; if ever Europe is to present some other spectacle than that of a brutal struggle for life, in which diplomacy is merely the registrar of decrees of violence; if ever the influence of the Christian nations of Western Europe on the backward races of the world is to become paternal and preservative; it will be through the Christian spirit, through which alone the common Father is recognised, and differences become complementary graces in the one body, and the capacity of all men for the higher life is perceived, and the glory of our common humanity outshines all occasions of enmity.

If we take the word Culture as summing up the higher life of the race, we may see how much the Christian spirit is required for its support.

Culture is sometimes opposed to Christianity; but the more we think of Christ as the restorer of humanity, the more we shall incline to identify His religion with culture rather than separate them. If culture be social not lonely, spiritual not sensual, harmonious not one-sided, self-giving not self-asserting, it is hardly to be distinguished from the spirit of Christ. And if we find that human nature throughout its history is always striving for this culture, and the progress of civilization is the growth of men and peoples in all that is humane, what is this but to acknowledge that man, in the untamed degraded state through which he is passing, groans and cries for Christ?

But (to follow out as a matter of history this process by which the needs of human society lead up to Christ and to the Christianized society), we must observe that the progress of culture is expansive, from the individual to the society, from the lesser society to the larger. The method of the training of the race is by mutual contact and the intercourse of nations; so men grow into that sense of brotherhood and the universal spirit without which human life and civilization is stunted. The family grows into the tribe, and the tribe into the nation; and thus men are drawn on from the most elementary and selfish needs to those in which their acquirements and enjoyments are those of others also, those which belong to larger and larger circles of interest, intellectual, artistic, moral, universal. Even the nation is not complete by itself. There is a national exclusiveness which engenders hate, and for which must be substituted that which is humane and universal. Towards this larger union the life of the world constantly and necessarily tends. The Asiatic empires represented this universality, though in a very imperfect form. They were accepted, not merely by the submission of the nations to force, but by the instinct of unity. As each in succession failed in its mission, it was succeeded by another more capable, and on the whole, more humane. Nebuchadnezzar is a nobler form than Sesostris, and Cyrus than Nebuchadnezzar. The Asiatic civilization gains its unity in the Persian empire, the Greek under that of Macedon; and the great attempt is made under Alexander and his successors to combine east and west, Europe and Asia, into one. Then comes the Roman, more capable than his predecessors of organization and universality. The Roman Stoic has a perception of the unity of mankind. The Roman legists know nothing of race-distinctions; and by them the outer form of an universal society was given to the then known world. But it was a form, a legal bond only. What was wanted by the great Roman organization was a spiritual force, to bind its members together[1]: and it

---

[1] This absence of a spiritual power in the Roman Imperial system is well

was precisely this which Christianity supplied, and which made it a bond of the new society when the Roman unity was broken up. That universality which was only a bare and formal outline in the Roman organization, which was a philosophical theory with the Stoics, became a reality and an enthusiasm in the early Christian Churches; for in them there was neither Jew nor Greek, Barbarian or Scythian, bond or free, male or female. This was rendered possible by the life and death of our Lord, and He therefore stands forth by right as the universal spiritual King. From Him a new beginning was made, since in Him it was shown that the true bond which men needed was not force nor thought, but love; and from the first century to the present day the leading portion of the human race has been aiming at a unity which can only be attained when Christian love is supreme. For want of such a bond the Roman Empire fell. By some partial recognition of such a bond, the Imperial and Papal system of the Middle Ages gained a certain power of cohesion. For lack of its recognition in the sphere of national and, still more, of international relations, discord and violence have reigned in Europe for many centuries. This spiritual bond is at this moment the great need of the world, the long-desired crown of our civilization, and the hoped-for guarantee of its permanence. And this spiritual bond the Christian spirit and religion alone can give.

I say the Christian spirit and religion alone, for

brought out in an Essay on Roman Colonies in Mr. George Brodrick's Political Studies (Kegan Paul and Co., 1879), and also in Dr. Congreve's Lectures on the Roman Empire of the West (J. H. Parker, 1855).

ultimately there can be but one religion. If the human race is one and is to be drawn into unity, it is impossible that there can be ultimately different religions. Nay, if we mean by religion the recognition of a divine unity and of a moral order, such a recognition may be at least dimly discerned behind the veil of many and strange doctrines in all countries and ages: and this recognition, we must believe, is everywhere destined to grow to its full, that is, its Christian form. Different modes of conceiving metaphysically of the one God, different ways of approaching Him, there still may be; but all must be bound together by a central moral principle. Different moral standards there cannot ultimately be. When the actual life of man as known and lived out in the world is acknowledged as the chief concern of religion, we have in this a central point on which all religious ideas converge, and by reference to which they may continually be tested.

The ideal of life, that is religion. When this is clearly seen, can we hesitate in saying that the ideal presented by the life of Christ is supreme? It is supreme in this especially, that it admits of comprehension and of growth. It is not necessary to oppose it to any of the ideals of life which any serious religious system sets before us. If they are, indeed, placed in rivalry with the image of Christ, so as to bid us discard it in their favour, Christians will naturally be tempted, as in past times, to disparage them. But we may think of them as 'broken lights' of the one true light, or treat them, as St. Paul treated Judaism, as school-masters to lead men to Christ; or, again, as national characteristics, destined to be numbered among the special *charismata* which give a local colouring to the central faith. No one doubts that our present Christian ideas are largely coloured by such influences as the Platonic and Aristotelian philosophies or the notions, even the fictions, of Roman Law[1]. Even in the New Testament we have to admit a local colouring of the schools of Jerusalem, or Alexandria, or Tarsus. And such a development and modification of the Christian system, as we are contemplating, is quite in accordance with the teaching of a 'diversity of gifts with the same spirit[2].' We shall ultimately have the one great ideal, that of the life of Christ, and one spirit, the spirit of Christ. But there will still be room for a Judaic and a Gentile Christianity, an artistic or a scientific Christianity, a Western Christianity, and one strongly coloured (much more strongly perhaps than we can at present conceive possible) by Oriental ideas; for Palestine is Oriental rather than European, and Christ belongs to the East at least as much as to the West[3]. To suppose that Christianity, as it at present exists among us, is to supersede all other systems or ideals would be to narrow fatally the life of mankind. But to believe that the central moral and spiritual principles which spring from the life of Christ, those which make us conceive

---

[1] See Note XIII, where a passage from Sir H. Maine's Ancient Law on the influence of Roman Law on the theology of the Western Church is quoted.

[2] See the teaching of St. Paul in 1 Cor. xii. and Eph. iv. on this subject, which admit of a much wider application than is commonly given them.

[3] See Note XIV. An extract from a Lecture by the late Baboo Keshub Chunder Sen entitled 'Jesus Christ, Europe and Asia.'

of the supreme power as fatherly love and righteousness, and of man's true life as a communion with that righteous and loving power—to believe, I say, that these principles must eventually be recognized as supreme, is not only reasonable but seems to be demanded by experience.

But these principles can never assert their supremacy merely as a philosophy. They must take form in human institutions. Christianity is not a mere spirit, a spirit unclothed, but it enters into the institutions of mankind and moulds or reforms them for its own purposes, and thus changes human society into the Church and body of Christ. And, since the progress of mankind is towards unity of organization (while allowing room for local differences), the result to which we look must be not only a universal Christianity but a universal Christian Church. The two factors, that of human organization growing to completeness, and that of the Christian spirit longing for an adequate body, thus find their meeting-place. That meeting-place must be a supreme Christian federation (a federation, the feeble beginnings of which we already see), with which all nations and minor societies will work in harmony. Thus we are brought round once more to the hope of a universal Church, which is synonymous with the human race organized in accordance with the Christian principle, and becoming, in all the relations of its component members, the home and organ of the Spirit of God.

The Church thus appears as the world transfigured by the Christian spirit of love. It will be the object of these Lectures to verify and impress this idea by showing how its realization has been aimed at in the religious development of mankind. It will not be attempted to do this by any exhaustive account of the religions of the world or of universal history, which would give these Lectures too great an expansion. If we believe that the Hebraic and Christian line of religious development is central and the others subsidiary, we may be content to keep to the main stream : for in this the Kingdom of God, which has been unconsciously sought by other systems, has been the object of conscious aim and practical effort.

The second Lecture, accordingly, will treat exclusively of Judaism. It will be pointed out that Judaism was not a religion merely but a polity, its aim being the establishment of righteousness in the relations of men within the commonwealth ; that the political and moral laws and the national organization form its central point, its kings and judges being in the fullest sense ministers of God. It will be shown also that this, rather than what is strictly called religious doctrine, formed the main subject of the Hebrew writings, and that the prophets were practical teachers and statesmen, urging continually upon the people and their rulers those just and loving relations in which the kingdom of God consists.

In the third Lecture the same purpose will be traced in the teaching of our Lord and His Apostles, and the founding of the Christian Church. It will be shown that this teaching was not meant to result in the formation of a separate society for the purposes of religious worship, instruction and beneficence, but in a world-wide society capable of embracing and transforming all other societies; and that, while it presents a deeper and fuller righteousness than Judaism, it still aims, like Judaism, at the righteousness of the nation as well as the individual, and, going beyond Judaism, at the blending of all nations into one grand organized brotherhood.

The fourth, fifth, and sixth Lectures will show how attempts have been made at three different epochs for the realization of this great organized brotherhood or universal Church; namely, first, in the conversion of the Roman Empire; secondly, in the mediaeval system from Charlemagne to Innocent III; thirdly, at the era of the Reformation. Of these, the fourth Lecture will describe the Imperial and Mediaeval efforts; the fifth, those of the Reformation and its adjacent periods, including the work of Savonarola at Florence, of Calvin at Geneva, and of the Jesuits in the revival of Catholicism, the system of Wolfgang and Erastus, and the attempts of Knox in Scotland, and of the Puritan colonists in America to found Christian communities. The sixth will show the same attempts made in a different form in England at the Reformation, with its results in our subsequent history.

The seventh Lecture will proceed on a different method. It will be an attempt to present the idea of a Christianized society, taking the various associations into which men naturally enter, and showing how each of these demands for its full development the spirit of Christ, and when thus developed becomes a branch of the Church universal.

The last Lecture will take a review of the present condition of mankind, in view of the hope of such a development, and will attempt to show by what changes each of the circles or associations into which society is divided may become branches of the Church, and society itself be changed into the kingdom of God.

I ask not merely for a candid hearing but for earnest and prayerful co-operation of thought. What is to be said in these Lectures is not a mere theory. It is an attempt also at practical guidance. In all investigations theory, and even hypothesis, are necessary[1]; for we must present a general statement of the facts and show the bond which connects them; but it must also be such as will shed a light on the pathway which we have to tread. It must do more in an investigation like the present; for Christianity is essentially progressive, and no theory or general statement of its purposes can be valid which does not teach us to look steadily into the future with burning and enthusiastic hope. It may safely be said that no such theory has as yet appeared as to the facts of Christian history, and consequently the Churches are to a certain extent working in the dark. But if by attending to the intimations of Scripture and reviewing God's dealings in the past, we can evolve a theory which adequately explains the facts, it will also serve as a means of quickening our hopes and our energies; and we may see Christians once more, with the primitive fearlessness and confidence, advancing to the spiritual conquest of the world.

[1] See Note XV. J. S. Mill on the use of hypothesis in scientific investigation.

LECTURE II.

THE JEWISH CHURCH.

> PSALM cxxii. 3-9. Jerusalem is builded as a city that is compact together: whither the tribes go up, the tribes of the Lord, unto the testimony of Israel, to give thanks unto the name of the Lord. For there are set thrones of judgment, the thrones of the house of David. Pray for the peace of Jerusalem: they shall prosper that love thee. Peace be within thy walls, and prosperity within thy palaces. For my brethren and companions' sakes, I will now say, Peace be within thee. Because of the house of the Lord our God I will seek thy good.

RELIGION consists in the relations of spiritual beings, their establishment, their maintenance, their exercise. Whether the word be derived from *Religere*, and signify pondering, or from *Religare*, and signify a binding together, the spiritual relation is that to which it necessarily leads. In the barest form, as a meditation upon God, or the world, or man, upon life or eternity, it constitutes a relation between him who meditates and that on which he meditates. But as the central unity before which all separate interests must bow grows upon his view, the demand for the establishment of relations between him and the organized and centred universe grows stronger and clearer. When he comes

Training in National Righteousness. 49

to know the central unity as the Father, as Love, then the relation between him and that unity becomes personal, spiritual. And this extends to all parts of the world, and especially to the relations of men to one another. They are all ultimately held fast by love.

Human history is necessarily the history of religion, because it is the history of human relations. The fault of history, as it has commonly been written, is, that it has dwelt too much on events, too little on human relations. Great events may pass and leave human relations much as they were. In any case, the human relations which cause or are caused by the event are of more importance than the event itself[1]. The more modern historians attempt to show us the real life of the people. It is a difficult task; but the man who has a genuine historical faculty will be exercised in it continually. We ask not merely, What happened? But, Why did it happen? And, What did the actors think or feel? And, What were the moral and social results? We are often tempted to cry in despair in the course of historical study, Who will lift the veil of mere events? Who will disclose to us the growth of spiritual principles?

In the preliminary Lecture of this course it was maintained that the destination towards which the Christian Church should direct its hopes and its efforts is an all-embracing community held together in all its relations by the Divine justice and love. The present

[1] See the remarks on this subject in the Preface to Green's 'Short History of the English People.'

Lecture will point out that just such a community, though in a limited and rudimentary form, is that which is presented in the Old Testament, as designed by the great teachers of Irsael, and partly realized in its history.

If we regard the Hebrew history as a revelation, that is, a disclosure of spiritual truth, it is because in it the spiritual principles are made distinctly to appear; and because the spiritual principles assumed or aimed at are true or growing towards truth. But the method of this revelation is not primarily by abstract statements, but through the life of the nation. It is not a system of theology, but religion realised in a social state which discloses the true principles of life and faith. Israel is not a sect but a Church.

Where, then, are we to find the life of the people? Chiefly in their laws. These form the centre round which the history turns. It is through the constitution of the Jewish state or Church, and the laws concerning just relations between man and man, concerning the family, concerning the righteous bearing of classes and individuals to one another, and concerning the administration of justice, that the central revelation is made. It is true that law is apt to be regarded as a mechanical form imposed upon men, and we contrast men's laws with their life, or their sentiments, or their songs. But if we regard law more philosophically in its close connexion with life, we may distinguish between that which is fictitious or merely imposed and that which is of genuine growth, springing out of, or accepted by, the better conscience of the people. We may also trace the spirit of the law and its central idea[1]. The Jewish records disclose a state in which the laws sprung directly from a consciousness of God overruling and indwelling.

The law of Israel was eminently spontaneous in its source. The attempts to show that it was derived from any foreign source have failed. It expresses the higher life of Israel alone. In no history do we see a clearer illustration of the saying that a constitution must grow, not be made. We may add that, just as in our own nation it is difficult to define the constitution precisely, and it has never been written down, but consists of a mass of relations partly understood or assumed, partly enshrined in actual laws, so it was with Israel. And, as Englishmen look back to the great charter as the seminal point from which their constitution was developed, so the Israelites looked back to Moses and Mount Sinai[2]. We may by this consideration to some extent allay the conflicts of criticism as to the exact date of the various laws, and of the books in which they are contained[3]. The phases through which the constitution seems to have passed are to some extent a development, to some extent an adaptation to new circumstances; and the fact that at one time the worship is diffused through the country while at another time it

---

[1] Montesquieu who first did this describes the laws appropriate to various social conditions, those of monarchy, or aristocracy, or republicanism. Though Montesquieu made the mistake of treating mankind as too plastic, and law too much as the formative principle in each case, yet his merit in tracing the spirit or underlying principle of the laws of each country cannot be contested.

[2] In each case, however, there was a previous development which made the assertion of the law possible.

[3] See Note XVI. An Excursus on the books of the Old Testament as a basis for history.

is confined to the central sanctuary, or that at different periods the magisterial, the prophetical, or the priestly power becomes prominent, or again, that the sacrificial office is first general, then Levitical, then strictly sacerdotal, only implies that the elements which were present from the first grouped themselves at different epochs in different ways. It does not follow from the fact that the laws as we have them now were not all written down at an early date, that they had no existence till they took their present form: the students of ancient law have shown us that law exists in the phase of instinct or of custom long before it finds its expression in a code[1]. And, further, the justice which the laws aim at is never complete. This is the case in other countries, but pre-eminently in Israel. The successive casts of the law which critics trace out are successive attempts to present and enforce the divine righteousness. But the ideal is never attained. As the history is a prophecy of a better state, so the laws are an effort to realize the better state. Even the precepts which were given for the hardness of men's hearts were, as it were, a pleading on behalf of a better feeling, of a righteousness to come.

The real convictions of a nation are best seen through their poetry, for the poet expresses the deeper feelings of those for whom he writes. What is it of which the Hebrew poets sing? The theme which is more than any other upon their lips is the law of Jehovah[2]. What, it is often asked, is this law which is sweeter to them than honey? When we read the Pentateuch, we are impressed and perplexed by the bulk of the laws of cere-

[1] See Note XVII on Customary Law.   [2] See especially Ps. xix. and cxix.

monial and of peculiar customs. But it is not of these that the Psalmists speak. In the Psalms there are a few faint allusions to ceremonial customs, such as the laws of drink-offerings of blood[1], or of forbidden food[2], or the purging with hyssop[3]; a few words about the new moon and solemn feast-days[4]; not a word about circumcision, not a word about the passover, not a word about the Sabbaths, not a word about ceremonial uncleanness. There is, probably, in modern hymns, eighteen centuries after Christ, more of artificial religion than in the Psalms written in the bosom of Judaism. But, on the other hand, almost every Psalm appeals to the law of plain justice, public and private. There are denunciations of those who break through the just relations established by the law, who persecute the poor helpless man[5], who oppress the fatherless and the widow[6]; there are ideal pictures of the just ruler[7], the just judge[8], the just king[9]; a delight in the feasts as politico-religious gatherings[10], a pride in the capital as the centre of the national life[11]; a constant and thankful reference to the events of their

---

[1] Ps. xvi. 4 : 'Their drink-offerings of blood will I not offer.'
[2] Ps. cxli. 4 : 'Let me not eat of their dainties.'
[3] Ps. li. 7.   [4] Ps. lxxxi. 3.   [5] Ps. cix. 16.
[6] Ps. xciv. 6.
[7] Ps. ci. This Psalm presents a picture of one who endeavours to rule his family, his court, and his kingdom according to the just law.
[8] Ps. lxxxii. 1-4 : 'God judgeth among the gods. . . . Defend the poor and fatherless,' &c.
[9] Ps. lxxii. 1-7 : 'Give the king thy judgments, O Lord. . . . He shall judge thy people with righteousness.'
[10] See especially Ps. cxxii : ' Our feet shall stand within thy gates, O Jerusalem. . . . Thither the tribes go up,' &c.
[11] Ps. xlviii. 12 : 'Walk about Zion, and go round about her,' &c. Ps. cxxii. 6, 8. 'Pray for the peace of Jerusalem. . . . For my brethren and companions' sakes, I will now say, Peace be within thee.'

national history[1]. It is the moral and political law, not the ceremonial, which is enshrined in the hearts of the people.

There is no such spectacle in history as that presented by this attachment to the law. The Eastern races bow down under their laws, or, as in China, accept them as an iron framework, or, as in the Buddhist system, leave the whole political life aside. The Greek was taught generally to reverence the Themistes and those who administered them; but, as to the laws of his own state, the ideals he builds are usually the contrary of the actual. Pericles describes in majestic language the character of Athens[2]; but Thucydides, who reports him, constantly shows his distrust of the Athenian laws, and is glad when the adverse fortune of war causes them to be changed[3]. The Spartan's law was to him a fate rather than a treasured possession. In general, Greek politics exhibit a restless desire for change[4], an oscillation between aristocracy and democracy, and a readiness to change the laws root and branch at the will of the dominant party. The Romans said that the good man was he who observed the decrees of the fathers, the laws and ordinances; but evidently such good men kindled no enthusiasm. Even in our own country, where the constitution deservedly inspires a warm affection and even a kind of worship, which has been expressed in the eloquence of Burke and the poems of Tennyson, yet no one has spoken of our laws

[1] Ps. xliv: 'We have heard with our ears, O God, our fathers have told us.' Pss. lxxviii, cv, cvi, &c.
[2] Thucyd. ii. 40-1.
[3] Thucyd. viii. 97.
[4] See Aristotle's Politics, especially Book viii.

II.] *Training in National Righteousness.* 55

with the glowing delight with which the Psalmist spoke of the laws of Israel. Nowhere else has it been felt that the law presented a divine ideal which was within the reach of a just ruler, and was at least partially realized in the better days of the nation; that it was like a tower in which all, but especially the weak, could find their refuge and their redemption; that it was a direct reflexion of the eternal righteousness. And the good man according to the law has the entire confidence of the people; he also is a worthy object of the Psalmist's praise[1]. The reason is evident, namely this, that the law was not merely prohibitory of certain crimes, but that it presented, in a practical form, an ideal of righteousness, not the righteousness which merely gives to each his due, but the divine righteousness, which goes beyond itself, which is touched with the spirit of sacrifice, which says, 'Thou shalt love thy neighbour as thyself.' The Hebrew law was loveable because it incessantly demanded care for the poor.

The paramount importance of the moral and political laws seems to have escaped the notice of most of those who have written on the Old Testament. Their minds have been mainly occupied with the historical events, or with the theology, or with the dates of the books; and the law has been examined with a view to the light which it might shed on these points. Even in Ewald its full examination is relegated to a separate work, the Antiquities. It has yet to be set forth in connexion with the history as the sure index of the

[1] See especially Ps. xxxvii. and cxii.

life of the nation, as the expression of their true relations and their religion.

Their land law was the basis of the system; and this rested distinctly on a religious sanction. The land was believed to have been measured out by Joshua by the line and the lot, and a portion assigned to each family. It was a sacred thing. 'The Lord forbid it' me, said Naboth to Ahab, 'that I should give thee the inheritance of my fathers[1].' There the family was to live according to the righteous law, so that each separate portion might be holy, and the whole might be a holy land. 'A full reward be given to thee,' said Boaz to Ruth[2], when she returned to claim her husband's inheritance, 'of the Lord God of Israel, under the shadow of whose wings thou art come to trust.' The land could not be sold for ever, because, so God is represented as saying, 'the land is Mine[3].' At the year of jubilee it returned to the family. We see how this passed into a spiritual idea when we find the Psalmist saying, of his whole estate temporal and spiritual, 'The lines are fallen unto me in pleasant places, yea, I have a goodly heritage;' or of God Himself, 'The Lord is the portion of mine inheritance[4].'

This religious value for the soil bred a wholesome agricultural industry—in that day at least the most moralizing of all pursuits. The Israelites were not traders like the Phœnicians—that would have brought them into a contact with the heathen for which they were as yet unfitted: nor freebooters and nomads, like the Ishmaelites—that would have hindered all steady

[1] 1 Kings xxi. 3.   [2] Ruth ii. 12.   [3] Lev. xxv. 23.   [4] Ps. xvi. 5, 6.

II.]   *Training in National Righteousness.*   57

civilization: nor manufacturers, like the Egyptians—
that would have demanded a more advanced state of
social organization than they were prepared for: nor
were they, except for one brief epoch, organized for
vast imperial enterprises like the Babylonians; these
were impossible in those ages, as the experience of
Solomon seems to show, without slave-gangs and
oppression[1]. They were to be a people of simple,
peaceable, industrious agriculturists, not exciting the
jealousy of their neighbours, and having little intercourse with them. They had officers[2] of tens and fifties,
hundreds and thousands; but these, though they served
also for war, were, according to their traditional constitution, appointed primarily for judgment and administration. They had towers in or near their cities[3] for
protection; but we hear of no regular fortresses till
the time of Solomon[4]. The wants of the people were
few and were supplied by themselves. There was
much equality among the people, as is the case where
each family possesses a portion of the soil; and the
few men who, like Nabal[5] or Barzillai[6], mostly by
keeping flocks and herds, obtained exceptional wealth,
were not separated from their neighbours by any strong
line of distinction. We find Saul, when he had been
designated as king, coming after the herd out of the
field[7]. It is said in one place that the poor should

---

[1] 2 Chron. ii. 17, 18.
[2] Exod. iv. 29; v. 14; xviii. 21, 22. Deut. xvi. 18.
[3] Judges viii. 17; x. 51.
[4] To Solomon is attributed the building of forts and 'store-cities' (1 Kings ix. 17-19; xi. 27).
[5] 1 Sam. xxv. 2.   [6] 2 Sam. xvii. 27-29.   [7] 1 Sam. xi. 5.

never cease out of the land[1]; but only a few verses earlier[2] the ideal is given, an ideal attained probably more nearly than in any other country, and which would have been still more nearly attained had the law been fully observed: 'There shall be no poor among you.' This equality was the condition of that brotherly feeling which plays so large a part in the hortatory portions of the law and in the Psalms.

This feeling of brotherhood was further maintained by the laws concerning the common relations between men. The whole system is instinct with it. Safety for life and property was guaranteed by the ten commandments. Just dealing in trade was a sacred obligation. 'Just balances, just weights, a just ephah, a just hin shall ye have: I am the Lord[3].' Respect for age[4], friendliness towards neighbours[5], dutifulness to parents[6], were all inculcated under the same majestic sanction; and the safeguards of domestic purity were again and again vindicated, by direct penalties for overt offences and the more deadly forms of lust[7], and by earnest statements of the will of God in more secret matters.

But the most special feature of the legislation of Israel was the regard which it had to the interests of the weaker classes of society. To abuse the deaf[8], to make the blind[9] go out of the way, were actions

---

[1] Deut. xv. 11: 'The poor shall never cease,' &c.
[2] Deut. xv. 4: 'Save when there shall be no poor among you: for the Lord shall greatly bless thee,' &c.
[3] Lev. xix. 36. [4] Lev. xix. 32. [5] Ib. 18. [6] Ib. 3.
[7] Deut. xxii. 21–24; xxiii. 17. Lev. xix. 29; xx. 10–22; xxi. 7–9.
[8] Lev. xix. 14. Deut. xxvii. 18. [9] Ib.

accursed. Of the poor it was said, 'Thou shalt not shut thine hand from thy poor brother, but shalt surely lend to him[1].' And this principle was enforced in a variety of ways. No one was to shut up his vineyard or his corn-field. If the path lay across it, the weary traveller was to be allowed to take handfuls of corn or grapes as he passed[2]. When the harvest came, the rich man was not to gather all the produce or to rake up every ear from the ground, but to let some remain for the fatherless and widows to glean[3]. The state of widows in every other country was miserable in the extreme, as it is in India to this day. In Israel it was the object of peculiar care, a care attributed to God Himself[4]. Further, when a poor man[5] had pledged his garment, he was to be allowed the use of it for the night; if he was in debt, no interest was to be charged him[6], and at the year of jubilee he was to be free[7]; if he had sold himself into slavery, he was not to remain beyond the sixth year, and his wealthier brother whom he had served was not to send him away empty at the close of his service, but to give him help to recommence his career as a free man[8].

It is true that polygamy and slavery are recognized by the Mosaic law; but no one can read it fairly without seeing that the effort throughout is to mitigate these evils. And they were mitigated. Malachi, the last of the prophets, protests against polygamy and

---

[1] Deut. xv. 7, 10.   [2] Deut. xxiii. 25.   [3] Deut. xxiv. 19-21.
[4] Deut. x. 18. Ps. lxviii. 5.   [5] Ex. xxii. 26.   [6] Lev. xxv. 36.
[7] Deut. xv. 7-9.   [8] Deut. xv. 12-15.

divorce altogether, as contrary to God's original purpose[1]. We read of no slavery in the Gospels. When it was attempted, some twenty-five years ago, to employ the Jewish law as a justification of slavery as it then existed in the Southern States of the American Union, a professor of history in this University showed, in a remarkable treatise[2], that no such comparison was valid; that the slaves in Israel were looked upon as brothers, admitted to the religious rites of the family, and cared for by the laws. The slave-law of Israel, if contrasted with that of Greece or Rome in the days of their greatest refinement, was that of solicitous mercy compared with utter neglect[3]. The slave in Israel was under the care of God; the slave in Greece or Rome was given over to the caprice of his master. It was not till the reign of Hadrian that laws began to be made to mitigate the slave's condition in the Roman world.

Nor is it the fact that an anti-social attitude was fostered by the laws of Israel. Almost all the restrictions upon the beneficence of the law came not from the law itself, still less from the spirit of the law, but from the selfish turn which was given to it by the later Rabbis. The law said, 'Thou shalt love thy neighbour;' 'Thou shalt hate thine enemy,' was an unauthorized addition. 'An eye for an eye, and a tooth for a tooth.' Did this authorize revenge? It was really

---

[1] Mal. ii. 14-16.
[2] 'Does the Bible sanction American Slavery?' by Goldwin Smith. J. H. Parker, 1863. This treatise, though the immediate occasion for it is happily a thing of the past, should be read by all students of the Jewish Law.
[3] Goldwin Smith, p. 17.

the enforcement of equal justice, a legal preventative for the oppression which would have made light of the maiming of the poor and helpless. The law of the cities of refuge recognized, no doubt, the blood feud; but it mitigated it. The Hebrew laws of war, at least in the Deuteronomic legislation, are singularly mild[1]. As to strangers, we may contrast the alien law of Athens in its prime, which allowed all foreigners to be banished or sold into slavery, a law actually put in force in the days of Pericles, when 5000 persons not of pure Athenian blood, who had crept upon the registers, were banished or sold as slaves[2], with the words of Deuteronomy, at least two centuries before[3], 'The Lord loveth the stranger;' 'The stranger that dwelleth with you shall be as one born among you, and thou shalt love him as thyself.'

Time will not permit me to do more than sketch the system of the laws of Israel. It will be interesting, when the critical questions which have hindered the work have been decided, as they now bid fair to be, to see a comparative digest indicating the development of these laws, a work which, if the estimate of them here made be confirmed, yields to few in importance. For that which underlies these laws is not, as with other nations, a self-contained righteousness, by which each man maintains his own rights and position, but a loving, and, as I may say, a missionary righteousness. The spirit of these laws is that which was confirmed and widened by Christ

---

[1] Deut. xx. Goldwin Smith, pp. 16-18. [2] Goldwin Smith, p. 49.
[3] Deut. x. 18. Lev. xix. 34.

Himself, who in His own person realized and fulfilled it, and through Whom it must be transplanted into all the relations arising between His followers. For the present, I propose to show that these laws form the centre round which (1) the constitution of the nation, (2) its theology, (3) its history, (4) its literature, revolved.

1. The constitution of Israel was exceedingly simple. The true political method was followed of leaving each family and each locality as much as possible to themselves. It is probable that there were elders and officers in every township, such as those mentioned as the heads of the people before the Exodus [1], or the judges described in Exodus xviii as being appointed by Moses on the advice of Jethro. There was probably a central council [2], of which the type is given in the seventy elders in the time of Moses; and there were great assemblies of all Israel held on special occasions. The government was local, and partly patriarchal, partly democratic. Similarly, there were local judicatures round the various local sanctuaries [3], where the law was administered by the Levites, and by others who from time to time rose to eminence. The Deuteronomic legislation [4] requires the appointment of judges and officers in every city; but the stress laid upon their appointment seems to indicate that their exist-

---

[1] Ex. iv. 29.

[2] Judg. xx. 2; 1 Kings xviii. 19. See this subject worked out in Ewald's 'Antiquities of Israel,' Sect. iii. 1, (1), The Nation and its Leaders.

[3] Deut. xvii. 9, 11; xix. 17, 18; xxi. 5. See also Exod. xxii. 8, 9, where the causes are to be brought 'to God' or to 'the judges.' Compare Ewald's Chapter on The Administration of Justice, 'Antiquities,' p. 310.

[4] Deut. xvi. 18.

ence had been precarious before; and we read of special attempts made especially by Jehoshaphat[1], to remodel the system of judicature, which had apparently fallen into abeyance. In the early democratic stage of the nation, the law seems to have depended for its enforcement partly on family authority, partly on the spontaneous election of officers by the people (as it is said in the song of Deborah, 'They chose new gods[2]') but mainly on the general sense of its beneficence entertained throughout the community.

The law itself was the thing of main importance. The interpretation and enforcement of it was secondary. The great judges who appeared from time to time, such as Deborah and Samson, Eli and Samuel, were raised up by the Divine Spirit, and recognized by the conscience of the people as interpreters of the law. The spirit of justice which was in them rather than any direct appointment, the spirit of their office rather than any fixed legal position, gave them their authority, as was the case also with the prophets. Even after the establishment of the kingdom, the spirituality of mind which was needed for the exercise of authority is the point on which the chief stress is laid. Judgment was not, as with us, a matter of exact law and precedent, but of intuitive perception. The judge must be imbued with the spirit of the law and of its Divine Author. 'The spirit of the Lord must rest upon him, the spirit of wisdom and ghostly strength, which will make him of quick understanding in the fear of the Lord,' so that he does not judge by

[1] 2 Chron. xix. 5-11.   [2] Judg. v. 8.

superficial appearances, but righteously, 'reproving with equity for the meek of the earth [1].'

But, though judgment and government generally was thus local and spontaneous, there were forces at work which made for centralization. The nation became habituated to united action, and thus required to strengthen the central power. For defence in war this was especially necessary; and the succession of wars described in the Book of Judges, culminating in the attacks of the Philistines, led on naturally to the kingdom. 'The word of Samuel,' even when he was young, 'came to all Israel [2];' in his later days he is said to have gone on circuit, and was reverenced equally in all parts of the kingdom. The spirit of brotherhood, which was fostered by the law, demands the discipline of a central authority to maintain unity. The historian, looking back to the time before the monarchy, described those days as evil days, when every man did that which was right in his own eyes [3]. This longing for a central authority, though it had something faithless in it, was due to what is commonly called a political necessity; and thus, if something was lost by it, something also was gained. Religion fastened on the new institution, and the king became the chosen agent of Jehovah. But his duty was, before all other things, to be a minister of God's justice, to maintain the law in its integrity. 'He that ruleth men,' such are the words of David, 'must be just, ruling in the fear of

---

[1] Is. xi. 2-4. Compare 2 Sam. xxiii. 3-7, and Ps. ci.
[2] 1 Sam. iv. 1; vii. 15-17.
[3] Judg. xviii. 1; xix. 1; xxi. 25.

II.] *Training in National Righteousness.* 65

God¹.' When we read the 101st Psalm, we have before us the picture of the king in his court and his kingdom, walking in his house with a perfect and upright heart, meditating on mercy and on judgment in the fear of God; seeking to gather round him all who were of a similar spirit, and to cast out all evil-doers from the city of the Lord. The main duty of a king in Israel was to further the observance of the law.

With the central administration of justice, the central sanctuary came into prominence; and Jerusalem, under David, became what its name still connotes in Hebrew history and song. Its acknowledged supremacy made it the sacramental emblem of the national life, and greatly aided those affectionate relations which it was the design of the law to establish; it became the centre of all interests and of all hearts in the national brotherhood. There had been from the first a national centre, the frequenting of which had greatly conduced to the spirit of brotherhood which it was the design of the law to foster. And this was strengthened, especially, by the ordinance of the national feasts. It is true that these feasts were not at first rigorously observed. The Passover, in particular, seems to have been celebrated as a family, not a national feast, till the days of Hezekiah²: the feast of Tabernacles was not celebrated at Jerusalem till the time of Nehemiah³. But even in Exodus we find the command that all should present themselves before the Lord three times in the year⁴. We find it laid to the charge of Jeroboam

¹ 2 Sam. xxiii. 3. ² 2 Chron. xxx. 1–5, 26. ³ Neh. viii. 17.
⁴ Exod. xxiii. 14–17.

F

that he had changed the month in which the feast of Tabernacles was held [1]. And Jeroboam found it necessary to make a central sanctuary—a double one in his design, but a single one in the issue [2]; for the instinct of the people, even in the North, was towards unity [3]. The earlier days between Joshua and David have been compared to the early part of the Middle Ages in Europe; and they resemble them especially in the fact that the central power of the nation was gradually forming; but when the system was fully developed, the power of the centre became supreme. The Psalmists and Prophets do not speak of Palestine, but of Jerusalem, and Sion, and the Temple. Thither the tribes went up: there was the throne of David. This centre of unity sank into the heart of the people, and passed into the circle of their spiritual experience, as the 84th, 122nd, and 133rd Psalms fully testify: 'Unto the God of gods appeareth every one of them in Zion;' 'For my brethren and companions' sakes, I will now say, Peace be within thee;' 'Behold, how good and how pleasant it is for brethren to dwell together in unity.' We have thus, in the fondness inspired into national relations, a preparation for the deeper and more loving relations of the universal Church.

These simple constitutional arrangements were adequate to the wants of an agricultural people cut off by their situation from the rest of the world. They did not contemplate a progress like that to which modern communities are impelled by their more

---

[1] 1 Kings xii. 32.   [2] Ib. 26-29.   [3] 2 Chron. xxx. 11.

complex conditions of life; and the inequalities of station, which caused disquiet and revolution in the Greek communities and in Rome, were less marked in Israel, and also less felt, since its life was national not municipal. The Hebrews further, being Asiatics, were less prone to change than Europeans. On the other hand, Israel had a superiority from the fact of being a nation not a city. While Greece was an aggregate of cities, with but a feeble bond of union, and Rome a single city, propagating itself by off-shoot colonies, each the image of the parent tree, Israel was a nation which, even in the time of David and Solomon, had attained a considerable maturity of organization. Though the strictly political life was comparatively weak, the moral education was profound. Conduct, it has been said, was the pre-occupation of Israel. 'These commandments thou shalt teach to thy children, and shalt talk of them when thou sittest in thine house, and when thou walkest by the way, and when thou liest down, and when thou risest up[1].' But it was conduct provided for by public law, the exercise of sound moral relations within the largest unity then attainable. To maintain this law and these relations was the object of the constitution of the people of Israel.

2. The law of moral and political relations was also the centre of the theology of the Old Testament. Israel has been called a theocracy. Unhappily the word theocracy has been commonly taken to mean a government by priests. This the government of Israel

[1] Deut. vi. 7.

never was. If at times a priest was ruler, as in the case of Eli or Ezra or the Maccabæan princes, this was almost solely from the personal eminence of the individuals. Moses was not a priest, nor Joshua, nor any of the great judges, except Eli, nor any of the kings. In the later history the High Priestly office attained a certain political supremacy: but in the princes of the Asmonæan dynasty it was an appanage of their military greatness; while in the latter days, when Judaism had become rather a sect within the kingdom or empire than an independent nation, the High Priest's power had to be exercised with deference to the Idumæan and Roman rule. In the New Testament the High Priests are Sadducees, while the chief influence in the nation is exercised by their opponents the Pharisees. The recent investigations into the Old Testament, which carry so much promise of certainty with them, tend to show that in the original law the priestly and sacrificial portion was inconsiderable [1], that up to the time of Hezekiah sacrifice was offered without blame in all parts of the country, that it certainly was offered by eminent men, like Samuel or Elijah, wherever they thought right, and possibly by the head of each family, as it had been by the patriarchs. They point with justice to the declaration of Jeremiah, that to the fathers when they came out of Egypt God had said nothing of sacrifice and offering, but only of obedience to the moral law[2]; for this seems to be borne out by the history. The second legislation also, of which Deuteronomy is the centre, is evidently

---

[1] See note XVI.   [2] Jer. vii. 22, 23.

moral and political, not priestly. That there had been a priestly tradition or Thorah is not doubted; and it is evident that this came into greater prominence in the later history, when the Books of Chronicles were written[1] and the Leviticus was put into its present form. But what was the purpose of this elaborate sacrificial system? It was, first, a witness to the need of reconciliation, a reconciliation not needed primarily for ceremonial defilement, but for moral offences, individual and national, which had brought ruin and captivity in their train: it was the means of satisfying the conscience which had broken the ordinances of justice. And it was, secondly, in a better sense than that in which the expression was afterwards used, a fence round the law, a set of peculiar customs by which the chosen people were kept separate from the moral defilement of the heathen, till their convictions should have grown to a more mature and robust independence. The *mere* ceremonialism, apart from moral good, finds no encouragement in the Old Testament. Against that all the prophets from Hosea onwards protest. But with the ceremonial in its due position they have no quarrel[2].

Moreover, the ceremonial system was a kind of sacramental vesture round the moral ideas expressed in the other parts of the law. The central thought of the ceremonial and sacrificial law is Holiness—the

---

[1] 2 Chron. xix. 8; Deut. xxxiii. 10.

[2] These opposite views of the ceremonial system are sometimes found in the same book. Compare the unsparing condemnation of the new moons and appointed feasts in Isaiah i, with the delight in the 'solemnities' of Israel in Isaiah xxx. 29; xxxiii. 20.

separation from moral evil, which is an attribute of both God and man : 'Be ye holy, for I am holy.' The place of worship, with its holy and most holy place ; the animals to be offered, of which excellence in their kind was the requisite ; the sweet odours and anointing oil, by which consecration was given ; the peculiar customs, which were often important sanitary laws[1]; the distinction of clean and unclean meats or conditions, were all of them typical modes (some of them of easy interpretation) by which this holiness or separation for the purposes of righteousness was enjoined. This holiness must be understood as identical with the conception of God and His will embodied in the Decalogue, which was entirely moral. The centre of worship was the ark, and the ark was constructed to contain the two tables of the moral law. It is thought that the fulness of the ceremonial system begins with Ezekiel. But to Ezekiel moral sanctity is all in all. That the Jews in later times made the ceremonial law a thing of importance *per se*, puerile, tyrannous, a fictitious righteousness which became the enemy of the true, was the witness of their degeneracy. They had missed the true meaning of the ceremonies, by seeking to make essential and eternal that which was only of relative and temporary importance.

The law, then, through which the nature of God

[1] See a remarkable Lecture by Dr. Richardson, F.R.S., in the 'Clergyman's Magazine' for March, 1881, on the Mosaic Sanitary Code. Dr. Richardson shows the superior healthiness of the Jews, the causes of which he traces to the observance of their law in the following particulars : (1) a yearly cleansing that acts as a safeguard from epidemic diseases, (2) the Sabbath rest, (3) immunity from syphilis through sexual morality, (4) the excellent provision for food and drink, (5) the care taken to shield and protect the enfeebled.

was made known to Israel, was the series of moral and political principles which established and maintained true relations among the people. It was not 'the law of commandments contained in ordinances,' but the law of righteousness which underlay the ordinances, and which took shape in ordinances—as modern research is proving to us—not once for all, but by successive adaptations of the righteous principle to the wants of successive ages. The law, thus understood, we may truly say, was the centre of the religion and theology of Israel. Religion, as we have maintained, is that which establishes true spiritual relations: and this was the function of the law. Moreover, the law, as thus understood, was directly from the mouth of God Himself: we may say more, it was God Himself as the Righteous One dwelling among His people. Jehovah is represented as making Israel His habitation, 'Jehovah his God is with him, and the shout of a king is among them;' as marching with His people through the wilderness, as settling with them in Canaan, His rest for ever, as inspiring their devotions. Examine for a moment the 68th Psalm, which represents the ideal march of Israel and their worship. The central fact of it is the moral and political law understood as a law of mercy. 'A Father of the fatherless, a Judge of the widow, is God in His holy habitation.' Thou, 'Jehovah, of Thy goodness hast prepared for the poor.' This was the truth that was to be proclaimed by the 'great company of preachers.' This gave the strength of unity to the nation, before which 'kings of armies did flee apace.' It was also the righteousness which lay at the centre of the constitution of the world, at the proclamation of which the hills leap up[1] and all nature acknowledges its king. This also is the centre of the worship of Israel. The God who sets the solitary in families, and brings forth those who are bound in chains[2], who loads His people with benefits[3], is He also whose goings are seen in the sanctuary, where the singers go before and the minstrels follow after[4]. Israel knows that he has attained the true centre of humanity and of the universe, not in a metaphysical conception of the Deity, but in moral and political righteousness.

We have noticed above the close connexion of the sanctuary and the judgment-seat. In the language of the law and of the Psalms the judge and the prince is a God[5]. To go to the tribunal is to go to God. God is in the congregation of the mighty, a God among gods, a Judge among judges[6]. He is also in the family. The Third Commandment, as the Jews reckon, belongs to the first table of the law. God is in the king's court and in the city, for justice and love are omnipresent. This was the theocracy, the recognition and worship of righteousness which is the presence of God among men.

There was, according to the truthful boast of the Deuteronomist, no nation that had such statutes and judgments, and who, consequently, had God so near to them[7]. The identification of the indwelling of God with the observance of those laws which made Palestine the Holy Land, may be specially seen in such words as

---

[1] Ps. lxviii. 16: 'Why leap ye, ye high hills? this is the hill which God desireth to dwell in.'
[2] Ps. 5, 6.   [3] Ib. 19.   [4] Ib. 24, 25.
[5] Ex. xxii. 8, 9.   [6] Ps. lxxxii. 1, 6.   [7] Deut. iv. 7, 8.

those which David uses to Saul, and in which he says that his enemies have driven him out from abiding in the inheritance of Jehovah, saying, 'Go, serve other gods[1].'

It is by this that we are to explain the peculiar relation of Israel to God. Taken generally, it is confessed by almost every student of the philosophy of history that Israel has a pre-eminent gift or faculty for righteousness. But righteousness is the manifestation of God among men, pre-eminently the righteousness which establishes just relations. If this be so, then the boast of the Deuteronomist is true: What nation has the Lord so nigh as the Lord our God is to us? What nation has statutes or judgments so just as all this law? Did any nation ever hear the voice of God speaking to them as we have heard? None, we may truly say. Where are to be found songs of righteousness like the Psalms, or pleadings for righteousness like the prophetical books? Greek philosophy was a guess at truth. The Indian religions are an intoxication with the sense of the Absolute and the Immense, to which human righteousness seems small and mean. But the religion of Israel is the recognition of God in human righteousness, the spiritual centre of the world. This God is indeed their God, and they His people.

It may well be that a growth is to be traced in the idea of God in the Old Testament. The Jewish Church,

[1] 1 Sam. xxvi. 19. The critics are apt to take these words as implying the belief that Jehovah had power in Palestine alone. A nobler and truer turn is given to them if we consider that in Palestine alone the divine law prevailed, while beyond its boundaries society was built up upon the unjust and immoral ideas of Syrian heathenism.

like the Christian, increases with the increase of God. That the original conception of Jehovah (for I hesitate, even before an academic audience, to use the more correct pronunciation Yahweh[1]) as current among the people, was extremely imperfect, that it was compatible with animal worship[2], with nature-worship, that the sacred books bear traces of a time when the sun was almost identified with God by the Israelites as by so many nations[3], that the worship of Jehovah at times was blended with the worship of Baal and the asherah, is evident; that it was often, among the people, the worship of an anthropomorphic, local deity, and was compatible with immorality and bloodshed, we learn from the denunciations of it by Isaiah[4]. But from Moses to Malachi, nay to John the Baptist and to Christ, the true religion of the prophets was constantly contending with the degraded ceremonialism and purifying the image of God. Jeremiah speaks of those who said, 'The temple of the Lord are these[5],' but who stole and murdered and committed adultery and burned incense to Baal, and walked after other gods (who sanctioned such things), and yet came and stood in the presence of Jehovah Himself, and declared that such abominations were permitted to them. Jeremiah told

[1] In the delivering of the Lecture the word Jehovah was used, which, though of bastard origin, carries with it so many sacred associations. I designed to use the word Yahweh in the printed book, hoping that these associations might gather soon around the correct word, but, finding that some doubt is still felt among scholars on the subject, I have retained the spelling Jehovah.

[2] Ex. xxxii. 5; 1 Kings xii. 28.

[3] A reminiscence of a stage in which the sun was the special emblem of Deity may perhaps be traced in the scenes of the passage of the Red Sea (Ex. xiv. 24), and at Mount Sinai (Ex. xxiv. 10, 17).

[4] Isa. i. 15; lix. 3, 13.   [5] Jer. vii. 4, 9, 10.

them that these were lying words, and that the only worship which Jehovah would accept was that of the sincere fulfilment of the moral law. 'If ye throughly amend your ways and your doings, if ye throughly execute judgment between a man and his neighbour, if ye oppress not the stranger;' that is, if you hold to the law which establishes true relations between men; then, the prophet says, Jehovah will own and bless you. Jeremiah declares to the king Jehoiakim, who bore the sacred name in his own, but was a follower of the debased worship of Jehovah, which was compatible with selfish luxury and neglect of duty and the law: 'Shalt thou reign because thou closest thyself in cedar? Did not thy father (the good Josiah) eat and drink and do judgment and justice? Then it was well with him. Was not this to know Me? saith Jehovah. But thine eyes and thy heart are not but for thy covetousness, and for to shed innocent blood, and for oppression and violence to do it[1].' The false Jehovah-worship, which was connected with heathenish practices, was marked precisely by the non-observance of the law of just relations. The worship of the true Jehovah is identified with the keeping of this law. The true prophetic religion was only represented by the better minds of the nation who strove ineffectually to subdue the false, until, after the great judgment of the captivity, which was rightly attributed to the non-observance of this law of just relations, it gained a complete recognition.

We may explain further, by the identification of Jehovah with the righteousness expressed in the law,

[1] Jer. xxii. 15-17.

the constant struggle with idolatry which the Old Testament presents. The false gods were representations of force or lust, of man's mere selfish greed; service was sometimes actually rendered to them by immoral practices, their worship was always compatible with such practices[1]. To be holy or consecrated to them often meant to be given over to some form of immorality. The name for the votary of the most hideous form of lust is 'the consecrated one[2].' And it is evident that the debased Jehovah-worship of which we have just spoken blended very easily with this worship of gods of lust and violence. The sin of Jeroboam opened the path for 'the statutes of Omri[3]' and the worship of Baal. Hosea figuratively describes the bride of Jehovah as saying of her vines and her fig-trees, 'These are the rewards which my lovers (the false gods) have given me[4].' He describes also how she burned incense to her Baalim, and decked herself with jewels, and went after them, and forgot her true lord. And therefore, he says, I will cause her feast days, and her new moons, and her sabbaths, and all her solemn feasts to cease[5]. These were the emblem of the debased Jehovah-worship which was verging upon Baalism. She is represented as calling the debased Jehovah by the name of Baali[6]. But the true Jehovah, he says, will betroth His bride[7] to Him again in righteousness, that is, not by this debased ceremonialism, but by the law of just relations.

[1] 2 Kings xxiii. 6, 7.
[2] Deut. xxiii. 17, where the word qadesh and its feminine are used for the votaries of lust in the two sexes.
[3] Micah vi. 16.   [4] Hosea ii. 12.   [5] Ibid. 11.   [6] Ibid. 16.   [7] Ibid. 19.

Thus we see that the theocracy, the true religion of Israel, the dwelling of God in His people, was identified with the practice of just relations. Through these God was known and worshipped.

3. We must trace the importance of the law in the political life and history of Israel.

It is evident that, so long as just relations were maintained among the people, and the life of simple agricultural industry contented them, they would prosper; and so long as through these just relations they were united, they would be strong to resist external enemies. But when lust and oppression, and the consequent evils of poverty and indebtedness, distrust and disunion prevailed, internal prosperity would be gone, and they would also fall an easy prey to their enemies. In the East in the present day, both in Turkey and in India[1], it has been observed that, where oppression and wrong relations prevail, population grows scarce, and the land becomes desert; but, where just rule prevails, population increases and the land changes to a garden almost as by magic. Even the amount of rain, on which all fertility depends, varies with the upturning of the soil, and the planting of trees, and the growth of crops. We can thus understand, without having recourse to miracle, how the non-observance of the law would result in calamity, and its observance in renewed prosperity. In Psalm cvii. 34, we read, 'A fruitful land maketh He barren for the wickedness of them that dwell therein.' In

[1] See Pearson's Life of Schwartz the Indian Missionary, chapters 17 and 20. Hatchards, 1834.

Isaiah [1] the land is described as at one moment bearing nothing but thorns and briars, so that the remnant left in it have nothing to eat but the honey of the wild bees or the butter of the wandering herds, and then at another moment the remnant that is left find the branch of the Lord beautiful and glorious, and the fruit of the earth excellent and comely for them [2]. The service of the false gods, and the debased Jehovah-worship, meant, as we have seen, injustice and oppression, discouragement, depopulation, parched lands, and general misery. The service of the righteous Jehovah, the practice of the true relations prescribed by His law, meant sober industry, glad confidence, smiling harvests, and universal prosperity. 'The wilderness and the solitary place were glad for them, and the desert blossomed as a rose [3].'

We may thus be led to an insight into the policy of the great leaders of Israel, the judges, the good kings, and the prophets. So long as Jehovah was worshipped and His law observed, Israel was a nation of peaceful agriculturists, inoffensive to his neighbours, strong through wealth and unity. So soon as the worship of the false gods and the debased Jehovah-worship, with their consequent evil customs, gained the ascendancy, the nation became weak and was easily subdued. It is thus that we may explain the often-repeated tale of the Book of Judges [4]: The children of Israel did evil and served Baalim; then Jehovah abandoned them to the dominion of the heathen; then they bore the cruel

---

[1] Isa. vii. 22-25.   [2] Ibid. iv. 2.
[3] Ibid. xxxv. 1.   [4] Judges ii. 11, 14.

yoke, until they cried to Jehovah, and longed once more for His just law[1] : at last a judge arose, some Deborah dispensing justice from under her palm-tree[2], some Gideon overthrowing the image of Baal, and summoned the people to the standard of Jehovah and of righteousness[3]. Then they arose in the strength engendered by returning unity and just relations, and prevailed and were free, and the land had rest.

We may admit that the attitude of unaggressive innocence was abandoned when the monarchy arose ; and in this we may sympathize with the protest of Samuel. No longer was Jehovah and His law to rule immediately, instinctively, enforcing its mild sway through the general conviction, and upheld in special instances by specially called judges ; but all was to be subject to a king, and a king meant caprice and luxury and war. Yet Samuel admitted that the new institution might serve the divine purpose if Jehovah and His law were obeyed. Otherwise, he said, you will be consumed, both you and your king[4]. The conquests of David are to be accounted for partly as a deliverance from intruders like the Philistines, partly by the natural state of the world at that time, in which each nation was, unless there were a special treaty, the perpetual foe of its neighbour. They may be palliated also to the conscience of mankind by the presumption that the rule of Israel was meant to be the rule of Jehovah Himself : the conquered races were to stretch out their hands to God. They probably partook, to a considerable extent,

---

[1] Judges iii. 7-10.   [2] Ibid. iv. 3, 4.   [3] Ibid. vi. 25-27.
[4] 1 Sam. xii. 13, 14, 25.

of the advantages afforded to all who lived beneath the laws of Jehovah. In the 16th chapter of Isaiah, Moab is urged to claim the protection of Judah in words which betoken just such a relation (I use Ewald's version); 'Let the outcasts of Moab dwell with thee; be thou to them a covert from the spoiler; for thus the extortioner shall be at an end ... and in mercy shall the throne (of Judah) be established, and he shall sit on it in truth in the tabernacle of David, judging, and seeking judgment, and hasting righteousness[1].' Such, there is reason to believe, was the spirit in which the higher mind of the nation looked at its conquests. But they probably had no wish for their extension, since the lower patriotism is with them always subordinate to the higher, the hope that their country may serve for the spiritual good of mankind.

The prophets were statesmen as well as religious teachers. They could not be otherwise if the true religion of Jehovah was what we have described. Their policy may be summed up in the evangelical words: 'Seek first the kingdom of God, and all shall be added unto you.' Hosea in the northern kingdom, Isaiah and Jeremiah in the southern, have each of them the same messages, though varying according to the time and circumstances. Let the people of Jehovah trust in Him alone: that is, let their confidence be in this, that they have His spirit of righteousness, and practise the just relations prescribed by His law; and let them refrain from entangling alliances with Egypt or Assyria[2]. The policy of Isaiah is specially to be observed. Palestine lay between

[1] Isa. xvi. 4, 5. [2] Hosea xiv. 1-3.

the two conflicting empires of Assyria and Egypt. He urges that Judah should take part with neither[1]. The way from the one to the other lay, not through the centre of Palestine, but by the sea-coast, and under Mount Carmel, and by the plains of Esdraelon. Had Judah remained a small, inoffensive, agricultural people, yet united and strong through their just relations, strong also in their mountain fastnesses of Libnah, Lachish, and Jerusalem, probably the great empires would have left them alone; or they might have made such terms as would have left them substantially independent. But, as soon as the suspicion arose, that, if left behind in the conquering path of Assyria, they would be secret allies of Egypt, the whole force of the empire of Sennacherib was directed against them. Even so, they were formidable enough under Hezekiah to brave the worst; and when, after the disaster which befell the Assyrian host, they gained a respite, it was not through Egypt, but through the unity engendered by the observance of the law that they prospered and maintained their independence. On the other hand, when, after the death of Josiah and the defeat of Necho by the Babylonians, the Empire was evidently supreme, and the Jewish state had not qualified itself through any full adherence to the just law for resistance, Jeremiah acquiesced in the submission of Judæa[2] and the payment of tribute; for thus alone could a modified independence be preserved, and the observance of the law be maintained. Ezekiel

---

[1] This attitude is seen, as regards an Assyrian alliance in Is. xxii., as regards the Egyptian alliance, to which Judah was most tempted, in Is. xxx. and xxxi.

[2] Jer. xxvii. 6, 12.

also reproved with all his energy Zedekiah's breach of his oath and pledged allegiance to Nebuchadnezzar[1]. Lastly, in the captivity, when, by the fall of Jerusalem, the last bond was severed which had bound the people to idolatry and the debased Jehovah-worship, the priestly system was drawn out by Ezekiel[2], which was afterwards confirmed by Ezra and Joshua, and the prophets of the return, Haggai and Zechariah, and was further enforced by Malachi. The object of this system, as we have seen, was to express the need of reconciliation for the abandonment of the law, and to deepen, by formal acts of consecration, the hold of the law on the conscience of the people. This may be seen especially in the Book of Malachi, the only prophet who distinctly urges the obligations of the priestly Thorah, the payment of tithes, the unblemished offering, the purity of the priests and the sons of Levi[3]. But in Malachi we find no contrast, such as we find in the older prophets, between the law of justice and the practices of worship. They are blended into one. The true law, the law of just relations, is both assumed and expressed by him as the matter of central importance. The judgment which he foresees will be a swift witness against the sorcerers, and adulterers, and false swearers, against those that oppress the hireling in his wages, the widow and the fatherless, and that fear not Me, saith Jehovah of the hosts[4]. And his last exhortation is to remember the law of Moses[5], not the priestly law, but the law as given in Horeb, with the statutes and the judgments, that is, the moral

---

[1] Ezek. xvii. 14, 18; xxi. 25.   [2] Ezek. xl-xlvii.
[3] Mal. iii. 10; i. 8; iii. 3.   [4] Ibid. iii. 5.   [5] Ibid. iv. 4.

and political law. This is his main interest, to support the true relations among men. In this he even goes beyond the Mosaic tradition by his denunciation of polygamy[1]. Thus the law was completed, and remained for the four centuries after Malachi the guide of the nation. It was this system, a moral kernel with a ceremonial rind, which was so energetically enforced in the synagogues, now springing up throughout the country, by the Pharisees. For these men, though they afterwards gave in to formalism, were at first both faithful and successful teachers. It was this law which Antiochus sought to destroy, because he knew it to be the very life of the nation. It was this system for which the Maccabæan heroes conquered or died; their constant testimony was this, that they laboured and bled in defence of the holy and honourable laws[2].

4. We must occupy one more position, namely, that the law which established just relations between men was the central and inspiring fact of the Hebrew literature. That literature divides itself into three groups—the law, the prophets (including the histories, except Chronicles), and the Hagiographa. Of these, the law was the recognized centre, that which first received the adherence of the whole nation as emanating from Divine inspiration, that which by some was alone accepted as of Divine authority. The prophets, as we

---

[1] Mal. ii. 14, 15.
[2] See the charge of Mattathias to his sons, 1 Macc. ii. 49-68: also the words of Simon, ib. xiii. 3; the testimony to Simon (2 Macc. iv. 2) that he 'was so zealous of the laws,' and the last words of Eleazar (ib. vi. 28) that he would 'leave a notable example to such as be young to die willingly and courageously for the honourable and holy laws.'

have already seen, have the law always at heart. The Hagiographa, especially the Psalms, are also mainly occupied with the just relations of the law.

If we go a little closer into the contents of these groups of books, this result will more clearly appear.

The simple stories of the Patriarchs in the Book of Genesis are tales of family life; and the purpose of the narrator is evidently by means of them to establish those family relations which lie at the root of the national life. As such, they are naturally referred to again and again in our Marriage Service. The Book of Exodus expands these relations in the nation, giving us the motive for them in the eternal name of God, and in His character as the Deliverer. The early historical books contain the account of the conquest of Canaan and the period up to David, written with the direct intention of showing how the life of the nation depended on the observance of the law. The prophets who wrote these accounts did that which the poetry of religion and its higher teaching ought always to do: they idealized the life of the people. We can measure, to use the words of a recent writer of great eloquence, 'the intimate union of Church and State in Israel, by remarking the religious character which belongs in that literature to such words as Jerusalem and Zion. The name of a city there suggests, not so much law-courts or even a king's palace, as the home of a God[1].' We may take the lovely idyll of Ruth, as exhibiting in the highest form the beauty of human relations as enjoined by the law. Similarly, we may take

[1] 'Natural Relig'on,' by the author of 'Ecce Homo,' p. 185.

the Book of Deuteronomy, which is now generally believed to belong to the age of the later Judaic monarchy, as exhibiting the law set in a poetical and prophetical framework. In the first eight chapters it is the prophet who speaks, in the centre the lawgiver, in the close the poet: and we have in it an epitome of Hebrew literature in its three branches, all circling round the law of righteousness. Even in the priestly books, Leviticus and Chronicles, we have not mere statements of ceremonies and laws of worship, but these set in a framework of stories, whether those of the kings, or the more ancient ones like that of Nadab and Abihu [1]; and these lead to the repetition of the chief political and moral laws [2], and their sanction by punishment and reward [3].

If we take next the prophetical writings, we find in them every variety of poetical, didactic, and historical composition, but all springing from one inspiration, that of the consciousness of God as a God who establishes and maintains true relations among men. The prophetical writings make also a special contribution to religious literature through their personal character. The personality of each prophet stands out vividly before us, and is in itself the most trustworthy witness, in its struggling and brave convictions, to the divine character of the righteousness which it enforces.

The Hagiographa are the parts of the collection most cognate to classical and modern literature. They comprise the Psalms, the noblest effort of lyric poetry which the world has seen; the Book of Job, a poem of philosophic reasoning comparable to Lucretius or the writings

[1] Lev. x. [2] Lev. xix., xxiv., xxv. [3] Lev. xxvi.

of Leopardi or Tennyson's 'In Memoriam,' but, as poetry, excelling them all; the Proverbs, which are a repertory of practical wisdom; the lovely dramatic idyll of the Song of Songs; and the book of soliloquies called Ecclesiastes; to which the Book of Daniel, the first Apocalypse, may be added, containing the rudiments of a philosophy of history. Yet each book is related to, and presupposes the law; the last written book, the Book of Daniel, as designed to encourage the patriots of the Maccabæan era in their devotion 'for the sake of the holy laws,' and as shadowing forth the destination of the Hebrew race in the establishment of the universal kingdom of God; the Book of Ecclesiastes, as returning after wanderings in the realms of wilfulness and doubt to the straight conclusion, 'Fear God and keep His commandments;' the Song of Songs, as the triumph of faithful love over licentiousness; the Book of Proverbs, as a commentary on the words, The fear of Jehovah is the beginning of knowledge; the Book of Job, as ending in unquestioning submission to the will of God, which, as has been pointed out, was ever to the Hebrews identical with the law. But the Psalms will ever be the chief evidence to us of the central position which the moral and political law held in the thought and literature of the nation. These free lyric compositions are religious in no strained conventional sense, but in this sense only, that the fear of God, the love of God, joy in God, gratitude towards God, are in the hearts of the poets and overflow from their lips. But the God of whom they speak is always Jehovah, the national God, the God of the law and of righteousness.

This is the case, not only in the didactic Psalms, like the 119th, or those which express, like the 1st, the praise of the good man whose delight is in the law of Jehovah, in which he meditates day and night; but, in historical Psalms, like the 105th, which celebrates, as the crowning mercy of the deliverance of Israel, their settlement in the Holy Land, 'that they might observe His statutes, and keep His laws;' in Psalms of nature, like the 19th, where the sun going forth in his glory is made the emblem of the law of Jehovah which is perfect, and His statutes which are sweeter than honey[1]; in Psalms of victory, like the 76th, where the triumph over Sennacherib is the uprising of God as the helper of the meek (the character always ascribed to Him in the law). The Psalms come from all epochs in the history of Israel; they are of all the characters that lyric poetry can assume; but the pervading thought of them all is the mercy, the justice, the redeeming love of the one God, whose law is enshrined in the life of Israel.

The Psalms, as poetry, form a specimen of art. They were joined with music and the rhythmic dance, which expressed the joy thrilling through body and soul in the presence of the Eternal. Israel was not an æsthetic people; but their best architecture, their costliest decorative art, their sculpture and embroidery and metal work, were lavished on the Tabernacle and the Temple, which was at once the place of approach to God and the centre of their political system. Whatever art they

[1] Compare Ps. civ, where the glories of nature suggest the contrast between the Psalmist who 'sings to Jehovah as long as he lives,' whose 'meditation of Him shall be sweet,' and the wicked who 'shall be consumed out of the earth.'

had, their whole intellectual and æsthetic nature, bore the impress of consecration to the God of righteousness.

It may be asked whether the whole moral life of Israel, which we have been attempting to describe, was not marred, so far as any application of it to the universal Church is concerned, by a mean national exclusiveness. The answer is that the impression of exclusiveness is given entirely by the ceremonial law, which is now ascertained to be mainly an after-growth, and of quite secondary importance. The moral law contains little that is exclusive. The political law, no doubt, bore partly the colour of its time and place, but was mainly, as we have seen, an effort at the establishment of just relations. This it is which gives it its high importance, for true righteousness is universal. It is also to be observed that at many epochs in the world nationalism is the truest universalism. There may be a catholicism which is merely sectarian, and an alliance of a whole continent which is only a tyrannical compact of its kings, and a fellowship in art or science which is no more than a bond of selfish and disdainful refinement; and none of these have the true spirit of universalism such as is exhibited by the feeling of brotherhood within a single nation, establishing just relations between its component members, drawing its various classes into one, and harmonizing all its public and private life. The true and universal religion, says Kuenen[1], must be born of the nation but rise above it. And this condition the religion of Israel fulfilled. The strangers within its borders were the special care of the

[1] Hibbert Lectures for 1882, Lect. I.

national God[1]. The prophets again and again announce that the people of God are those, and those alone, who have the righteousness of God among them, and that Israel when unfaithful is no more His people[2]. There is nothing sectarian about the prophets. The condemnation of the Assyrian tyrant in Isaiah is not the sectarian or nationalist complaint that he has oppressed Israel, but this: 'Thou hast destroyed thy land and slain thy people; the seed of evil-doers shall never be renowned[3].' The prophets also keep in sight the hope that other nations will share in the favour and service of Jehovah, as when Isaiah represents Him as saying: 'Blessed be Egypt My people, and Assyria the work of My hands[4];' or, when Malachi says, 'From the rising of the sun to the going down of the same, My name is (or shall be) great among the Gentiles, and in every place incense is (or shall be) offered to Me, and an holy worship; for My name is great among the heathen[5].' The true relations which the law establishes are the heritage of the world. In this sense the prophecy has been fulfilled that the law of Jehovah shall go forth from Jerusalem to many nations[6].

Perhaps it may be said that Jewish history is the history of one nation only, a small nation, without the secular greatness which belongs to Greece or Rome, and that the interest in it is somewhat fictitious or conventional. There has, no doubt, been much that is

---

[1] Ex. xxii. 21; xxiii. 9. Deut. x. 18, 19. Ps. cxlvi. 9.
[2] 2 Kings xvii. 22, 23. Jer. ix. 13-16; xliv. 26, 27. Ezek. xvi. 3, 48-53. Hosea iv. 6.
[3] Isa. xiv. 20.   [4] Isa. xix. 25.   [5] Mal. i. 11.
[6] Isa. ii. 3. Mic. iv. 2.

conventional in the study of the Old Testament, since the chief stress has often been laid on the predictive element in prophecy or the external resemblances of ceremonial or history to events in the Christian dispensation; and events and characters have been studied without any philosophical estimate of their true place in history, while the law which established true relations has been neglected. But study the history of the three races (we can spare none of them), and ask which of the three presents an ideal of life of the most central importance and the most applicable to ourselves[1]? The ideal of the Greek was versatility, Ἐπὶ πλεῖστα εἴδη τὸ σῶμα αὔταρκες παρέχεσθαι[2]. That of the Roman, Imperial power, 'Parcere subjectis et debellare superbos[3]'; that of Israel, Righteousness, 'Open ye the gates that the righteous nation, which keepeth the truth, may enter in[4].' We learn much, no doubt, from Aristotle's *Politics*, and from Roman constitutional history. But the Greek republics, whatever their form, were an aristocracy superposed upon a mass of slavery. Roman history resulted in a despotism, a useless patriciate, and a pauper proletariate. The Jewish community was a brotherhood bound together by a worship and a law of righteousness, and it gave

---

[1] Mr. Goldwin Smith has, in articles in the 'Contemporary Review' and 'Nineteenth Century,' asserted that the Jew as the worshipper of a tribal God can never be a trustworthy citizen of a Christian nation. That depends on the question whether the Old Testament is interpreted by the Jews of the present day as it was in the Rabbinical schools or as it was in the Sermon on the Mount. The latter I believe to be generally the case. On this point mainly depends the answer to the question, whether the Jewish race will bear the high place for which it seems destined in the Christian society of the future.

[2] Thucydides, ii. 41.   [3] Virg. Aen. vi. 854.
[4] Is. xxvi. 2.

birth to the righteousness which is owned as complete where that of Rome and of Greece fails. The ideal we seek in modern times is that of a national community knit together in all its relations by righteousness and love, and caring especially for its weaker members. This neither Greece nor Rome did, but only the Jewish nation. Let those who would make Christianity merely a religious system apart from the common life of men, those who ascribe to it a sacerdotal or a dogmatic basis, those who conceive of God as apart from human relations, and of religion as a merely individual connexion with Him, see to it, that they do not fall below the Hebrew ideal. Those who appreciate that ideal most fully, and dwell most on the divine element pervading it, will see very clearly that it points to none of these as its proper development, but to an all-embracing society, including the whole range of human interests and binding all men and classes and nations together in true relations, which are the work and the expression of the Spirit of God.

In the present day there is too great a tendency to disparage the religious importance of the Old Testament, and to doubt its value as an educational instrument, or as a medium for the teaching of practical life. This is, to a large extent, a re-action from the overstrained notions which attributed to it an exact historical accuracy and a perfect sanctity. The Rationalismus Vulgaris, which has been applied with success to destroy such notions, was in its right, and had received abundant provocation. But the fuller and higher criticism of later years which has come to us from Göttingen, from

Leyden, from Aberdeen (may we not say also from Natal, at least in the later volumes ?), if it has displaced some parts of the fabric of our religious ideas, has also readjusted them. When the smoke of controversy has passed off, we shall find that the more historical treatment of the Old Testament greatly enhances its religious value for us. It is true that we must make a distinction between various parts of the Old Testament. Christ and St. Paul have taught us this. There are some parts which have already been recognized as unsuitable for reading in our churches, and this process may be carried further. Other parts can only be read with profit if we apply to them constantly a kind of philosophy of history; and this will be more possible with the advance of general education. But, if what has been said in this Lecture be true, not only will the Psalms and the prophets gain through the appreciation of their historical surroundings,—a process which will be greatly furthered by the forthcoming new version of the Old Testament, and by the more open study of Hebrew literature in our universities,—but the whole of the Old Testament will be recognized as possessing the highest educational and political value. Through its connexion with Christianity, it knits together the old and the new world without a breach of continuity. And it exhibits the stages of human progress, and also its drawbacks, its incidental failures, its atoning penalties and sacrifices, in a manner which strikes all ages and both sexes, and goes direct to the heart. It is also of extreme value as presenting religion as a matter of public and national concern, which has often been prevented by a misreading of the New Testament. And if the political and moral aspect which I have attempted to restore to prominence be maintained, this will make it still more precious in an age of political changes. For we have in it both a constant stimulus to the reform of our social state, and at the same time a direction for our efforts and a safeguard against our excesses. We may enter upon the path of democratic progress, which seems to open before modern communities without fear, if we apply, like Savonarola, the spirit of the prophets to uphold and to guide it; for no nobler effort can be made in the political sphere than that which they made, to direct the national action towards the raising of the poor and the weak, and the promotion of brotherly relations throughout the community in the name and in the fear of God.

LECTURE III.

THE NEW TESTAMENT CHURCH.

St. John xviii. 37. Pilate saith unto Him, Art thou a king then? Jesus answered, Thou sayest that I am a king. To this end was I born, and for this cause came I into the world, that I should bear witness unto the truth. He that is of the truth heareth My voice.

The establishment of a true theocracy or reign of God, by which, as we have shown, is meant, not a government by priests, but a recognition of divine righteousness in all the relations of life, is the purpose of the whole course of human development. We are not following any narrow or conventional plan when we trace this development in the facts revealed in the Jewish and Christian Scriptures; for the world of our day is led by Western Christendom, and an understanding of Christendom must be sought in the study of the Christian origins, and these again cannot be understood apart from the Old Testament. Other systems, European or Oriental, are accessory; here alone is the main line of development. The principle of life which the Scriptures set forth is brought face to face with those of Greece and Rome, and to some extent of the East, in the early Christian history.

I will not say that the one destroys the others; but it absorbs them ; it vindicates itself as supreme, partly by contrast to them, partly by its power of assimilating them. But the battle-ground, or point of contact, is not that of philosophical disquisition, but of the establishment and maintenance of human relations : for this is the true subject-matter of religion ; in this lies the kingdom of God. If Judaism and Christianity (which we may take as one whole) formed a peculiar religion, that is, a special system of doctrine and of worship, it could never take the position which experience shows it capable of taking. It is the object of these Lectures to show that it is something different from this, that it is a central principle of spiritual life, which develops into relations, and through these again into organisations and communities; and that, being this, it is capable of becoming, and has constantly sought, and is now seeking to become, the harmonizing, co-ordinating and saving principle of human society universally.

It has been pointed out in the last Lecture that the centre of the Jewish development, of its laws and constitution, of its theology, its history, its literature, was the consciousness of God as a power of righteousness, abiding amongst the people by the law of just relations. This was the true theocracy. This theocracy, it was shown, was cast in various forms suited to the various epochs of the national history; it was necessarily national not universal at first, and was bound up with peculiar forms, which, though they had a moral interpretation, yet constituted a fence round the inner and moral law, thus giving to its votaries an exclusive character, and to righteousness and obedience to God a formal and limited meaning. But it was also pointed out that the moral law has in it the character of universality, and that the development into universality was contemplated by the prophets as the object of aspiration, if not of direct endeavour.

The time came when this universal moral power, nourished within the womb of Judaism, was to come forth into light. Christianity is born from the Jewish Church as Christ Himself from a Jewish mother; and though the separation of the child from the parent was full of sharp pangs, the life of the one passed over into the other. The theocracy in Israel was the righteous God abiding in the nation. The theocracy in Christendom was to be the same righteous power abiding in mankind. The righteousness is at once deeper and fuller; deeper, because, to become universal, it must touch the springs of human action, not the mere rules of national custom; and fuller, because, starting from the central principle, that of love, it must show itself all-pervading, applicable to all, subduing and embracing all, binding the world into one.

The inwardness of the Christian righteousness has been recognized; it has been characterized in our day as the special method of Christ [1] : but its extension and

---

[1] M. Arnold, *Literature and Dogma*, p. 195: 'No outward observances were conduct, were that keeping of the commandments, which was the keeping of a man's own soul and made him enter into life. To have the *thoughts* in order as to certain matters, was conduct. This was the 'method' of Jesus: setting up a great unceasing inward movement of attention and verification in matters which

goal have been little dwelt upon. We have known, to use St. Paul's words, the depth and the height of the love of Christ, but not its length and breadth. Men see in Him the Saviour of their own lives. We must show that He is the Saviour of the life of the world, the Founder of a society which is to embrace all mankind in a fellowship of righteousness.

It is true that the first and main effort of His ministry was to renew in men's minds the consciousness of the Fatherhood of God, and the inner and spiritual life, the life of gratitude and affection, which flows from this consciousness. He and His disciples were members of the Jewish Church, and it was not the first and essential part of His office to revolutionize

are three-fourths of human life, where to see true and to verify is not difficult, the difficult thing is to care and to attend. And the inducement to attend was, because joy and peace, missed on every other line, were to be reached on this.'

Mr. Arnold seems to be content with this inwardness, and to consider that it cannot and ought not to work itself out into a social system. 'Mr. Froude,' he says, (*Lit. and Dogma*, p. 95) 'thinks he defends the Puritans by saying that they, like the Jews of the Old Testament, had their hearts set on a theocracy, on a fashioning of politics and society to suit the government of God. How strange that he does not perceive that he thus passes, and with justice, the gravest condemnation on the Puritans as followers of *Christ!* At the Christian era the time had passed, in religion, for outward constructions of this kind, and for all care about establishing or abolishing them.'

Contrast with this, *Natural Religion*, p. 187: 'Is it true that, whereas the ancient religions, including the Jewish, were closely connected with public and national life, Christianity is different in kind, being purely of the nature of a philosophy, and intended only as a guide for the individual conscience? ... It does not appear that Christianity has ever wished or consented, except under constraint, to be such a religion. Its nature is misrepresented when it is reduced to a set of philosophical or quasi-philosophical opinions; its history is misrepresented when it is described as a quiet spiritual influence, wholly removed from the turmoil of public disturbances, and spreading invisibly from heart to heart. Its rise and success are closely connected with great political revolutions.' P. 197: 'Look almost where you will in the wide field of history, you find religion, wherever it works freely and mightily, either giving birth to and sustaining states, or else raising them up to a second life after their destruction.'

existing institutions. He gave intimations, no doubt, of the changes which must be wrought by the working out of the universal principle which He inculcated —the conversion of the Gentiles, the universality of His kingdom; and, as the enmity of the Jews against Him deepened, of His own self-sacrifice, of the destruction of Jerusalem, and of the upraising of a new and spiritual temple. But He did not excite His hearers by dwelling upon any of these. He spoke of them only to the inner circle of His followers, and with the reserve imposed by His spiritual objects. There was to be nothing of that which is called in our day sensational. Speculation on wonderful events to come was not to outstrip the conviction by which the minds of His servants were to be prepared for them.

Nevertheless, the events were present to His mind, and He was concerned to prepare His disciples for them. He declared, and with more frequency and impressiveness towards the end, that He was come to send a fire upon the earth[1], that His disciples would be delivered up[2], expelled from the Jewish synagogues[3], brought before Gentile rulers. And here we may trace the need for the formation of the Church. His disciples were to go forth as sheep among wolves. Was there to be no fold or shepherd, no organization in which they could support one another? We can hardly doubt that the great prophecy of Matt. xxiv. expresses His thoughts about the future. When the great tribulation there spoken of should come, and Jerusalem should no longer afford them any shelter, was there

[1] Luke xii. 48.   [2] Mark xiii. 9.   [3] John xvi. 2.

to be no social system to succeed that of which Jerusalem had been the centre? The fabric of the ceremonial law must crumble away, as the political law had well-nigh done. It had crumbled away already in our Lord's estimation, for He never urges its obligations, and, so far as the record informs us, He never practised more than its central ordinances. What was to come after, when the fabric of the law, which had seemed to the Jews like the eternal ordinances of nature, should have vanished away? Was each man to build up an intellectual home for himself? Were the simple believers to confront the Western school of philosophy, or the theosophies of the East, or the stupendous power of Rome, without guides or leaders? Our Lord saw multitudes already taking the kingdom of heaven by storm [1]; the fields were white to the harvest [2]: and He bade His disciples pray for labourers to gather them in [3]; the Greeks who sought to see Him at the last Passover, called forth some of His deepest and most far-reaching sayings [4]; His last injunction to His apostles was, that they should make disciples of all nations [5]. Was He content to look forward merely to a tumultuary aggregate of individuals, and not to an organized society? Some such questions—though we must not bring all our later thoughts within the scope of our Lord's ministry—must have presented themselves to His mind; and the answer He gave to them was the foundation of the Church. There are many of His sayings, especially in the parables, which show

[1] Matt. xi. 12. Luke xvi. 16.   [2] John iv. 35.   [3] Matt. ix. 38.
[4] John xii. 23-26.   [5] Matt. xxviii. 19.

how His mind dwelt upon the future destinies of the body of His disciples [1], and which must have come back to them for their guidance when they began to organize the Christian community.

We may compare our Lord's dealing with the subject of the Church or organized body of believers, with His dealing on some other matters of importance. Take the question of public worship. There is hardly a word about it in our Lord's discourses. Yet we cannot doubt that, though its position has been greatly exaggerated, it is an integral element in the life of Christians; and, as such, it must have been present to the mind of Christ. We must presume, therefore, that He gave no injunctions concerning it, because the general principles of prayer which He unfolded, and of which the Lord's prayer is a type, and the transference, which was sure to come, of the customs of the synagogue to the church, were deemed by Him sufficient, under the guidance of the Divine Spirit, without any express directions. Or, take another instance, that of the doctrine of equality, the abolition of the difference between Jew and Gentile, bond and free, which to St. Paul was the very essence of the Gospel. A few intimations, such as the parable of the Good Samaritan, or the welcome of the Greeks at the last Passover, and the absence of all that is distinctively Judaic in our Lord's teaching, were all that He left to guide the disciples in a matter of absolutely vital moment to the infant community. Similarly, as regards the Church itself, our Lord spoke little of it, as indeed He spoke

[1] Matt. xiii. 24-30; 31, 32; 33. Mark iv. 26. Matt. xxii. 11-14.

III.] *Beginnings of the Universal Society.* 101

little of any outward institution. The time for direct guidance in such matters was not come. But the principles of justice, and mercy, and love, of which Christ's teaching is full, the common need of men for an organization of some kind, the previous existence of the Jewish state—these were the materials with which the Church had to work at the beginning of its development. At the other end lies the dominion over all mankind which Christ claimed. But as to what lies between, there is hardly a word in the way of actual command. A rudimentary organization suited to the rudimentary needs is established; but the disciples are left free to adapt it, and to build up new institutions within it, according to the new circumstances that may arise. That our Lord, in the forty days before the Ascension, when He spoke of the things of the kingdom of God, gave intimations as to the principles which should guide His followers, is a very natural supposition. What is certain from the silence and subsequent action of the Apostles is that He gave no definite directions for the organization of the Church.

Our Lord belonged to the Jewish commonwealth, which, as has been pointed out, had at the base of all its relations a consciousness of the divine righteousness; and that righteousness had formed, and had at various times changed, the laws. In this sense, Israel had represented the kingdom of God on earth. The key of the kingdom was in the hands of the Scribes and Pharisees [1], whose extra traditions and whose fence around the law had rendered the kingdom inaccessible to those without,

[1] Matt. xxiii. 13.

and formal and hypocritical to those within. Our
Lord's first effort, therefore, was to infuse a spirit of
reality into relations which had been thus formalized:
and at the outset the hope might well have been entertained that, as changes had been made before, so, without any violent revolution, the simpler and more universal truth, and the social state flowing from it, might
displace the cumbrous and artificial system then existing.
It is interesting to imagine the possible course of events
had this hope been realized: how the Jews might have
become the apostles of a simple human righteousness
and the belief in the One God to mankind, and the
sacrifice of a laborious and a successful life, instead of
that of an ignominious death, have been the means of
reconciling the world to God. But selfishness was too
deeply ingrained to yield to such a process. The sin of
man required for its extirpation the Sacrifice of the
Cross. Nevertheless, it is certain that Christ made the
attempt to win the Jewish nation by persuasion, not by
death. He began His ministry by announcing Himself
as the herald of a spiritual jubilee [1], and declared that
the prophet's announcement of an era of deliverance
was fulfilled that day in men's ears; and He lamented
at the close of His ministry that the nation had not
known the day of its visitation [2].

This refusal was the turning-point of the history of
the Jewish nation. It was also the turning-point in
the development of the infant community of Christ's
disciples, which changed from a sect into a Church
or kingdom. The attempts which had been made in

[1] Luke iv. 18, 19, 21. [2] Luke xix. 44.

III.]   *Beginnings of the Universal Society.*   103

earlier times to reform the Jewish community had been made by sects, or small bodies of like-minded men. Isaiah had had his special disciples [1]. We trace in Jeremiah's and Josiah's day a small society of godly men bent on restoring true piety in Israel [2]. The Chasidim [3], and later on the Pharisees [3], were sects. Even John the Baptist gathered a company of disciples, who at first rivalled those of our Lord, and who, notwithstanding his own readiness to pass away, remained, as we read in the Acts of the Apostles, for many years [4]. Our Lord, accordingly, from the first, allowed His disciples to baptize and enrol converts, and the number of adherents to what might then have been called the sect of Jesus was large, as St. John reports [5]. But when the opposition of the Scribes precluded the hope of the conversion of the nation, a new creation became necessary. The kingdom of God must be taken from the wicked husbandmen, and given to a nation who would yield the fruits of righteousness. Let us trace this process.

First, the tone of the teaching grows more peremptory. If we may, with Neander [6], consider the Sermon on the Mount as a kind of epitome of the earlier teaching, we may take its authoritative tone and clear definition of the Master's position as significative of this new departure [7], 'I say unto you.' Next (or with Luke immediately before), we have the call of

[1] Isaiah viii. 16.
[2] 2 Kings xxii. 12-14.   See Stanley's *Jewish Church*, ii. 518.
[3] Ib. iii. 327-9, 376-8.   [4] Acts xix. 3.   [5] John iii. 26.
[6] *Life of Christ* (Bohn's Standard Library), p. 240.
[7] Matt. v. 22, 28, 32, 34, 39, 44.

the twelve, the number being that of the tribes, and signifying the formation of a new Israel. We find these twelve set apart for special training under the Master's eye. 'He ordained twelve that they should be with Him[1].' As a part of this training we may note the trial mission recorded in Matt. x, where they are sent forth to cast out devils, and to heal diseases, and to proclaim that the kingdom of God is at hand. The charge which was given them is evidently designed to prepare them and others for a lifelong service far beyond the range of the Galilæan towns. Simon Peter was early recognized as their leader; and he, with James and John, came to form an inner circle through whom the Master revealed the more secret passages of His life and thoughts. Round the Master gathered a larger and less defined company, some of whom, like the family in Bethany, remained in their own homes, some followed Christ wherever He went[2]. The circle of the most immediate followers were all, in spirit at least, perhaps actually, required to give up all that they had. 'He that forsaketh not all that he hath cannot be My disciple[3].' The tie which bound them together was faith in their Lord, the faith of St. Peter, 'Thou art the Christ, the Son of the living God[4].' This faith was synonymous with absolute devotion, a devotion attested by baptism into His name, and subsequently by the Lord's Supper. And this devotion implied, even in those who did not belong to the inner

[1] Mark iii. 14.

[2] This has been ably worked out by the aid of a well-instructed imagination by the author of *Philochristus*.

[3] Luke xiv. 33.

[4] Matt. xvi. 16.

circle, a readiness to give up all at any moment: 'He that hateth not father and mother, yea, and his own life also, cannot be My disciple[1].' This new Israel was built up on a spiritual basis and directed towards spiritual ends. Its princes are the meek, the poor in spirit, the peacemakers, those who suffer for righteousness' sake, and those who are willing to be the servants of all. Those whom we honour now as the founders of the kingdom and its typical characters, went with Christ from place to place, having no other object than to learn and teach the truth; they had no certain dwelling-place, and were supported by a common fund furnished, probably, in part from the original possessions of those who, like Matthew, actually gave up all, and in part from the contributions of well-wishers. This did not imply asceticism, though even asceticism in the East, as shown by the Buddhist sects, is a far easier yoke than in the West, and the disengagedness also of a teaching and mendicant body is not so difficult under the simpler conditions of Eastern life as it would be in the complex social state of the West. But it involved an absolute abandonment of all selfish and ambitious aims. To this society, unlearned as its members were, but having its conscience purified by faith and unselfish love, Christ declared that the keys of the kingdom of God, before held by the Jewish Rabbis, were transferred[2]. Their conscience was the reflex of the divine truth and love which no longer dwelt with the rejecting and rejected nation. Their decisions were

---

[1] Luke xiv. 26.
[2] Matt. xviii. 18; comp. ch. xvi. 19. John xx. 23.

to take the place of those of the faithless Sanhedrin of Israel[1]. This was no mere form of words : for in the society so framed the Spirit of Christ has lived ; it has been, as the Epistle to Timothy calls it, 'the house of the living God, the pillar and ground of the truth[2];' and the principles which it has announced, and has striven, though weakly, to practise, are those by which all mankind even now are judged. It is the body of which He is the inspiring soul. In the just and loving relations of its component parts are expressed the mind and will of the Father.

The establishment of the Church as a kingdom was the final gage of the battle. The Sadduçaic party of the priesthood, the Pharisaic party of the Scribes and Pharisees, trembled, the one for their power, the other for their influence. Either Christ or they must go down. To believe in Jesus now meant not merely general trust in His teaching, but practical adherence to the new kingdom, the rudiments of which were already formed. All the spiritual teaching of our Lord thus gains a keener edge through the thorough and immediate application which must be made of it. The parables, which now form the staple of the teaching, with their double aspect, attracting and repelling, describe the fortunes of the Kingdom[3], the qualifications of those who enter it, the presence of good and bad within it[4], the growth from the little seed to the great

---

[1] So we may understand the words about binding and loosing in Matt. xviii. 18-20, following as they do immediately on the appeal to 'the church' prescribed in the case of obstinate wrong-doing.

[2] 1 Tim. iii. 15.   [3] Matt. xiii. 23.   [4] Ibid. 24, &c.

tree[1], the sifting process which each great judgment-time would bring with it[2]. Then follow the denunciations of those in authority among the Jews[3]; for the influence of the teachers and rulers of Israel is gone for all who enter the new kingdom. The conflict which is thus set up grows more intense towards the close of the ministry. The last year is one of incessant strife. At the beginning of it there come down from Jerusalem into Galilee Scribes and Pharisees[4] to stir up the people against Christ, and they succeed. The little band of believers are found constantly in the outskirts of the country wandering almost as exiles[5]. Herod also begins to be alarmed. Christ Himself plainly foresees and accepts His doom. 'It cannot be,' He says, 'that a prophet perish out of Jerusalem; I do cures to-day and to-morrow, and the third day I must be perfected'; and He steadfastly sets His face towards the fatal city[6]. The great prophecy of Matthew xxiv. points plainly to the doom of the old system, and the deliverance which this would effect for all who own the true King. The death of the King is the condemnation of the murderers; the stone which the builders refused shall be the headstone of the corner[7]; and they who resist it and on whom it falls shall be ground to powder[8]. The King Himself will come with power and great glory[9] in the clouds of heaven (the well-known metaphor for a coming in spirit and in power) for the deliverance of His subjects, and

---

[1] Matt. xiii. 31, 32.　　　　　　　　[2] Ibid. 30, 47, 48.
[3] Matt. xxiii. 13. Luke xi. 42.　　　[4] Matt. xv. 1. Mark vii. 1.
[5] Mark vii. 24, 31. Ibid. viii. 27. John x. 39, 40. Ibid. xi. 53, 54.
[6] Luke xiii. 32. Ibid. ix. 51.　　[7] Matt. xxi. 42.　　[8] Ibid. 44.
[9] Luke xxi. 27.

the burning of the rebellious city[1]. The kingdom of God shall be taken from the wicked husbandmen and given to a nation which will yield the fruits of righteousness[2].

No doubt this idea of the kingdom was misunderstood by both friends and foes. They alike supposed that the Master was aiming at a dominion to be gained and exercised by means of force, for the temporal advantage of Himself and His followers. From all such ideas Christ resolutely withheld His countenance; and every reader of the Gospels understands the childish mistake of those who wished the Saviour of men's souls and of the world to imitate the debased patriotism of Judas of Galilee or Barabbas, and who quarrelled for places on the right and left of the King. But it is almost, if not quite, an equal misunderstanding to think of the kingdom as merely the assertion of a moral principle without any care for its social and political results. What Christ demands is the carrying of the principle into its fullest practical effect, the entering into all the relations of life under His leadership, the bringing of every sphere of human existence under His spiritual dominion. It was for this purpose that, at the close of His ministry, when His approaching death made the attribution to Him of selfish ambition no longer possible, He accepted the part which He had before refused, and allowed Himself to be borne into Jerusalem with the triumph of a king.

We are here at the very centre of our subject, which we may best bring into relief by giving an answer to

[1] Matt. xxii. 7.   [2] Matt. xxi. 43.

III.] *Beginnings of the Universal Society.* 109

the question: What did Christ mean by saying that He was a King? In the remarkable words recorded in the fourth gospel, and also in the early document called the Acts of Pilate [1], we have our Lord's own answer: 'Thou sayest that I am a King; to this end was I born, and for this cause came I into the world, that I might bear witness to the truth. He that is of the truth heareth My voice [2],' becomes, that is, my spiritual subject. And, again, 'My kingdom is not of this world.' Does this imply, we ask, that the Church or Kingdom of Christ is to exist solely for certain objects which are to be marked off as spiritual, apart from the organization of human society which is to be regarded as profane? I think not. We cannot thus cut human life and society in two. Indeed, experience shews that it is impossible. Nor do the words of Christ demand it. We may well interpret the expression 'this world' as meaning the present evil condition of the world, which is essentially transitory; and we may understand the assertion to mean, 'My kingship does not belong to the present evil state of things in which empires are built up by fraud or force; it will build up an empire of its own on the true principle of love.' Moreover, How shall we define a purely spiritual kingdom? Shall we take as purely spiritual functions prayer, and teaching, and beneficence? But each of these, as functions of a community,

---

[1] *Acts of Pilate*, or, *Gospel of Nicodemus*, i. c. 3, and ii. c. 3. This Apocryphal book is believed to be the one referred to by Justin Martyr in his Apology (A.D. 139). It contains the passage alluded to in the text in words varying but slightly from those of John xviii. See, upon this, Tischendorf, *When were our Gospels written?* p. 83. The Apocryphal Gospels are published in English by Mr. B. Harris Cowper (Williams and Norgate, 1867).
[2] John xviii. 37.

has necessarily a secular side. On the other hand, the organization of human society, where it is in a healthy state, cannot be conceived of otherwise than as spiritual. The assertion of a spiritual society is well-grounded, but it extends to the whole organization of mankind. The assertion, on the other hand, of a *merely* spiritual society is one-sided. It has, indeed, a certain truth in it, but not the whole truth. Let us try to estimate this.

The truth aimed at by the assertion of a society which shall be merely spiritual is this—First, that the beginning of all Church life is a spiritual influence which may be called faith, or sympathy with goodness, or aspiration ; and we must add that this spiritual influence is not bound up with the existence of any organization, not even of the baptized community, since our Lord spoke of the other sheep which were not of the fold [1], of the children of God which were scattered abroad [2]; and we see the Church influence outside as well as within the baptized community; but, Secondly, that the kingdom of Christ is not dependent on the intrigues and selfishness which so commonly actuate human organizations, those established for worship quite as much as others ; and that, so far as it takes shape in human organizations, it must be constantly freeing them from these evil influences : Thirdly, that the discovery and vindication of truth is the supreme matter, the working out of this in human relations coming afterwards : and, lastly, that this vindication of truth, and the expression of it in worship and teaching, is one of those spheres,

[1] John x. 16.   [2] John xi. 52.

like family life, or, in modern times, the press, which lie almost entirely without the sphere of law.

But we cannot go beyond this point. To suppose that Christ meant by His kingdom a purely ideal state, which would have no earthly expression as a society, and would only realize itself in another world, is to say that the Apostles and all subsequent generations of His followers misunderstood Him. But as soon as we admit the existence of a Christian society trying to realize God's kingdom in the world, we get beyond the sphere of that which is commonly understood when men speak of a purely spiritual society, namely, prayer and teaching and beneficence. Each of these leads us beyond itself: for worship is the echo and the expression of the prayer, 'Thy kingdom come, Thy will be done *on earth* as it is in heaven;' and Christian teaching necessarily occupies itself with human relations; and beneficence is the first attempt to set those relations right. Those who have prayed together, and have been stirred by Christian exhortation, and have banded themselves together in the Sacrament for the service of God and man, rise from their knees with the question 'What are we to do to bring about that better state for which we have prayed?' The answer to this has often been: Let us give to the poor and do the seven acts of mercy. But all such acts of mercy, to be effectual, go forth into wider and wider circles. The efforts to diminish poverty and disease lead direct into the sphere of politics. The wish to establish right feelings and sound relations among men is nothing, unless it reaches up to the sovereign community, and uses the national organs for its purpose.

There lies the great power, the universal means of Christian well-doing. Can it be supposed that Christ, who claims the supreme dominion, meant that His followers should carry on the good efforts prompted by His Spirit only in those spheres in which they are small and ineffectual, and that, just at the point at which they may become effectual and partake of the redeeming character of universality, they should pass them over to another power which is to be for ever strange to Him[1]? That is impossible; and, if so, we can set no bounds to the purposes of our Lord, and the functions of His Church. We must take in a simple and literal sense His claim of universal dominion.

The task then of the society which Christ founded is to bring about His universal dominion. It is to make the kingdoms of the world to be kingdoms which are not of *this* world. The present evil condition of the world, in which force and fraud reign, is to be replaced by the new and better state in which it will be no longer *this* world, but the world of God and of righteousness. The evil æon or sæculum, the reign of selfishness, is that with which Christ's kingdom stands in opposition. The effort of the Church is to exorcise the evil spirit which enslaves human life, and which makes the present æon to be 'the present evil æon[2].' So far as this is done, the Church succeeds in its mission. Moreover, its methods are primarily those of persuasion, always those of truthfulness. When Christ resisted the temptation to take the kingdoms of the world on condition of worshipping the Tempter, we may justly

---

[1] See Note XXIII, Dr. Arnold on the Church.   [2] Gal. i. 4.

interpret this as meaning that He rejected the methods of violence and deceit, and deliberately chose those of persuasion and laborious self-sacrifice as the only way of establishing His empire. The same methods He enjoins upon His followers, not to the exclusion of discipline among themselves or of self-defence, but as the rule, and as the path to be always preferred. We have learnt that coercion is no remedy ; not that it is not sometimes necessary, but that the root of evil is moral and social, and must be removed by moral influence, by a change of mind, by the introduction of just relations.

Further, we may say that our Lord's words constitute a political revelation. Government is essentially a moral and spiritual process, it is only secondarily one of compulsion : and it is directed ultimately not to material but to spiritual ends. Just as Socrates constantly taught the Athenian youths who were embarking in a political career that the object of political life was to do good to the citizens ; so, in an ampler manner, our Lord would show us that the true kingdom or community is that in which divine righteousness finds a home and human relations are knit together by the fear of God. It was the expansion of the Jewish ideal; not the destruction of the law of just relations, but first its purification and then its wider application. The Christian Church, the universal empire of our Lord, is the new Israel in which the Gentiles are made fellow-citizens of the household of God : it is Israel transfigured and spiritualized and made capable of embracing the world.

We must trace out the process of building up the Society which had this universal aim.

First, Christ Himself is the centre and inspiring force of the new spiritual kingdom. He realized in His own person and presented the type of all the chief relations of human beings. As towards God He showed what the relations of a son should be to the universal Father, and He draws all men into these relations; in the family He represented that prince of family virtues, subjection or deference; in the nation He exhibited that exalted patriotism which makes a man desire that his country should save mankind; while His care for the poor and weak furnishes the aim in which all true government should be constantly occupied. In social intercourse we see in Him a frank heartiness, and at the same time a deep concern for the spiritual end of such intercourse. In the smaller circle of His friends, and in His special love of St. John, we see the brotherly relation in its most attractive form. In all these relations we discern the higher form of self-sacrifice, not the casting away of self, but the imparting of self to others for their good. This is the central spirit of the Christian society and its first manifestation. The Church, which is the body of its founder, must be the expansion of the heart of Christ in the larger sphere of social relations.

We have seen that our Lord demanded in His followers the absolute giving up of self and of all that self implies. This is, in the first place, the giving up of the heart to God which is the aim of every religious revival, and which means, in Christ's sense, the substitution in the mind and purpose of the universal good for selfish objects. But this passes into a social requirement. The whole status of those who believe in Christ is merged in their membership in His kingdom.

There is no limit, external or internal, to this requirement. If this seems on one side a socialistic or hyper-socialistic demand, or on the other side one which must conduce to tyranny, and in either case to interfere with human independence, it must be modified by saying that it can only apply primarily in the spirit and intention of our actions, and can become practical only so far as the society is really Christian. But with these reservations we must accept it without hesitation. We are no longer our own, but belong entirely to Christ and to His Church. The society of which He is the inspiring power exists not for the protection of body and goods alone, but to train us to use spirit and soul and body and possessions alike for Him and for our brethren. So far as the Christian society is really Christian, so far we can give up to it all that is personal; not only our money to taxation, our social relations to be ruled by laws, our persons to the conscription and to death in war, but all personal property, personal interests, our own life and separate existence. The individual interest wanes and the universal interest grows. We merge ourselves in Christ and in the community in which He lives. We can do this, I say, so far as the community is really Christian, for we know that in losing our life we shall find it; we ourselves are living integers in the society, and a really Christian society gives back to its members all that it receives from them, and will never trench on the just domain of individual freedom. The first Christians at Jerusalem for a little while felt in themselves the power to do this. No one said that anything that he had was his own, but they had all things common [1]. In this they anticipated the final working out of the divine principle in society. The Church could not maintain itself at that exalted level, and after eighteen centuries we are still far from regaining it. But the Christian community is still one in which the brother of low degree is to rejoice in that he is exalted, and the rich in that he is made low [2]. Towards this ideal we can see a progress throughout the Christian centuries, and we may cherish an unshaken faith that it will go on to completion. We tend to a universal brotherhood perfected by the Christian spirit.

How then were the members of this new commonwealth, who entered it with free but absolute submission, to be governed? It might seem at first sight as though Christ cared only to assert principles, and that He was careless as to their practical application. And undoubtedly, the highest laws of the kingdom are such as are contained in the beatitudes, or such as have been traced out by the author of *Ecce Homo*, the law of philanthropy, of edification, of mercy, of resentment, of forgiveness. The lawyer may criticize this by saying that such laws lack a definite penal sanction. But in a spiritual society not only is the conscience sensitive towards God, but it feels and asserts the principles which Christ proclaimed, as with a knightly sense of honour. In such a society at its highest perfection the public sentiment of which each man is conscious would do the

[1] Acts iv. 32.   [2] James i. 9, 10.

work of discipline. Each member would feel in the averted glances of his brethren and the loss of their esteem a power which restrained him (apart from any actual punishment) from injustice or violence or lust. But our Lord, though He declined to be a judge or a divider in special causes[1], yet gave indications that the divine principle must be applied, and that the community which He founded must not shrink from the actual decision of cases, and the formation of rules and laws. He Himself, in the case of divorce, did not hesitate to speak distinctly, even peremptorily[2], and showed the result which must flow from the Christian spirit in contrast to the general selfishness of the marriage relation both in the East and the West, and even in the Mosaic law itself[3]. Nor need we find a difficulty in ascribing to Christ Himself the prescription of the methods for the settlement of quarrels among His followers, as contained in Matt. xviii, if we bear in mind that, as with so many of His words, it is the method not the rule which we are meant to follow. That is, He would say, 'Do not be judge in your own cause; take others who are not blinded by self-interest to determine the question. Only when you have exhausted all such efforts to set things right can you be justified in treating the man you think to have injured you as distinctly in the wrong, and needing like the publican or heathen repentance and reclamation.' This is a good instance of the way in which Christian principle can guide us in many domestic affairs, in political and social relations, in international

---

[1] Luke xii. 14.   [2] Matt. v. 31, 32.   [3] Matt. xix. 3-12.

dealings, in the making and enforcement of laws. The principle which Christ enjoins is capable of an application to awards and judgments in the most general sense. It results in such rules of moral and political conduct as these : let self-interest be banished as much as possible wherever you have to form a judgment; be conscious of your own liability to undue prejudice ; let others decide rather than you ; and again, to carry the principle into the wider sphere, let all have their proper share in the national representation ; appeal to a neutral tribunal if such can be found ; invoke arbitration before you draw the sword. It is a mistake to confine the application of such a principle to a single punishment like that of excommunication, which some have held to be the foundation of Church-discipline, while others have believed it to have been never practised in primitive times. The principle must be applied in a larger sense. It is a witness that Christianity is broadly human, and the Church capable of guiding and assimilating all human institutions.

It is true that, while the Church was first making its way in the world, this great social capacity was restrained. The Church was hemmed in by a vast organized society which had power over a large part of the Christian's life. The first need of the infant community was instruction. Our Lord Himself was principally a teacher. The Apostles gave themselves to the word of God and to prayer[1]. But the teaching function needs much less organization than has been commonly assumed. In the Constitution of the Synagogue no

[1] Acts vi. 4.

formal office of teaching existed. The instruction was given by any scholar with any pretensions who presented himself for the occasion [1]. And this, no doubt, was followed in the early Christian communities which arose out of the Synagogue. And, accordingly, so long as the element of government was greatly subordinate, there was little organization. It was the practical needs of the Church as a body of men living together, not the needs of worship or of teaching, which gave birth to the permanent organization. Even the great change under which Episcopacy sprang up, if it was caused by doctrinal requirements, was caused by them not because new doctrines caused differences of opinion, but because they caused schisms, and rent asunder the body which should be united [2]. Consequently, while the infant community chiefly needed instruction (though the function of government was never wholly absent) the organization was slight and precarious [3]. Our Lord gave no injunctions about it of

---

[1] Stanley, 'Jewish Church,' iii. 462.

[2] The word αἵρεσις, which has passed into a technical sense as heresy, was always used in early times for a schism or division, as in 1 Cor. xi. 19 : ' There must be also heresies (margin "sects") among you.' St. Paul is speaking of the lack of unity in those who ought to be one body at the Communion.

[3] The belief that teaching was not confined to the bishops and Presbyters in the primitive church is confirmed by the discovery (since the delivery of these Lectures) of the 'Teaching of the Twelve Apostles,' which shows that in the middle of the second century there still existed Prophets and Apostles to whom special authority in teaching was accorded ; but also that all who were capable of teaching could do so. There is no restriction in such passages as these (Sections 11, 12, 15) : ' Whosoever cometh and teacheth you all the things aforesaid, receive him.' 'Afterwards by putting him to the test you shall know him.' This is confirmed by what is said of the Bishops : ' *They too* minister to you the ministry of the prophets and teachers; therefore despise them not.' (Farrar's Translation, 'Contemporary Review,' May, 1884.)

perpetual obligation. We can gather from His actions no more than that there must be order of some kind, and an order suited to the circumstances. He sent out the Twelve, two and two, during the Galilæan ministry, and the Seventy to prepare His way in His last journey to Jerusalem: but both these orders passed away. The Seventy were for a temporary occasion; the Twelve were the first Judaic mould of the Church; but after the election of Matthias their number was never filled up, and, at the age when our Gospels were put in their present shape, there would seem to have been considerable doubt as to the original list. We may trace a rudimentary organization of the Church during our Lord's ministry, a leadership in Peter, an inner circle of trusted followers in the Three, the rudiments of a ruling body in the Twelve, a management of the common purse, Christ Himself acting as Governor; and we may see that the Jewish officers who collected the Temple tax, recognized Him as the head of the community by the question, 'Doth not your Master pay tribute [1]?' But it is evident that for the general purposes of government these rudiments were quite inadequate. The Church must adapt itself to the wider society which it tends to assimilate, and must take upon itself successively the forms of the family, the club, the synagogue, the municipality, the nation, the empire, the universal federation, binding these forms to its divine purpose, infusing into them all the Spirit of Christ.

The later part of the New Testament reveals the first attempts at the organization which was needed

[1] Matt. xvii. 24.

for the larger society or kingdom of God, first among the Jews, secondly among the Gentiles. In each case we see the effort to organize a society complete in all its parts, or at least preparing for completeness. There are no limits prescribed for its functions, such as would certainly have been set with the greatest care if the society had been meant to exist only for prayer, and teaching, and beneficence; unless, indeed, we take beneficence as including all mutual well-doing, in which case the goal of a universal society is reached directly, for we then include in the scope of the Christian Church the whole social and political life.

The first event is the organization of the Church after the Day of Pentecost. The life of the little society, ' the number of whose names was a hundred and twenty[1],' was not changed at once. It was still almost a family life. But the family is a microcosm, and contains in itself the rudiments of the general and national society. The believers ate at a common table, where, at the common meal, they commemorated the death and resurrection of their Lord[2]. Into the fund for the support of this common table they cast their whole living[3]; and by doing so they gave themselves up completely to the society. They were, of course, outwardly amenable to the Jewish law; but they felt that the existing fabric of society was tottering around them. The great day of the Lord announced by the prophet Joel had come. It is true that the change to the new social state, the new world of Christendom, did not come in a moment: but the first believers were, as little as possible, members of the

[1] Acts i. 15. [2] Acts ii. 46; 1 Cor. xi. 26. [3] Acts iv. 34, 35.

Jewish state, as much as possible citizens of the new kingdom.

This state of things, a kingdom within a kingdom, was not unknown in the East. The organization of society has there been always much less thorough than in the West. The Jewish state itself was a kind of *enclave*, an 'imperium in imperio,' first under the Persian, then under the Macedonian, and later under the Roman dominion. As now we see in Syria communities which are to a certain extent autonomous, such as the Druses and Maronites in Lebanon, and indeed throughout the Turkish empire the religious communities have also a civil organization, and the taxation is made through their heads; so, to some extent, it was in the first century. It was easier therefore than it would be with us for an infant community to manage its own affairs as a nation within a nation, having no settled boundary line between its own attributes and those of the larger society by which it was surrounded. The administration of the common fund, when this fund was the whole living of the society, must have embraced almost all the functions of government. The story of Ananias and Sapphira [1] exhibits the faithful bringing their offerings to the feet of the Apostles, and the Apostles sitting as a permanent council for the management of affairs and for judgment, the Sanhedrin of the new Israel, realizing already the promise, 'Ye shall sit on twelve thrones judging the twelve tribes of Israel [2].'

Of the great change that was coming the first believers were dimly conscious. They clung, indeed,

---
[1] Acts v. 1, 2.   [2] Matt. xix. 28.

III.] *Beginnings of the Universal Society.* 123

to the hope that the Jewish nation would by a corporate acceptance of Christ become the Church ; and this might seem adverse to the hope of universalism. Yet the demand for baptism into the name of Jesus, if complied with by the nation, would of itself have made Christian universalism, and not Jewish restriction, the law of the national life. This demand was therefore felt by the blind leaders of the nation to be subversive; and the people as a mass went with their leaders. There were, no doubt, those who still conceived of the new community as a Jewish sect. This was its legal position, of which St. Paul availed himself in his defence before Felix, when he said, 'After the way that they call heresy,' that is a sect (a way perfectly legitimate and understood), 'so worship I the God of my fathers[1].' There were also, up to the taking of Jerusalem, the Jacobean and hyper-Jacobean party, who were ' all of them zealous for the law [2],' that is the law as taught by the Rabbis. But as early as Stephen's time the more far-seeing had begun to take a bolder attitude. They perceived that much, or rather all, in the fabric of Judaism must undergo a change. On the other side, to the Jewish leaders and the mass of the nation, the idea of founding a community, not on positive institutions and peculiar customs, but upon the principles of faith and love and justice which are common to all men, and in the presence of which Jew and Gentile were equal, seemed not only the height of infatuation but positive treason, a speaking against Moses and the temple and the law. This feeling had, no doubt, underlain their hatred to

[1] Acts xxiv. 14. [2] Acts xxi. 20.

Christ Himself, and had been the cause of His death. At a later time, St. Paul, in his oration on the temple stairs, which was arranged with so much tact, gained a hearing till he spoke of being sent to the Gentiles, but at that word they cried out, 'Away with such a fellow from the earth[1].' Stephen vindicated himself at his trial, not by denying that great changes were at hand, but by appealing to the changes which had confessedly taken place before, from Ur to Charran, from Charran to Palestine, from Palestine to Egypt; from the patriarchs to the law, from the tabernacle to the temple. Yet even Stephen did not give up the hope that the Jewish nation as a nation might be saved: and we find the same feeling[2], half hope, half regret, in St. Paul, who, however, shews early in his career a prophetic foresight of the destruction of Jerusalem[3]. It was not fully made clear that the Church must undertake by itself, independently of the Jewish organization, the task of forming a righteous community in which Judaism had failed. It is in connexion with these hopes and fears that we may best understand the disputes in the Apostolic Church concerning the keeping of the law. Those who supposed the Christian Church to be only a Jewish sect, desired that every part of the law should be kept as a fixed matter of obligation. Those who, like St. Paul, understood it to be a new creation, might yet be willing, with him, to observe the customs so as to keep the door open to the last for the entrance of the Jewish nation into the Church. But, as the cup of Jewish obstinacy was filled to the brim, it became

[1] Acts xxii. 22.   [2] Acts xxii. 17–22.   [3] 1 Thess. ii. 14–16.

evident that the Church must no more be hampered by a regard to Jewish traditions; and the fall of Jerusalem finally set it free.

Christendom, then, as a distinct attempt to realize the kingdom of God on earth begins with the communities founded by St. Paul. It is in them that we find the Christian principle of life developing itself into relations, laws, institutions. All therefore that relates to their constitution and their action upon the world is of primary interest for our subject. It is evident that they took their shape at first from the synagogue; and so far they perpetuated the Jewish traditions and the law of just relations which lay at their centre. But, existing as they did in the cities of the Roman Empire, they had also the form of the Hetæriæ or clubs with which those cities teemed, and so took in something of the secular life of the empire and its associations. To the first of these origins belongs the name of elders given to their officers, to the second that of 'bishops,' and these were used interchangeably throughout the Apostolic age[1]. The word 'Ἐκκλησία, by which they called themselves, is associated with both origins. It is the equivalent for συναγωγή in the dialect of the Septuagint. But it also recalls the assemblies of the Greek Republics.

What then, we ask, was the object proposed by these Societies? Was it simply teaching and prayer, or was it the conduct of the general life? If we look back at their Judaic origin, it is evident that the synagogue

[1] See Titus i. 5-7: 'That thou shouldest ... ordain elders in every city ... if any be blameless ... for a bishop must be blameless.' Acts xx. 17: 'He called the elders of the church, and ... said unto them ... Take heed to ... all the flock over which the Holy Ghost hath made you bishops.'

was the attempt to realize, so far as circumstances allowed, the national idea in its completeness. 'The whole congregation,' or Synagogue or Church 'of Israel' is the ordinary expression for the nation, not merely as gathered for worship, but as a company or community in the most general sense. The Greek equivalent for this, ἐκκλησία, is the word used in the Grecian cities for the general assembly of the whole sovereign state when met to deliberate on the affairs of their common life, and is contrasted with the smaller council or βουλή. It is quite a mistake to suppose that ἐκκλησία implies a select body called out as separate from the rest. It is the whole body of the citizens, called out from their homes to engage in the most general interests of the State. The Jewish synagogues were, no doubt, mainly occupied with teaching, and prayer, and almsgiving. But this was because of the peculiar position of the nation when they arose. Their organization was a little counterpart of the national Sanhedrin [1], which had

[1] 'The Sanhedrin was established in Jerusalem after twenty-five years' war by Simon Ben Mathathia (142 B.C.). The business of this institution was the administration of law (Handhabung der Rechtspflege), and its president was called the Nasi. Next to him stood the first President of the Judicial Tribunal (Gerichtsvorsteher), on whom in course of time civil processes specially devolved. In Simon and his successors we find an equal care for the spiritual and the outward.' (Zunz, Die gottesdienstlichen Vorträge der Juden, pp. 37-8. Berlin, Asher, 1832.)

'The synagogue probably answered the purpose of the town hall as well as of the church of the district. Each synagogue accordingly had its own small municipal jurisdiction, with the power of excommunication and exclusion, and extending to the right of inflicting lashes on the bare back and breast of the offender.' (Stanley, Jewish Church, iii. 462.)

'Les synagogues étaient de vraies petites républiques indépendantes; elles avaient une juridiction étendue. Comme toutes les corporations municipales jusqu'à une époque avancée de l'empire romain, elles faisaient des décrets honorifiques, votaient des résolutions ayant force de loi pour la Communauté, prononçaient des peines corporelles dont l'exécuteur ordinaire était le hazzun.' Renan, Vie de Jésus, 136 (later ed. 140).

all the supreme attributes, deliberative, judicial, and administrative. Their system of discipline was limited by no defined boundary, but was designed to enforce the law as a whole. Had the nation been free, this organization would have served for all purposes of local government, as well as for those of worship and instruction.

If we take the Gentile origin of the infant churches, and regard them as clubs for mutual beneficence, what limit can be set to such beneficence? Only the limit of the possible. Those who belonged to the society pledged their whole life to it. If they did not cast into a common fund, like those at Jerusalem, their whole substance, they looked on all that they possessed as held in trust for Christ and their brethren. They were not only, to adopt a modern expression, 'Romans if you will, but Christians first.' The Deacon of Vienne[1], who, when tried for his life, would make no other answer to all the questions as to his name, his race, his occupation, than the one word Christianus, expressed the absorbing interest which all true believers had in the Christian community. If they were, like the Jewish settlements, πάροικοι, and the origin of the word parish is a body of sojourners, it was because they looked constantly for a new state of society which was to emerge out of the old. And if this hope was at first the hope of a heavenly rather than an earthly state, it gradually

---

[1] Ὁ δὲ Σάγκτος τοσαύτῃ ὑποστάσει ἀντιπαρετάξατο αὐτοῖς, ὥστε μηδὲ τὸ ἴδιον κατειπεῖν ὄνομα, μήτε ἔθνους, μήτε πόλεως ὅθεν ἦν, μήτε εἰ δοῦλος ἢ ἐλεύθερος εἴη, ἀλλὰ πρὸς πάντα τὰ ἐπερωτώμενα ἀπεκρίνατο 'Ῥωμαϊκῇ φωνῇ· Χριστιανός εἰμι. Τοῦτο καὶ ἀντὶ ὀνόματος, καὶ ἀντὶ πόλεως, καὶ ἀντὶ γένους καὶ ἀντὶ παντὸς ἐπαλλήλως ὡμολόγει, ἄλλην δὲ φωνὴν οὐκ ἤκουσαν αὐτοῦ τὰ ἔθνη. Euseb. Hist. Eccl. v. 1.

became, like the hope of the prophets, a longing for a practical righteousness here, and the resolute attempt to attain it in all the relations of life.

The more we study the history of the early Christian communities, the more clearly these two things stand out; first, that their organization is adapted to their needs with entire freedom; secondly, that the work of government among them was quite as important as that of teaching or worship.

The Apostolate was the first office, but, as we have seen, was put aside when the Jewish destination of the Church ceased. The word Apostle remains in St. Paul's Epistles as a venerable title, applied to men who did a work similar to that of the original Twelve in the founding and guidance of Churches without being fixed to any one place [1]. The Seven came next, whether we call them formally an order of Deacons, or look on the office as personal, and instituted for the emergency described in the sixth chapter of the Acts. In any case, we read nothing more of Deacons until the Epistle to the Philippians, unless we except the female 'Servant of the Church of Cenchrea [2].' In the first Epistle to Timothy they appear ; from the Epistle to Titus they are absent: from which we may gather that they were commonly adopted in the later part of the first century, but were not regarded as indispensable. The next

---

[1] Romans xvi. 7; 1 Cor. xii. 28, 29; 2 Cor. viii. 23; Ib. xi. 5. The newly discovered work, 'The Teaching of the Twelve Apostles' shows that this use of the word Apostle lasted on far into the second century. But this document shows also that the authority of those who bore this name was then but slight, and that the need of their erratic ministrations was diminishing.

[2] Romans xvi. 1.   [3] 1 Tim. iii. 8-13.

office was that of the Presbyters. The Church was to have its own rulers as the synagogue had; and this seems to have been recognized as soon as the rudimentary institution of the Apostolate was found inadequate, both at Jerusalem and Antioch and in the Mission Churches[1]. But in the first Epistle to the Corinthians we have an enumeration of offices[2], or at least of functions, in which there is no mention of either presbyters or deacons, nor do such officers appear in the argument of these Epistles, though in the questions of discipline and administration and the collection of funds with which these Epistles abound, it would have been hardly possible to avoid the mention of them had they existed. The whole condition of the churches was plastic: Apostles and Prophets are placed side by side with teachers, powers, helps, governments[3]. Whatever actual offices may have existed, they are regarded by St. Paul rather according to the general effect which they in common with others might produce upon the life of the Church than as permanent orders. Out of them all emerge in the time of the Pastoral Epistles, the two offices of Deacons and Presbyters. Later on (perhaps some thirty or forty years after) we find the episcopal office rising to pre-eminence above the presbyterate. But this, and the causes which produced it, and the changes in an office the name of which has at various times in Christian history been made to cover functions so different as those of the chorepiscopus, the city bishop, the diocesan prelate, lie beyond our immediate scope. It is sufficient to note that the Episcopate, like

[1] Acts xi. 20; xv. 4, 22; xiv. 23. [2] 1 Cor. xii. 28. [3] Ibid.

K

the other offices, was due, not to any formal appointment which it would be impious to alter, but to providential necessity; and that a similar necessity has constantly changed its form. This necessity, and the Spirit of Christ, that is of sound judgment, have throughout been the guides in the organisation of the Church, which is not bound to any one type, but has power to adapt its institutions to the needs of mankind and its own position in the world.

The other important matter to be noticed is the paramount position which the function of government occupies in the early churches. The original Deacons had nothing to do with teaching, although some Deacons became eminent teachers. Their duty was to regulate the distribution of the common fund. The Presbyters were, like those of the Jews, rulers of the community. In the enumeration of Church functions in the first Epistle to the Corinthians [1], and in a similar but shorter enumeration in the Ephesians [2], prominence is, no doubt, given to the teaching functions, those of the prophets and teachers. This was but natural in infant Societies, the first object of which was to perpetuate the life and teaching of Christ. But the 'powers,' 'the gifts of healing,' the 'helps,' the 'governments,' are agencies for the conduct of the general life of the community, the 'Pastors' in the Ephesians standing between the two groups, occupied both in teaching and in ministration. Similarly, when St. Paul speaks to the elders of Ephesus [3], he addresses them as shepherds tending a flock, which, according to both its classical and its

[1] 1 Cor. xii. 28. [2] Eph. iv. 11. [3] Acts xx. 28.

biblical associations, implies the gift of general supervision as exercised by kings and magistrates rather than that of teaching and of prayer alone; and his address closes, not with an exhortation about prayer and preaching, but with the commendation to them of a disinterestedness like his own as to money matters [1], and an exhortation to remember that the duty of Christians is to labour and support the weak, and to impart freely to others. In the Pastoral Epistles the normal duty of the elders is to rule: those who rule well are to have double honours [2]; those who add to this the less common function of teaching are specially to be honoured. The Elder or Bishop must be apt to teach, but still more apt to rule [3]. The qualities required of him—vigilance, sobriety, hospitality, disinterestedness, experience, the capacity to rule as tested by ruling his own family—attest the governor rather than the preacher or the liturgist.

As to teaching and public prayer, every index points to its being free, under the general rule that all should be done decently and in order. In the synagogue the function of teaching was confined to no special class: the ruler of the synagogue invited any competent man to address those assembled, and the Church, no doubt, adopted this custom. In Jerusalem the Apostles chose these functions as the most important, whether intrinsically or for the time, for themselves [4]. But there is nothing to limit these functions to the Apostolic office. The Deacons, though appointed to serve

[1] Acts xx. 33-35, 19-22. [2] 1 Tim. v. 17. [3] Id. iii. 2-7. Titus i. 7, 8. 1 Tim. v. 1, 2, [4] Acts vi. 4.

tables, at once began to teach, some of them with eminent publicity and independence[1]. Those who were scattered abroad, in the persecution that arose about Stephen[2], went everywhere preaching the Word, even to Antioch[3], where the Apostles would have greatly hesitated to send them, and began spontaneously to preach to the Gentiles. Later, in the Corinthian Church, every man 'had a psalm, or a doctrine, or an interpretation[4];' and there is no suggestion by St. Paul when he took order in this matter, that teaching and prayer belong to a particular class. Even as late as the Pastoral Epistles, when the Presbyterate is fully formed, the writer's direction is only that *men* should lead in prayer, and that no woman should teach in the public assemblies[5]. It was only by degrees, as reflexion brought doctrinal differences, and increasing numbers required stricter order, that these duties were confined to a particular class, and that Bishops first, then Presbyters, and later even Deacons, came to be occupied mainly or solely with prayer and teaching[6]. It would seem that it was long before this change occurred. The Parochial system was formed, not on the basis of teaching and worship, but on that of government. The superintendent of a parish, in the beginning of the fifth century, was called not Doctor but Rector[7].

This ruling function had a constantly widening field

---

[1] Acts vi. 9, 1c.   [2] Acts viii. 1, 4.   [3] Id. xi. 19.
[4] 1 Cor. xiv. 26.   [5] 1 Tim. ii. 8. Ib. 11, 12.
[6] See the account of the formation and changes of these offices in Dr. Hatch's Bampton Lectures, and the note at p. 160 of this volume.
[7] See Sulpicius Severus, Dial. i. 4. Ecclesiam illius loci (Bethlehem) Hieronymus Presbyter *regit*.

of exercise even in the Apostolic times. In the Pastoral Epistles, we read no longer of a small and poor community, but one in which various classes exist, in which many are wealthy, in which also there are various orders of officers, not only Presbyters or Bishops and Deacons, but orders of women Deacons[1] and widows. The exercise of discipline has become a vast labour, comparable to that of Moses and the elders of Israel at Mount Sinai. The Apostolic deputy, Timothy or Titus, is sent not merely to regulate worship or teaching, but to take order in the affairs of the community generally[2]. And if the sentiment of St. Paul[3], that it was a shame for the infant Church to bring its matters before the heathen tribunals, was generally adopted, we can understand that the rulers of the Christian community had a large sphere of labour traced out for them.

If we ask by what law such matters were decided, we may well suppose that the Christian spirit of itself suggested the principles of all true government, and that, as with the judges of Israel, judgment was with the Christian elders mainly a spiritual faculty. But it is of the nature of legal procedure to become fixed, and to appeal to rule and precedent. Some such rules we find laid down in the Epistles to the Corinthians and the Pastoral Epistles, such as the directions concerning mixed marriages in the Epistle to the Corinthians[4], or those concerning the marriage of presbyters and deacons[5],

[1] 1 Tim. v. 9, 10; iii. 11. It is possible that γυναῖκας in this passage ought to be translated (as by the Revisers) merely 'women.' But it seems more likely that some special women are meant, and that they were Deaconesses, the passage before and after having reference to servants of the church.
[2] 1 Tim. i. 3, &c., &c. Titus i. 5.
[3] 1 Cor. vi. 1–6.
[4] 1 Cor. vii. 12–16.
[5] 1 Tim. iii. 2, 12.

and the admission and conduct of widows, in the Epistle to Timothy [1], all of which were at a later period appealed to as the ground of Ecclesiastical laws. The Old Testament would also be consulted, especially in matters relating to the family. But, no doubt, the customs and laws of Roman, or Greek, or Jewish society would also be adopted so far as they were not anti-christian in their tendency. Thus a body of Christian customs and rules of life grew up, through which the Church attempted to renew human life, and to establish on earth those just relations in which the Kingdom of Heaven consists [2]. The family was the chosen field of its influence, but all parts of human life came under its cognizance; not only the relations of its members to one another, but their bearing towards those who were without. It was a beginning of a new world, a world of tenderness in contrast with the callousness of heathen life, of laboriousness in contrast with the luxury and idleness of Roman citizens; a world in which murder, and adultery, and fraud, as we learn from Pliny's letter to Trajan [3], were forbidden, not by an external law, but by the conviction and the longing for purity which bound the citizens themselves together; a world from which the corrupting public shows were banished, and in which the slave became a brother and a free man in Christ; a world in which the antipathies of race and condition were to be obliterated, and of which love was

[1] 1 Tim. v. 2-16.
[2] For the Christian Church existing as a state within a state, see Lecky, *Eur. Mor.* i. 468.
[3] 'Quod soliti essent (Christiani) . . . sacramento se obstringere . . . ne furta, ne latrocinia, ne adulteria committerent, ne fidem fallerent, ne depositum appellati abnegarent.' Plin. *Ep.* xcvii.

III.] *Beginnings of the Universal Society.* 135

to be the supreme law. The ideal was but partially reached at best. Yet many of the Christian customs passed eventually into the laws of the empire, and, later on, into the public sentiment of Christendom.

It is the Church beginning thus to form itself which is the basis of the ideal Church of St. Paul and St. John. Already, in his prison at Rome, St. Paul describes himself as joying and beholding the order of the Christian community at Colossae[1]. This working out of righteousness in the organized life of believers gives substance to all that he says of the Church as the body and the bride of Christ[2], the fulness of Him that filleth all in all[3]. It is impossible to apply such words as these to a body which is limited in its scope. The Church of St. Paul and St. John is the complete humanity, for nothing short of this can be the fulness of God. When, further, we enter upon the glowing vision of the Apocalypse, we find that what is before the mind of the Seer is a holy city[4], a society of just men, which is the counterpart, on the one hand, of the corrupt Jerusalem, and, on the other, of the polluted Babylon[5]. These two represent the world under the dominion of the debased Judaism and heathenism. The New Jerusalem is the world under the dominion of Christ. Like the visions of the older Prophets, it has its realization, not in a heavenly state beyond this world, but in a progressively righteous state in this world. Nor is it a society for worship and teaching that the Seer has before his mind; (there is no temple in the New Jerusalem[6];) but the

[1] Col. ii. 5.   [2] 1 Cor. xii. 27. Eph. v. 25-32.   [3] Eph. i. 22, 23.
[4] Rev. xxi. 2.   [5] Rev. xviii.   [6] Id. xxi. 22.

transformation of the kingdom of this world in which unjust relations subsist into a kingdom of God in which just relations will subsist: this is the object for which Christ goes forth conquering and to conquer.

We may add that this throws a clear light on the expectation of the Coming of our Lord in the Apostolic age. It would be vain to deny that in certain passages St. Paul repeats the language of ancient prophecy with a kind of literalism. The voice of the archangel, and the trump of God [1], and the saints caught up into the clouds, can hardly be explained otherwise than as a literal expectation of things never destined to be fulfilled. Nor can we deny that such literalisms are among the integuments which had to fall off when the age of childhood was past. When we look, however, at the words of our Lord Himself we have no similar difficulty. The angel with the great sound of the trumpet [2] gathering the elect from the four winds is evidently the ministry of the Gospel going abroad through the world before the great crisis of the destruction of Jerusalem. The end of the 'age [3],' about which the disciples ask, is the end of the Jewish dispensation. The passing away of heaven and earth is the rolling away of the existing fabric of society. The Coming of the Son of Man in a cloud [4] (an image borrowed from Daniel) is the triumph of Christ over the world-powers of Judea and of Rome. The apostolic visions must be interpreted in a similar way. The day of the Lord is the great crisis of history, when Church and world must pass through a purifying furnace of suffering. And,

[1] 1 Thess. iv. 16, 17.   [2] Matt. xxiv. 31.   [3] Ib. 3.   [4] Ib. 30.

beyond this, stands forth before the Seer's eye the new state of society, the abode of divine justice, the new heaven and earth wherein dwelleth righteousness.

How, then, was this result to be brought about? Partly, no doubt, by the influx of converts, and by the growth of the kingdom itself; partly by the general influence of Christian doctrine, the leaven leavening the whole lump. But, partly also, as a consequence and accompaniment of these processes, by the appropriation of human organizations, which, by the infusion of the Christian spirit, came to realize the Church idea, and thus to become Churches themselves. The most striking instance of this is the appropriation of the family, which, being itself a microcosm, presents a typical specimen and a commencement of the whole process. The family was, both among Jews and Gentiles, to a large extent the home of selfishness. By the facility of divorce, the absolute power of the father, and slavery, selfishness reigned supreme. So much was this the case that, even when Christianity had been three centuries at work, the family life was still worldly enough to make many of the great fathers despair of its redemption. But, in the New Testament, we find the family life recognized as the natural abode of the Gospel-spirit, and becoming, to use the words of St. Paul, 'the Church which is in the house.' 'Our Lord,' said Clement of Alexandria, 'said that where two or three were gathered in His name, there was the true Church. Who are these two or three, but the father, the mother, and the child[1]?' For the investigation we are now pursuing, the passages which

[1] Clem. Alex. Strom. iii. 10.

speak of the family are the most precious in the New Testament. In our Lord's ministry we find occasions in which the whole household passes into the Church. In the Acts and Epistles this is still more frequent. The family of Cornelius[1] and the family of the Philippian jailor[2] are the two most familiar instances. The promise of salvation through faith is not to the individual alone, but 'thou shalt be saved *and thy house*[3].' If we ask how a family can be said to become a church, we have but to go for an answer to the passages in the Ephesians[4], Colossians[5], and the first Epistle of St. Peter[6], in which the effect of Christianity upon the various sections of the household is described. We see there the Christian spirit of mutual deference and respect establishing true relations between husband and wife, parents and children, masters and servants. We have but to picture to ourselves a family living according to the Apostolic prescription, and we realize in the circle of the family what the Church is meant to be, society transformed by the Spirit of Christ. We have there the kingdom of heaven taking shape before our eyes.

We must extend this to all other circles of human life, to social and commercial intercourse, to societies formed for the increase of knowledge or of art, but most of all to the sovereign state. As it is said by sociologists that the family is the miniature of the State, so also the family which has become a Church is the miniature of the State which has become a Church.

---

[1] Acts x. 44-48.   [2] Id. xvi. 32-34.   [3] Ib. 31.   [4] Eph. v. 22—vi. 9.
[5] Col. iii. 18—iv. 1.   [6] 1 Pet. ii. 18—iii. 9.

The language of St. Paul[1] and St. Peter[2] concerning the sovereign state reveals to us the true destination of political society. When all officers of State are looked upon as ministers of God, and all orders of men who compose the state are brought within the action of Christian brotherly kindness, we see political society as a whole already transformed in the mind of the great Purposer. The ideal stands out before us in the words 'Honour all men, love the brotherhood, fear God, honour the king[3].' The whole fabric is there in the germ, already recognized as divine in its essence and in its destination. It is for those who are the special messengers of Christ not so much to change its organization as to breathe into it the Spirit of their Lord, and thus to convert it into a Church. That is the task of the growing Christendom.

The history of Christendom, therefore, until the final condition at which we aim is reached, must be the record of an imperfect state, a becoming not a being. If the perfect state is that in which the Church and mankind are one, both must be constantly undergoing change. We may apply to them the words of Hebrew prophecy, 'I will overturn, overturn, overturn it, until He come whose right it is, and I will give it to Him[4].' Any theory which claims to be complete, while dealing only with the existing materials, must by its very terms be in error; and everything that can be said truly will appear vacillating and inconsistent. It is as in a country which is being gradually conquered, as, for instance, in the winning back of Spain from the Moors

[1] Rom. xiii. 1-7. [2] 1 Pet. ii. 13, 14. [3] 1 Pet. ii. 17. [4] Ezek. xxi. 27.

in the seven centuries from Charles Martel to Ximenes. Who can fix the exact limits of the conquest? At one moment it may seem that a line can be drawn, on either side of which stand the opposing armies and people. Yet, even so, the parts occupied by the invading hosts may merely submit, or may be in rebellion, or, again, may be governed with their own free consent; while on the side occupied by the defenders some may sympathize, languidly or actively, with the invaders. At another time no line at all can be traced. In such a state of affairs, the territory may be said to belong to one party or to the other, according to the views of the narrator, his information, or his temperament. At one moment the invaders seem ready to be surrounded and destroyed, at another the whole land seems theirs. The inhabitants and the invaders alike will give the most varying accounts of the state and prospects of the country. Who, during such a struggle, would undertake to give an accurate description of it? Or what description which holds good for one moment could fail to be false in the next? No one can give such a definition of the Church in its relation to mankind as will hold good for all time. It is a growing organism with universal capacities, destined to embrace the world, yet still far from accomplishing its destiny.

But these two things seem to follow as practical conclusions from our review of the work of the Founder, and of those who planted the Church during its earliest age. First, since Christ demanded the complete allegiance of His followers, our duty is to strive that whatever calls itself by His name should be absolutely holy.

Secondly, since Christ also gave the promise of universal dominion, we need never doubt that we are fulfilling His will by opening wide the gates of the city which were to be shut neither day nor night, and embracing within its hospitable area more and more of the organisms which make up the complete humanity.

LECTURE IV.

THE IMPERIAL AND MEDIÆVAL CHURCH.

REVELATION vi. 2. And I saw, and behold a white horse: and he that sat on him had a bow; and a crown was given unto him: and he went forth conquering, and to conquer.

THE Christian Church, at the close of the Apostolic age, went forth to conquer the world, and it was armed for this vast enterprise with all that was essential. First, it had a body of authoritative documents; for though the New Testament Scriptures were not gathered in a volume receiving general consent till the later part of the second century[1], the Old Testament, understood in the sense which Christ and the Apostles had given to it, was in the hands of all, and the various documents which afterwards made up the New Testament were sufficiently known to present to any inquirer a clear embodiment of the Christian scheme. Secondly, the Christian Church had the rudiments of a complete society. It contained within itself a principle of life which was at once a close bond between its members and an expansive force; and it had a perfectly free constitution, which rendered it capable of growing into

[1] The Muratorian fragment, which shows that the Canon of the New Testament was at Rome at that date substantially as we have it now, is believed to have been written about the year A.D. 170. Westcott's *Hist. New Test. Canon*, p. 185.

United Christendom attempted. 143

a State, an Empire. Thirdly, it had an organization, and officers, whose duty it was both to keep alive the Christian traditions by a worship and teaching centred in the personality of Christ, and to exercise discipline and minister to the wants of all classes of the community, especially the poor. Lastly, it had, what is far the most important, the ideal of the life and spirit of Christ, the inspiring power of the whole organism. This ideal was partly derived from the Scriptures, both of the Old Testament read in a Christian sense, and of the New as recording the life of Christ; it was also partly a matter of tradition; but it was most of all to be seen in the life of the Church itself. Christians were themselves the living epistles, known and read of all men[1]. For the promise to which they appealed was not that a certain defined type should be impressed on them, and through them on mankind, but that the Spirit, which blows where it lists, should guide them and convince the world. The design of the Christian community was not to substitute itself for the organized society then existing, but to blend with it, to breathe a new spirit into it, and finally to be so fused with it as to transform it into the body of Christ.

The first thing which had to be done, and which was accomplished in the first three centuries, was to produce conviction, to impress upon the conscience of mankind the belief that the spiritual power which wrought in the Christian Church was divine and therefore supreme. There was no design of outward conquest, but of persuasion. The conviction, when

[1] 2 Cor. iii. 2.

once thoroughly impressed, was capable of renewing the whole life, first of the individual, then of the community. It was capable of rebuilding the whole of human society; it drew in its train all that is needed for society, the establishment of just relations, systems of law, political constitutions, a strict and peremptory discipline. Indeed this discipline was from the first unhesitatingly and impartially applied to all the members of the Christian society. But as regards those without, persuasion was the sole legitimate agency. Of what then was it designed to persuade men? Of this above all, that the moral ideal presented in the life of Christ was supreme. For this, as we have said, is the centre of the whole organism. All else may change, but, so long as the moral and spiritual supremacy of the Life and Spirit of Christ remain, Christianity is living, and whatever is necessary for its full expansion will follow in due time.

It is true the Christian faith has often been set forth by means both of ordinances and of statements which may easily be divorced from the moral ideal to which they relate: when thus divorced they lose their power over the conscience, and provoke wonder at the contrast between the greatness of the work to be done and the triviality of the means by which it is sought to compass it. But the moral centre is always discernible, to those who are patient enough to watch for it, in the forms and the teaching which have held fast the Church and convinced the world. The Sacraments are designed to perpetuate the memory and realize the indwelling of Christ, to make His life the life of the community; and all the Church-ordinances to bind men in the brotherly relations which flow from union in righteousness. The early Christians, as Pliny's letter shows [1], bound themselves in the Sacrament not to swear falsely, or to commit theft, or adultery, or withhold money that was entrusted to them. And the teaching, when its symbolical expressions are rightly understood, always represents the supremacy of the moral ideal. If it was asserted that Christ rose from the dead, and the doctrine of the resurrection was the foundation of the Church, this was based on the conviction of the sovereign nature of His holiness. The Holy One, it was said, could not be held by the chains of death: the resurrection was the assurance that the divine righteousness which was manifested in the life of Christ was supreme in the world. If the immortality of the soul was taught, this was grounded on the assurance that the principle in man which is capable of righteousness and of redemption is divine, and therefore destined to endure. If the divinity of Christ was asserted, this was the assertion that He was morally supreme, the true image in humanity of the eternal power of love. If, again, faith was proclaimed as the saving power, it was a moral faith, a union of the heart and life with Christ. The whole Christian teaching is the presentation by various means of the moral ideal of the life of Christ to mankind [2].

[1] See the words quoted in Lect. III, p. 134.
[2] There is a tendency, especially in Germany, to take these doctrinal conceptions as something ultimate in the minds of the writers who first gave them expression. But it is truer to regard them as presentations of the central and underlying moral

What then, we may ask, was this moral ideal, or rather, what did it mean to the believers and to those whom they strove to convert? Was the self-sacrificing love, by which we can most nearly express it, a new moral type, perfectly clear to all believers of every age, and set forth so distinctly as that all men could apprehend it? and was it meant to be placed in contrast with all other moral types, and to displace and destroy them as evil? It would be truer to say that in this the saying of Christ holds good, 'I came not to destroy, but to fulfil.' We perceive this the more distinctly the more history and philosophy unfold to us the secret of ancient religions and of individual and national character. But in the early church it was not unrecognized. The Western Fathers, indeed, like Tertullian and Jerome, depreciated all morality but the Christian. But those of the East, especially the earlier Alexandrine teachers, Clement and Origen, placed the great heathen moralists amongst those who had prepared the way of Christ. It is true that when that which is perfect is come, that which is in part must be done away. To linger in an inferior moral state when a higher has been presented becomes sinful. It is true also that the Christian ideal is that before which all others must pale. But it overcomes all other moral systems, not by denying their suitability to the times of comparative ignorance, but by outshining and absorbing them. It was noticed by Dr. Chalmers[1] that when St. Paul wrote to

truth, varying with the thought of the age, and sometimes, as is shown by the difference between the different groups of St. Paul's Epistles, with the various experiences of the same teacher.

[1] Commercial Discourses. Disc. I. (Collected Works, vol. vi).

the Philippians that they should, for the completion of their Christian life, think upon whatsoever things were honest and just, lovely and of good report, whatsoever was deemed a virtue and worthy of praise[1], he was using the common terms of Greek ethics, and urging his converts to assimilate the ideal which was recognized in the society around them.

But, it may be said, the motive at least was new, and the motive really determines the ideal. The Pagan philosophy bade men seek these qualities because they were humanly good, the Christian religion from love to God. This, however, is only in part true ; for the love of God was not wholly absent from Paganism. It may further be said that the moral ideal acknowledged by the society of Greece or Rome had at its root a proud independence, while Christian goodness demands a sense of sin and the belief in an atonement. But here again we cannot ignore the sense of sin[2] presented by some of the Greek tragedies and their early myths : and if we follow the development of Greek thought, we find at its final issue in Neo-Platonism a longing for purity and for the image of God. Even humility, which is often taken as distinctively Christian, may be found in writers like Marcus Aurelius ; and self-sacrificing love, at least for country and for friends, has many representatives in the Greek and Roman world. But we may justly say that Christianity laid a stress upon these which had never been felt before. No

[1] Phil. iv. 8.
[2] 'In the assertion of Original Sin the Greek Mythology rose and set.' Coleridge, Aids to Reflexion, p. 211.

one had said with the same emphasis such words as these: 'Blessed are the meek and the pure in heart, for they shall see God;' nor 'Except a man be born again, he cannot see the kingdom of God;' nor 'Except a corn of wheat fall into the ground and die, it abideth alone, but if it die it beareth much fruit;' nor 'God is love.' The self-sacrifice of Greek and Roman times is found in exceptional heroes, that of Christian times is much more widely diffused. The Decii gave up life that Rome might conquer her enemies, Christ and His followers that the hearts of all men might be won to God and to love. It is true also that Christianity brought the moral qualities into their proper harmony, raising into prominence those which are most widely humane, that it made the true motives operative, and that it imparted to men the assurance that ultimate and divine truth had been reached and would prevail. This last gave the Church that unconquerable hope which more than anything else overcame the world.

No student of the moral world in the first centuries of the Christian era can fail to be struck with the fact that moral ideas, both true and false, appear at the same time in very different places and connexions. Similarities may be traced in the language of St. Paul and of Seneca; Marcus Aurelius and Epictetus have much in common with the ideas of the Christians whom they ignored or persecuted. Plutarch's religious and moral principles have a cast which indicates a progress in comparison with Stoics like Brutus or Cato, comparable to that from the Pharisees to the Apostolic fathers, and in general we may observe that when Christianity is advancing heathenism becomes serious and turns to the unseen world for satisfaction[1]. It is natural to ask, whether this progress is the direct result of Christian teaching, and its expressions taken from the Gospel[2]. At a later time it may be asked whether asceticism was imported into the Church from the Eastern religions where it prevailed before. It is no impeachment of the truth of Christianity or of the zeal of its emissaries to observe the manner in which moral ideas spread through the world,—a matter which is seldom rightly conceived. That direct teaching of the primary truths is the most important channel of propagation is true. 'How shall they hear without a preacher?' But influence and example also go for much: and again both teacher and taught are subject to forces, partly arising from their circumstances, partly from causes which we cannot trace, and which form what has been called a climate of opinion. Moreover, the phrases and the arguments used on some chance occasion lie as germs in the mind, and spring to life almost unconsciously and are reproduced when circumstances occur to fructify them, often in complete forgetfulness of their source. Thus it may happen that the same expressions occur in two writers who have never seen one another; and the influence of different persons and

---

[1] See Merivale's Conversion of the Roman Empire (Boyle Lectures for 1864), especially pp. 86 ff., pp. 111 ff., and the whole of Lecture VI.

[2] The problem of the relation of the sentiments of the great Roman Stoics to those of the New Testament is discussed by Bishop Lightfoot in his Essay on St. Paul and Seneca in his book on the Epistle to the Philippians. It seems hardly necessary to attribute to them so much knowledge of the Christian writings as is implied at p. 28 of that volume.

schools may be reciprocal and extensive without their either consciously acknowledging or consciously ignoring their mutual obligation. But he who believes that the progress of mankind is all one, and springs from one source, and who is content to assert for Christianity not an exclusive position, but a primacy among beliefs and moral systems, will conduct the inquiry into the method of the evolution of truth and goodness without any anxiety: nor will he assume that Christianity stands or falls with the assertion that all good is visibly connected with the teaching of the Church. It is enough that the moral ideal which Christianity enshrines has shown itself capable of either including or assimilating all that is permanently good in human nature.

Yet it is more true that Christianity gives a stimulus to good than that it discloses a moral ideal. Faith rather than the faith, truth rather than the truth, is that to which it incites us. As to the ancients the divine was always surrounded by a cloud, which partly hid partly revealed it, so it is with the divine moral ideal. Indeed, when we speak of God as a moral being, we know that no morality such as exists between man and man can be a full measure of His nature. And so when we speak of the divine moral ideal which is presented in Jesus Christ, though this is more tangible, it has yet a side which is always beyond our grasp. It is in this way that we may understand the ideas of the Buddhists and Quietists, who appear to be at times indifferent to moral good and evil, in their absorption in that which is, as they say, beyond both. To suppose that God is in any way indifferent to good and evil is to belie all that we are taught by revelation, or by nature rightly understood. But we may as Christians readily confess that what seems to us good or evil may often wear a very different aspect in God's sight; that there is often evil which we have not perceived corrupting what seems to us purely good; and again, that there is 'a soul of good in things evil.'

The importance of these remarks will be evident if we cast a glance upon the history of the conversion of the Roman empire. For, first, we find that the Church is in contact with a system of life which it is impossible to stigmatize as absolutely evil. Secondly, that influences such as the Alexandrian philosophy, the Roman law and administration, Oriental mysticism and asceticism, were taken in to the exposition of Christian doctrine and the development of the Christian society—some of them from the very earliest days: and necessarily so, for they were wrapped up in the human language which Christianity must use, and in the human life with which Christianity must blend. But, thirdly, what is far the most important, we find the Christian ideal itself varying from age to age. To the Church of the earliest centuries it meant a childlike submissiveness and fidelity: to the age of the great fathers and their successors, from the fourth to the eighth century, it meant mainly asceticism; from Charlemagne to the end of the Crusades it meant mainly the spirit of chivalry; and from thence to the Reformation it meant mainly the clerical virtues. In the Eastern Church the ideal has been that of correct doctrine; in the Western, good discipline. I have put this as strongly as possible, so as to mark how great the change has been at various times in the moral ideal itself, which is the living kernel of the whole system. Such a statement needs, indeed, to be modified by the acknowledgment that, through all these forms of the moral ideal, Christian love, and faith, and beneficence (this last the most constant factor) were presented to the world. But, if we compare the ideals of life presented by an apostolical father like Polycarp in the second century, a monk like Macarius or Hilarion in the fourth, a hero like Charlemagne in the eighth, a clerical administrator like Pope Innocent III in the thirteenth, and a promoter of liberal learning like Gerson in the fifteenth, it might almost seem as if we were reviewing a series of different religions, rather than different forms of the same. Yet each of these appeared to the men of their own day as the model of Christian excellence. Christians would have pointed to each in turn and said to mankind, That is what we wish you to become. These observations should make us, in the first place, very tolerant of diversities, even as to that which seems most important and central; in the second place, it should make us feel that our own conception of Christianity is probably far from complete, so that we must not dogmatize as if we and our age had nothing more to learn. Thirdly, it should make us feel that Christianity can leave full liberty to moral science and gratefully encourage its researches. The impulse which the Gospel gives, the desire to fulfil God's will in union with the sacrifice of Christ, may be all its own. But what is the will of God has not been disclosed all at once, but is left to be ascertained more and more as human knowledge and experience clear the pathway before us. And, lastly, we should look upon the whole Christian development as a striving upwards, a fuller perception from age to age of the scope of redemption, a gradual assimilation of the various elements of social life ; a process which is subject at times to at least apparent stagnation, and even to retrogression, but, which is never for any long period turned back in its progressive course.

We take self-sacrificing love as the nearest expression we can give of the Christian ideal ; and this, though clothed in many forms, has been constantly present. It must indeed be admitted that it is much easier to see the differences in the ideal of life in different ages than its constancy in reference to this standard. Who would take as an expression of love an ascetic of the fifth century, or a crusader of the twelfth, or an ecclesiastic like Hildebrand or Becket, or one of the schoolmen ? Yet it is certain that each of them had in some way before his mind the image of Him who said, ' Hereby shall all men know that ye are my disciples, if ye have love one to another.' A second constant factor of the Christian ideal is faith in a fatherly and redeeming God ; but this also is subject to vast changes. God is at one time the redeemer of Israel ; then of those within the Church's pale ; only in a vague uncertain manner of the world. He is the redeemer from His own jealous wrath, or from a world which is itself left to perish. He is the redeemer of the individual rather than of society. He is the redeemer from personal misery rather than from sin. These divergences from the ideal, as we are able to conceive it, go very deep, and there are many others of a similar kind. Yet it would be quite untrue to assert that a Christian of the Israelitish type of St. James of Jerusalem, or one of the ascetic type of St. Jerome, to whom even the Christian family was a mere scene of worldliness destined for destruction; or again, of the type of Thomas à Kempis, whose only motive might seem to be to save his own soul from misery, was destitute of all perception of the universal love of God. A third factor, and one easy to recognize, is beneficence. This again has varied in its forms. It was in the earliest times directed to the relief of distress within the church itself; later on to the redemption of captives and the alleviation of disease; then to the founding of monasteries as centres of Christian enlightenment; later again to the building of colleges, schools, and hospitals. At one time it has applied itself to the emancipation of slaves, at another to the conversion of the heathen. It has often been narrow and misguided, and has never frankly identified itself, as beneficence in Israel did, with the action of the general community: but it has, nevertheless, been at all times a reflexion of the divine compassion, an extension of the life of Christ. The differences we have traced do not make us lose the sense of unity of purpose. We may say more. The inherent vitality of Christianity is shown in its capacity to survive the ideals in which it has represented itself. The ideal of each age passes. But it leaves something behind. It has presented some element of tenderness or strength to the conscience, some 'substance and evidence' to the faith of mankind. Its body dies, but its soul survives. And therefore we may rightly, as we touch upon the various ages of Christian history, dwell mainly on the positive endeavours or attainments of successive generations, laying little stress upon the failures, which are only too evident, or upon the controversies by which those failures were exposed, but marking what progress was actually made, and what new elements of human life were assimilated by the Church.

We may take the three factors which have just been mentioned, self-sacrificing love, faith in a redeeming God, and beneficence, as the central points of the Christian ideal. This ideal has been partly presented, partly made effective, by the memory of the life of Christ and by His spiritual indwelling: and the destination of the Church is to make this ideal universally operative, so that it may be accepted by the convictions of all, and may work itself out in the life of mankind; to preside over the process by which it is to become the co-ordinating power of all society and of all human occupations, the stimulus of knowledge, of art, of industry, the sanction of all that is lovely as well as of all that is useful. But it must be observed that the Church has in each age been strangely unconscious of this destination. It has imagined that, if it could bring all characters within some special mould, it would have done its work; or it has taken hardly any care for the mass of mankind, and has been contented to save some few out of the general destruction; or it has thought

of the blessed state as belonging entirely to the world
to come; or it has aimed at a dominion of the clergy.
At no age has it distinctly set before itself the task of
bringing mankind universally in all their relations under
the dominion of Christ. Only to a few minds, at rare
intervals, has the idea of a Christian commonwealth, of a
Christian world, presented itself, and then almost always
only to be abandoned. If this feebleness of conception
is disheartening, we may on the other hand derive
encouragement from it: for it shows that the capacities of Christianity, so far from being exhausted, have
in their largest field of exercise yet to be brought
into play.

The famous chapter of Gibbon, in which the causes of
the spread of Christianity in the first three centuries
are described, however suggestive it may be of the historian's own scepticism, and though an invidious turn
is given to each of the causes, may yet be taken as indicating substantially the points of contact at which
the Church's influence was felt, and through which
it won upon the convictions of mankind. It will be
seen, as we touch upon them, that the presentation
of the moral ideal of Christianity is that which gave
them force.

The first cause is the inflexible and even intolerant
zeal of the Christians. It would seem that this is exaggerated. It is true that certain of the Christians,
like Tertullian, protested against the most innocent
customs, if even remotely connected with heathen observances; but this is contrary to the teaching of St.
Paul. It is certain that even in the fourth century,

when Christianity was in the ascendant and had begun to persecute, the intermarriage of Christians and Pagans was not uncommon, and social intercourse went on freely between them[1]. But the earnest conviction which underlay the inflexible zeal of the Christians presented that for which the better mind of the Empire was craving, an assured moral resting-place. And the protest against idolatry, though it sometimes passed into intolerance, was in the main a salutary reproof, carrying on the process begun among the Greeks by Socrates and Plato, against the unworthy conceptions of God, an appeal to the better sense of mankind.

The second cause stated by Gibbon is the doctrine of immortality, and of a quickly approaching judgment in which the Pagans should be destroyed. No doubt various extravagant notions mixed themselves with the simple belief of judgment and immortality. But the foundation of these beliefs was profoundly moral. The belief in the permanence beyond the grave of the life of righteousness begun here is the counterpart and support of the belief in the eternal and absolute character of righteousness. That the vices of the non-Christian world must bring about its destruction was a moral conviction expressed in the burning words of St. Paul, and which was vindicated by the event, first at Jerusalem then at Rome[2].

The third cause assigned by Gibbon is the miraculous

[1] See, for instance, Jerome's account of the heathen priest Albinus, whose daughter Læta was married to the son of Jerome's friend Paula, and whose granddaughter, the younger Paula, is described as lisping Halleluia on the knees of the heathen grandfather (Jerome, *ad Lætam*, Ep. 107, ed. Vall.).

[2] See 1 Thess. ii. 15, 16. 2 Thess. i. 5-9; ii. 8.

power attributed to the Church. This we can scarcely estimate. It is certain that it is acknowledged by Christian teachers to have ceased at an early period. But, whatever the influence of this belief may have been, it was the witness of a larger belief, that of a Divine power inherent in the Church. This belief has been fully vindicated. The Son of Man was seen in the progress of the Church, according to His own words, 'Coming in the clouds of heaven with power and great glory.'

The fourth of the causes specified by Gibbon is the virtuous lives of the Christians. This is the central fact from which all the rest gained their validity. It is important to note the special features of this virtue, which flowed direct from a belief in the supremacy of Christ. It was the virtue not of a sect or a nation, but partaking of the character of universality. This distinguished it from the current virtue of both Jew and Gentile. It was also not a customary nor enforced virtue, but original, and a matter of conviction; and this conviction was an enthusiasm for goodness, existing not, as heretofore, in a small class of cultivated men, but among the simple, the female sex, the slaves. Moreover this virtue was tested in the most signal manner by persecution. In that great trial the true quality of virtue, real manliness, was evoked; it was seen that the meekness which distinguished this period of the Church was compatible with the most heroic energy and endurance.

The last cause enumerated by Gibbon is the attention which was paid to the government of the Church. This is a point which must receive special attention from those who believe in the universal capacities of the Christian Church. The Church was the Christians' fatherland. To it they gave themselves up entirely. Into it they poured their offerings. And the fund thus created was administered by the officers of the Church, who were elected by the members with a special regard to their probity. A community which had such attractions was eagerly sought after. In the misery which pressed on the whole Roman world it was a harbour of refuge for the helpless. A rigorous test was therefore necessary for the admission of members, a rigorous discipline also for those within its pale [1]. But to its sincere members it was a city of the saints, a new Jerusalem, a kingdom of God, the laws of which were on a level with the convictions of the citizens. And whereas the subjects of the Roman empire had been accustomed to submit 'for wrath's sake' to the iron rule of the imperial officers, confessing, perhaps, its necessity and even its justice, bowing down before its dread majesty, the Christians could feel that the laws of their community were the laws of God and of Christ; they regarded their bishops and presbyters as ministers of God doing them good in body and in soul, and could follow them with reverent and enthusiastic loyalty.

In this last cause of the influence of Christianity we may see the rise of something more than moral influence. It is impossible that a large society should be held together without some system of rewards and

[1] See Pressensé, La Vie Ecclesiastique aux 2me et 3me Siècles, ch. iii.

punishments. St. Paul had said that[1], though Christians were not to judge those who were without, they were to judge those that were within : and this is precisely what came to pass. So long as men were outside the Church, the Church acted upon them only by means of persuasion. But so soon as men came' within its pale, it acted upon them by means of discipline. Gibbon points out very rightly the fact that the government of the Church acted upon its members by both reward and punishment. Here we find the Church passing out of the condition of a sect or teaching body, to take upon itself some of the functions of the State, with its laws and their appropriate sanctions. It is vain to assert that the Christian communities were governed by merely spiritual motives. The rewards of its members were those of a constant share in the Church's benefactions, and admission to, and promotion in, the hierarchy. The Epistle to Timothy had said, ' Let the elders that rule well be counted worthy of double honour[2].' Promotion and increase of emoluments are here clearly designated. The same epistle had given rules for the support of widows, and these rules served for an example of the general treatment of the poor[3]. It is not necessary to traverse again the ground so adequately occupied by the Bampton Lectures of 1880[4].

---

[1] 1 Cor. v. 12.   [2] 1 Tim. v. 17.   [3] Ib. 3-16.
[4] The Organization of the Early Christian Churches, by the Rev. E. Hatch, D.D. These Lectures show (1) How the organization of these communities grew up naturally according to their needs and circumstances; (2) How the Bishops and Presbyters, originally administrators and disciplinarians, gradually acquired control over the teaching and all other parts of the Church system. The strong animadversions called forth by these Lectures are but one of many proofs of the difficulty which men have in conceiving (1) of the Spirit of God as acting through

It is evident that the early Church was, on its temporal side, a vast brotherhood for mutual beneficence, rapidly absorbing into itself the functions of the State. But in such a State punishments keep pace with rewards. Deprivation of office, exclusion from the benefits of the society, these were no spiritual censures, but loss of the means of existence [1]. And when excision from the brotherhood took place, it was not, as excommunication would be if practised among us now, a somewhat arbitrary exclusion from an ordinance from which, for whatever reason, the larger part of the Christian community refrain, but a process more comparable to what was in Israel the cutting off from the congregation, or in the states of the ancient world the exterminatio, the compulsory loss of all that makes life dear. In later times excommunication was easily defied, and bishops excommunicated each other with impunity. Even of the Pope, Hincmar of Rheims in the ninth century said, 'If he comes to excommunicate he will himself go away excommunicated [2].' But, when the sentence, like that pronounced on Henry the

the general sense of the community, (2) of Government as being essentially a spiritual function.

[1] See Bingham's *Antiquities*, B. xvi, on the Discipline of the Church. He says, indeed, that the discipline consisted only in depriving men of the privileges gained by baptism, and that the Church had only a spiritual sword. But he gives immediately (B. xvi. c. 2) the case of Paul of Samosata, who was deprived of his office and refused to give up the episcopal house at Antioch. The Church not having power to execute its own sentences invoked that of the heathen emperor Aurelius. But the sentence of the Church was deprivation of a livelihood and a house. To call this a merely spiritual censure is a misnomer. Moreover, Bingham himself points out (B. xvi. c. iii. § 11) that, as early as the fifth century, 'congruous stripes' were recognized as a common punishment for ecclesiastical offences.

[2] 'Sic excommunicaturus venerit, excommunicatus abibit.' See Guizot, 'Civilization in Europe,' Lect. vi. p. 183.

M

Fourth of Germany by Hildebrand, was consonant with the convictions, or the animosities, of the larger part of the people, it fell on the offender with a crushing weight as to both his spiritual and his temporal estate. It was not ambition, nor a lack of spirituality of mind which made such bishops as Cyprian great disciplinarians and founders of an ecclesiastical code, but the natural and necessary development of a society. And it is evident that, so soon as such a society should become a sovereign state, or get the power of a sovereign state into its hands, it would be folly and hypocrisy in it to hesitate to use all the powers of a temporal ruler to enforce its legal discipline [1]. Nor would this derogate from its character as a spiritual society, provided that conviction and teaching remained free, and that Christian goodness, not selfish advantages, was the aim of the government.

But such a state of things demands several conditions. It demands first that discipline should be concerned with those moral offences which discipline can properly touch, that it should be as little as possible concerned with theological error: secondly, that there should be a large tolerance in matters of faith, penalties being assigned, in the case of laymen, only to open acts such as blasphemous and insulting conduct, and, in the case of religious teachers, to the most palpable inconsistency with the system under which they serve; thirdly, that the legislative, administrative, and judicial functions

---

[1] It will be pointed out later on what is the truth underlying the assertion that religion has nothing to do with coercive law, and in what sense it may properly be maintained that the law should not interfere with religion. See pp. 258-260 and Note XXIII.

should be definitely recognized as divine functions or ministries. That these conditions must eventually be complied with in every Christian commonwealth, and recognized by the Christian conscience as just, seems to follow from our conviction of the permanence and comprehensiveness of the Church. That they have not commonly been recognized, and that the tendency of those who look on the Church as a limited and separate community has always been to make theological error the chief object of discipline, and still to wish to make it so when it has become impossible, and moreover that the constant tendency of Clerical authority has been to overbear and crush out individuality, must, I fear, be admitted.

The settlement arrived at in the time of Constantine has been by some considered as the beginning of the Church's corruption, by others as presenting the normal relation of the Church and the State. We may look upon it as the first attempt made by a sovereign state to bring human life under the dominion of Christ; a very imperfect attempt, it is true, but one which needs to be repeated again and again, in one form or another, till it succeeds; an attempt which has been repeated in many ages and many ways, notably in the time of Charlemagne, and again in the time of the great Popes of the eleventh and twelfth centuries, and at the Reformation: and which it is the task of the present day to attempt again with fuller knowledge and under new conditions. If what has been said in the last and present Lecture be true, if government or discipline in the Church is an inherent necessity and one of its most important functions, Church life cannot possibly be confined to regions with which law is not concerned. As the Church expands and becomes a great society, it requires a fuller, and at last a complete system of law, which must be accepted and administered as Christian law, and obeyed 'not for wrath but for conscience' sake' as an ordinance of God. The only question, therefore, which we can raise is whether the action taken at any given time to give effect to this growing necessity was wise, far-seeing, and corresponding to the actual needs.

Historians are very apt to accept a kind of fatalism; and, when any mistaken course has been followed, to point out the advantages which have ensued, and thus to leave the impression that what was done was inevitable and, however wrong, still fortunate. It is, no doubt, the province of the historian to show any incidental good which has resulted from a mistaken action. But it is hardly his province to infer that all the possible evil consequences must certainly have followed on the right action. If Hildebrand, it is said, had not destroyed the family life of the clergy, the clergy would have become a caste. Possibly; but also possibly not. And the remedy for a caste might have come much sooner and more easily than that for clerical celibacy. The refusal to sully the family by making the unmarried state the model of excellence might have had, in connexion with the growing chivalry, an elevating effect upon the whole social condition of Europe, the good results of which might have vastly outweighed any possible dangers of a caste. We may excuse those who acted mistakenly, but it is not necessary to glorify their mistakes.

In the case before us, that of the relation of the first Christian emperor to the Church, we cannot but believe that, had his imperial duties been recognized more fully as a Church function, many mistakes and conflicts would have been avoided, and the effect of Christianity on the Empire would have been both sounder and more extensive. Had it been acknowledged that human justice in its highest and Christian sense is the thing chiefly aimed at by the Church, the effect would have been to sanctify the government of the Empire. It would have been possible to take adequate guarantees for the independence of Christian worship and teaching beneath the general protection of the imperial rule: and the power of Christianity to breathe a spirit of justice and of holiness into human relations might have been preserved without the fatal dualism, which has, with few exceptions, frustrated the very design of the Church by separating religion from common life.

The Church, during the persecutions, had acquired the habits of a sect. It is true that something of public life and public spirit had been evoked by the secular side of Church life; but it was not perceived that this was its proper field of expansion; there were causes, to be specified presently, which made it lay greater stress on correctness of doctrine than on the right conduct of life; and when the moment came at which the Church leaders might have advanced to claim the general life of mankind for Christ, they shrunk back. Like the Jews of the first century, they knew not their day of visitation. They cared for the formal guarantees of Christianity, for its correct statement, for the provision made for its worship, above all for their own order; they willingly used the imperial power for these purposes, and it was for these that it was least fitted; but they cared nothing for the righteous government of the state and for the general welfare of mankind. Constantine himself held an ambiguous position [1]. At one time he was the supreme bishop to whom all appealed; at another he refused to take his place in the Council at Nicæa till a sign of permission had been given by the Bishops [2]; he was afterwards believed to have taken the lowest place among the assembled fathers [3]. And this was due to the attitude of the Church leaders, who made the Church appear rather as the organ of a peculiar cult surrounded by unreal mystery, than as the open arena of universal goodness. We may trace, no doubt, a large and beneficial influence of Christianity in the laws of Constantine [4]. But it is partly ceremonial, as in the law for the observance of Sunday, partly clerical, as in the laws for the immunities of the clergy: and, where it touches morals, it often, as in the law imposing the penalty of death for adultery, crudely enforces the Mosaic law upon a society unprepared for it; so that Justinian's legislation three centuries later has in this case to revert to the earlier Roman law.

[1] See Stanley's 'Eastern Church.' Constantine's awe of the clergy, 142. Conflict of character, 231. His part in the Council of Nicæa, 147.

[2] Milman, 'Hist. of Christianity,' ii. 367.

[3] This belief is constantly found in the letters of Hildebrand, who grounds upon it his views of the superiority of the clergy to the lay-power.

[4] Gibbon, chapter xliv. Milman, Lat. Christ. Book iii. ch. 4.

One principal cause of this is to be found in the doctrinal controversies. The mind of the Church having been exercised in its earlier days by the strange Gnostic heresies, which had set before men a false moral ideal, partly ascetic, partly licentious, it had been thought necessary, and perhaps was so, to guard against this evil tendency by exact statements of the Christian tenets. These, indeed, were not reduced to formulas imposed upon the Churches generally. The Gnostic controversies left behind them no creeds and no formal anathemas. But the tendency to doctrinal disputes had been engendered, and, in a large community which had but a limited sphere of public action, it grew apace. The clergy being now a formed and separate class, organized for worship rather than for life, grew speculative and disputatious. And the fact that the imperial government, though doing the work of Christian discipline, was not recognized as a Church function, made a further separation between life and doctrine. Thus the Christian teachers were withdrawn still further from that close intercourse with the life of the general community which might have made them a really redemptive agency.

The ascetic tendency, which also began to operate about this time, confirmed this withdrawal from general influence[1]. When it was taught that the height of Christian excellence was to be found in a solitary life, and in breaking away from all social bonds, it is evident that the influence of the Church on society must be

[1] The subject of asceticism is treated with great fulness of historical illustration by Mr. Lecky, 'European Morals,' ch. iv.

most seriously impaired. It was almost in vain that Ambrose and Chrysostom preached against the vices of the age. The homilies of Chrysostom, no doubt, are full of excellent precepts of morals and of piety. But so long as the real object which lay behind was a life of separation and of celibacy, the effect was necessarily slight: for, men would argue, it is of little importance to form good habits unless we are prepared to put away our wives and live in monasteries or in deserts. And the ascetic ideal was almost universal at the end of the fourth century.

Connected with this was the transference of the view and aim of the Church from this world to the world to come. This, which had been forced upon men in the time of the persecutions, was not given up when the door was open for present influence. Instead of bringing the sanctions of the world beyond the grave to bear upon the establishment of universal justice and love, the other world was made the object of direct and exclusive longing. The present life was dwarfed; and it was taught that eternal happiness was to be gained and misery avoided by constantly dwelling upon eternity in a separate life of prayer and mortification. This will account for the fact that the great fathers of the end of the fourth century had so little effect on society. Their influence was great on the monastic and clerical system, but feeble on the general life. They stimulated no high thought and endeavour, and they had no successors. Even Ambrose[1], whose great influence was used in

---

[1] For Ambrose, see Gibbon, ch. xxvii., and the article Ambrose in 'Dict. of Eccl. Biog.' by Mr. Llewelyn Davies.

some degree for public purposes, forms no exception to this statement. His successful embassies were to avert an immediate danger to the Church, and had no ulterior aim or effect. His excommunication of Theodosius for the Thessalonian massacre, and his disapproval of the penalty of death inflicted on the Priscillianist heretics, were motived to some extent by a superstitious feeling about bloodshed as distinguished from other forms of punishment [1]. He was regardless of family ties in his ascetic preaching [2]: he would not allow Arian worship in Milan: he was the instigator of the persecuting edict of Theodosius against heathenism, and his first rebuke to the Emperor was a condemnation of his noble tolerance in requiring a synagogue which had been destroyed by violence to be rebuilt.

We may here touch upon the absence of any real patriotism and public spirit in the Church leaders. When Alaric sacked Rome, Jerome and his friends at Bethlehem felt the shock; but it was a matter of mere wonder and awe to them. It did not quicken them to any thought as to the future of the empire and of mankind. It is sometimes thought that Augustine's great work 'De Civitate Dei,' which was caused by that awful event, is a kind of prophecy of the Christian state of society which was to arise on the ruins of the Empire. It is nothing of the sort [3]. He defends Christianity against the charge that it had brought on the ruin by averting the protection of the gods of Rome; he shews that the gods had never protected Rome, and that the

[1] Lecky, 'European Morals,' ii. 43.   [2] Ib. 140, 141.
[3] See the analysis of the De Civ. Dei in Note III, and the extracts there given.

only protection from the horrors of the sack had been in the Christian churches. But his theory is that the city of God is a separate state which has been growing up, first in the kingdom of Israel, then in the Christian Church; that it has nothing to do with the general life of mankind : and he looks not for the renewal of society by its influence, but for a vast conflagration which will burn up the existing fabric of the world and make it fit for the eternal habitation of the saints. It is evident that a theory such as this would operate not to strengthen the good principle in the common life of men but to weaken it. It would make Christians not the salt and the light of the world but a race of timid separatists.

These great fathers gave the tone to the Church of the middle ages. The ideas of Augustine are the prelude to the *Dies Iræ* and the *Hora novissima, tempora pessima sunt, Vigilemus*, of Bernard of Morlaix. The figure of Ambrose withstanding Theodosius is the constantly recurring image of the opposition between the clergy and the government, or as they are mistakenly called, the spiritual and temporal powers. This opposition or contrast was the necessary consequence of the refusal of the great opportunity offered to the Church in the era of Constantine. The Church leaders resolved that the Church should remain a separate body. The laws which it had had before the Empire became Christian were not to be merged in the imperial law. The Church was still to have its own system of canon law, its own penalties, its own judges. It was a complete *imperium in imperio*. If, as we have maintained, systems of law are efficacious in upholding a moral and political ideal, we have here the attempt to mould society and character in a special form not in harmony with, but in contrast to, the general life of mankind.

The unreal character of such a system, its opposition to what we must hold to be the divine constitution of society, is apparent throughout the mediæval history. It is true that the Church being composed of both laity and clergy, it might seem as if lay influences must always act as a corrective upon clerical separatism. But, unhappily, the clergy had now become separate in their action and their interests from the laity. During the era of the persecutions it was often necessary to concentrate power in the hands of the Church officers. There were times, if we may trust to the language of the Ignatian Epistles, when each bishop became almost a dictator; and, partly from the necessities of the case, partly from the growth of sacerdotal ideas, it became customary for the bishops to take counsel amongst themselves alone[1]. Cyprian, indeed, declared that he would do nothing without the laity[2]. But that befell him and his colleagues which has so often befallen the clergy and other rulers. Being trusted, and being able to act better on behalf of the community than they could for themselves, the bishops were constantly tempted to

---

[1] Cyprian's view of his position is thus described by Archbishop Benson ('Dict. of Eccl. Biog.' art. Cyp. p. 741). 'Each Bishop is elected by his own Plebes. Hence he is the embodiment of it.' 'The Bishop is in the Church, and the Church is in the Bishop.' 'They have no other representative in councils, he is naturally their "member."'

[2] Cyprian, Ep. v. 4 (Ed. Baluze). Solus rescribere nihil potui, quando a primordio episcopatus mei statuerim nihil sine consilio vestro et sine consensu plebis meâ privatim sententiâ gerere. See also Ep. xvii.

act alone; no habit was formed in the laity of taking part in Church affairs, which, indeed, became too technical for them; and, when the day of liberty came, it seemed quite natural that this should continue. No one thought of proposing that the laity should be admitted at the Council of Nicæa. Thus the hierarchical and sacerdotal principle, with all its evils, grew apace, and the bishops were cut off from the salutary check of lay advice and control.

This system of separation gained a vast increase of strength from the rise of the Papacy. When the Roman Empire of the West passed away, the hierarchy was left standing. When the whole social system was broken up by the invasion of the barbarians, the clergy alone remained to pilot the ark of Christian civilization across the flood. When social organization began to form again, a central power was needed to which men might appeal. Even when the Papacy was despised at Rome itself, it was held in honour abroad; and when great men held the reins, their power became almost unbounded. Originally the mouthpiece of the decrees of the Church, the Pope gradually gained an independent power; and his decrees, like those of the emperors before him, became laws. Innocent III. is said to have promulgated no less than 4000 such decrees. And, lest decrees issued to suit emergencies should not carry due weight, the Popes sanctioned, if they did not create, in the later part of the ninth century, the stupendous forgery of the False Decretals. These documents which imposed on all Christendom for the six centuries and a-half before the Reformation, are the most remarkable instance of a successful fraud that the world has ever seen[1]. They are partly documents transparently spurious, such as a letter from Clement of Rome to St. James of Jerusalem, partly genuine letters of the early popes, with insertions from Scripture and from some forty other sources designed to promote the purposes of the compiler. These purposes appear to have been—1st, to add to the power of the bishops as against the metropolitans; 2nd, to do away with the chorepiscopi in the interest of diocesans; 3rdly, to strengthen the whole clerical system as against the imperial and national governments. For all these purposes the unknown author exalts beyond measure the power of the Papacy. These Decretals formed henceforward the solid nucleus of the system of papal decrees, which were gathered by Gratian in the twelfth century, and by Gregory the Ninth and others at various times up to the year 1484. When we read such lives as those of Hildebrand or of Becket, we see how vast a power these documents possessed. On the Dotation of Constantine[2] and similar documents, which are incorporated with the Decretals, Hildebrand grounded his attempt at universal empire. We read of Becket, when in his banishment at Pontigny[3], that, though often fasting and reading the Psalter and Epistles, his chief study was that of the Canon Law and Decretals, by which he justified his vast sacerdotal

---

[1] See the Preface to Hinschius' edition of the Decretals. Leipzig, 1863.

[2] Hildebrand often alludes to the Dotation. See especially his letter to the Archbishop of Metz showing that he has power to excommunicate the Emperor (Monumenta Gregoriana, March 15, 1081).

[3] Robertson's Biography of Becket, pp. 167, 168.

pretensions, and nerved himself for his disastrous struggle with the king.

We touch here upon the great question of what are called the two powers, a question which produced the unceasing strife between the Pope and the Emperor in the centre of the Middle Ages, and between the clergy as a corporate body or class and the general government, in many countries, especially in our own; a question which has gained fresh importance in our day, not only from the revival of clericalism in England, and of Ultramontanism abroad, but also from the claims of Free Churches among Protestants, and from the attempt of M. Comte in his Positive Philosophy to vindicate the separation of the two powers as a fundamental principle of sociology. It will be seen that the tendency of the present Lectures is hostile to such a separation, and favourable to unity in the moral ideal, in actual life, in law, and in government. If that which was said in the last Lecture is true as to the meaning of the words of Christ, 'My kingdom is not of this world,' no such separation of powers was contemplated at the beginning; and, indeed, the original theory of the Mediæval Church was that not so much of the separation of the temporal and spiritual powers, as of their harmony and co-operation. Let us look at this question in its various aspects.

First, we may draw a distinction between the moral ideal which we cherish within, and the practical attainment which we can reach either individually or in society. It is evident that the outward is but a faint copy of the inward. To subject the inward to the outward, to bind down the ideal to that which is practically attainable, would evidently be a disastrous course. Any external power, then, which hinders the free working of conviction, or sets a limit to the expression of opinion, except so far as it would be injurious to others, is doing wrong. There is a region of the soul which must remain inviolate from the incursions of any external power. But it would be equally wrong to keep the moral ideal out of all contact with the external life. The two must evidently act in harmony. And this applies to all our convictions, political, social, scientific, as well as religious. But this region of conviction must be kept inviolate as much from the decrees of the Pope and the clergy as from those of the king or parliament. History shews us that it is the clerical power, by its councils, decrees, inquisitions, excommunications, rather than the lay power, which has interfered with conscience and its free expression. This, therefore, which is an exceedingly important matter, cannot come to the aid of the principle of the separation of the powers.

Secondly, it is of great importance that religious teachers should not be interfered with unduly in the expression of their convictions, so that they may impress the truth upon their hearers. But here again we may see that bishops, church assemblies, and, in our day, pew-renting congregations, have, more constantly than parliaments or judicatures, set themselves to bias the Christian minister. There are many other spheres of human life, especially the family, but also trade, the arts, the universities, which ought to be left as free as possible, though their general status must be ruled by external laws. The chief concern of law in all such matters is to mark out and protect a sphere in which their energy may have free scope. If the general government has interfered too far with any of these (but it is necessary to recall again the fact that it is the clerical body which has been most inclined to interfere), it has stepped beyond its province. But no one would think that, in order to obviate the danger of such interference, a separate jurisdiction must be set up for each of these spheres of life. If so, we should have not two but many separate powers.

Thirdly, we may introduce the supposed contrast between the Church and the State. But this was not really in question in the Middle Ages. It was then, as indeed it has mostly been since, a question between the clergy and their adherents on the one side, and the general body of churchmen on the other. In modern times, indeed, there is a difficulty in assuming that the Church and the nation are coterminous, though the difficulty is not insuperable, and it may be justly maintained that they are so interwoven that more injustice would be caused by treating them as separate than as one. But the mediæval theory of the Church and the Empire was based upon the supposition that the Emperor and all his subjects were Christians and members of the Church.

This theory may be stated thus[1]. Christendom forms one great whole, in which there are two chief

---

[1] In the statement of this theory, and generally in what is said as to the mediæval system, I have made much use of Professor Bryce's 'Holy Roman Empire.' See especially ch. vii.

functionaries, the Pope and the Emperor, each in a different way its head. Each power is instituted by God. The one is to rule over men's bodily, the other over their spiritual interests. Both spring from the old Roman Empire, which, having become Christian, was at once Empire and Church. In one sense the Church enfolds the Empire; in another, the Empire enfolds the Church. The two powers must support each other, and are mutually necessary. The Emperor sanctions the Pope's election, the Pope crowns the Emperor. The Emperor protects the Pope, and the clergy, and the spiritual courts; and these in return support the authority of the Emperor over his subjects. This theory, though it did not wholly correspond to the facts, had much in it, considered as an ideal, which was sound. Even before the conversion of the Empire, it had occurred to Church writers like Tertullian [1] that the Empire had a divine function, that of maintaining peace within its borders, of just rule, of saving society from anarchy. Later, we find Optatus, Bishop of Milevis, in Africa, speaking of the Christianized Empire still more distinctly in these terms. We catch an echo of the same idea in Aquinas [2], who, in his book De Regimine Principum, declares that the Emperor Augustus was

[1] Tertull. Apol. cap. xxxii, Necessitas nobis orandi pro Imperatore quod vim maximam universo orbi imminentem (ab eo) scimus retardari. Ad Scapulum cap. 2. Colimus Imperatorem ut hominem a Deo secundum, et quidquid est a Deo consecutum, solo Deo minorem. Optatus De schismate Donatistarum, lib. iii. c. 3, in Migne's Patrologia, xi. col. 999. His argument is against Donatus, who repudiated the Imperial authority, saying, 'Quid est Imperatori cum ecclesiâ?' 'Non Respublica,' says Optatus, 'est in Ecclesiâ, sed ecclesia in Republicâ est, id est in Imperio Romano . . . Super imperatorem non est nisi Deus.'
[2] De Reg. Princ. l. iii. c. 10., Aquinas' Works (Venice, 1787), Vol. xix.

God's vicegerent in ruling the world when Christ was born into it.

The sacredness of secular justice and its ministers is fully admitted in this theory. Dante, in his De Monarchiâ[1], calls upon the Emperor, Henry of Luxemburg, as the successor of the Roman Emperors, and as God's vicegerent, to regulate the discordant communities of Italy. The Popes, indeed, from Hildebrand onwards, are apt to ignore the sacredness of kingly justice[2]. Hildebrand even speaks of it as having its source in the robbery of those who originally set themselves up as kings, in contrast to the Papal power which was instituted by Christ Himself. It would seem that the title of the Holy Roman Empire[3] was originally taken by Frederick Barbarossa as a protest that his rule was as sacred a thing as that of the Pope with whom he was then in controversy. And other sovereigns upheld their rights under the same high sanction[4]. This sacredness of the Emperor as the source of law was strongly asserted by the agents of Frederick II. at the Council of Lyons in 1245[5], in opposition to the claim of Innocent IV.

[1] See the sketch of the argument of the De Monarchiâ in Bryce's 'Holy Roman Empire,' pp. 265-7.

[2] See Hildebrand's letter to Hermann of Metz of Mar. 15, 1081, in the Monumenta Gregoriana, in which he proves that the Pope can excommunicate Kings, § 4, Jaffé's Ed. pp. 456-7.

[3] The origin of the title is discussed in Bryce's 'Holy Roman Empire,' pp. 199-203.

[4] See Henry II's expression to the Bishop of Chichester in the case of the Abbey of Battle, 'Tu pro Papæ auctoritate ab hominibus concessâ contra dignitatum regalium auctoritates mihi a Deo concessas calliditate argutâ niti praecogitas.' Wilkins' Concilia Mag. Brit. i. 431.

[5] See the account of this Council in Milman's 'Latin Christianity,' vol. vi. 239-244, and Frederick's letter to the Princes of Christendom, p. 245. See also

to judge him. His proctor, Thaddeus of Suessa, withstood the whole episcopal assembly in the name of a superior justice. But, in the beginning, the Popes had amply recognized the sacredness of the Imperial rule. When Leo III. crowned Charles the Great at Rome on Christmas Day 800, the coronation was an admission to a sacred Church function[1]. The Emperor was ordained a deacon, and received the cup of the Communion with the priests, and was arrayed in the stole and dalmatic. Thus consecrated he exercised his power as a minister of God; and so he deemed himself throughout his reign. Even before his coronation he presided at the Council of Frankfort[2], though the legates of Hadrian I. were present. The decrees of the council, the canons which relate to such things as the proscription of the worship of images, as well as the statutes on affairs of state, are sent forth in Charles's name. In his Capitularies[3] Charles demands that all officers of his empire shall swear allegiance to him, as binding themselves to live 'in the holy service of God, to do no violence to the clergy, and to widows and orphans and strangers, seeing that the Lord Emperor has been appointed, after the Lord and His saints, to be a defender of all such.' Crimes are denounced, as in the Mosaic law, as sins. 'The whole cycle of social and moral duties,' says Bryce[4], 'is deduced from the obligation of obedience to the visible, autociatic head of the

the account of the vindication of the rights of Louis of Bavaria against the Pope by William of Ockham. Milman, viii. 104; ix. 147. Also the argument of Marsiglio's Defensor Pacis in Creighton's History of the Papacy, vol. i. 37.
[1] See Bryce's 'Holy Roman Empire,' pp. 106, 112.
[2] Ibid. 64.   [3] Ibid. 65–6.   [4] Ibid. 66.

Christian state.' It was in the name of God that he undertook his thirty-five expeditions of conquest, reducing under the dominion of Christian civilization the tribes in the North and East of Europe[1]; and, wherever he conquered, he planted monasteries as fortresses and centres of Christian enlightenment. The theory of the Mediæval Church and the Christian Empire was well illustrated by its founder as regards the functions of the Emperor. Nor did the impulse given by the founder die with him. It bore fruit in many ways, even when the Empire itself had become a shadow, in the sense of unity which it imparted to Christendom, in the heroism of the early crusades, in the chivalrous feelings and enterprise which were the redeeming features of feudalism, in the repression of private war, above all, in the recognition of the sacred Christian character properly belonging to government, as it was realised in men like Alfred in England, or St. Louis in France.

Nor can it be said that the other part of the theory, that which regards the clergy, was unreasonable or impracticable, if its conditions were observed. There is no reason why the clergy should not have one supreme head, their guide and leader, speaking in their name, declaring what they as a body of teachers and learned men think right, and urging it by the appropriate means of persuasion. With adequate safeguards the institution of the Papacy might have been a true spiritual power without the evils which attended its actual working. But for this purpose it must give up

[1] Bryce's 'Holy Roman Empire,' p. 69.

its claim to a separate jurisdiction; it must subject itself to the condition which Charles desired for the clergy generally[1], and look upon all its possessions merely as endowments, not as conferring external power; and it must, in its organization and outward action, be subject to the law of the State or Empire in which it is placed.

But this was not the meaning of the theory as apprehended by the Pope and the clergy. The germ of a different system was introduced when Pippin gave the Roman States to the Pope. Though his position was long ambiguous, yet he was, even in Charles's day, a territorial sovereign. As soon as the influence of Charles himself is withdrawn, the Papacy declares itself a great world-power. The fiction of the Dotation of Constantine which was incorporated into the Decretals[2], gives the Roman States to the Pope, not as a mere endowment subject to the law of the empire, but as a kingdom. Constantine is made to say that he goes to live at Constantinople because it is not fitting that the earthly emperor should have power in the principality of the priests, and because the head of the Christian religion is established by a heavenly emperor. He gives the Pope his imperial palace of the Lateran, makes him wear the crown which he had worn himself, and the diadem and frigium[3]; and recites how the Emperor has held the rein of the Pope's horse, and fulfilled the office of a groom for him.

[1] Bryce, pp. 66-7.
[2] Isidorian Decretals (Ed. Hinschius), p. 249. The passage alluded to is at p. 253.
[3] Mitra Constantini Imperatoris candidi splendoris, ornamentum capitis phrygio colore prætextum. Du Cange.

This was not a spiritual power, but an earthly power upholding itself by spiritual sanctions. Moreover, as in Constantine's Dotation the clergy are made to ride in company with the Pope, so throughout Christendom they are to partake of his inviolability, to be subject to no law but his. Thus the bishops, though feudal lords, owned a divided allegiance: and the clergy claimed an immunity, even in criminal matters, from the law of the realm[1]. The Ecclesiastical Courts were held throughout Europe in the name of the Pope and the Bishops, and claimed authority, 1st, over all clerical suits ; 2nd, over all suits in which clergy were concerned ; 3rd, over all questions of marriage, legitimacy, succession to property, and tithes ; 4th, over all who had made religious vows, and over widows, orphans, and minors; 5th, over all matters having a religious side, as adultery, fraud, or perjury; and 6th, over all questions which the suitors agreed to submit to them. The revived study of Roman Law in the twelfth century was indeed at first welcomed by the clergy ; but it was soon found too imperial, too little clerical, and it was discarded except where it might serve to fill up lacunae in the canon law. It was further held also that all temporal jurisprudence was bound to frame its decrees with due deference to the superior authority of the ecclesiastical. Thus a vast jurisdiction arose, the rival, often the master, of the imperial and national jurisdictions. We have before us no longer a spiritual and a temporal

---

[1] The facts relating to the clerical jurisdiction are well summed up in the Article Canon Law in the Encyclopædia Metropolitana. See also Milman's 'Latin Christianity,' vi. 165.

power, but two rival temporal powers, each aspiring, though on different grounds, to universal dominion. Innocent IV. in his controversy with Frederick II. says: Christ has given to the Pope not only the pontifical, but the regal power, having committed to St. Peter and his successors the reins both of the earthly and the heavenly empire, as is sufficiently shewn by the plurality of the Keys[1].' Boniface VIII. at the Jubilee of 1300 appeared in imperial robes, seated on a throne, crowned with the diadem; and, laying his hand on the half-drawn sword, said to the pilgrims, 'Ego, Ego sum Imperator[2].'

Then arose the question which of these two great temporal powers was supreme; and here superstition, aided by the False Decretals, gave the victory almost always to the Pope. In Hildebrand's statement[3] entitled 'Quid valeant Pontifices Romani,' he asserts that the Pope has power to excommunicate, to form new dioceses; that he alone may use the imperial insignia; that his feet alone are kissed by all the kings of the earth; that his name is alone recited in the churches, and is the supreme (unicum) name in the world. He may depose emperors, he may supersede bishops. He alone may preside at a Council. No book of Canons may be made without him. He may be judged by none. All great causes in all churches must be referred to him. Finally, the Pope has never erred and is sinless[4]. Hildebrand claimed of great kings like

[1] Quoted by Milman (Lat. Chris. vi. 240). [2] Bryce, Holy Rom. Emp. p. 109.
[3] A Memorandum (Dictatus Papæ) of the year 1075, given in the Monumenta Gregoriana, p. 174.
[4] Gregory quotes, for the sinlessness of the Pope, the words of Ennodius at a

William the Conqueror[1] that they should obey him. He was feudal lord of Naples. He claimed to be owner of all parts of Spain which should be recovered from the Mahometans[2]. The words, 'Regnante Jesu Christo,' with which his decrees begin, imply the assertion that, through his Vicar the Pope, Christ is actually ruling the world. In his letter to Hermann of Metz[3] in vindication of his power to excommunicate the German king, he says that it cannot be doubted that priests are the fathers, and consequently the masters, of kings and princes; and he so far depreciates kingly rule as to declare that it is invented by secular persons who ignore God, and has its origin from plunderers. To such claims as these it was in vain for the Emperors to oppose force or right. Their power could rarely reach the Pope; but the subtle power of an excommunication or an interdict could dislocate all the relations of families and of kingdoms. The history of the struggle of the Papacy and the Empire is one of almost constant success for the clerical power.

It is by no means to be denied that the Papal and clerical power was the instrument of vast benefits to mankind. Indeed, it may be observed that, wherever clerical claims have been strongly asserted, as in the time of Hildebrand and of Innocent III, or in the time

Synod at Rome held by Pope Symmachus. These words are given in the Decretals (Hinschius, p. 666). See also a quotation to the same effect made by Gregory in his letter of Mar. 15, 1081 (in Monumenta Gregoriana), in which he shews that he has power to excommunicate the Emperor.

[1] Gregory to William, Ap. 4,.1074 (Mon. Greg.).
[2] Letter in Mon. Greg. dated Ap. 30, 1073.
[3] Mon. Greg., Mar. 15, 1081.

of Laud in England, or even in the present day when they have been partially revived, they have produced in the first instance a sense of dignity in the clergy, which has been a real moral power. When Hildebrand at Canossa took the Sacramental cup and said that, if he were guilty of the crimes laid to his charge, he prayed that God might strike him dead, he was perfectly sincere[1]. He knew that the King, whom he challenged to make a similar declaration, could not do so without falsehood. He felt himself morally his superior. And no doubt he believed that the clergy, if purged from marriage and simony, were also the moral superiors of the temporal authorities, and were capable of ruling mankind for their good. Nor was his belief wholly false, though it was exaggerated. The mediæval system, dominated as it was by the clergy, accomplished a great and beneficial change in the social life of men[2]. It abolished slavery, emancipation being made a distinctly religious act. Through the chivalrous virtues which it fostered it made the position of women not merely satisfactory but honourable. It did much to curb blood-revenge and to abolish private war. Moreover, the Church law was often superior to other codes. Guizot has remarked[3] that the laws of the Visigoths in Spain, which issued direct from Ecclesiastical Councils, had a special pre-eminence in all criminal matters, and, in respect of punishments, anticipated many of the

[1] See the account of the events at Canossa written by Gregory himself to the Princes of Germany. Mon. Greg., Jan. 28, 1077.
[2] An interesting résumé of 'Humane Progress under Christianity,' chiefly in the Middle Ages, is given in Mr. Loring Brace's *Gesta Christi*.
[3] Guizot, 'Civilization in Europe,' Lect. vi. p. 167.

ideas which through Bentham and other jurists have entered late into modern legislation. The Church Courts were at certain epochs much purer than those of the State, and legitimately attracted jurisdiction to themselves. Further, the opposition of the clergy to the temporal rulers was often the opposition of reason to brute force; it was a salutary check even where it was no more than rivalry. Lastly, the world can never forget the great missionary zeal displayed by men like Boniface or St. Gall, or Adalbert or Raymond Lull, by which the borders of Christendom were in the most legitimate manner extended[1]. The mediæval attempt to bring the world under the dominion of Christ, with all its faults, was a grand effort of the Christian spirit.

What, then, were the causes of its failure? For that it failed is only too evident. First, the fatal dualism which it introduced into life. Human nature is not two, but one. However purely spiritual may be the conception of Christian goodness, it must work itself out into the whole life, and harmonize not divide it. As a consequence of the unnatural division, the so-called spiritual power became worldly, and the cause of perpetual strife[2]. The line of cleavage is to be traced

---

[1] See the account given of these and other mediæval missionaries in Neander's 'Memorials of Christian Life,' part iv.

[2] 'By a law to which it would be hard to find exceptions, in proportion as the State became more Christian, the Church, which to work out her purposes had assumed worldly forms, became by the contact worldlier, meaner, spiritually weaker.' Bryce, 'Holy Rom. Emp.,' 107-8. Mr. Bryce seems here to attribute the increasing worldliness of the Church (that is the clergy) to union with an increasingly Christian State. This seems a paradox. The true cause is that the clerical system has used the support of the State for the maintenance of a separate

everywhere, in politics, in law, in common life, in international relations. Italy, the seat of the Papal power, was, for the sake of that power, kept divided down to our own day[1]. Tyndale the Reformer[2] points out that the interests of the Papal and clerical power had been the pretext of almost all the wars of his day. Our own generation has witnessed one great war at least springing from the same source. The Papal power has constantly been an element of discord, rarely, if ever, an arbiter of peace.

But, secondly, the theory on which the mediæval system proceeded involved the supremacy of the clergy as a peculiar and privileged class. They were to be kept separate by means of celibacy from their fellow-Christians, maintaining a superhuman standard of self-denial, so that they might exercise, as from without, a discipline of righteousness upon society. But what was the result? At first, as I have pointed out, the system imparted to them a sense of dignity; but afterwards it made them pharisaical, then tyrannical, then corrupt and incapable of bearing the wealth which had been lavished upon them. At the close of the Middle Ages the clergy, the monasteries, and the Ecclesiastical Courts were thoroughly debased. The Papal chair was gained by bribery, and was occupied by

---

position in which (the true interests of human life being now administered by the State) it has been more and more absorbed in the pursuit of the interests of a class.

[1] See this drawn out in Milman's 'Lat. Christ.' B. iii., c. 4, last two pages. 'Whatever it may have been to Christendom, the Papacy has been the eternal, implacable foe of Italian independence and Italian unity.'

[2] 'Obedience of a Christian man,' in Tyndale's Doct. Treatises (Parker Soc. Ed.), pp. 186-7.

Roderick Borgia. We have here the nemesis of the unnatural exaltation of the clergy, their separation, their supremacy.

We must add to this the perversion of the Christian ideal, which the supremacy of clericalism infallibly brings. Church work, church life, church ideas, became something quite different from Christian goodness. Lovers of Gothic architecture cannot fail to notice how many of the great towers of churches, cathedrals, abbeys, were built in the fifteenth century, and even early in the sixteenth. The great judgment of the Reformation fell upon some of them, as at Bolton Abbey, before they were completed. The clerical supremacy had directed men's minds to an extent quite unnatural to the building and adornment of churches. The reproach of William Tyndale [1] the Reformer was well-deserved, that the Papal clergy had so 'crope into men's minds' as to make them think of nothing but the building of great steeples like that of Tenterden, while the adjoining harbours were neglected ; and that the functions of commerce and patriotic energy were in abeyance because of the exclusive absorption in a fictitious religion, in 'Pope-holy works.' This indeed is the worst effect of clericalism, that it draws away the consciousness of dignity and of holiness from common life. We have seen how deficient the great Church-leaders of the fourth and fifth centuries were in patriotism and in the

---

[1] Tyndale's answer to More, pp. 77-8. In this passage Tyndale cleverly turns into a solid argument More's well-known jest about the building of Tenterden steeple having caused the rising of Goodwin sands and the silting up of Sandwich harbour.

attempt to found a true City of God. In the Mediæval Church the great effort of the clerical leaders, almost the whole effort from Hildebrand onwards, is to induce men not to consecrate their lives to God, but to be obedient to the Pope and the clergy. This was the ruin of the ideal of the earlier time, the time of Charlemagne, in which the whole life of man, the monarch and the laws were holy. Men were now taught to despise their common life, which is the ordinance of God. Christianity ceased to be the inspirer of hope; there was no sense of progress, no longing for the establishment of the Kingdom of God.

But I have noticed that, not only does Christianity survive its own limited ideals and create fresh ones, but that the outworn ideals are not wasted—their souls survive. The ideal of the early part of the Middle Ages gave to the world the notion of the unity of Christendom, the belief in a great organized Christian Society which is above all nationalities, of a Holy Empire, the rulers of which rule in the name of God. The two parts of this vast unity, though in practice they were constantly opposed, in the theory were mutually helpful, the two pillars on which the fabric rested. The realization of this ideal failed then, and no attempt has since been made to renew it, except by the feeble efforts of diplomacy. Since the Holy Roman Empire ceased to be a reality, a struggle for life has gone on among the states which have portioned out its inheritance. War has been constant; and, where it has ceased, the suspicions and preparations for war have been a burden which has now become almost unbearable. If ever this state of things is to pass away, it must be by some means like that which floated before the vision of the nobler spirits of the Imperial and Mediæval Church, a vast Imperial or federal community, with Christ as its unseen head, in which the spiritual aspirations of men will blend with their practical efforts for the establishment of true and Christian relations.

Lastly, we may notice how, though the Middle Ages were unconscious of progress, progress was going on. During the ten centuries from Romulus Augustulus to Charles V, Europe was changed from Barbaria into Christendom. The changes from Barbarism to Imperialism, to Feudalism, to Nationalism, constitute a genuine and salutary progress. Though the Empire succumbed to the Papal Power, the rising nations contained the germs of spiritual independence. However repressive of individual liberty the Church-system may have been, we must put to its credit such genuine revivals of religion as that which produced the Preaching Orders. The disputes of Scholasticism, however barren they may appear to us, raised questions to which the Reformation was to give the answer, and trained the mind of the Church to deal with the new learning when it arose. The spirit of freedom and enterprise was growing. Printing was invented. The introduction of Greek literature awoke the critical faculty. The discovery of America gave a vast impulse to commerce and a new range to thought. Wycliff and Huss, though they were scorned by the ruling clerical powers, had not lived in vain. Men like Colet and More, the disciples of the new learning, con-

ceived an ideal more in accordance with that of the
New Testament, and, from beyond the waning glamour
of the Mediæval Church, the more solid form of the
Christianity of the Reformation was coming to view.
It may indeed have seemed, when the Catholic system
of the Middle Ages fell, that the last effort of the
Christian Church had failed ; and the fifteenth century
seemed to bear out the complaint. The Church was
confessed at the Councils of Constance and Bâle to need
reform in the head and in the members, but the reform
seemed to be impossible ; and in the atmosphere of the
Renaissance it could be believed that religion had died,
and that learning and art, without morality, must
henceforth suffice for mankind. We now know that
that epoch was the prelude to the greatest outburst of
the Christian spirit, except that of the first century,
which the world has ever seen. The spiritual needs of
men cannot be suppressed, and the resources of God are
infinite. Age after age the Christian spirit renews the
attempt to bring mankind under the dominion of its
true King. It casts aside the systems of the past only
to weave a more fitting vesture for the new generation.
'They shall perish, but thou shalt endure. As a vesture
shalt thou change them, and they shall be changed,
But thou art the same, and thy years shall have no
end.'

LECTURE V.

THE CHURCHES OF THE REFORMATION.

REVELATION i. 19, 20. Write the things which thou hast seen, and the things which are, and the things which shall be hereafter; the mystery of the seven stars which thou sawest in my right hand, and the seven golden candlesticks. The seven stars are the angels of the seven churches; and the seven candlesticks which thou sawest are the seven churches.

THE attempt to reduce the whole world under the dominion of Christ must be made in each successive age according to its special powers and opportunities. The efforts of the past must be studied in order to throw light upon the future. We write the things which we have seen in history, that we may better write of the things which are and the things which shall be hereafter. If we find in the past grounds for warning, we find none for despair. Where the attempt to make the world Christian has failed, the failure has never been absolute; and the vision which men have sought to realize has been made more vivid to mankind by the attempt. The Imperial Church under Constantine and Theodosius failed partly because the world was not ripe for the great change: though the conviction of mankind had been won, the heathenism of its life presented too strong a resistance. It failed also in part because the attempt which it made was only partial. It did not face the complete problem. The Mediæval church under Charles and the great Popes seemed much nearer to success. Nominally indeed it succeeded; and for some six or seven centuries it held Christendom together. But it failed and fell; partly because of the fatal dualism, the contrast between the spiritual and the temporal, which, except in its highest ideal, it presented; partly because, in fact, it became a system not of a Christian Church and a Christian Empire, but of two rival worldly powers, each aiming at a dominion which could not belong to both; partly also because the triumph which the Papacy gained over the Empire was the triumph of the clerical order, who were quite unfit to rule, and who did not even understand the meaning of the Kingdom of God. The Mediæval system, long hollowed out and become destitute of spiritual force, was blown to pieces by the Reformation.

Yet the Imperial and Mediæval Church left behind it the idea of unity, and of an organized social system of which Christianity should be the inspiring power; and towards the realization of this idea the churches of the Reformation were bound to work. Only they must recommence the process from another side. The Imperial and Mediæval Church had insisted too exclusively on the principle of unity. It had made little account of the nation; it had trampled upon the individual. But the New Testament had represented the Spirit as working first in the individual, afterwards in the community.

And it had spoken not only of the Church, but of the Churches. The mystery of the Apocalypse is not that of a single spirit, but of seven ; not of one candlestick, but of its seven branches. The unity of Christendom must be one in which all its component parts have their full rights and their free development. The great tyrannical Empire-Church was shattered. The work of reconstruction must begin anew with the separate national churches. This was the task of the Reformation.

It is one of the greatest of historical errors to represent the Reformation as primarily a negative movement[1]. All great movements of reform have in them a negative element, and it is the first which strikes the eye. But no movement can live on negation. The Ten Commandments are negative, since almost all of them say, Thou shalt not ; but at their root lie the central affirmations of all religion and morality. Our Lord's teaching was negative in its denunciations of the Pharisaic system, but its strongest negations gained their force from the

---

[1] M. Guizot (*Civilisation in Europe*, Lect. xii.) seems to limit the effects of the Reformation to the enfranchisement of thought. It had no effect politically, he says, but 'it abolished and disarmed the spiritual power, the systematic and formidable government of thought.'

M. Comte's dislike of Protestantism is well known. He habitually speaks of its 'purely negative doctrine,' 'the anarchical character of its principles,' &c. See especially *Positive Catechism* (Congreve's translation), p. 415.

This view of the Reformation finds its extreme expression in the lately published work of Ed. v. Hartmann, *The Self-Destruction of Christianity and the Religion of the Future*. 'Its task,' he says (p. 12), 'in relation to the dogmatic of Christianity is one of absolute negation, destruction, and tearing down.' 'Catholicism sought to preserve the corpse with the appearance of life; the historical task assigned to Protestantism was to dissect the corpse limb by limb, and to obtain the public recognition of the fact that it was actually dead.' He says in his Preface, ' I recognize Ultramontanism as the true representative of historical Christianity, and its championship against modern culture as the last effort made by historical Christianity for its own preservation.'

underlying demand for a worship in spirit and in truth. The sun in the spring-time is negative, in that it breaks up the frost barriers by which the world has been held fast; but the heat which destroys is life-giving. And so the Reformation pulled down only because of its eager resolve to rebuild a sounder fabric. In whatever aspect you look at it, it was primarily constructive, only secondarily and by necessity destructive.

The Reformation was the uprising of positive religious conviction. The assertion of the doctrine of justification by faith was the demand that each man should himself look up directly to the Eternal, realizing his personal responsibility and claiming without intervention the divine forgiveness and grace. Incidentally it was negative; for, if this conviction was personal and immediate, it could not be a matter of ceremony and of system; and therefore the whole fabric of mediæval superstitions fell before it.

The Reformation, again, was the beginning of a great era of popular enlightenment. The Renaissance was intellectual and artistic, the means of culture to the few; the Reformation was religious and popular. When Luther and Tyndale gave the Scriptures to the laity, and demanded that every man should have the faculty of reading them given to him, they awoke a thirst for knowledge in the people, which has resulted in popular education and popular power. Incidentally the follies of monkhood and the unreal system of the school-philosophy were shattered. Erasmus, in his Encomium Moriæ, laughed to scorn the absurdities which had been the intellectual aliment of the preceding centuries.

But if the Dark Ages passed away, it was not so much because men mocked at their darkness, as because a truer light was shining around them.

The Reformation, further, was the uprising of the laity. The requirements of a conscious and independent life were too serious to be held under the dominion of the clergy. Property was no longer to be kept in the dead hand. There was more to be done with men's substance than to build church-steeples and chantries. But, if they used their wealth for other than ecclesiastical purposes, it was because they were learning that those other purposes embodied the will of God. Similarly the corruptions and delays of the Ecclesiastical Courts could no longer be tolerated by those who had caught sight of simple justice, human and divine. But if the appeals to Rome were abolished, and the powers of the Ecclesiastical Courts were curtailed, it was because the ordinary courts of the realm had become purer and more efficient, and men had gained courage to say that justice is itself divine, and to seek it where they saw it could be found, not where the superstitions and forgeries of the past had directed them. The Renaissance had made the laity as well as the clergy eat of the fruit of the tree of knowledge, and learning was no longer hid in monasteries. What the laity read in the classical literature aided their emancipation. And further, the wave which brought Plato and Thucydides to the shores of Western Europe brought also the Greek Testament. Such men as Valdes in Spain, or Paleario in Italy, began with classical knowledge and passed on to religion. Above all, the lay life was gaining spiritual vigour. This alone ensured the emancipation of the laity from clerical trammels. Men like Thomas Cromwell in England, or Ulrich von Hütten in Germany, earned the name of 'Malleus Monachorum' or of ' Pfaffen-Feind[1],' not from a mere iconoclastic impulse, but because they had before them the ideal of a non-clerical Christianity.

And, lastly, the Reformation was an uprising of the national spirit. The end of the fifteenth century is the epoch at which the chief European kingdoms attained their organic form[2]. No one can read the writings of Luther without seeing how his appeal is always, consciously or unconsciously, to the German nation to assert themselves against the Pope beyond the mountains[3]. A great part of the English Reformation is the uprising against the degrading yoke of Italian ecclesiastics. The Dutch Republic freeing itself from Spain is a parallel instance. There was, as we may say, a national faith, a spiritual power arising in the local divisions of Christendom ; and it was this alone which enabled them

[1] Ulrich von Hütten, being in exile on the island of Ufnau on the lake of Zurich, on account of his resistance to the Pope and his supporters in Germany, expressed his confidence in the goodness of his cause in a poem, the first verse of which contains the expression quoted in the text :—

'Ich hab's gewagt mit Sinnen
Und trag des noch kein Reu,
Mag ich nit dran gewinnen,
Noch muss man spüren treu,
Damit ich mein', nit ei'm allein,
Wenn man es wollt erkennen,
Dem Land zu gut, wiewohl man thut
Ein Pfaffen-Feind mich nennen.'

See Buchheim's Deutsche Lyrik, p. 16, and Note at p. 345.

[2] This is fully drawn out in Guizot's *Civilisation in Europe*, Lect. xi.

[3] See especially his appeal to the German nobility, translated by Wace and Buchheim in *First Principles of the Reformation.*' (Murray, 1883.)

to throw aside the fiction of the Empire and the yoke of the Pope. And, more generally, whereas the mediæval idea, which largely influenced the aims of European life, had been that of a single great Empire, which in its later phases had become the instrument of Papal domination, now the national centres regained their importance. In the time of Charlemagne or of Frederick Barbarossa, or even of Rudolph of Hapsburg, the life of Europe resided in the central power which overlay the local. In the time of Francis the First and of Henry the Eighth, the vital force resided in the national organisms, which had now become conscious of their strength and had shaken off a yoke no longer necessary to their practical wants or their imagination.

In all cases, first comes conviction and a sense of power, the spiritual power that sees, and longs, and wills; then comes the negative result, which says, We can no longer have the power which we feel within us stunted or baffled; we will no longer endure thraldom or unreality.

It has been said by Guizot[1] that the main fact of the Reformation is contained in the word Liberty. This Liberty he takes, in common with many, in a somewhat negative sense, that is, as an assertion that the power of the Papacy and of the clergy was gone. But, if the real force which broke the chain was Christian conviction, the result could not possibly be merely liberty in this negative sense, the liberty to think as men pleased unfettered by clericalism. The liberty of the Reformation is that which would have been expressed in Greek

[1] *European Civilisation*, Lect. xii.

not by the word ἐλευθερία but by the word ἐξουσία. It was the free course given to a new spiritual power. And the central fact of the Reformation is the action of this spiritual power, first in the assertion of truth and the resolve to make it prevail, and then in a new attempt to build up the general life on a Christian model. This is seen by the zealous manner in which the Reformers everywhere addressed themselves to the people, by their efforts to put the Bible unreservedly into the hands of the laity, by their zeal in enforcing the main principles of Christianity by preaching and by church systems for the training of the general life, by works such as Luther's homely Postills, or like Tyndale's Obedience of a Christian Man, in the latter of which the true non-ecclesiastical justice is brought out in contrast with the clericalism by which it had been overlaid; and, lastly, by the distinct attempts, to some of which I design to call attention to-day, to form society afresh on a Christian basis.

Nor is it true, as Guizot has further said, that the reformed doctrine cared nothing for the form of government, and never tried to assert practical and popular liberty. No doubt some Protestant countries have been governed without popular forms; but even in these Protestant Christianity has always been favourable to popular rights; it has modified the government and given it a right direction, as in Germany, Denmark, and Sweden; and in the end, unless it lose its vitality, it must bring about a popular constitution. In England, Scotland, Holland, Switzerland, and the United States, it has been the parent of vigorous constitutional liberty; while the opposite tendency, which covered up truth under ecclesiastical forms, has led to subserviency and despotism, as in Spain, in Austria, and in France under the old régime. It is not too much to say that popular government flows naturally in due time from the acceptance of the religion of the New Testament, where it is untrammelled by ecclesiastical traditions. And we shall see that some of the most signal attempts to Christianize the life of communities have been accompanied with the placing of power in the hands of the people.

This is indeed an essential feature of the modern period which begins with the Reformation. Its Christian and public life reposes on popular conviction. Efforts like those of Charlemagne or of Hildebrand were vast conceptions, but they were imposed from above upon the world[1]. Efforts like that which built up the Dutch Republic or that of Geneva were in the truest sense popular. Whatever the power of the Empire and the Papacy in their day, they dealt with men only from afar. They could not respond to the needs of the conscience, which was grasping truth for itself and tending to self-government. But the municipal and national organizations were close at hand, ready to be

---

[1] It may be said that in some countries the Reformation was similarly imposed, as in the North German States or in England. But the similarity is deceptive. In each case the popular conviction was at least abreast of the action of the sovereign. In Germany the people followed Luther immediately, and men like Frederick the Wise of Saxony allowed themselves to be won gradually with the people. In England, though the people were long undecided, yet the more worthy part was inclined to sympathize even with the doctrinal reformers. In the national movement, which abolished the power of the Pope, the King acted in the main as the trusted leader of a united people.

moulded by the new spirit. It was in the life of cities and of nations that the revived Christian truth was to find its expression. Even in the fifteenth century we find the beginning of this process. The Empire becomes more and more a single hereditary kingdom, and ceases to overbear the separate nationalities; the Papacy is judged at Constance and at Basle. The European kingdoms take their distinctive forms, not only for general purposes, but as separate national churches. The Church of England, indeed, had never wholly lost its nationality. The German Church, in which the leaven of Huss and of Tauler was working, was beginning to feel its incompatibility with that of Rome; the church of the eastern nations broke finally away. The Gallican tendency first took shape under the Pragmatic Sanction of St. Louis[1], and later in the Concordat of Francis I. No doubt this tendency to national Christianity is not final; universality, not nationality, is the goal. But, since universality had become unmeaning, and the universal powers mere chimæras, the only sincere attempts, the only attempts which could respond to the awakening thirst for righteousness and veracity, were those directed to the purification of cities and of nations.

We may recall one such attempt, far back in the Middle Ages, that of Arnold of Brescia at Rome[2]. The disciple of Abelard, Arnold had breathed the free philosophical atmosphere of the Paraclete, and had learned to

[1] The Pragmatic Sanction embodied in the ordinance of St. Louis, of March 1268, is described in Milman's *Latin Christianity*, bk. xi. ch. 4.
[2] See the account of Arnold in Milman's *Latin Christianity*, iv. 373-412.

distrust both the ecclesiastical and the imperial domination then existing. He determined to invoke the free convictions of the Roman people to remedy the abuses of clerical government. The Romans, under his direction, expelled the Pope, and for thirteen years (1142-1155) governed themselves as a Republic. The clergy were, under his system, simple ministers of the Gospel, and the Pope simply the head of the clergy. Arnold perceived the sacredness of popular government, and endeavoured to educate the Roman people to its exercise. The idea of Arnold was far more serious than that of Rienzi, two centuries later, which was a fantastic antiquarian revival. But he was several centuries before his time. The Society of Rome was chaotic and full of factions. It had expelled the Pope to gain not righteousness but licence for its turbulence. It had no consciousness of its own responsibility or of the divine nature of justice and of government. Moreover, the Empire was then in the height of its vigour, and such anti-clerical hopes as existed centred in the imperial seat then worthily occupied by Frederick Barbarossa. The Republic of Arnold was a rebellion against the Emperor as well as against the Pope. The Emperor claimed and took possession of the city. He treated Arnold with contempt; he could believe in the holiness of the Roman Empire, but not in the holiness of a Roman Republic. He disdainfully handed Arnold over to the Pope, whose officers slew him, and his body was burned and thrown into the Tiber. Yet that must have been a great soul, which, nearly two centuries before Dante, and nearly four before the Reformation, conceived, and in some degree realised, the idea of a free popular government as an organ of the Spirit of God. The idea, though derided by the Emperor and the Pope, was sown deep in the heart of the church, to spring up again after many days in those whose career we have now to describe.

In Savonarola, at the end of the Middle Ages, on the very margin of the Reformation, the idea of a Christian city took definite shape. Those who believe in a Christianity which can blend with and inspire public life, will never tire of studying his career[1]. A fervent believer in Christ, and in the whole church system which represented him to the world, he regarded that system as the expression of a divine moral power, as may be seen in his books on the Triumph of the Cross and the Simplicity of the Christian Life. He was possessed of all the learning of the Renaissance; he held a noble philosophy; and he was by no means alien, as has been supposed, to the artistic spirit then active in Italy, but held a moral theory of art which did much to save it from frivolity and degradation. Yet he maintained above all the supremacy of faith and holiness. In an age in which it was possible for Roderick Borgia to be

[1] The facts relating to Savonarola are mainly taken from the Life by Villari (Horner's translation), and from the article by Dean Milman in his collected Essays. I cannot refrain from bearing testimony to the exactness of the representation of his work which is contained in George Eliot's *Romola*. I subjoin the principal dates of Savonarola's career to aid in the appreciation of his work. Birth at Ferrara, 1452. Enters Dominican Convent at Bologna, 1475. St. Mark's, Florence, 1582. First success as preacher at Florence, 1490. Prior, 1491. Roderick Borgia, Pope, 1492. Lorenzo de Medici dies, 1492. Piero de Medici driven out, 1494. New constitution of Florence, Dec. 1494. Charles VIII invades Italy, Aug. 1494; at Florence, Nov. 1494. Savonarola excommunicated by Pope, May, 1497. Medicean conspirators executed, Aug. 1497. Savonarola condemned by Pope, and inhibited by Signoria, March 1498. Executed, May 23, 1498.

the head of Christendom, he not only presented an example of a saintly life, which bears comparison with that of Dominic or of Francis of Assisi, or of the Fra Angelico of his own San Marco, but was, unlike them, moderate, tolerant, appreciative, good on every side. He was eminent in counsel and administration, so as to become Prior of his convent; and was so fully trusted as to be allowed to make St. Mark's of Florence independent of the Dominican province of Tuscany. He came to Florence from Ferrara by the invitation of Lorenzo de Medici, who knew the fame of his talents, and even in some sense was touched by the spell of his influence. In him lived again the spirit of the Hebrew prophets, their moral power, their spiritual insight into futurity, their firm faith in a redemption for the people as a whole, their deep sense at the same time of the actual wickedness around them, and their awful denunciations of swiftly coming judgment.

The Italian Republics, after many political vicissitudes, had at the end of the fifteenth century mostly fallen under the sway of powerful families. Partly from a desire for deliverance from the alarms of a turbulent democracy, partly from weariness of political change, they had purchased repose by the abandonment of liberty. At Florence the old republican forms remained, but, as at Rome under Augustus, they were so used as to be practically annulled. They were superseded by an unrecognized cabal of the friends of the Medici. The rule of Lorenzo was externally splendid, but often unjust and cruel; under it political and moral virtue were dying. Savonarola, whose power was silently growing, refused to accept the fatal alternative of despotism or licentious democracy. He held before his own eyes and those of the people the vision of a tempered liberty inspired and sobered by religion and morality. If that could be restored, Florence might become a City of God. When he was summoned to the death-bed of Lorenzo, he made three conditions of his absolution, (1) that he should believe firmly in God's mercy; (2) that he should forgive his enemies and make restitution to those whom he had defrauded; (3) that he should restore liberty to Florence. By this last request, which was refused, he showed how closely, in his conceptions, political justice was bound up with true religion[1].

Under Lorenzo's son, Piero, public affairs were neglected; the tyranny of a weak youth was more keenly felt than that of his able father. Savonarola became more vehement and more pronounced in his preaching. He had predicted the deaths of three Italian rulers—Lorenzo of Florence, Innocent VIII of Rome, and Ferdinand of Naples—and they all died within two years. He announced his vision of a drawn sword in the heavens, with the legend 'Domini gladius super terram cito et velociter,' and the threatened descent of Charles VIII of France soon confirmed his words. When Piero was expelled, and the Florentines needed an adviser, Savonarola became practically dictator of Florence (1494–7). He was so constantly appealed to by the Signoria or governing Committee, that he at last

[1] The accuracy of this account of the last interview between Lorenzo and Savonarola has been questioned. It is carefully discussed by Villari, who shows good reason for his belief that it is authentic.

summoned the whole City to the cathedral to hear the counsel which he gave them as being (and indeed it was) the righteous will of God. He demanded, (1) that they should always have the fear of God before their eyes; (2) that the Government should be for and by the people themselves, the benefit of the State being preferred to the particular benefit of individuals; (3) that there should be an amnesty and obliteration of all past feuds; (4) that a Grand Council should be established, consisting of all whose families had gained full rights of citizenship, by which all officers should be elected, and the consent of which should be necessary for the enactment of all laws. This Council was also to elect the governing Committee or Cabinet, the Signoria, which might be changed every month. All this was done according to the prophet's advice. His advice was also followed in the matter of taxation, in which he recommended a Decima or fixed property tax, and gained the assent of the people to it by warmly urging that to give to the State was to support their common father; in the question of appeals, where, however, by diverging on one point from his wise advice, and giving the appeal in cases of treason not to the smaller council of eighty but to the larger one of a thousand, the citizens laid up for themselves a store of troubles; in the formation of a Commercial Code, and in the institution of a workman's bank, or Monte di Pietà. The religious spirit breathed by Savonarola into the Republic elevated the whole compass of political action. The law of political appeals was prefaced by these words, not dictated by the Friar, but freely adopted by the Signoria:

'Inasmuch as it is of the greatest utility in a well-conducted Republic, that unity and concord should prevail, and in order to walk in the footsteps of our Lord, who always spoke of peace . . . . and as we have been warned by the supernatural events which we have witnessed in the formation of this government, and have seen how great is the mercy of our Lord vouchsafed to us, we are bound to imitate his mercy ;' therefore they decree the amnesty and the right of appeal.

The influence of Savonarola lasted for four years (1494-8), during which the Republic was justly governed, and supported under great reverses and distress; and the Friar gained, through the respect which he inspired, good terms for the city from the king of France. He organized societies of old and young for the reformation of morals; and at each Carnival, amid the chanting of hymns which had taken the place of the lascivious songs of Lorenzo, he burnt up the instruments of folly and vanity, which had been heaped together by the converts, after the manner of St. Paul at Ephesus. Yet he had a presentiment that his success was fleeting. He said constantly that the cause would one day succeed, but that he would have the martyr's crown. The Pope (Roderick Borgia, Alexander VI) alternately flattered and condemned him, but was steadily intent on his destruction, as Caiaphas on that of Christ. The Medicean party were on the watch to upset the government and bring back the old corruption; their party, the Arrabbiati, within the city longed to restore the age of licence: and the continuing distress exasperated the citizens and made them restless. Though Savonarola took no part in the Government, but merely supported it by his advice when called upon, all faults were laid to his charge. At last a Signoria hostile to him was elected; the Pope excommunicated him and demanded that he should be condemned; and in one of those hours of the wicked and the power of darkness, which have occurred in the history of so many of the deliverers of mankind, the author of so much good, with those who had most faithfully stood by him, was hurried, with mock trial and torture, with cord and flame, to his death.

Savonarola died a martyr to his attempt to make Florence a Christian city. Shall we pass an adverse criticism on his career, and say that it would have been better had he not, as the expression is, 'meddled in politics?' Shall we say that he should have contented himself with the reformation of individuals, and left on one side the question of the welfare of the State? Let us take care lest the condemnation which such a criticism implies fall on those we should be least inclined to condemn, and in particular on three careers to which that of Savonarola in different ways bears a strange resemblance,—the careers of Jeremiah, of John the Baptist, and, with reverence be it spoken, of Jesus of Nazareth. The attempt to establish the social and political relations on a religious basis is the most divine work given to man. It is an attempt in which to fail is better than to succeed in any other. It is an attempt which must be renewed again and again, each time, let us hope, under better conditions, until it succeeds; for it is the attempt to give effect to the Redemption of the World.

Less than forty years after the death of Savonarola, on the other side of the Alps, on the other side also of the great historical cataclysm of the Reformation, in the little Republic of Geneva, the same attempt was renewed, with a narrower scope, perhaps, but with larger results. In the year 1536 Calvin[1] arrived in Geneva, and from that time till his death in 1574, with the exception of an exile of two years (1539-40), he was the chief director of the public life of the Commonwealth. His first object was to lay a religious basis for all the relations of men within the state. He drew up a Confession which embodies in broad, general terms the Christian faith as then understood by the Protestant Churches. It has hardly anything in it of the doctrines with which his name is specially connected, although he had already written the Institutes of Theology. Every citizen was required to sign this Confession[2], so that the Church and the State were identical as to their component members. Rousseau, when he went to claim his citizenship more

---

[1] The facts relating to Calvin are taken mainly from Bungener's Life (Edin. 1863). I subjoin, as in the case of Savonarola, the chief dates of Calvin's career :— Birth at Noyon in Picardy, 1509. Curé of Marteville and Pont l'Evêque, 1529. Resigns 1534, and publishes Institutes at Strasburg, 1536. At Ferrara with Renée, daughter of Louis XII, 1536. At Geneva, 1536-8. Strasburg, 1538-41. Married 1540. At Geneva, 1541, till his death, 1564. Burning of Servetus, 1553.

[2] Rousseau describes in his Confessions how he went to Geneva in the year 1754 to take up his position as a citizen. It was necessary to sign the Confession of Faith. 'Je pensais,' he says, 'que l'Evangile étant le même pour tous les Chrétiens, et le fond du dogme n'étant différent qu'en ce qu'on se mêlait d'expliquer ce qu'on ne pouvait entendre, il appartenait en chaque pays au seul souverain de fixer et le culte et ce dogme inintelligible, et qu'il était par conséquent du devoir du citoyen d'admettre le dogme et de suivre le culte prescrit par la loi.' Consequently, he went through the prescribed course of instruction from the pastor of his parish, and appeared before the Consistory to make his confession, after which he was admitted to the communion, and, being thus restored to his rights as a citizen, he attended a general council and took the oath of admission as a member of the Republic.

than two centuries later, signed this Confession. So completely was the State acknowledged to be a Church, that the monogram of our Lord (IHS) was inscribed on all public buildings, on the standards, and on the coins. The Prince Bishop, who for many years had gained a power at Geneva comparable to that of the Medici at Florence, had been expelled in 1535, and, unlike the Medici, though he tried to return, found no favouring party strong enough to aid him. The old Government of the city retained its recovered independence, and was a body ready for the spirit which Calvin infused into it. It consisted of a General Council of all the citizens, and of a great Council of 200, and a small Council or Cabinet, both of which were elected by the whole body of the people in their General Council. In the year following the expulsion of the Bishop (1536), the Government took an oath to abide by the Gospel as the foundation of its laws, and thus a foundation was laid on which Calvin, who arrived the same year, could build. At his suggestion was established the Venerable Company of Pastors, to which the direction of worship and doctrine was confided, and the Consistory, by which all ecclesiastical discipline was exercised. There was also a body of Deacons, who were Hospitalers, and provided for the sick and poor. These bodies had no coercive power; but they wielded the potent weapon of excommunication, they had the recognised right of delating offenders to the magistrates, (a right best known from its exercise in the case of Servetus,) and of tendering advice or remonstrance as to the making and administering of the laws. The laws passed under this régime were often exceedingly severe. The attempt was made to enforce by penalties the whole range of the moral law, and to keep the Church-Republic free from all taint of heresy. But they expressed the conviction of all that was best in Geneva and in the reformed Christendom; and some of the most severe laws date from the era before the Reformation. There was a party of Libertines, with whom Calvin entered into conflict, refusing them admission to the Communion, and, the Government taking their side, he went voluntarily into exile; but within three years he was entreated to return, and from that time he was supreme.

The energy and devotion of Calvin were boundless, in pastoral work, preaching, writing, receiving the strangers who flocked from all parts to Geneva as to a city of refuge. He founded the College, now the University; he instituted the system of religious instruction, through which every Genevese Protestant still passes, and the system of pastoral visitation and diaconal ministrations to the sick and poor which, with some changes, still exists. Under him Geneva became the model state, the spiritual capital of the reformed Christendom. The spirit, indeed, which he infused into it was not the spirit of Christ in all its fulness. It was not the spirit of love, but that of stern justice, which knows God as a law-giver and a ruler, and assents to his decrees and his righteousness with mind and heart, with full conviction and entire devotion. He died worn out with mental and spiritual toil, commending to the Pastors and to the leaders of the Government the continuation of his work. That work, though deficient in tenderness, yet through its elaborate consistency, and the systematic conviction which it represents, held the republic together. For three centuries the little Protestant city endured, almost unchanged, in the midst of a continent the larger states of which were subject to tyranny and superstition, the home of freedom and of reasonable religion, and the constant channel of these blessings to mankind.

In the last fifty years many changes have occurred, the constitution becoming a pure democracy, all tests being abolished both for the system of Government and for the system of worship, the Roman Catholic Church being placed on an equality with the Protestant, and the whole apparatus of public worship becoming a less conspicuous and less powerful element in the community. But even now most of Calvin's institutions remain and enjoy the respect of the people generally; so that when, in the year 1880, it was proposed to abolish the maintenance by the Republic of the system of public worship, the proposal was rejected by a vast majority of the citizens, who, after long and vehement discussion, voted on it by universal suffrage[1].

I have spoken of Geneva as illustrating in the most marked way the attempt to frame a Christian polity for a single city. Other similar attempts were made with a not dissimilar result in several of the other Protestant

[1] For information as to this remarkable vote, its causes and its circumstances, I may refer to an article written by me in the *Contemporary Review* for August, 1882, entitled 'Church and Democracy at Geneva.' For the present condition of the Church at Geneva, I may refer to an article by Professor Bouvier, in the *Modern Review* for January, 1884, entitled 'Protestantism in Geneva.'

v.] *Efforts for a Christianized Society.* 213

cities and Cantons of Switzerland, in Berne, Zurich, Neuchatel, and Lausanne.

Meanwhile an attempt was being made, on a much more extended scale, and in a totally different direction, to restore the unity of human life in Christendom, I mean the attempt of the Jesuits to revive the Mediæval idea of Catholic unity under the new conditions established by the Reformation[1]. Like the Reformers, the Society of Jesus left the cloister to live among men; like them, it desired that religion should dominate the whole life of mankind; like them it wished to reorganize society; but, unlike them, it believed that this was to be effected by restoring the power of the Papacy. It seemed as if, through the inroads made upon the old church unity, all unity whatever would be destroyed, and Christendom become a disintegrated congeries of separate fragments. The Christian religion, instead of being, as it had been in the days of Innocent III, the strong power of coherence which bound men and nations into a connected whole, seemed in danger of being dissipated into endless sects, each nation, each city, having its own form of religion and of life, often antagonistic to that of its neighbour. The higher unity which arises from the Christian spirit freely playing upon the common life of men had not presented itself to the founders of the Jesuit Society; it had indeed not fully actuated the Reformers, who contended, each of them separately, for truth, with very little attempt at

[1] Most of the facts relating to the Jesuits are taken from the *History of the Jesuits*, by B. N. (Burns and Oates, 1879). Loyola was born in 1491. His conversion was in 1521. The society was formed at Paris in 1534, and founded by the Pope 1540. Loyola died at Rome, 1556.

union. To the Jesuits this higher unity amidst diversity would have appeared very shadowy, as indeed it does even now to all but a very few. But, if the old dogmatic religion and the clerical system was to be the basis still of human life and international unity, what body could undertake the task of restoring it, but the Roman clergy acting under the Pope? The clerical system had indeed received a great wound, but the wound might be healed; the lost countries might be restored as in the former days, as in the time of Hildebrand and of Innocent; and fresh conquests might be won among the heathen, through which the rebellious subjects of the Papacy might be shamed back into their allegiance.

The Jesuits had some great advantages. For them many of the questions which perplexed the Reformers had no existence. The limit between the temporal and spiritual domain had been settled long ago for them in the subjection of all rule and authority to the Pope. While Protestant piety often tended to limit the sphere over which religious thought could range, they could take in all spheres of human interest; and their zeal for learning was great and fearless. While Protestants were perplexed at times by moral and spiritual difficulties, such as that in which Luther was involved as to the bigamy of the Elector of Hesse, or the dispute with the Zwinglians about the Sacrament, all was made clear for them by the Papal decrees and by the subtle system of casuistry which they built upon them. And, further, while Protestants had enough to do in establishing a new religious system at home, the zeal of men like

v.]   *Efforts for a Christianized Society.*   215

Fràncis Xavier, transcending the course of the most ambitious commerce, was carrying Christianity into the furthest East, into the wilds of Central Africa and into South America. Lastly, while Protestantism was hardly conscious of its ultimate goal, and hardly had the conviction to claim successfully the whole of human life, the Jesuits knew exactly what they wanted, and made imperative demands upon man's entire obedience. Hence Protestant quietism, like that of Jacob Böhmen, resulted only in personal peace and withdrawal from active life : Jesuit quietism, as taught by Molini, gave the whole outward man, body and soul, to be used or cast away at the will of the ruling power of the Order, and in promotion of its great objects[1].

For a time it gained a wonderful success. The Order[2] multiplied rapidly. Though none but active members were admitted, they numbered, at the end of forty years from the foundation, more than five thousand. They had by that time arrested the Reformation in Italy, Spain, Hungary, Bohemia, Poland and Belgium. They were intriguing for the re-conversion of England and Scotland. They had founded Colleges everywhere. The stupendous work of the Bollandists, the Acts of the Saints, was commenced. Xavier had died at Sounian on the coast of China (Dec. 2, 1552). The Mission to Paraguay was beginning (1586), to be followed by the Mission of the Brahmin-dressed De Nobili (1609) in India, of Ricci and Ruggieri in China, of Valignani in

---

[1] The decision allowing the views of the Molinists was given in 1606.
[2] The order was founded by the Bull of the Pope, Regimini militantis Ecclesiae, Sept. 27, 1540.

Japan[1]. In the Thirty Years' War most of the chief leaders on the Catholic side, the Emperor Ferdinand, Maximilian of Bavaria, and Tilly, were pupils of the Jesuits. A Jesuit, John Casimir, was for twenty years king of Poland (1643-1663); a Jesuit, Balde, was the patriot poet of Alsace. We must credit the Jesuits further with the revived life and force of Roman Catholicism generally, and with the attempts made even by those who were most opposed to them, like the leaders of the Gallican Church in 1682, to bind great communities of men by the Catholic bond. Even where Catholicism was rejected, Jesuitism gained the respect which is inspired by fear.

What was the fundamental fault which caused its failure? It was, in one word, a lack of faith in human nature. Human life was to be denaturalized, not developed. It was to be overlaid by an extraneous power. And the Catholic unity at which Jesuitism aimed was to be not one of freedom and truthful conviction, but one of subserviency to positive institutions, at the head of which stood the Pope. The best work, probably, ever done by the Jesuits was in Paraguay. There the whole country was subject to their sway and ruled as a Christian community. They developed its resources, discovering many useful products, such as chinchona, bark, caoutchouk, vanilla, rhubarb. The Indians were brought by them into such a state of docility, that it was reported by the Bishop of Buenos Ayres in 1721, that not a mortal sin was committed in a year in the whole country. They forbad the slave trade; and,

[1] Sent by the third General of the Order, Claudius Aquaviva, who died 1615.

v.] *Efforts for a Christianized Society.* 217

though compelled to train the Indians for self-defence, had the weapons locked up in an armoury as soon as the attack was over. But the people were no more than grown-up children. They were not allowed the use of money; European commerce was forbidden among them; and, on the opening of the country to freer external intercourse, the whole system of the Jesuits melted away. The Jesuits were an army suited only to a special emergency. It has long been apparent from a full experience to Catholic as well as Protestant nations, that the rule of the priest, at which they aimed, is impossible. The effort to establish it can be nothing now but sectarian, the parent of division and of hypocrisy. Nevertheless the attempt which the Jesuits made was originally the prompting of a piety which embraced a larger area than that within the province of their opponents. The church of the future must aim, as the Jesuits aimed, at unity, and at the bringing of the whole man under the dominion of Christ; but it must be a unity brought about by free conviction, respecting the spiritual liberty of its component parts, compatible with very large differences of form, above all acknowledging the sacredness of human life and social institutions, and making Christ not an external King but the inspiring guide of mankind.

If now we turn once more to the Protestant Churches, we must notice an effort of a different kind to give a unity of direction to human life, which, though never recognized as the distinct principle on which a Society or even a sect was organized, has been widely influential. I allude to the tendency represented by Zwingli and the pastors of Zurich, which was formulated by the Reformer of Basle, Wolfgang Musculus[1], and afterwards energetically maintained by Erastus of Heidelberg[2]. Its chief assertion is, that the Magistrate of a Christian state is not to be regarded as holding an office outside the Church, but within it: that in a Christian commonwealth all matters of rule and external order whatsoever should fall under the control of the ruler, and that the ruler should be recognized as an office-bearer of the Church. The sentence from Wolfgang Musculus prefixed to Erastus' Theses is this: 'Omnium vero nocentissimus error est quod plerique de Magistratu Christiano haud aliter sentiunt quam de dominatu profano, cujus potestas tantum in profanis sit agnoscenda.' This thesis may be said to be almost the direct contrary of that which is popularly understood as Erastianism. That word is commonly used as signifying the theory that a ruler, whether Christian or not, has a right to prescribe the religious belief of his subjects. Erastus maintained on the contrary, that, when the ruler was a member of the Church, he ought to be regarded as the ruling officer

[1] Wolfgang Musculus was born in 1497 at Disuze, in Lorraine, and became a Benedictine Monk. He settled at Basle in the early days of the Reformation, and died at Berne in 1569. His 'Common Places' were translated into English by John Man of Merton Coll. Oxford, and published in London, 1578.

[2] Erastus (Thomas Lieber) was born at Baden in 1524. He studied at Basle and Bologna, and afterwards practised medicine at Heidelberg, where he was also professor, and privy councillor to Frederick Prince Palatine. He returned in later life to Basle, and died there in 1583. His Theses, published in 1568, form a small volume, not very accessible to the English reader, though often published in the 15th and 16th centuries. He wrote a Confirmatio Thesium in reply to Beza in 1569. This work may be found in a volume entitled *Explicatio Quaestionis Gravissimae* (Amsterdam), 1649. The Theses were published in English (Simpkin and Marshall, 1844) by Dr. Robert Lee of Edinburgh. An account of Erastus and his works may be found in Mr. Llewelyn Davies' *Theology and Morality* (King and Co. 1873).

within the Church. His contention had reference to the vast system of Church law and Church courts, which had sought in the Middle Ages to supersede the ordinary administration of justice, and had produced a confusion in men's allegiance. The corruption of this system had greatly contributed to bring on the crisis of the Reformation, but in some Protestant countries it was then being sought to re-establish it by means of the power of excommunication, vested in the ministers of public worship. Erastus maintained (wrongly perhaps) that no such power had been used in Apostolic times as an engine of discipline. But he fully admitted that, so long as the Church existed in a non-Christian Commonwealth, it must have its own domestic system of discipline. When, however, the Commonwealth itself and its ruler were included within the Church, Erastus maintained that all such discipline must pass under the general law of the community, and all offences must be cognizable by the ruler, whose office was now converted into a sacred ministry. The Word and Sacraments he declared to be not subject to any power[1]; it was the only duty of a Christian ruler to take care that they were duly maintained. If questions arose about such matters in the administration of justice and of discipline, it would be the ruler's duty to consult the clergy and professors as experts, and to guide himself by the Holy Scriptures[2]. 'We sum up thus[3],' he says, 'that in a Christian Commonwealth there is one universal ruler, to whom is committed by God the external government of all things which belong

[1] Conf. Thes. B. iii. 140.   [2] Theses, 73.   [3] Conf. Thes. iii. 128.

either to the civil life or to the life of Christian piety; that the right and authority of rule and jurisdiction has not been committed to ministers or to any others.'

There are two things which have been misconceived in the views of Erastus and his coadjutors. First, it has been supposed that they would establish a tyrannical authority over conscience, and that in matters of religion they would overbear by external force those who have special qualifications for exercising spiritual influence. But, on the contrary, they confess that the region of conviction is one over which no man has power; they would leave conviction as free as possible. They would recognize, no doubt, the principle confessed by the Church of England, that councils for ecclesiastical legislation cannot be called without the will of princes, and they would assign to the ruler the duty of taking care that the decision should be that of the whole Church; but they would also recognize the necessity of giving full weight to the authority of the clergy and other experts in the formation and administration of religious laws[1]. It is only in the forum externum, the sphere of enactment and enforcement, that they would attribute an ultimate power to the ruler. The other misconception is the supposition that the views of Erastus regard the ruler as an external power superior to the Church, whereas they simply regard him as the chief officer within the Church for all matters of external conduct. 'The distinction of ecclesiastical and profane laws,' says Wolfgang Musculus[2], 'can find no place among Christians. The Magistrate himself is holy and

[1] Theses, 73.   [2] Wolfgang Musculus, 'Common Places,' p. 1318 (London, 1578).

not profane, his power and laws holy, his sword holy.' It is manifest that what was contemplated in this system was not, as has been supposed, two powers or communities, the one worldly, the other professing to be heavenly, of which the worldly because of its physical force was to domineer over the heavenly, but one Christian Church or community, the government of which should be under one head. They wished to avoid what Peter Martyr[1] called the Biceps et monstrosa Respublica, in which men would be distracted in their allegiance between opposite claims upon their consciences.

This system has had its main effect in Germany, though it is hardly distinguishable from that of the Reformation Settlement in England. The chief fault which we may trace in its operation in Germany is a fault not of the system itself but of the general method of government. In all matters, ecclesiastical and civil alike, there has been in Germany too minute a regulation of affairs, and too little confidence in the people themselves; and the government has consequently appeared as an external power which caused discontent by imposing its will upon the Church, whereas the fault has really lain in a wrong balance of powers within the Church itself[2]. That there are many spheres in life, the chief of which is the formation and expression of

[1] Peter Martyr's views on this subject may be found in his 'Common Places,' Part iv. c. 5 (p. 61), and his Commentaries on Judges xviii. and 1 Sam. viii.

[2] See Note XVIII, in which are given, first, some extracts from Baron Bunsen's Life, showing the arbitrary power over religious affairs which he sought to correct; secondly, extracts from the introduction to the law of 1880 for the regulation of the Prussian Church, showing the modifications now adopted of the former system of absolutism.

religious belief, with which no government ought to interfere, except so far as to ensure their proper development, is a political principle of the utmost importance; and this principle has often been ignored by those in authority, by none so much as by ecclesiastical rulers. But to call this ignoring of the proper bounds of coercive authority by the name of Erastianism is unmeaning. To the system of Erastus, and of the great reformers who agreed with him, it is difficult to see what objection can be made. That system is one more of the many attempts, partially, but for the reasons above given only partially, successful, by which Christians have sought to bring human life into harmony through the redemptive power contained in the Gospel, to raise the government of men in the whole range of its operation to the dignity of a function of the Church.

I now turn to the religion of our English race, and I take, besides the main stream of it which will form the subject of the next Lecture, two important and largely successful attempts at the great object; the establishment of the Presbyterian régime by Knox in Scotland, in the latter part of the 16th century, and the foundation of Puritan communities in the early part of the 17th century in New England.

The movement of Knox in Scotland was eminently national. He addressed himself, not mainly to individuals, but to the Queen and the Estates of the realm. Religion was to be a matter of public concern. The scene at Edinburgh in the year 1581, in which the Confession of Faith, the Protest against Rome, and the

National Covenant were ratified, is worthy to be compared with the Jewish Covenants in the days of Hezekiah and Josiah[1]. The Estates professed their resolve to stand by the settlement of the realm made at the Reformation, and they concluded their deliverance in these solemn words: 'Because we cannot look for a blessing from God upon our proceedings except with our profession we join such a life and conversation as beseemeth Christians who have renewed their covenant with God, we therefore faithfully promise for ourselves, our followers, and all others under us, both in public and in our particular families and personal carriage, to endeavour to keep ourselves within the bounds of Christian liberty, and to be good examples to others of all godliness, sobriety, and righteousness, and every duty that we owe to God and man. And, that our union and conjunction may be observed without violation, we call the Living God, the searcher of our hearts, to witness; most humbly beseeching the Lord to strengthen us by His Holy Spirit for this end, and to bless our desires and proceedings with a happy success; that religion and righteousness may flourish in our land, to the glory of God, the honour of our King, and the peace

---

[1] The fundamental documents of the Scotch Church are to be found in a volume entitled, 'The Confession of Faith, Larger and Shorter Catechisms,' &c. (Glasgow, F. Ore and Sons, 1843). The National Covenant or Confession of Faith of 1581 is there given (pp. 287-298). It should be distinguished from the Solemn League and Covenant made in 1643, which is also in the volume (pp. 299-306). The National Covenant contains an enunciation of the Acts of Parliament by which the Presbyterian system was established.

A spirited description of the restoration of the National Covenant in 1638 is given in Stanley's Lectures on the History of the Church of Scotland (Murray, 1872), p. 73.

and comfort of us all.' In a word, the whole nation here profess their faith and their firm resolve to pursue Christian righteousness. It was an attempt to make the Scottish kingdom a Kingdom of Christ and of God.

I need not dwell on the vicissitudes of the Scottish Church and nation, which are so closely bound up with those of our own. We all know how the settlement then made stood firm, so as to resist the designs of Charles I and of Laud, to which the English Church succumbed; how its success made Presbyterianism for a time the form of English as well as Scottish religion; how, after the Civil War and the reigns of Charles and James II, it reasserted itself in Scotland and has maintained itself ever since. I will content myself with pointing out how far it succeeded, how far it failed, in the attempt to make the Christian religion in Scotland the basis of the national life.

The words of the Covenant which I have read shew that Christian righteousness was the main thought of the actors in that memorable scene. But, owing to the preoccupation of men's minds with the controversy with Rome, and the fact that the chief instrument of Roman tyranny had been a peculiar form of doctrine and of worship, the idea of doctrine and worship was much more prominent than that of good government. Almost all the Acts of Parliament to which the Covenant refers are for the establishment of the Presbyterian form of worship and discipline. They revoke all laws made in former times in favour of idolatry, superstition, and the Papistical Kirk; they provide that all Papistical priests and their adherents shall be punished with ecclesiastical and civil penalties as common enemies of all Christian governments; they condemn all erroneous books, and forbid superstitious ceremonies, and ordain that those who use them shall be punished, on the second fault, as idolaters. This absorption in the question of public worship and ceremonies necessarily throws into the shade the yet more important matters of men's relations to one another and to the society, the body of Christ, in which they live, in the practice of which relations consists the genuine service of God, the proper outcome of the worship in spirit and truth. And, though such relations would naturally result from Protestant Christianity sincerely adopted, and have indeed largely resulted from it, yet, the stress not being laid on this result, religion failed to gain the hold upon men's consciences which it would have gained if identified with a righteous public life. Also, the extreme severity of the laws against Popery could not but create a spirit of harshness in the minds of the people very widely different from the spirit of Christ. Righteousness without love is not Christianity; and to enact laws of extreme severity in the name of God must give men a wrong idea of the Divine character. When the heated iron had cooled, a hard form remained, which made religion rather a peculiar mould in which character was cast than a living spirit and conviction.

And yet no one can doubt that the effect on the national character of Scotland was real, permanent and noble. If the Presbyterian system had been somewhat more plastic, that effect might have passed into the universality which is the chief note of the full Christian development. In one point, indeed, it contained the germ of this, namely, in its zeal for education in all its branches. Scotch philosophy, Scotch enterprise, the original impulse given to knowledge by Hume and Adam Smith, the culture evinced by Burns and by the peasantry who could appreciate him, the enlightened philanthropy of Chalmers, the generous sacrifice made for conviction by the Free Church Pastors at the Disruption, as well as the more liberal movements of Scotch religious thought which the present day has brought forth, are all of them effects of the fine institutions of Christian instruction which had their roots in the Presbyterian Church-system. It was said, indeed, by Macaulay that the Scottish parochial schools were established for the narrow purpose of inculcating Presbyterian orthodoxy alone, and that, contrary to the intention of their founders, they had ministered to general culture[1]. But their object was to train the nation in the apprehension of the will and righteousness of God; and, as knowledge widened, the conception of the will and righteousness of God widened also. The test of a religion lies not so much in its immediate results as in its capacity for such changes as may adapt it to the needs of successive ages. There is nothing which should prevent the impulse towards knowledge engendered by Presbyterianism from lending its powerful aid in

---

[1] 'History of England,' ch. xxii. 'To the men by whom that system was established posterity owes no gratitude. They knew not what they were doing .... their own understandings were as dark, and their own hearts as obdurate as those of the Familiars of the Inquisition.' Vol. iv. p. 192 (small edition).

furthering the true and full religion of Christian life and culture.

I turn now, lastly, to the most notable and most promising example of the attempt to bind the whole fabric of human life into one Christian system, an attempt made on a virgin soil, under no social fetters, but with full powers of self-development in the community, the attempt of the Puritan settlers in New England[1]. They left the old country because they did not deem it possible in the England of the early seventeenth century to live such a life as they believed that God demanded, or to worship Him as they believed He required to be worshipped. It was the time when the Book of Sports was read in the churches by command of the King and the Bishops, in defiance of the growing convictions of the Church; the time of the Courts of the Star Chamber and the High Commission, from which there was no appeal, which possessed legislative and judicial functions in combination, before which men could be forced to accuse themselves, and in which the whole system of Anglicanism, though a large part of it was conscientiously believed by the most Christian half of the nation to be contrary to the will of God, was enforced by brutal and degrading penalties. The Puritan emigrants went forth to a land not so much of liberty as of righteousness, where they could live and worship

[1] The facts relating to the New England Colonies are taken from Palfrey's 'History of New England,' Cotton Mather's 'Magnalia,' Bancroft's 'History of the United States,' Elliott's 'New England History,' and Leonard Bacon's (Jun.) 'Genesis of the New England Churches.' I may refer also to a lecture by Professor Goldwin Smith, 'The Foundation of the American Colonies,' given at Oxford in 1860 (Jas. Parker, 1861).

according to the will of God[1]. They were not actuated, notwithstanding their sufferings, by any hatred of England, or even of its government. It is recorded of the founders of Massachusetts that, as they lost sight of the Land's End, they cried out, not 'Farewell, Babylon,' but 'Farewell, dear England[2].' The Pilgrim Fathers, who sailed from Delft Haven in Holland in 1620, after many years' exile at Leyden[3], before they landed at Plymouth in New England, signed the following declaration, which was to serve as a basis for their common life[4]: 'In the Name of God, Amen. We, whose names are underwritten, the loyal subjects of our dread Sovereign King James, having undertaken, for the glory of God and advancement of the Christian faith, and honour of our King and country, a voyage to plant the first colony in the northern parts of Virginia, do by these presents solemnly and mutually, in the presence of God and one another, covenant and combine ourselves together into a civil body politic, for our better ordering and preservation and the furtherance of the ends aforesaid;

---

[1] See, besides the declaration of the Pilgrim Fathers given in the text, the Church Covenant of Massachusetts (July 30, 1631), in which it is said that the members desire to live 'under our Lord Jesus Christ as our head, in such sort as becometh those whom he hath redeemed and sanctified to himself. We do solemnly and religiously, as in his holy presence, promise and bind ourselves to walk in all our ways according to the rule of the Gospel, and in all sincere conformity to his holy ordinances, and in mutual love and respect to each other, as man and God shall give us grace.' Elliott, in the account of the colony of Salem.

[2] Elliott, p. 143.

[3] The congregation of John Robinson came originally from Boston in Lincolnshire. They left England in 1607, and settled first at Amsterdam. In 1609 they removed to Leyden, and in 1620 a large part of them sailed from Delft Haven in the *Mayflower*. The declaration given in the text was signed by forty-one heads of families in the cabin of the *Mayflower* off Cape Cod, on Nov. 11, 1620.

[4] Elliott, p. 102.

and by virtue hereof to enact, constitute and frame such just and equal laws, ordinances, acts, constitutions, and offices, from time to time, as shall be thought most meet, and convenient for the general good of the colony, unto which we promise all due submission and obedience.'

We see from this declaration that what was aimed at by the settlers was to live in just relations one to another in the sight of God, and according to His will. For this purpose, every member of the community was to have a voice in the management of the common affairs; so that the spirit of equal brotherhood, the foundation of all civil and religious justice, reigned supreme among them from the first. Nor was their system so narrow and dogmatic as is sometimes represented. The pastor of the congregation by whom the Pilgrim Fathers were sent forth, John Robinson, in his parting exhortation to them on the shore at Delft Haven in Holland, while he urged them to stand fast by the general teaching which he had given them, yet gave them these two notable injunctions: first, that if they found that anything which he had taught was contrary to God's word, they should cast it aside: secondly, that they should look incessantly for fresh truth beyond that which he had taught. 'I am persuaded,' he said, 'that the Lord hath yet more truth to spring forth from His word.'

The history of their struggles in the wilderness against hunger, cold, and disease, and the hostility of their savage neighbours, is a story of Christian heroism fit to compare with that of any age. After the first few years the settlements rapidly multiplied. They attracted to themselves a large proportion of the simple Christian worthies of Puritan England, men of faith and sturdy independence, self-controlled, law-abiding and industrious, lovers of liberty and, so far as toleration was then understood, respecters of the rights of all. Their laws were grounded on the laws of Moses and those of their English forefathers. Most of the great Saxon institutions were reproduced in the new world—trial by jury, representative assemblies, parochial government, freedom of speech and of writing[1]. In most of the colonies none but the Church-members had rights of citizenship, so that Church and State were conterminous. There were many positive laws, in which religion, morals, manners, dress appear side by side in a way that to modern ears sounds grotesque. Yet the law was among them a reflection of the Divine justice as they understood it[2], and directed them to a life full of zeal for righteousness and for the common good. Within sixteen years of the landing of the Mayflower, within nine years of the foundation of Massachusetts, the university town of Cambridge was founded. Every township was bound to have an elementary school, every hundred families a grammar school. Within twenty years of the first landing the colonies had so multiplied that, when com-

[1] In the directions given by the Company, by which the colony of Salem was founded, it is provided, 'That all be kept to labor in their several employments as the only means to reduce them to a civil, yea, a godly life.' It was also ordered that 'A registry be kept of what is done by every familye,' so that 'no idle drone be permitted to live amongst us.' Elliott in his account of Salem.

[2] 'The first intention of Government in the Massachusetts and New Haven Colonies was to establish a Theocracy, to insure the rule of the saints, and the first legislation was, in a good degree, intended to promote religion. They looked to the Mosaic Law and found their model.... This idea gave the clergy a mighty influence, and stamped the character of the State.' Elliott, p. 174.

bined for mutual defence, they would put into line a thousand men.

Can we say that in this, which I have called the most notable of the experiments of the Reformation Era, the object was fully attained of binding the whole life of the community together by the power of Christian righteousness? Not altogether, certainly; but more nearly than in the other instances which have been cited. There were, however, several things which militated against its completeness, of all of which one thing mainly was the cause.

As in all the instances on which we have dwelt to-day, the Church or Commonwealth had not emancipated itself from the exaggerated stress still laid on public worship, its forms, its special doctrines. Worship and doctrinal forms had not yet their just relation to the whole Christian life. They were viewed as something apart; and a special discipline was instituted to preserve their purity under an order of ruling elders; it was not as yet fully acknowledged that the true discipline is the law of the Christian Commonwealth and the true ruling elder the Christian magistrate. The close system, the test for membership, which was adopted, suitable as it might be to a small community which was little more than a family, was not suited to regulate the same community when growing into a nation, still less when receiving a large and miscellaneous population of immigrants. Even those who shared generally the Puritan belief felt their discipline irksome. A clergyman who had settled in the neighbourhood of the Massachusetts colony refused to cast in his lot with them. 'I came here,' he said, 'to be rid of the tyranny of the Lords Bishops: and I do not intend to subject myself to that of the Lords Brethren[1].' There was a pettiness in the subjects with which church-discipline dealt, which was degrading to the Christian life, and which also engendered constant strife and often persecution. There was difficulty, from the very first, in reconciling the Plymouth Colonists, who were Brownists or Separatists, with the Colonists of Massachusetts, who desired a National Church with something of the old parochial system though with Puritan forms. Opinions like those of Mrs. Hutchinson, which partly resembled those of the Baptists, partly those of the sect termed Brethren in the present century, were held to make it impossible for the maintainer of them to remain in the Colony[2]. Roger Williams, who demanded an absolute licence of opinion, was driven to found the separate colony of Rhode Island, of which Cotton Mather, the learned minister of Boston, said, that 'it was a colluvies of Antinomians, Familists, Anabaptists, Anti-Sabbatarians, Arminians, Socinians, Quakers, Ranters, and everything but Roman Catholics and true Christians[3].' Quakers were whipped at the cart-tail in several towns of New England. The story of the burning of witches at Salem is known to all. To no one, unless it were Roger Williams, did it occur amidst these mutual condemnations, to ask whether those whom

[1] W. Blackstone. The story is given in Elliott, in his account of the colony of Salem.

[2] A curious account of the discipline administered in the New England churches is given in Leonard Bacon's (Sen.) account of the First Congregational Church in Newhaven.

[3] Elliott, in his account of Rhode Island.

they denounced were not just men who feared God and wrought righteousness.

From such a state of things several issues were possible, and were attempted. It was possible to go forth further into the wilderness, and, with a few saintly companions, to live a more entirely separate life. That was the course adopted by Davenport, the founder of Connecticut[1]. He had left his church in the City of London, because it was impossible for him there to carry into effect the godly discipline which he deemed essential. He went into the wilds, that he and his followers might live according to the will of God. He set up at Newhaven, in the meadows near the harbour, a community which would admit none to their membership but those whom they deemed to be truly converted. But again the difficulty pressed, which arose in all these communities, from the accession of fresh colonists. The Church relaxed its discipline. 'It went,' according to the expression of Davenport, 'into the parish way,' that is, the way of counting as Christians all within a given circle who professed a Christian belief. He left his flock and his ministry, acknowledging that he had failed, and lived in retirement at Boston till his death.

But it was possible also to widen the basis of membership; and this was done gradually as the colonies of the Bay of Massachusetts united into a single state. The toleration was not speedy nor full; but Presbyterians and Independents learned to look on each other

---

[1] These facts are taken from Leonard Bacon's (Sen.) volume on 'The First Congregational Church at Newhaven.'

as brothers, and a century later were so little at variance that the Independent Jonathan Edwards could be President of the Presbyterian College of Princeton. The provision for public worship still remained a principal occupation of the government, so that even to a very late epoch a tax was levied, which was distributed, according to the wishes of those who paid it, among the various institutions for public worship.

A third way was that adopted by Roger Williams in the foundation of Rhode Island. This was the principle of universal toleration, at least of Protestants, which was confirmed by the Charter received from England in 1663. Those who took part in the government must be members of some one of the churches. But the laws which they made had nothing to do with worship; they had reference to their common life alone. Their code concludes with the words : ' Otherwise than is here forbidden, all men may walk as their consciences persuade them, every one in the name of God.' And this is in the main the system which has been adopted throughout the American States. It is manifest that establishments existing solely for a special form of worship can only be maintained, in a large commonwealth which is self-governed and has various forms of worship, as purely voluntary societies. It is now an integral article of the American constitution that no state shall have the right to set up an established church.

Thus it might seem as if the attempt made originally in the American colonies to bind men's lives into one by the sanctions of religion had failed, since it has resulted in the absolute severance of the life of worship from that of the commonwealth. But this is only in appearance. The effect of the Puritan religion upon the general life has been and is immense. It was in the early days the connecting link with the English nation, if not with the English government; and the witness for successful liberty which it bore was the support of those who were struggling for liberty on this side of the Atlantic. It lessened the jealousy which began to arise in the end of the seventeenth century between England and her growing colonies, it gave them a common cause in the struggles against the Roman Catholic nations in the wars of the eighteenth century; and, when the Revolution came, it mitigated its ferocity. The American Revolution, in contrast with the French, was sober, not vindictive, religious, not destructive. And to the same religious influence we owe the speedy restoration of harmony and even of Christian brotherhood which, through God's mercy, is now almost complete.

The final condition of religion in America it would be quite as difficult to predict as in any other country. Even the attempt to separate the apparatus of public worship from public and official life is by no means finally decided, for prayers are offered in Congress, and religious observances exist in many of the public schools. As regards the more important matter on which we are dwelling, the enterprise of bringing the general life under the influence of Christian principle, in no country is the need of a new departure with this as its goal more strongly felt[1].

[1] See the article on 'Religion in America,' by Mr. J. L. Diman, in the Centennial number (250, Jan. 1876) of the *North American Review*.

There are two views which the experiments dwelt upon in this Lecture suggest to different minds, with the expression of which, as given in the conclusion of two American histories of New England, I will close the review of the Reformation era and of the attempts then made to build up Society on a Christian basis. The first, I venture to characterize as the negative view rendered necessary by the controversies of former ages and the excessive scope then given to the sphere of public worship and of doctrine. The second opens out the prospect of a higher synthesis and harmony.

'We find,' says Leonard Bacon in 'the Genesis of the New England Churches,' 'that American Church history is essentially the history of voluntary churches, the history of tendencies and conflicts which have come to the result that now every American Church forms itself by elective affinity, the principle of separation. We find that it is the history of Christianity working towards its own emancipation from the secular power; and that it is at the same time the history of the State learning slowly, but at last effectually, that it has no jurisdiction in the sphere of religion, and that its equal duty to all churches is the duty, not of enforcing their censures, but only of protecting their peaceable worship and their liberty of prophesying.'

That might be a complete statement of the matter if the Church were a society merely for public worship and its accessory functions. But if it is, as has been here maintained, an all-embracing society, the principles of which are designed not merely to influence all human life, but to blend it into one harmonious whole, a larger lesson is needed, which is thus described by Elliott in his New England History, p. 135 :—

'The day had come when a few brave men could take this step in the advance towards freedom, the step of establishing a Church without priestly forms, free to work out its ideas into life and action, and not be swallowed up and lost. The day had come when Democracy was possible in the Church, foretelling its coming in the State; a day yet certain to be, when the State shall assimilate to the Church, and the true religious spirit, pervading all men of all classes, may leaven even politicians, when Church and State shall be as one.'

LECTURE VI.

THE ENGLISH CHURCH AND COMMONWEALTH.

Isaiah xxvi. 1, 2. We have a strong city; salvation will God appoint for walls and bulwarks. Open ye the gates, that the righteous nation which keepeth the truth may enter in.

WE have examined, in the last Lecture, several of the attempts which were made at the era of the Reformation and in the succeeding century to rebuild the shattered unity of society, whether by directly restoring the mediæval idea, or by the sounder process of local and national christianisation; and we have traced the effect of these attempts upon the modern world. This Lecture will be devoted to the same attempt as made in our own country. No excuse is needed for devoting so much space to a single country; for not only is the condition of England by far the most important matter for Englishmen, but also the attempt we are tracing out has been made here on a larger scale and with fuller success. In no other country has religion so fully blended with the national life. And commentators on universal history, like Guizot or Comte, have felt it necessary to turn from the general course of their disquisitions in order to

Christian Nationalism. 239

bestow a peculiar attention on the working out of the great experiment in England in the sixteenth and seventeenth centuries.

It is instructive to observe that all the Reformation documents, legal, constitutional, liturgical, send us back to the early Saxon times. When Saxon England became Christian, church and commonwealth became one. When the Heptarchy passed away, and the unity already existing in the organization for worship extended also to the organization for external government, the King was supreme over a kingdom and church combined. The barons and bishops sat side by side in the Witanagemot. Earl and bishop judged together in the Shiremoot or County Court. And, though this last arrangement was altered by William to satisfy the Roman Court to which he owed his crown, the King, as representing the whole nation, still claimed a supremacy over clergy and laity alike[1]. The struggle between Henry II and Becket, and the Constitutions of Clarendon, bear witness to this[2]. And this claim was distinctly made as a religious claim in the name of God. When Henry II in the question of

---

[1] It is, indeed, probable that William felt himself better able to manage the clerical estate as a separate body through a Norman archbishop introduced by himself than as forming part of the general community. See Stubbs' Constitutional History, i. pp. 304-7.

[2] The Constitutions of Clarendon (1164) give the king a very large power over the clerical estate. In particular they prescribe that elections to all the greater ecclesiastical offices shall be held in the king's chapel by those whom he summons, and with his consent. The course of ecclesiastical appeals is prescribed just as in the Reformation statutes, except that the final decision is to be made by the king's decree in the archbishop's court: 'Praecepto regis in curiâ archiepiscopi controversia terminetur, ita quod non debet ulterius procedere (i. e. to Rome) absque assensu Domini Regis.'

Battle Abbey[1] was opposed by the Bishop of Chichester, he made use of these remarkable words, which sound as an anticipation of the Reformation : 'Tu pro papae auctoritate ab hominibus concessâ contra dignitatum regalium auctoritates mihi a Deo concessas calliditate argutâ niti praecogitas.' This claim was not consistently maintained, especially in the fifteenth century, when Henry IV and his successors, to gain the support of the clergy to their doubtful title, and through fear of Lollardism as a political power, yielded something of the authority entrusted to them on behalf of the nation. Yet even then the statutes of Praemunire and of Provisors put some check upon both the foreign and the domestic clericalism. But at the Reformation the ancient kingly power was reasserted, and was more distinctly than in previous times felt to represent the will of the nation, which now moved in its regained unity under King and Parliament together.

It is sometimes said that in Germany the Reformation was religious, in England political. This is, like all epigrams, exaggerated : for the German Reformation owed much to the national spirit rising up against the foreign domination of the Pope[2]; and in England the spiritual conviction wrought by the reading of the Scriptures and the teaching of men like Bilney and William Tyndale, was the real underlying power, without which King and Parliament would have acted

---

[1] A.D. 1157. An account of this may be read in Pearson's 'Early and Middle Ages of England,' pp. 351-2. See the scene fully described in Spelman and Wilkins, i. 431. They quote from MS. Chron. Abb. de Bell., pp. 91.

[2] See Luther's Address to the German nobility in Wace and Buchheim's English edition of Luther's Primary Works. (Murray, 1883.)

in vain if at all. Nevertheless the political aspect of the English Reformation is that which most strikes us; and it is this which most needs to be set forth in a clear spiritual light. Nor is the task difficult to those who believe in the Divine character of political rule, and in the unity of the sacred and the secular in the Christian nation.

There are some persons to whom the word Political conveys a bad and worldly sense. It is connected in their minds with selfish scheming. So far as the Reformation movement in England was tainted with such a spirit, it was, no doubt, debased. But from no great movement which has ever taken place, not from the career of Constantine, of Charlemagne, or of Hildebrand, not from the English or the American Revolution, not from the great struggle for the suppression of slavery, has this evil spirit been wholly absent. And this remark must be impartially applied to all church movements. Few of the actors in them have been wholly free from ambition or self-seeking. It must be the task of Christians to detach from politics this selfish taint, first in idea, then in fact. We must maintain that just laws, just policy, just relations among men, are amongst the most sacred of all things. The political life is, no doubt, a neutral term, and must take its character partly from the motives of the agent, partly from the nature of the πολιτεία to which it is applied. But when this πολιτεία is a great Christian community, then every measure which relates to it affects directly the kingdom of God; and we must credit its rulers with a sense of responsibility as office-bearers in the church. Such a community is the body of Christ, and its internal relations expressed in its laws are the means by which its master-builders provide for its edification. What is political then becomes most properly Christian, and the statesman is a minister of Christ.

And this was the view of things on which the English Reformation proceeded. The more thoughtful men throughout the nation awoke to the consciousness that the Papal power had disorganized the Christian community. The clerical system of Canon Law had become corrupt and oppressive. The Papal influence was a perpetual source of disturbance and division. And when the nation rose up under its King to put an end to Papal usurpations, and to reassert the ancient authority of the Crown, that is of the nation, over its own ecclesiastical affairs, when the King was substituted for the Pope, and English law and administration for the Papal decrees and judicature, this was a great step towards the substitution of Christian righteousness for unrighteousness. It was the counterpart, in public affairs, of the assertion of the need and power of faith in the individual soul: for that bade the individual no longer depend on the hierarchy, but look up to the Eternal justice for pardon; this was an act of national faith, the assertion that, in the ruling of the church and realm, the nation need not depend on an exotic system emanating from the Bishop of Rome, but had the right and duty of acting freely in the presence of the Divine rectitude.

Take the first great national act, which preluded

the English Reformation, and drew all the rest in its train, the abolition of appeals to Rome. No doubt, the special case over which the battle was fought, the King's divorce, was one of more than doubtful justice; but a good cause does not necessarily suffer from the special case in which its principle is asserted, as may be seen in the conflict against general warrants in our later political history, which turned upon the legality of the arrest of Wilkes for his infamous publications. And it would be difficult to say that Henry and his advisers were not sincere in the belief that the failure of heirs to the throne was a witness that the marriage with Catherine was invalid, and ought to be dissolved. But, further, it was perfectly well known that the reasons why the divorce was not granted were not that it was wrong or immoral, or contrary to precedent or law, but that the Pope was seeking some advantage for himself, and that he was afraid of the Emperor. The Universities were favourable to the King's cause; and that which was needed was a just tribunal. Hence the First Act of Appeals (24 Henry VIII, c. 12), which asserts that all such causes shall be decided within the realm, and that the English spiritualty are fully competent to deal with them, expressed the conscientious conviction of clergy and laity combined. It required that causes relating to tithes, matrimony, and wills, all affecting seriously the social relations of men, should no longer be subject to the jurisdiction of the Pope, but to that of the King. The appeal was to be only to the ecclesiastical courts of the archbishops in England, by whom it was to be finally determined. The Preamble to the

Act vindicates the competence and rectitude of the English as contrasted with the Papal judges.

The further steps were taken in the same interest, that of the introduction of simple justice in the place of ecclesiastical fictions, and of national unity in the place of a divided rule. The unjust power of the Pope was gone as to matrimony, wills, and tithes; it must go also as to all other matters. In the next year, therefore (1534), the Second Act of Appeals (25 Henry VIII, c. 19) subjected all ecclesiastical causes of all kinds to the process prescribed by the first Act[1]. That Act, however, would have left each metropolitan as the final recipient of appeals in his own province. Contradictory judgments might have been pronounced, and the supreme authority, though not foreign, might still have been anti-national. An appeal, therefore, was given in all causes to the King, from whose Court of Chancery Delegates were to be appointed in each case to determine the cause. But, again, it would be useless to abolish appeals to the Pope if the papal decrees could still be accepted as laws. The Canon Law, therefore, was subjected to revision by a Commission composed equally of clergy and laity, in order to determine what parts of it might be retained as consonant to English law; and, though the Commission led to nothing, it has ever since been a maxim that the Canon Law is only admissible in England so far as it is consonant with the laws or

---

[1] 'The words are (§ 3), 'That all manner of appeals, of what nature or condition soever they be of, or what cause or matter soever they concern, shall be made and had,' as in the Act of the previous year.

recognized usages of the nation. Thus at one blow fell the vast superstructure of Papal domination, which had been so largely tinctured by forgery, by usurpation, by corruption, and had distracted the consciences of men. The ecclesiastical courts were to be henceforward the courts of the King, that is, of the nation; the ecclesiastical law was to be the King's, that is, the nation's, ecclesiastical law.

But, further, if the English clergy might frame fresh laws apart from the nation, the whole evil system, or one equally unjust and anti-national, might grow up again. The Submission[1] of the clergy made in the Convocation two years before was therefore incorporated into the law which restored the just balance of powers in the Christian commonwealth. The clergy were no longer to have an independent power of making ecclesiastical laws. They were to be ministers, not lords, of the church. It was enacted that the Convocations of the clergy should only proceed to business when a licence was given them to do so, that they should only discuss such subjects as were specified in the licence, and that their decrees should be subject to the King's consent. By a subsequent Act[2] the King was declared

[1] The Submission of the clergy was made on May 15, 1532. The First Act of Appeals passed on April 10, 1533; the Second Act of Appeals March 28, 1834. See Stubbs' Hist. Appendix to the Report of the Commission on Ecclesiastical Courts, pp. 32-34.

[2] 26 Henry VIII, c. 1. The Act purports to be declaratory and corroborative of a power well known and acknowledged. The King is to be 'reputed the only Supreme Head on earth of the Church of England, called Ecclesia Anglicana,' and 'shall have full power and authority to visit, repress, redress, reform, order, correct, restrain, and amend all such errors, heresies, abuses, contempts, and enormities, whatsoever they be, which by any manner of spiritual authority or jurisdiction ought or may lawfully be reformed ... any usage, custom ... or any other thing or things to the contrary notwithstanding.'

Supreme Head of the Church of England, and not only was all power of whatever kind which had before been exercised by the Pope assigned to him, but all the clerical system in all its parts placed under his control.

It cannot be denied that the process of committing all power over the ecclesiastical estate to the personal discretion of the Sovereign went to an excessive length, and that it was afterwards abused[1]. The King was empowered not only to repress all kinds of heresies and enormities, but to declare what was to be accounted as heresy. In these enactments lay the germ afterwards developed into the Courts of High Commission. Such powers are only defensible on the ground on which a dictatorship is found necessary in times of danger. But the constitutional principle of the King's supremacy is one of vital importance in view of the unity of human life and of the commonwealth which we are vindicating. The King represented the whole church. He was the head of the whole

[1] See the Commissions for the exercise of the episcopal office given by Henry to Bonner, and by Edward to Cranmer. Burnet's 'Reformation Records,' Pt. i. B. 3, No. 14, and 'Records,' Pt. ii. B. 1, No. 2. They assume that all episcopal jurisdiction, including the power of ordination, resides in the Sovereign, and is committed by him to the bishops. Bonner's Commission assumes, further, that the King had committed the power of ordination, together with the rest of his ecclesiastical power, to Cromwell, and that it is only because of the Vicegerent's numerous occupations that the power of ordination is transmitted to the bishop. Cranmer's Commission assumes that the power may be revoked, and should from time to time be restored to the King, and regranted at his pleasure. These assumptions as to the exercise of the supreme power are instances of the temporary dictatorship. But that all jurisdiction of all kinds emanates from the Sovereign was acknowledged very generally. It is admitted by a writer so anxious to rehabilitate the credit of the English clergy during their struggle to retain power as Mr. Dixon. See 'History of Church of England,' from the abolition of the Roman jurisdiction, by R. W. Dixon, M.A., (Smith, Elder, and Co., 1878,) i. 56–9.

community, not of one section of it. The principle of the Royal Supremacy means that the Christian community as a whole, represented by its Sovereign, is to be supreme over all its parts. It implies that the clergy are not to be regarded as a separate class having an independent power over the church, but as the ministers of one important church-function, which is to be exercised in harmony with the rest, and subject to the will of the whole community. It recognises that the will of Christ resides, not in the ministers of public worship acting separately, but in the whole brotherhood, to which alone we can apply the words, 'His body, the fulness of Him who filleth all in all.' And this is consonant with the most ancient opinion and usage of the church: for apostolical and evangelical precedent, as shown in such words as 'Tell it unto the church[1],' or by St. Paul's conduct in the case of the incestuous man at Corinth, is in favour of admitting the whole body to a voice in ruling and in judgment[2].

We must add one thing more as involved in this assertion of the Royal Supremacy, the ultimate supremacy of the lay over the clerical element within the church, whenever the two came into collision; and especially of the lay interests, those of just government, over the clerical interests, those which circle round the function of public worship. The English sovereigns have never taken holy orders, nor assumed to ordain or to administer the Sacraments in their own persons. Yet they are heads or supreme rulers in the church; and they are this in their lay capacity. In

[1] Matt. xviii. 17.　　　[2] 1 Cor. v. 4, 13; 2 Cor. ii. 6, 7, 10.

the Act 37 Hen. VIII, c. 17, which provides that laymen may be judges in ecclesiastical courts, it is expressly stated that this is consonant with the general constitution, 'seeing that the King is a layman [1].' This implies a recognition of the fact that the secular life, the business of the great mass of Christian men and women, is that which is the supreme function of the Church. The ministry of public worship exists for the sake of human duties, that these may be fulfilled in the spirit of Christ, not these duties for the sake of public worship. The Church, though bound together by common prayer and the sacraments, exists for the higher purpose, expressed in one of the noblest of our prayers [2], 'That every member of the same, in his vocation and ministry, may truly and godly serve the Lord.'

We may sum up the Reformation settlement, then, in these terms. The whole body of citizens, which was called by one collective term, 'This Church and Realm' (a single word followed by a verb in the singular number [3]), moved together under its sovereign ruler. All its acts were those of one great Christian commonwealth or church [4]. This great community resolved

[1] End of § 1.
[2] Second Collect for Good Friday.
[3] See, as an instance, the third question in the Service for the Ordination of Priests: 'Will you minister the Doctrine, etc., of Christ, as this Church and Realm hath received the same?'
[4] In the celebrated discussion between Roman and Protestant divines in Westminster Abbey in the year 1558, attended by the whole Parliament and presided over by the Lord Keeper, the Reformed Divines, among whom were Scory, Cox, Horne, Grindal, Guest, and Jewel, undertook to defend as their second thesis, 'That every particular Church has authority to institute, change, and set aside rites and ceremonies.' They begin by defining the meaning of 'Church.' 'And, first, by

VI.]   *Christian Nationalism.*   249

to manage its own affairs in all respects independently of the Pope, and of the clerical system of the Middle Ages. Its faith was not bound to the Roman church system, but was a faith in God, in truth, and in righteousness. And, further, within its own borders it was determined that the ministers of public worship should not separate themselves from the rest of the community, but should be, in matters relating to public worship and teaching, as in other matters, subject to the Sovereign power of the realm or church, owning that the part exists for the sake of the whole, that the function of public worship is designed to minister, and is subordinate, to the general life.

It was this settlement which involved the reform of public worship and the standards of Christian teaching. Into that I do not enter here, wishing to redress the balance which has been displaced by the tendency commonly shown to regard the changes in public worship and teaching as in themselves constituting the Reformation. This reform of the standards of doctrine and of worship must be for us, however important, only one amongst many salutary instances in which the growing demand among the people for reality and simplicity in the conduct of life found its expression in the Acts of the Sovereign and the Parliament.

The settlement, which I have described, was approved by all the progressive spirits of the day. It was approved by Henry, who, with all his faults, was a thoughtful and far-seeing statesman, laborious, deeply

every particular Church they mean every kingdom, province, or country, which is formed into a distinct society.' Collier's 'Ecclesiastical History,' vi. 207.

sensible of the demands of the national conviction and of the important issues involved in the Reformation. It was approved by Thomas Cromwell, who undertook as the King's Vicar-general the conduct of the Reformation, and who presided in the Convocation. It was approved by Cranmer and his colleagues, who marked their sense of the supremacy of the Crown by accepting from Edward VI new commissions for the exercise of their office[1]. But it was not official men alone who approved it. The principle of the Royal Supremacy was forced upon the most thoughtful men of the sixteenth century. It was approved not only in the next generation by Hooker, whose theory might have been an afterthought upon an established order of things, but in the early dawn of the great movement by Tyndale, the Translator of the New Testament, the most courageous and the most independent of the workers and martyrs of the English Reformation[2].

Tyndale formed his opinions almost alone. He was influenced probably, in his early manhood at Oxford, by Colet. But Colet had no thought of the great changes that were at hand; Tyndale distinctly foresaw and aimed at them. He was probably thirty-seven years old when Luther's first protest rang through Europe, and was then tutor to a family in Gloucestershire. But he formed the purpose even then of translating the Scriptures into English: and within nine years, amidst many difficulties, he executed the task so

---

[1] See p. 246, note.
[2] See 'Life of Tyndale,' by Rev. F. Demaus, a work of considerable critical merit, published by the Religious Tract Society.

VI.]   *Christian Nationalism.*   251

simply and in a manner so well adapted to the English
people that subsequent revisers have done no more than
correct in details his admirable version. He found every
one averse to his project. The Bishop of London (Tunstal)
refused to aid him, and afterwards tried to destroy his
work. He was driven from England, and even from
Cologne, and had to publish his translation at Worms.
Even when he was well known, and maintained a controversy with More on at least equal terms, he lived as
a fugitive at Antwerp, in constant danger, till, by the
machinations of his adversaries, he was arrested, tried,
and put to death by burning [1]. Such a man, suffering
under the disfavour of the King, and protesting, as he
did, against the Divorce, could have no undue bias in
favour of the Royal Prerogative. Yet in his works are
scattered the germs of all that is meant by the King's
Supremacy. In his book against More[2] he points out
the evil of the existing state of religion in that the lay
life, the life of commerce and of government, had been
neglected and esteemed vile or unclean, while all that
had been counted as religious was the building of vast
churches, chantries, and monasteries, and the performance of deeds which in derision he called Pope-holy
works. In his book entitled 'The Obedience of a
Christian Man [3],' Tyndale points out how the clergy, by

[1] Tyndale was born about 1480. His translation of the New Testament appeared in 1526. He suffered in 1536, his last words being, 'Lord, open the eyes
of the King of England.' In 1537, the English Bible, mainly from his translation,
was placed by the King's order in the churches. How much of the Old Testament
beyond the Pentateuch, which is wholly his, was translated by him is uncertain.
[2] Parker Society's edition. See especially the remarkable and witty reply to
More's jest about Tenderden Steeple and Goodwin Sands, at pp. 77, 78.
[3] Published about 1528.

maintaining a jurisdiction of their own, and by establishing sanctuaries and immunities for all who, by saying a verse of Scripture in Latin, could claim the benefit of clergy, had brought corruption and lawlessness into the state; and he calls upon all princes to remedy these abuses [1]. The lay law of the realm he identifies with the law of God; the lay power he takes as God's special ordinance. 'See,' he says of the clergy, 'how they divide and separate themselves. If the layman be of the world, so is he not of God. If he believes in Christ, then is he co-heir with Christ, and hath the Spirit in earnest, and is also spiritual' (that is one of the spiritualty). 'The King,' he adds, 'is in the room of God; and his law is God's law, and nothing but the law of nature and natural equity, which God graved in the heart of man [2].' Even in matters of religious knowledge, the special province of the clergy, he would have laymen associated with them. 'If any question arise about the truth of the Scriptures, then let them judge by the manifest and open Scriptures, not excluding the laymen, for there are many found among the laymen which are as wise as the officers [3].' 'This is a book,' said Henry, when a copy belonging to Anne Boleyn was brought to him by Wolsey for censure, 'for me and all Kings to read [4]:' and we cannot doubt that the thoughts contained in it contributed largely to frame the King's policy.

---

[1] Tyndale's 'Doctrinal Treatises' (Parker Soc. ed.), p. 180.
[2] Obedience. 'Doctrinal Treatises,' p. 240.
[3] Id. 240, 241.
[4] See the curious and instructive story in Demaus' 'Life of Tyndale,' 212-15, taken from Strype's 'Eccl. Mem.' i. 172.

Yes, the English Reformation was political. This was the true polity which underlay it, the right and just relation of the various powers within the Christian commonwealth towards one other. If any proof were needed that it was a serious work, and that the Royal Supremacy was a religious principle, in the assertion of which earnest men were obeying the Divine Spirit, it would be found in the fact that the political changes, equally with those relating to doctrine and worship, were advocated by the holy zeal of Tyndale and sealed with his blood. The ideal of the saint and martyr was one with that of the politician.

The system which we have thus described, the supremacy of the nation over the organization for public worship and its functionaries, must be examined somewhat more closely and critically. The organization for public worship, it will be seen, is treated under this system, not as forming a separate community inserted into the larger secular community, and enjoying a divine sanction which the larger community does not possess, but as fulfilling one function of the great community which itself, and as a whole, possesses this divine sanction. There has always been a tendency, chiefly, I venture to think, springing from want of clearness and boldness of thought, to mistrust this view, which attributes the sanctity of the Church, or Body of Christ, to the whole community. The clergy especially, most of all when left, as they frequently are, outside the main current of the popular life, are inclined to this mistrust. They look upon the organization which they conduct as so sacred that it must stand alone and self-governed in the midst of human society. In the Roman communion this has been most fully the case; and it has resulted in varying relations between the organization over which the clergy preside and the general community; sometimes in Concordats between them, sometimes in the repression of the common life under the dominion of the priest, sometimes in open hostility, rebellion or counter-tyranny on the part of the representatives of the general community, especially on the part of the male sex. In our own country this contradiction has been less acutely felt owing to the clear assertion of unity at the Reformation; and the clergy have for the most part acquiesced in the established system, partly from conviction, partly from feeling that under this system they at least 'enjoyed much quietness,' and a liberty in the exercise of their calling which possibly they might not under any other. But at various times, notably in the time of Laud, and again in our own day, there has been a tendency to the assertion of clerical powers incompatible with the Reformation settlement. In the time of Laud the system was, as it were, turned round. The governing power of the nation, which should have exercised control over the clergy, was made to work their will as a power separate from the nation. The government became clericalist. In later times the acquiescent tone has predominated, until the clericalist movement begun in Oxford fifty years ago: but this revival of clericalist claims is now again before the world, and its demands must be discussed with all fairness. The Societies also, whether of the Presbyterian, Independent, or the Wesleyan type, which are sometimes spoken of as separate churches, but are really societies for worship, teaching, and beneficence operating within the general Christian community or church, have often, through the injustice to which they have been subjected, and which still endures though only in its social form, been inclined to charge their wrongs upon the system of Christian nationalism and to demand its destruction. Thus from different sides, and with different objects, the demand for a separation of the organization for worship from the general life has arisen; some of those who make the demand aiming at a clerical supremacy in all matters termed religious with the support of the general government, some at a complete severance, which is often supposed to be a system of freedom, but which would, at least in a vast Episcopalian community, almost certainly result in the dominion of the clergy. It is necessary, therefore, to consider whether the union of the system of public worship with the general government is so grounded in truth and in Christian principle as to have the promise of vitality.

It is said that, for the sake of the purity of religion, the system of public worship must be held apart from the general life. But experience shows that there is great spiritual danger in such a separation. A society which is mainly clerical, and which is occupied almost exclusively with those parts of life which belong especially to the clergy, is almost sure to be petty and unjust. And it becomes so, just because it is cut off from the common life of men, the sphere in which justice and civilization have free play. But, further, religion is in its own nature most sociable. It cannot abide in a state of seclusion. It languishes and dies if it has not free vent. Its only healthy existence is that of a permeating spirit which appropriates and quickens all that it touches. The whole life of man is essentially religious; and politics, the sphere of just relations between men, especially become religious when conducted in a Christian spirit. Nothing can be more fatal to mankind or to religion itself than to call one set of things or persons religious and another secular, when Christ has redeemed the whole. It is especially erroneous to suppose that the clergy alone represent religion. They have their special function, which, rightly exercised, should be the highest of all. But others have also their vocation and ministry. Every calling which is so exercised as to become a service to God and a spiritual benefit to man is a sacred ministry, and he who works in it is a minister of Christ. To attempt, therefore, to treat clergymen and pastors as the sole ministers of religion is to take the heart out of the Christian community. Such a tendency is sometimes spoken of as that which exalts the church. In reality what it does is to exalt the clergy, at least in appearance, beyond their just measure; but the church it enfeebles and destroys.

It is, further, assumed that the clergy, or the worshipping body taken by itself, bear witness in their isolation for the liberty of conscience. The great Popes and Archbishops of the Middle Ages, it is said, were the only men who resisted kings and emperors, and who asserted a spiritual power in opposition to the selfish and worldly power then ruling in secular affairs; and, it is implied, this selfish and worldly spirit will always remain dominant in secular affairs, while the succession of these great clerical potentates, and of their protest for liberty of conscience, falls now to synods and church-assemblies: these are needed in modern times, it is supposed, to resist the tyrannical materialism of secular government, and to maintain spiritual freedom. But it may well be doubted whether the clerical power was ever the sincere advocate of liberty of conscience. What the great Popes of the Middle Ages aimed at was not liberty of conscience for the worshippers, but a vast imperial dominion for themselves and the clergy, a dominion having very little that was religious in it, but using religion as the instrument of its power. Even if we concede that there was something favourable to liberty in the claims of clerical independence in the Middle Ages, such claims have almost ceased to have any spiritual value since the laity awoke to a sense of responsibility at the Reformation. They have served for the most part, whether abroad or in Great Britain, in Roman Catholic or in Protestant countries, merely to consolidate and enforce the existing system; their advocates have contended zealously for their own rights. In doing this they have sometimes incidentally served the cause of freedom. But it would be difficult to point out at Trent or at Dort, at Westminster or at Edinburgh, an occasion in which they had sincerely asserted individual or general liberty.

That which seems to be aimed at in all the assertions

of the need of ecclesiastical separation is that there is a sphere in which law and government have no right to interfere, but in which individual men, or companies of men freely associated, must think and act for themselves. There are many departments of human life in which this is the case; and religious conviction, though a pre-eminent, is by no means the only instance. But let it be asked, as to any of these spheres, from which of the two powers, from the clergy or the general government, has the chief danger to liberty arisen? The answer must in almost all cases be, From the clerical side. In the Middle Ages the Albigenses and the Waldenses were slaughtered by lay swords, but under clerical incitement. So it was with the persecution of the Lollards and of the Hussites, with the massacre of St. Bartholomew, with the expulsion of the English Puritan ministers in 1662, and of the French Protestants in 1687. It has been in the repression, not in the exaltation, of the clerical and ecclesiastical power, that the best hope of liberty has lain. If we take the analogy of other departments of life, in which there should be immunity from minute police regulations, the answer becomes plainer still. The family life, literature, science, art, trade, are instances of this. Political experience has shown that it would be very wrong that the government should interfere in the conduct of family life as was attempted in some of the Greek Republics, where the time of marriage, the number of children, even the meals which the citizens should take in common, were prescribed by law. But in modern times it is the clerical, not the lay power from which there has been the danger of interference with the sacred freedom of family relations. It would, again, be monstrous for the government to prescribe what books should be written or read. The censorship and the prosecution of authors for anything but libel and a few marked offences against the community have disappeared. It is the clerical power at Rome, and the governments influenced by it, which have, in modern times, presented the most flagrant instances of such attaints upon freedom. It would be wrong, again, for the government to interfere with the pursuit of knowledge, to forbid enquiry, to encourage some and discourage others of the fields of human thought; and the same thing may be said as to art. But if the history of these departments of life be examined in such a record as that of the History of Rationalism [1], it will be seen that the false notions with which clericalism had overlaid them have almost always been the retarding element in their development. And, as regards trade, while governments have often, through a mistaken notion of advantage to the community, or to particular classes within it, fettered commercial intercourse, it is the clerical influence which for ages made the larger operations of commerce impossible by declaring that the taking of interest was by the law of God forbidden.

It is a discovery of political science that with all these departments of life the central government should interfere as little as possible. Does that mean

[1] 'History of the Rise and Influence of the Spirit of Rationalism in Europe.' By W. E. H. Lecky, M.A. Longmans.

that it should not assert its supremacy over them, and should refrain from making laws for them? By no means. Its true function in these departments of life is to guarantee their free and beneficial development, to establish general laws in accordance with their recognised requirements, to intervene when their machinery has got out of gear, or when new conditions arise, and to present an impartial tribunal for the settlement of disputes. No one thinks it necessary that each of these departments should have a separate organization endowed with indefeasible rights. They are none the less free because the central government assures their just internal relations and their free development. Precisely the same may be said of the organization for public worship. The central government has at times, no doubt, interfered with it unduly. But what it ought to do, and has for the most part done, is to guarantee its harmonious exercise according to the convictions of those for whom it exists. And this it has for the most part done in England with general approval, in contradistinction to the usurped authority of the Pope over the nation, and also to the no less usurped authority of the clergy over the laity.

If it be asked whether there must not be a special system of law for clerical discipline, the answer is, that the analogy may be followed of professions like the army and navy, or of special systems of law such as those by which Admiralty suits are decided; and that, as in those cases, it is well to have the advice of experts. But, since clerical discipline is a much less simple matter than that of the army or the navy, and affects the general welfare much more widely, it is right that the ultimate appeal should be to a tribunal representing the nation. If it be asked how the laws which govern the organization for public worship should be framed, the answer is that the constitutional course is that such legislation should be prepared by a Royal Commission, on which lawyers and other laymen as well as clergymen should serve, but that the laws themselves should be passed, as Hooker says, by the national organs alone [1]; and for this, though the advice of the clergy may rightly be asked, as the advice of the college of physicians for a medical Act, yet their consent is not indispensable. If it be asked, further, how the details of ritual and of parochial organization should be decided, the answer is that in the original settlement such matters were partly laid down by the central acts of uniformity, that a strong visitorial power was held to reside in the Bishops, as is shewn in the visitation of Ridley in London in 1550[2], which has gradually been extinguished; and that all things not settled by these means were left to the discretion of the individual clergyman; but that the analogy of other departments would point out as the true policy the gradual relaxation of uniformity, and the relegation of such matters to local discretion, and the calling forth of lay interest and lay power in the localities.

[1] See Note XIX.
[2] 'Injunctions given in the visitation of the reverend father in God, Nicholas, bishop of London, for an uniformity in his Diocese of London, in the fourth year of our Sovereign Lord King Edward the VIth, A.D. 1550,' in Cardwell's 'Documentary Annals of the Reformed Church of England,' i. 81.

If, further, a question be raised as to the legitimacy of the Royal Supremacy from the fact that, through the progress of the national development, it is no longer the Sovereign who is supreme, but the Prime Minister and the Parliament, the answer is that the laws of the Reformation era were themselves framed by Parliament, and that Parliament then represented a nation in which far less unity of sentiment prevailed in such matters as were then dealt with than in the England of our own day; that the Sovereign had power as representing the nation, and that the Prime Minister and the Parliament of our day represent the nation more fully; and that it accords better with the genius of Christianity that these matters should be determined by the great Christian brotherhood as a whole through its representatives than by the individual Sovereign. And if, further, it be objected that neither the electors nor the elected are all of them Christians, much less all of them worshippers according to the Act of Uniformity, the answer is that in all such matters we must take the general sense of the community, not looking minutely at exceptions, and that experience shews that the more the community is trusted as a Christian body, the more it will prove itself capable of acting unitedly as such, and will grow into its full capacities as a branch of the Christian Church.

We must race, by reviewing the salient facts of English history during the last three centuries and a half, how far this ideal of the national supremacy and Christian unity has been preserved, how far abandoned or ignored.

In the time of Henry himself the system was fully maintained. It was furthered by the masterful spirit of the King, though at times marred by his violence. But the redeeming feature of Henry's rule, as afterwards of Edward's and Elizabeth's, was that on the whole it was in harmony with the general conviction of the nation. His changes of mood and action reflected for the most part those of the people. Acts like the abolition of the Papal Jurisdiction, the Suppression of the Monasteries, the Laws of Appeals, and the placing of the Bible in the churches, were acts of the Church, however they may have been regarded by the clergy. If the Act of the Six Articles represents one of those reactionary impulses to which the English nation has always been liable, on the other hand, the feelings of the nation were consulted when, in the end of Henry's reign, the services were translated and a beginning was made of an English Liturgy. The Litany remains to us in the form in which he himself, with Cranmer's assistance, cast it, a monument of the combined political and religious movement. In it the king and the clergy, the lords of the council, the magistrates, and all orders and degrees of men stand side by side as the object of our prayers, constituting in their unity a branch of the Catholic Church; and the national well-being and political justice are recognised as amongst the primary objects for which the Church exists.

In the reign of Edward the problem of the national and ecclesiastical unity was simplified by the fact that the convictions of the young monarch were in accordance with those of the ecclesiastical leaders, and that the bishops were in harmony with the reforming movement which had now become popular. There were indeed two dangers, the one that through the covetousness and indolence of statesmen the reformation movement might be turned into a channel of mere destructiveness, the other that the ecclesiastical influences about the young King might lay the foundation of a new clericalism. Both were on the whole avoided. The secularization of ecclesiastical estates, so far as it had gone, was ratified; but the wastefulness and violence of men like Admiral Seymour was checked, and Northumberland's misrule, had Edward lived, would have been soon suppressed. The Articles of Religion were sanctioned as a general statement of the beliefs on which the English Reformation had proceeded, reflecting its moderation, not to say its compromises and its hesitancies; the Second Prayerbook also was accepted, though with evident reluctance, and a clear indication of unwillingness to enact changes of the system of worship beyond what was absolutely required[1]. But the book of reformed ecclesiastical

---

[1] See the words of the Preamble of the Act, 6 Edw. VI, c. 1: 'Where there hath been a very godly order set forth by the Authority of Parliament for Common Prayer, &c. ... within this Church of England, agreeable to the Word of God and the primitive church, very comfortable to all good people.... And whereas there hath risen in the use and exercise of the aforesaid Common Service in the Church, heretofore set forth, divers doubts for the fashion and manner of the administrations of the same, rather by the curiosity of the minister and mistakers than of any other worthy cause, therefore as well for the more plain and manifest explanation thereof as for the more perfection of the said order or Common Service, in some places where it is necessary to make the same prayer and fashion of service more earnest and fit to stir Christian people to the true honouring of Almighty God; be it enacted,' &c.

laws, which would have imposed abstract theological statements and minute and puerile directions upon the country as laws, and would have restored a clerical tribunal for ecclesiastical appeals, was put aside as savouring too much of clericalism[1].

We may pass over the reign of Mary as one of mere reaction and confusion, which yet was of service as a testing time. Unhappily, there is a tendency, after revolutionary proceedings like those of Mary's reign, to rebuild too hastily all that has existed before.

But the long and glorious reign of Elizabeth was one in which the value residing in the united action of the whole Commonwealth for furthering its healthy development was fully tested and confirmed. The Queen had, indeed, far too little faith in liberty, and watched with jealousy instead of sympathy the growth of Protestant conviction, which in the next generation carried all before it. But the toleration which she exercised was great and many-sided. The fault of her administration lay in her determination to keep ecclesiastical affairs under her personal control, instead of allowing the system to be freely moulded by the

---

[1] The final draught of the Reformatio Legum was made by Cranmer and Peter Martyr, their six colleagues lending apparently but little assistance. The first section repeats in several parts the doctrinal statements of the Thirty-Nine Articles, sometimes, as in those about Predestination, making them more stringent. As an instance of the unreal character of these proposed laws, we may take the section on Idolatry, in which 'Pestiferæ artes' are condemned and 'Gravissimæ pœnæ' are denounced against them, but without any specification of the penalty; or the section on Marriage, in which is a proposed law headed, 'Ut matres propriis uberibus infantes alant.' The proposal as to appeals to the Crown is that they should be decided, in extreme cases, by the provincial Synod, that is, the Convocation; otherwise by three or four bishops appointed for the particular suit by the Crown. It is evident these proposals were unfit to pass into law.

convictions of the people expressed through the Parliament. She introduced a personal rule in ecclesiastical affairs, which, in the hands of her feebler successors, who did not know when to give way, led to the great convulsion of the succeeding century. Yet she finally yielded, with however bad a grace, when Parliament showed its determination to deal with questions of worship or of doctrine, as in the passing of the Act which required the signature of the clergy to the Protestant Articles of Religion [1]. In the whole of the complications, political and religious, which culminated in the deliverance from the Armada, the Queen and the nation were at one. No nobler or more truly English statesmen ever lived than those whom she chiefly trusted, Burleigh, Walsingham, and Sir Philip Sidney. And the best proof of the security of the people under her rule, of the repose and satisfaction of the national heart, is to be found in the free and bright spirit of culture, which makes us look back to 'the spacious times of great Elizabeth' as the springtime of English literature.

The great work of Hooker, written towards the close of Elizabeth's reign, the theory of which has been sometimes regarded as a speculation, is really a true representation of the facts as they then existed, and a just inference from them. He grounds the principles of government, not on any infallible Biblical or ecclesiastical statements, but on universal justice; and he draws the inference from them that no form of ecclesiastical organization is of necessary and divine

[1] 13 Eliz. c. 12. An Act for Ministers of the Church to be of sound religion.

authority[1]. His conviction of the unity of the nation, expressed in the famous sentence that the same persons constitute the Church and also the Commonwealth [2], must be understood in a general sense, which would make it equally applicable in our own day, since he was writing of a time in which Roman Catholics sat in the Upper House of Parliament, and the Puritans were a growing element in the Lower. His statement, thus taken, holds good throughout our modern history, as does also his inference that the national organs alone can justly frame laws for the Church-system. Yet the result of his work was not in accordance with his principles. He was succeeded by an era in which everything was done by those in power that was most contrary to his contention, one in which the Episcopal form of Church government was held to have divine sanction, in which the making of ecclesiastical laws was violently taken out of the hands of the national organs and placed in the hands of the clergy alone. And the reason for this is obvious. The keen point of Hooker's argument is turned exclusively against the Puritans. He has not a word to say against the arbitrary power exercised by the Crown in ecclesiastical matters, nor against the oppressive

---

[1] Eccl. Pol. III. xi. 7 : 'I therefore conclude that, neither God's being author of laws for government of His Church, nor His committing them unto Scripture, is any reason sufficient wherefore all churches should for ever be bound to keep them without change.' xi. 16 : ' Unto the complete form of church polity much may be requisite which the Scripture teacheth not, and much which it hath taught become unrequisite, sometime because we need not use it, sometime also because we cannot.' He goes on to say that the reformed churches of Scotland and France have not that government by bishops which he considers most scriptural, but that this is not by their own fault, and that they are right in accepting 'that which the necessity of the present has cast upon them.'   [2] B. viii. i. 2.

character, then already making itself felt, of the Courts of High Commission, nor of the growing assumptions of clerical power as existing by divine appointment[1]. These things, which caused such disasters a few years after his death, were as completely contrary to his principles as was the assumption of the Puritans; yet he fails to notice them. Every part of the Prayer Book, even those which were afterwards altered, some even in the decade following his death, is equally supported by his stately periods[2]. Even abuses in the Church system, such as pluralities, are defended[3]. The mistake of the Genevan system in imposing on the Church an order of ruling elders is exposed[4]; but there is not, in substitution for this, a frank recognition of the Christian ruler as a Church officer and a minister of God, responsible for the administration of a branch of Christ's

[1] The extreme doctrine of the divine and exclusive sanction of episcopacy appears to have been first broached in a sermon by Bancroft at St. Paul's in 1588. The sensation caused by this was considerable: but there is no consciousness in Hooker's great work of any danger from this exaggeration.

[2] For instance, B. v. ch. xliii. is on the objection made by the Puritans to the lack of special forms of thanksgiving in the Prayer Book. Hooker defends this omission vigorously; but the Hampton Court Conference, though it treated the Puritans harshly, saw that the objection was valid, and the forms of thanksgiving were added. This was only some seven or eight years after Hooker wrote.

[3] B. v. ch. lxxxi. 6, 7. The defence of pluralities is abstractedly reasonable; but when we read the list of Laud's and Williams' promotions in 1611 in Perry's 'History of the Church of England' (i. 196), (Laud held, apparently all at one time, three parishes, two prebends, an archdeaconry, and a deanery, and Williams had as many or more), we see that Hooker is blinding himself and his readers to a vast abuse.

[4] Eccl. Pol. B. vi. It appears from the notes of Hooker's pupil, Cranmer, that this was almost the central part of the work as Hooker wrote it; but in book vi, as it has come down to us, topics such as the power of the keys and repentance, which seem to have been meant to lead up to the question of the ruling elders, are treated, and the subject itself is never reached. It is possible therefore, that the recognition of the Christian ruler as the true ruling elder may have formed part of Hooker's scheme; but Books vi-viii were for a long time supposed to be lost.

kingdom. There is, indeed, in this great work, little of that political sense, the association of which with religion is the only hope for the right conduct of public affairs; and consequently, though it must always remain a treasury of thought on the subject with which it deals, it did little to prevent the storm which was then ready to darken the horizon.

Men were casting about for a stable, if possible an infallible, support for their faith and practice. That of the Pope and the clergy had been thrown off by the better part of the nation; and the substitute for it was the Bible. It is impossible to exaggerate the power which the Bible exercised over the minds of Englishmen in the latter part of the sixteenth and the early part of the seventeenth century. It has been graphically described for this generation in the History of the English people[1]. But it was thought that the Bible could give, what the Pope and the clergy had professed but had failed to give, what nothing indeed can give in an absolute sense, a direct guidance to individuals and communities, not in the way of principles, but in that of laws and rules. It was not yet understood that men's conduct, private and public, must be determined by the conscience and the reason, in that region of human responsibility into which neither minister nor Bible can enter; that men must, in humility and prayer, make use of Scriptural principles, of the advice of Christian leaders, of the precedents of the past, of all the lights which God vouch-

[1] See a fine passage on the influence of the Bible in Green's 'History of the English People,' ch. viii, beginning.

safes to us; but that ultimately the task of determining their course must be decided by their own independent judgment.

The Puritan was technically wrong in supposing that the Genevan model was to be found in the Bible, and that it was divine and necessary truth. But even in this he was not wholly wrong, since thus he was led to follow the democratic constitution of the early Christian societies and their simplicity of worship. In his serious interest in life and government, in his aspiration to an ideal community, such as those attempted in New England, he was wholly right. His profession of Calvinism was not a mere speculation. It was a protest against the self-will which had loaded the Church with unauthorized ordinances. What God had ordained, that alone he would follow. It is true the Puritan was mistaken in supposing that he could find the Presbyterian system in Scripture, and that this was the sovereign will of God. Yet this mistake might have been made clear to him, as indeed it was made clear in another way and at a later date by the Independents; it might have been made clear through the ordinary processes of Christian constitutionalism, had he been met fairly with temperate and reasoned opposition. But how was the Puritan met by those in authority? By the revival of a theory of divine right in the Episcopalian clergy unknown to the reformers or the Elizabethan divines, and known only up to that date in the assumptions of the Papacy[1];

---

[1] See the account in Perry (i. 46-8) of the works of Bishops Bancroft and Bilson. Of Bilson's 'Treatise on Church Government,' he says, 'It is the first

VI.]   *Christian Nationalism.*   271

by the alliance of this ecclesiastical assumption with the claim for a divine right inherent in the Sovereign apart from the nation[1]; by the practical comment upon these assumptions which was offered by the tyrannical injustice of the courts of the Star Chamber and High Commission; by the claim of the clergy in their Convocations to determine alone (as in the Canons of 1604[2] and of 1639[3]) all matters of the organisation of divine worship and of moral discipline for the whole nation; by a refusal to listen to the voice of the laity as expressed in Parliament[4]; by the introduction of

work of Anglican Divinity which asserted and argued the necessity of the apostolical succession to constitute a church. Without episcopacy there can be no lawful ordaining of ministers, and, by consequence, no lawful administering of the Word and Sacraments.'

[1] See the Canons of 1606, commonly called Bishop Overall's Convocation Book (given in Cardwell's 'Synodalia,' p. 330), which asserted the divine right of the King in such an extreme manner that even James I. saw that their publication would make him ridiculous, and refused to sanction them.

[2] The chief part of these Canons relate to matters of public worship and the discipline of the clergy; but these were points of vital importance in the beginning of the 17th century. There are canons also on schools and universities, matters of matrimony and of wills, which affected the general body of the laity. 'The publication of the Canons in 1604,' says Cardwell ('Synodalia,' p. 585), 'added greatly to the causes of disquiet which already existed in the Church of England. They were strongly opposed on legal grounds. Up to this period the cause of the church was successfully defended by Archbishops Whitgift and Bancroft; from this time it sensibly and constantly declined.'

[3] The parts of the Canons of 1639 which excited most discontent were—(1) The canon (v) against sectaries, requiring that all who objected to the Prayer Book, or wrote against it, or did not attend the church service, should be sought out and presented to the bishop to be punished. (2) The 'Etcetera Oath,' which was to be administered to all the clergy, and which bound them never to assent to any change in the government of the church 'by archbishops, bishops, deans, and archdeacons, &c.,' as then established. (3) Canon vii, 'On certain ceremonies,' which prescribed bowing towards the east on entering and leaving the church. These canons were passed after Parliament had been dissolved, the Convocation at the same time granting a benevolence to the King (the Parliament having refused any money grant) to enable him to carry on a war against the Scotch.

[4] The Commons protested against the Canons of 1604, refusing a conference

principles which seemed, not without reason nor without actual examples, to lead back to Romanism; and by the insistance upon these in a blind and obstinate temper, even up to the moment when the nation was on the verge of civil war. When the Parliament, as the great lay synod of the nation, attempted resistance and remedy, the House of Commons was dissolved, the King resorted to illegal means to raise money, and the Parliamentary constitution, the pledge of Christian liberty and brotherhood, was held in abeyance for eleven years [1]; to all of which the clergy gave their active consent. Is it to be wondered at that Puritanism grew bitterer and more sectarian? or that in the Civil War, in which the King and the clergy were ranged together against the liberties of the country, moderation and justice disappeared?

And yet it is clear that Puritanism, in the extreme form which it was driven to assume, was by no means the dominant power from the first, even in the progressive part of the nation. It was only by degrees, and unwillingly, that the Parliamentary leaders yielded to it. The lives and experience of Pym, of Hampden, of Eliot, of Dering, and of Milton, shows this quite clearly. They began as a constitutional opposition within the Church system, the forms of which they

with the Convocation, and passed a bill, which was cut short only by a prorogation declaring that no such canons could be enacted without the consent of Parliament. Lingard, vi. 26.

[1] 1629-40. The Commons in 1629, before adjourning, passed a resolution, directed against the arbitrary proceedings of the King and the clergy, that they who make innovations in religion, or who enact or pay subsidies not granted by Parliament, are enemies of the kingdom.

admired, while of its culture they not only partook but were the choicest examples. Even when, in the year 1827, Parliament resisted the claim made by Laud through the Royal declaration prefixed to the Articles of Religion, that the Convocations should regulate questions of doctrine, its language was that of a body of churchmen expressing themselves with firmness but with moderation[1]. 'We claim,' they said, 'for the truth that sense of the Articles of Religion which by public act of the Church of England and by general and concurrent exposition of the writers of our Church hath been delivered to us.' It seems clear that, if Parliament had been allowed in a constitutional manner to settle these questions, it would have settled them with moderation. The fatal fault, the constant provocation to violence, lay in the claims of the clergy and the King, which were in all cases extreme and short-sighted, and in many cases actually illegal. That they acted conscientiously we need not doubt, as Becket acted conscientiously in his struggle for the immunities of the clergy. But, as Becket's struggle and death only adds a pathetic tone to our condemnation of the forgery of the false decretals, on which he relied as having a divine sanction, so do the executions of Charles and of Laud to our condemnation of the false system of clerical power on which they depended, and for which they died.

The ideal of the nobler minds who eventually supported the Puritan cause was an England ruled by the laws of God, united and free. There is nothing to

[1] Perry's 'History of the Church of England,' i. 396.

make us doubt that the pursuit of this ideal would have left room for the development of all that was noble and refined in the nation. Pym and Hampden were two of the most cultivated gentlemen of their day. But both unity and freedom were destroyed by the King and the clergy, and men were driven into a sterner and more morose frame of mind. It would be wrong to judge the King and the clergy by the standard of political knowledge to which we have attained. Yet foresight, and a just apprehension of facts and tendencies, are the qualities rightly required in rulers; and such a just apprehension was not impossible in the days of Pym and Eliot, of Falkland and Chillingworth, of Cromwell and, we may add, of Hobbes. The blame must be thrown on that false idea of the Christian Church, which takes it for a separate society, having a sanction different from that of the general community, a society established mainly, if not solely, for worship and its adjuncts; and which attributes exclusive power in this society to the clergy. The Puritans, indeed, shared both these ideas to some extent. To many of them the substitution of one form of religious worship for another, of the Genevan model or of independency for the Episcopalian and liturgical system, was of more importance than justice; and the discipline which such men desired to establish would have been more irksome if less truculent than that of the old Church system. When, therefore, deprived of the checks exerted by the opposite party, and driven into an extreme position, those who had fought for constitutional liberty were left to rule under the direction of a dominant Puritanism, they also became a sect, with a limited ideal differing from that of the nation, often hypocritical, often oppressive; and the nation welcomed the Restoration as giving a promise of a state of things more consonant to its true aspirations.

Puritanism, then, passed away. But, as with the other experiments we have described, though its body was dead, its soul lived on. Beneath the superficial orgies of the Restoration might be found a nation serious, industrious, and resolved to be free. Beneath the wave of persecution in which Puritanism seemed to have been submerged, was a living Puritanism, which created a state of unrest until it was recognised by the Revolution settlement. Then the liberties for which the Puritans had fought arose from their graves and asserted themselves. Even the Cavalier Parliament of 1661 had acquiesced in most of the great constitutional principles, the denial of which had occasioned the Civil War[1]. All government or jurisdiction by the King alone, or by the clergy without the subsequent sanction of Parliament, was definitely condemned. The attempts of Charles the Second to evade the principle of the national sovereignty and of James the Second to override it were successfully resisted and finally overcome by the Revolution; nor has this principle ever since been seriously questioned. The constitutional enthusiasm of Burke, or Fox, or Hallam, the liberty of America, the Reform Act of 1832, are all the direct consequences of the Long Parliament and the Revolution. In this all England has acquiesced. The

---

[1] Green, 'History of English People,' ch. ix, sect. vi, first paragraph.

policy of Pym, which made the voice of the whole Christian country, expressed in the House of Commons, supreme, is the policy which has won its way to full acceptance. The Crown still forms a central rallying-point, the Peers a regulative reserve, the Convocations an influence. They can never become rival powers. In the supremacy of the House of Commons is realised the unity of the Christian Commonwealth. By this just relations between the political powers are established, and just relations between the members of the great brotherhood are guaranteed. In the observance and perfecting of such relations the establishment of God's kingdom on earth consists.

It may be thought that the Revolution, by finally recognising the liberty of the various Christian denominations, made a rift in the unity of the Church. We must gratefully acknowledge this liberty, and must recognise that it was even greater in fact than in the direct scope of the Toleration Act. But it is not a just inference from this liberty that it involved the breaking up of the religious unity of the nation. If religion consisted in common worship alone, it might be true to say that the Revolution made England a country of many churches. But, if the true religion is that by which men act, we may justly assert that our Church has never been divided. England has since the Revolution been more united on the basis of Protestant Christianity with divers forms of worship than it ever was before on the basis of enforced uniformity. On the matters of the chief practical importance the vast mass of the country is at one, and forms one commonwealth, one Christian

Church. It is true that at the Revolution, through the baneful influence of clericalism, then in a specially acrid mood on account of its recent loss of power, the better policy of Comprehension was defeated. The worship of our non-conforming fellow-believers was merely tolerated; they were not invited into union. But the fact that uniformity of worship was abandoned as impossible does not destroy our unity. The true statement of what was effected by the Toleration Act is this, that the Church of England conceded freedom of worship to all private societies among its members. It was no longer to be essential to membership in the Church or Commonwealth that men should worship according to the established forms. They might combine as they would for prayer and mutual edification. It is much more essential that those who form one community should feel and act together than that they should worship according to the same forms. The differences between English Protestants, which are far less than they seem, and which are made to seem considerable mainly through the peculiar position and action of the Episcopalian clergy, will yield in due time, we may be sure, to the real unity of Christian sentiment and its corresponding action which is constantly growing amongst us; and English Christianity, in its formal expression as well as in reality, will be one.

It may also appear to the superficial observer of our history that during the eighteenth century religion was in abeyance, while political life alone was vigorous. But, even taking religion in its more restricted sense, such an assertion would hardly be correct. It is true that, owing to the disputes about worship and church government which had distracted the seventeenth century, there was a disinclination to move such questions in the eighteenth. But even as a profession, and even among the upper classes, religion was still powerful [1]. As a spiritual influence upon the mass of the people it was still more so. It had a strong hold upon the national conscience, even where its rites were least frequented; and the succession of great teachers never failed. Law was a disciple of Ken, and Wesley of Law; and thus we reach without a break the Evangelical Revival. But it is true that much of men's interest which in the seventeenth century was occupied with questions of worship and church government was in the eighteenth turned to the sphere of politics, to realise there an equivalent for the piety which, with all its nobler features, had had an unfortunate issue in ecclesiastical controversy and in war. When a modern historian asks the question, whether the higher life of England owes more to Wesley or to Chatham [2], it is clear that we are invited to compare two modes, very different, yet practically one, by which the nobler spirit, which is inseparable from that of Christ, gained a fuller hold upon the life of the nation. The triumphant energy

---

[1] See 'The English Church in the Eighteenth Century,' by Abbey and Overton (Longmans, 1878); especially a discussion on the general condition of religion and morality in the Introductory chapter.

[2] Lecky, 'History of England in the Eighteenth Century,' ii. 517. 'From about the middle of the 18th century a reforming spirit is abroad, and a steady movement of moral ascent may be detected. The influence of Pitt (Chatham) in politics, and the influence of Wesley and his followers in religion, were the earliest and most important agencies affecting it.' See the whole passage, and the eighth chapter generally, which is almost wholly devoted to the character of Pitt.

with which in his earlier days Chatham inspired the nation, before so inert and aimless, the lofty assertions of liberty which marked his later life, must be reckoned as genuine products of the Divine Spirit. In the next generation, while Wilberforce was beginning his great work of religion and philanthropy, Edmund Burke, and Charles Fox in the second period of his life, with a religion less conscious but yet worthy to be compared with that of Wilberforce, were raising the whole tone of politics out of the slough of corruption into which it had fallen, and were laying the foundations of the pure public life of this century.

Nor ought we to omit, while speaking of the development of England as a great Christian brotherhood or church, to glance at the more general and secular life as an integral part of its Christian progress. We have spoken above of the culture and euphuism of the reign of Elizabeth. Development of this kind was arrested in the next century by the absorbing interest in matters of worship and by the events which led up to the Civil War. But in the sphere of law and constitutional relations great and beneficial progress was effected during the seventeenth century[1]. The substitution of tenure in fee simple for tenure by military service, the Habeas Corpus Act, the creation of a standing army as the servant of the nation not of the Sovereign, the

[1] Substitution of tenure by fee simple for tenure by military service, 12 Charles II, c. 24. Habeas Corpus Act, 31 Charles II, c. 2. The Court of High Commission abolished by 16 Charles I, c. 11 : the abolition confirmed by 13 Charles II, c. 12. Convocation ceases to be a taxing body in 1664, by a general agreement, not by statute. The abolition of all fetters upon the Press, 1679. Independence guaranteed to judges, 12 and 13 Will. III, c. 2. The Bill of Rights (1689), 1 Will. and M. sess. II, c. 2.

abolition of the High Commission and all similar Courts, the independence guaranteed to the judges, the removal of the taxing powers of Convocation, the better system of general taxation accompanying the first dawn of political economy, the maturer constitutionalism which dates from the Bill of Rights, all served to bring about more equitable and brotherly relations between men and classes within the Christian commonwealth. In another field, another sphere, as we may rightly call it, of Church energy, vast progress was made, the sphere of natural science and its application to industry. The foundation of the Royal Society (1660), and the great discoveries of Newton[1], preluded the series of triumphant inventions in which England has mostly led the way. The steam-engine, the methods of cotton manufacture, the railway and the telegraph, have changed the relations of human life, while the successive revelations of astronomy, geology, and biology have equally changed the methods of human thought. The modern life of England has, indeed, been marked by a slighter development of the arts, and especially in later times of the Drama, than might have been expected. The national energies have been concentrated on business and politics and the pursuit of science. The serious spirit also has not completely found its way to the alliance with and encouragement of the Arts. But our line of poets has marched even with the general advance. The progress in medicine and in surgery has been little short of triumphant. And when we look at the sphere of trade and colonisation, we are in

[1] Newton's 'Principia,' finished 1685.

the presence of a development which irresistibly recalls the primæval command, 'Be fruitful and multiply, replenish the earth and subdue it.' How can we, who take that command as a part of the divine impulse communicated from the first to mankind, refuse to recognise this important form of human activity as a function of the Christian Church? If, further, we are right in viewing human relations as the special object for which Christian Society and the Church exist, we shall recognise as Christian achievements the reforms of the criminal law, the successive acts by which one class after another has been brought within the pale of the constitution, still more the great movements of national education and of public philanthropy which more recent years have witnessed. We are conscious of a grand progress in our national history, and we gain the conviction that our commonwealth is able, through the whole range of its functions, to discharge the duties of a Christian Church. And this should be an imperative call of the divine voice to us, to put away the discords which arise from religion in its narrower sense, and to embrace the wider and more truly Christian religion, which has for its object the hallowing of the whole life of the nation.

It is sometimes said that the consideration of these larger questions and the optimistic hopes which they inspire blunts the sense of sin, with which the Church has primarily to deal, and without which there can be no adequate sense of redemption. But the treatment of the nation as a Christian Church also opens out a fuller view of our shortcomings; and this induces a

sense of sin as poignant as that which the Hebrew
prophets sought to arouse when they spoke of Israel as
the bride of Jehovah, and upbraided her for her unfaith-
fulness. That the effort for freedom in the seventeenth
century should have eventuated in a military tyranny;
that our Church should have been so blind as to drift
into the senseless wars of the eighteenth century, and
take part in its shameless greed of territory; that it
should have grasped at the hateful Assiento[1], which
made England the chief slave-carrier of the world; that
Ireland should have been tyrannically treated to gratify
the jealousy of English traders, and that Protestantism
should there have been linked to persecution and oppression; that we should, through our light-minded
injustice, have parted from America with bloodshed and
mutual wrath; that we should have had no wisdom to
discern the true meaning of the French Revolution;
that our poetry and art should have been so often degraded by impurity and by mercenary motives; that
the blessed discoveries of natural science should so often
have been resisted in the name of religion; that our
vast empire should bear in so many places the marks of
covetousness and of violence; that the free public life
of the last century should have been disgraced by the
most cynical corruption; that, while wealth was increasing amazingly, pauperism should have advanced
with almost equal strides; that drunkenness should
have become a national habit still requiring a special
organisation to overcome it; all this is the reproach

---

[1] The Assiento, or agreement for the carrying of slaves, was granted to England for thirty years by the treaty of Utrecht.

which we have to bear, and which, if we had the spirit of the prophets, would make us cry aloud and spare not, and summon the nation to the lamentation of bitter repentance.

But the times of that ignorance, we may say, God winked at. He now calls us to a new life. It is not our duty to reproach our fathers, but to take care that we with fuller light do not fall into a like condemnation. We may trace a great part of the evils of the past generations to the fact that the general life of the nation was not recognised as the life of a Christian Church. It was thereby deprived of Christian sanctions, and treated by the clergy and many of the most religious men as secular and profane. Experience everywhere shows that, where any set of persons and any sphere of life is degraded in the estimation of mankind, as the occupation of the tax-gatherers in Judæa in the time of Christ, it is almost sure to become irreligious, and to fulfil the evil prophecy which has gone out against it. But, as it was the special aim of Christ to seek out and to save that very class of men, so it should be the office of all who sincerely follow Him to redeem those spheres of life which have been specially supposed to lie outside the range of His influence, and to raise them, by His spirit, to dignity and holiness. They have done much for themselves; but, owing to the false limitations of the Church, they have sometimes exaggerated their own importance, sometimes drawn away the interests and the worship of men, so as to break the unity of our common Christian life. It must be the aim of the Church of our day to widen itself out so as to embrace them, and to raise them to their highest honour and use by bringing them into direct contact with the Saviour of the world.

There is no more animating thought in the whole range of spiritual aspirations, than that of a nation in which one spirit should rule, in which all classes of men should move with a common and a righteous impulse. All popular enthusiasms have a charm which is little short of irresistible; and we are so made that the love of our country and devotion to its interests is a natural instinct as well as a Christian virtue. Our country demands us; and we are, in any but our worst moods, ready to yield ourselves to its service. The defence of Greece against the Persians, of England and Holland against Spain in the 16th century, of France in 1793 against united Europe, the uprising of Germany against Napoleon in 1813—what a grand spectacle does each give us of a nation strong through enthusiastic union. Yet these present but a feeble image of that which would be seen were a whole nation to be possessed with the love of God and of Christ as their acknowledged national bond, and each citizen to take for the quickening purpose of his own life the determination to build up, so far as his influence extends, the life of the great brotherhood to which he belongs, and of every sphere of action which it contains, and of each of his fellow-citizens, in justice and the fear of God.

LECTURE VII.

THE CHRISTIAN BASIS OF HUMAN SOCIETIES.

EZEKIEL i. 15–20. Now as I beheld the living creatures, behold one wheel upon the earth by the living creatures, with his four faces. The appearance of the wheels and their work was like unto the colour of a beryl; and they four had one likeness; and their appearance and their work was as it were a wheel in the middle of a wheel. When they went, they went upon their four sides; and they turned not when they went. As for their rings, they were so high that they were dreadful; and their rings were full of eyes round about them four. And when the living creatures went, the wheels went by them: and when the living creatures were lifted up from the earth, the wheels were lifted up. Whithersoever the spirit was to go, they went, thither was their spirit to go; and the wheels were lifted up over against them; for the spirit of the living creature was in the wheels.

THE genius of Christianity requires us to conceive of the spiritual not as separate from, but as interpenetrating and vivifying the material; of God, not as separate, but as a spirit pervading the universe; of the human soul, not as separate, but as penetrating and transforming the body; of redemption, not as making men separate by removing the redeemed into a different sphere of existence, but as drawing them with all their surroundings into holy and loving relations; of the Church, not as a separate body, but as seeking always, and destined finally, to embrace the whole race of mankind.

The purpose of God, which we have been endeavouring to follow out in these Lectures, must be held fast. That purpose is described in the words of St. Paul: 'That He might gather together in one all things in Christ, both which are in heaven and which are in earth;' or in the vision of the Apocalypse, which places the Lamb in the midst of the throne, and in concentric circles round him the redeemed humanity and the various orders of the creation. To guard against mere archaism, we may state this in the simplest terms. It implies that the Christian spirit of universal, self-renouncing love is, and must show itself to be, the supreme power in the world; that its operation is first to raise men individually out of moral evil or selfishness, and then to bind them together by a spiritual bond; that this bond is the uniting power in all the various circles into which human society is subdivided; that all these rings and circles of life, these wheels within wheels, must be united by the same power into one great comprehensive brotherhood; and further, that the whole material world, which becomes more and more subject to man, partakes through him of the same redeeming influence; so that finally the spiritual and the material worlds form together a perfect harmony. We may express this also in theological language, thus: That the manifestation of God in Christ, acknowledged and believed, redeems man and transforms him in all his relations, to God, to other men, and to outward nature, and issues in a spiritual unity, of which God in Christ is the centre, and in which all the creation in its various degrees partakes. This, we say, is the purpose of God.

We are also His offspring. We are made in the image of God, and can enter into His thought and purpose. The man who apprehends it finds the world made new to him; he sees it ideally as it is in the Divine intention; and, further, he becomes a fellow-worker with God, an organ of the Divine Spirit, in bringing it to pass. He feels himself no longer isolated and no longer aimless, but a conscious member of a vast spiritual whole, of which every part conspires for the execution of the Divine purpose: and every minor society in which he is associated with his fellow-men he looks upon as undertaking some department of this great enterprise.

We need make no distinction at this point between those who are confessedly and consciously Christians, and those who are not yet awakened to this sublime calling. The love of God and his purpose of grace embrace us all. The spirit of God and of Christ is working upon every conscience, though the result of this working is infinitely varied. We all accept the fact that the spirit of Christ was in the prophets, and that it wrought upon the Jewish nation at large in the ages before Christ came. St. John's doctrine of the Word, without which nothing was created, the Light which lighteth every man, and that of St. Paul, that

God is not far from any of us, since in Him we live and move and have our being, enables us to extend this belief to mankind universally. There is, to use a phrase of grammar, a proleptic, or anticipatory, Christianity, of which we may see traces deep down in the convictions of the various races of men. It shows itself partially and fitfully in their religions, but more in their philosophies, their family life and their laws. In these God has always had a witness among them. Christ came in the fulness of time. The ground was laid on all sides in preparation for Him; the human race was growing towards Him: so that we must look at the whole human development as one, and on the Christian spirit as the root of all that is good and true in it, and on Christ Himself as its crown.

But, besides this proleptic Christianity in ancient times before Christ came, there is also an unconscious Christianity in modern times, by which men are being trained for the eventual recognition of God in Christ. Within the recognised boundaries of the Church this is fully acknowledged. It forms the justification for the original admission of whole families within its pale, in which, if there were not, as is sometimes argued, little children, there were certainly immature members like the slaves, who were in this stage of unconscious Christianity[1]. It forms also the substratum of truth

---

[1] John iv. 53: 'Himself believed and his whole house.' Acts x. 2, 24, 44: 'Cornelius, a devout man, and one that feared God with all his house.' 'Cornelius had called together his kinsmen and near friends.' 'The Holy Ghost fell upon all them which heard the word.' Acts xvi. 31: 'Believe on the Lord Jesus Christ, and thou shalt be saved and thy house.' Ib. 33 : 'He was baptized, he and all his, straightway.' Ib. 34 : 'He rejoiced, believing in God with all his house.'

beneath the doctrine of baptismal regeneration which is so untenable when baldly stated; that is, that those who have been brought up within the Christian community imbibe into the very texture of their moral nature some of the primary assumptions of Christian morality. But ideas and moral influences pass, as by some subtle form of commercial exchange, from man to man and from nation to nation, through all the forms of human intercourse, without as well as within the pale of Christendom. It is impossible to look at the wide diffusion of goodness and not to admit its existence in many different modes, in connexion with or apart from the actual confession of Jesus Christ. The heads of the organisations of professed believers have often been too slow to recognise this, and the want of its recognition has been greatly to the detriment of the Church.

We can find no standing ground until we identify Christianity with moral goodness, and the Christian Church, in its idea and ultimate development, with the whole moral, social, and political system by which the human race is growing to its fulness. But this does not imply that the true condition of things which we thus describe is already realised, or that the divine spirit is diffused at once and equably throughout the

This last case is a striking one, since it is impossible to suppose that the women, children, and slaves composing the house of the Roman jailor could give more than a simple assent to what the head of the family had done. The manner in which v. 31 is quoted is a mark of the difference between a merely individualistic Christianity and the social Christianity now making itself felt. It has usually been quoted only as far as the words, 'thou shalt be saved.' If we add the concluding words, 'and thy house,' we get the idea of faith, which is given in these Lectures.

U

mass. The principle of Election must be acknowledged as that by which the whole process is carried on; not an election to happiness but to service; not an election in an exclusive sense, but as the medium of blessing to all. The race of Israel from Abraham downwards was the elect race to whom, in the first instance, God made himself known; but the promise, for the sake of which they were called, was that through them all families of the earth should be blessed. Similarly, the Greeks, the Romans, the Oriental nations, the Germans, have had their special gifts of mind or of art, of social or political capacity, which were also destined to become universal. We have learnt to interpret the dealings of God in these matters more fully through historical and ethnical research, and through the comparison of languages and religions.

But further, this doctrine of Election extends to all the various special spheres of human life. Each department or circle has as its leaders those in whom the spirit of the society dwells in the fullest degree. But their election is not for themselves, but that through them the rest may be taught, led, influenced, inspired, until the whole body is brought up to the level of its leaders. Nay, to follow St. Paul's teaching, each man has his gift, which is for the common use, to edify others by sharing it with them.

If we apply this doctrine to the Church in the wide sense which we have given to it, we need not scruple to take into our view the whole human race without exception, since we confess that all have been redeemed, and that upon all the Spirit of God is playing and finding an entrance here and there in ways far beyond our knowledge. We may trace in every part of the human family those who are shown by their lives to be partakers of the Divine spirit, whether consciously or by the proleptic and unconscious processes which we have described. But we look upon those who consciously partake of this spirit, who confess God as he has been manifested in Jesus Christ, and who enrol themselves in the company formed for the purpose of making Him known to men, as the specially elect portion of the race or church of mankind. These are destined or appointed to communicate the Divine Spirit to all mankind, and to be the channels of salvation to the world.

It is with this elect portion that we have chiefly to do. But it is necessary to keep the rest in mind, lest, when we speak of the Christian nation, or of societies formed for art, or science, or commerce, as branches of the Church, or again of the universal Church as coextensive with mankind, we should find a stumblingblock in the fact that there are some belonging to each of these circles who do not consciously acknowledge the Christian name. The possession of the spirit, not the name, is the matter of importance, though we must seek to make these two conditions coincide. And even where the spirit is but dimly manifest, we must regard those who in any degree possess it as the immature members of the family. The Church is universal in the fullest sense, and its essential character is that of its most characteristic members, of those who most fully partake of the Christian spirit. That spirit we may speak of either as the spirit of the universe, or of humanity, of Christ or of God. The universal spirit, since humanity is the crown of the universe, is the spirit of humanity. The spirit of humanity, since Christ is the head of humanity, is the spirit of Christ. The spirit of Christ, since Christ is one with God, is the spirit of God.

It is true that the Christian Church has not for the most part understood the high calling which we thus vindicate for it. Those who confess God in Christ have usually been inclined to limit their view of His kingdom, or to adjourn the possibility of its full extension to a future world. But the Apostolic Church, though compelled by circumstances to a limited scope of action, distinctly contemplated this extension. It has been the mistake of each successive age to deny it. It must be the privilege of our own age to recognise it and to give it effect.

The Christian Church, then, is absolutely universal. It works through selected individuals, societies, nations, for the good of the whole body, with a view to make it one spiritual unity. Whatever the Christian spirit touches it transforms and ennobles. It connects it, first in thought, then actually, with God and with Christ, who are felt by spiritual minds to be present everywhere and in all things. Each effort of knowledge is an effort to know some part of God, that is, to know his will, that will which is another expression for love. Each art is a representation of some phase of that beauty which is part of the Divine nature, the calm and joyous side of love. Each effort of culture, whether of the mind or of the earth, is the extension of a humane and a Divine influence over some fresh sphere. Each mode of human intercourse, whether for social purposes or of direct utility, is a field for the cultivation of mutual affection, of human and Christian love. Thus to the spiritual mind everything undergoes a change, and is converted from neutral or evil associations to become moral and spiritual, Christian and divine, first in the thought of the believer, then in actual reality.

But, further, we must introduce here what may be rightly called the Sacramental idea—that which makes outward and visible things the channels of inward and spiritual blessing. The societies of men are bound together by the outward objects with which they deal; the family by the primary needs of life and objects of desire, scientific societies by the particular studies, whether material or historical, with which they deal; literary and artistic societies by music or poetry, sculpture, or painting, or architecture; and others in similar ways. But these objects are not to a Christian mere brute matter. They have been changed by the alchemy of religious thought and feeling. They become to the Christian apprehension the means through which God and the human spirit are perceived, and spiritual blessings communicated. Each object of science reveals not only the law of its existence but a part of God's nature. Each art reveals not merely natural beauty but human feeling, which also is divine. The family life is full of the outward and visible signs of love, and love is of God. The common partaking, appropriation, and enjoyment of these, therefore, makes them also partakers of each other and of God. These things become the channels through which love, and beauty, and truth, and all that constitutes the human and divine excellence, enter into us. They are also the means to us of aspiration and of prayer, by which we associate ourselves with God and Christ, and reach out towards the promised unity, the establishment of the kingdom of heaven. Thus the whole Church, including humanity in its widest sense, and every several organisation within it, contains the materials of constant worship, communion, and edification. It is not too much to say that he who thus appropriates the world realises at every turn the inner meaning of the words, 'Take, eat, this is my body.'

If we add to this the Christian doctrine of the universal priesthood of believers, we may justly speak of each of those who work in the several departments of human life as ministering to their brethren in a holy office. And if we bear in mind the teaching of the Apostles, that the service of God is not so much that of any formal function, not even of public prayer, as that of a life pervaded by the Christian spirit, we have in the various rings or circles of human society so many branches of the universal Church, each having its organised church worship—the priest, the prayer, the sacrament, the service [1].

---

[1] Rom. xii. 1 : 'Present your bodies a living sacrifice, holy, acceptable unto God, which is your reasonable service' (λογικὴ λατρεία). James i. 27: 'Pure religion' (θρησκεία καθαρά) 'and undefiled before God and the Father is this, to visit the fatherless and widows,' &c. The two words which most clearly expressed formal worship to Jews and heathens are thus claimed, not for the public worship of the Church, but for the devotion of the life.

But, further, we must look upon the Church, not as a single and simple organism, the members of which are only attached by the bond of faith to the central society. We must look on the Church as enfolding and including a vast number of organisations, each of which partakes of the character and vitality of the whole. We are not simply members of the Christian Church, but members of the Church of England; not simply units in the great body of humanity, but citizens of our own country; and not this only, but members of orders, families, colleges, associations, professions, within the Church. We must strive neither to narrow ourselves down to our specialism, nor lose ourselves in a vague universalism. Our affections must be made vivid by their direction to home and country, but they must be enlarged by devotion, like that of our Lord, to the good of mankind. The truest Christian life is that which works earnestly in its special calling, while yet having an eye to the general good: or rather, since we are taught first to pray, 'Thy kingdom come,' it is a life which begins with an appreciation of the great result, and, by keeping this in view, redeems and raises the special service in which it is engaged. The Church idea, that of a society bound together for the furtherance of the divine purpose and the making known of God's fatherly love to all mankind, must be reproduced in each society formed within it, and become its vivifying element. It is said by biologists that in every organism there are innumerable gemmules circulating, which are of the same character as the whole, and which are capable under certain circumstances of reproducing it[1]. So, within the vast organism of the Church of Humanity, which is the body of Christ, there exist many minor organisms, each bearing and reproducing the character of the whole, and the image of Him who formed it.

The individual is a microcosm. The single man is stamped with the image which is seen in larger proportions in humanity itself. In the redeemed man we have before us a little copy of the redeemed humanity, which is the Church. Look for a moment at the process of the redemptive work in him, and you see the character of it in the Church at large. The evil, the ruin from which we are redeemed, is best expressed by the word Selfishness, the narrowness of mind and heart which exalts the individual and his own circle of interests to the exclusion of all that is beyond him, of God and of humanity. The restoration[2] consists in the reverse process, the attaching of self to the larger unity, the losing of self, so far as this is possible to a moral being, in God and man, the self-forgetting, universal love. In the former state, the part is everything, the whole is lost; in the latter, self is subordinated to the supreme Unity and to those circles of life through which the supreme Unity is manifested to us. Self is subdued,

---

[1] See Darwin's Provisional hypothesis of Pangenesis in his 'Changes of Plants and Animals under Domestication,' ch. xxvii. pt. 2.

[2] I do not enter here upon the doctrine of the Atonement, but confine myself to the effects of the Atonement on human life; and I use the word Redemption in this sense, as is commonly done in Scripture (e. g. in the expression 'Waiting for the redemption of the body,' Rom. viii. 23). The Atonement, however, as self-sacrifice, is the heavenly counterpart of the earthly effect described in the text. This, as pointed out by Coleridge, 'Aids to Reflexion' (p. 244), seems to be the meaning of the 'earthly' and 'heavenly things' in John iii. 11-15.

and God and Christ reign within us. This also is true spirituality of mind. A carnal mind is that which estimates men and things only in relation to self and selfish interests; a spiritual mind is that which estimates men and things, including itself, in their relations to the supreme unity, which is no other than God. And similarly, a spiritual energy is that which seeks to appropriate itself, and all men and all things within the range of its power, to God.

There is a certain sphere over which our personality ranges, consisting partly of our own faculties of mind and body, partly of that portion of the human race with which we are personally connected, partly of outward nature, our possessions, or those things with which our tastes, dispositions, and circumstances connect us. In this sphere lies our work, our enjoyment, and our influence. The spiritual mind is shown in thinking of this whole sphere and its component parts, and in feeling about it, in its relation to God and Christ and the true interests of humanity. The spiritual energy is shown in working upon it, appropriating it, enjoying it, using it, with the design of consciously connecting it with God and with the interests of men, so that it may fulfil its functions as a part of the universal harmony. This is the process in which we are engaged, the more consciously the more we ourselves are swayed by the divine Spirit. It is never wholly absent from our thought or energy; but, on the other hand, it is never wholly complete and triumphant.

The Church is the society of those in whom this process is being accomplished, or who may hereafter become subject to it, of those who are conscious or unconscious Christians; a twofold category which is absolutely universal, since all men necessarily sustain a relation to God and to their fellows, and all are subject, consciously or unconsciously, to this process of redemption. But, just as in the individual there is always a large part of his powers which as yet has felt feebly if at all this redeeming process, so in the universal society, which is the Church, there is always a large number of persons, and often whole spheres of human interest, which as yet have not been brought under the dominion of the saving principle. No circle of social life is wholly subject to universal, self-renouncing love. We must, indeed, assert that this love shows itself in many different ways, not in one alone, that it is here a devotion to knowledge, there to beauty, or again an absorption in social life or in business. We are, to use an expression lately coined to express a stage in the history of religions, Henotheists, or Kathenotheists[1], still. We find the true faith and love coloured by special circumstances, and appearing as love of wife and children, of friends, of great and good men, of our country. But, however widely we may recognise its operation, we still see vast fields which it has yet to conquer.

What we have to trace, therefore, is the capacity of the various societies or unions formed amongst men for being the abodes of the Holy Spirit rather than

---

[1] 'Henotheism, that is, a belief and worship of those single objects, whether semi-tangible or intangible, in which man first suspected the presence of the invisible and the infinite.' Max Müller, Hibbert Lect. 260.

the fact that they have actually become so. The Church and all its branches and circles are always growing into full existence. It is this which makes it so difficult to define the Church. It is this which makes any full definition of it such as has been offered here, namely, that the Church is the whole human race in all its modes of life inspired by the Spirit of Christ, though it is offered as an anticipation and a hope rather than a thing realised, seem to many exaggerated or absurd. But it is this also which makes any definition which stops short of this necessarily inadequate. It has been pointed out in the previous Lectures that from its first beginning the Church, though it was but a germ, was the germ of an universal society. But it has been also pointed out that this germ has been unequally developed, and, like a child which has some of its organs defectively nourished, has thereby run great danger of its life. We have to show how it may regain its full vitality, and embrace and vivify all the various circles of human life.

There are seven such circles which we may trace out within the great circle of the complete humanity, which forms the eighth.

1. The organisation which exists for public worship, and which is often, but mistakenly, identified with the Church.

2. The family.

3. The society formed for the common pursuit of knowledge—the University, the School, and the Learned Society.

4. The fellowship in artistic pursuits.

5. Social intercourse.
6. The intercourse of business, professions, and trade.
7. The Nation.

To which we add as the eighth the Universal Society of Humanity. We have to point out how each of these realises, or rather ought, for the complete fulfilment of its object, to realise the Church-idea, that is, to be the embodiment or manifestation in social relations of the universal, self-renouncing love of Christ and of God.

1. The organisation which exists for the conduct of public worship, to which are joined Christian exhortation and works of beneficence, might be thought to be in no need of such a demonstration. Is not this organisation itself the Church? Is it not to this that we must apply all that is said of the Church as being the body and the bride of Christ? To this we must answer unhesitatingly in the negative. So little is it right to identify the Church with the system of public worship that it is possible to imagine a Christian Church entirely without it. Indeed, it may be maintained that this is the ideal of Christianity: there is no temple in the New Jerusalem[1]. If the presence of God could become all-pervading, formal worship would no longer be needed, or would at least undergo a great change. And further, as a matter of history, if we consider how constantly the system of public worship and teaching has been a narrowing and dividing influence, the parent of confusion, of quarrels, of persecutions, of wars, we shall entirely refuse to identify it with the Church itself. We may further observe

[1] Rev. xxi. 22. See the views of Rothe quoted in Note XX.

that the tendency of modern thought and practice is increasingly to restrict its sphere. If, then, we believe it to be destined to be permanent, still more if we think it the highest of all the modes of human society, there is assuredly none which more needs to vindicate its capacity to be the organ of Christian universality.

Certainly, it can never be the organ of universal love so long as correct definitions of the great objects of faith and of the spiritual processes of redemption are made the test of fellowship: for these are matters which must always appear different to different minds, and which, indeed, are incapable of definition. Nor can it be, so long as the forms of organisation are regarded as essential, nor so long as so much of Christian teaching is taken up, as it frequently is now, with speculations about another world; nor again, so long as it is looked upon mainly as the means of individual rather than of common good. The common worship of the universal Church must tend constantly to unity, not to division; it must include all who acknowledge the supremacy of the Christian spirit. Its language must be that of the invitations, 'Come unto Me all ye that are weary and heavy laden, and I will give you rest;' 'Whosoever will, let him take of the water of life freely.' It must set forth the spirit and life of Christ as the great object to be sought; it must inspire men with a longing for these. Compared with this all forms of organisation and all positive institutions must be held to be of quite secondary importance. It must not adjourn the hope of eternal life to another state of existence, but must help men to realise the divine now in their common life. It must promote not a selfish spirituality, but a love which expands to the full measure of that of God. Those who minister as its leaders must imbue themselves with this universal spirit, and become the examples and the channels of it to all whom they lead.

We say that the organisation for public worship, exhortation, and mutual well-doing, is capable of this universality; that it is capable of it in the highest degree, and that it is capable of imbuing all the other organisations with it. Let us show this in reference to its various functions, which are Common Prayer, the Sacraments, Christian instruction and beneficence. Each of these would, in the ideal we are contemplating, partake of, and minister to, the spirit of Christian universalism.

The prayers of the universal church must be inspired with the chief of all prayers, 'Thy Kingdom come,' the undertone of which must be heard through every special petition. They must lead the worshippers to forget self as much as possible by bringing the general interests of men before their minds. They must pray not only for the rulers and the laws, but for the elevation of the poor, for the progress of knowledge and art and literature, for union among the nations of the West, and for their influence over the weaker races of mankind. Worship must be, to be brief, a bringing before God of the real needs of the whole community: the hallowing of life in all its branches must be conducted here in the way of aspiration.

The Sacrament of Baptism will be regarded, first, as

the bringing of a new member into the brotherhood to which the universal love of God is made known ; and, secondly, as the consecration of the individual to God and to the brotherhood. The Sacrament of the Lord's Supper will be regarded not merely as an individual partaking of Christ, but as the means of realising his life in the life of the community. It is the means by which the society distinctly asserts itself as a society belonging to Him, appropriates Him, imbibes His Spirit: the means by which it realises the fellowship of His members, and strengthens itself for the task of imparting His Spirit to mankind. But it does all this as a function of the universal society, not for the actual worshippers alone, nor as if the Sacrament were an unique ordinance without extension or counterpart beyond itself. It is the symbol or representation of the whole life, and the centre of a sacramentalism which extends through the whole range of human existence. As a commemoration, it associates with the central work of the Redeemer all redemptive efforts, and all manifestations of universal, self-renouncing love which have been seen throughout the whole course of history. As an offertory, it brings material offerings, an earnest of the whole harvest of the material world, to consecrate them to the service of God and man. As a sacrifice, it demands and ensures the spirit of sacrifice throughout the whole community. As a communion, it concentrates, in thought, all the modes of human intercourse which we have specified, and ensures their becoming the channels of spiritual good through the sympathy which, like an electric current, it sends through their linked hands. It shows also the means by which this may become effectual, namely, by making outward and visible things universally the signs and the means of inward and spiritual grace; the means, that is, by which men may recognise in each other, and transmit to one another, the spirit which flows from their union with Christ.

Similarly, the instruction given in connexion with Divine worship, an instruction in which as many as are competent should be invited to bear their part, must be in harmony with the objects of the universal community. It must show the Christian spirit as a power pervading all things, and must help men to realise it in all their occupations. It must bring the universal interest to ennoble each separate endeavour. It must explain to men the facts of human life, and the events both of the past and of the present in connexion with the general destination of the Church. This will furnish a constant supply of illustrations, which are also a kind of sacramental media. The examples of Scripture and of history enable us to see the universal principle in the particular instance, and become the means by which men recognise truth and convey right feeling one to the other, and thus promote Christian fellowship. This is especially true of the great Example which must always be the most prominent subject of our teaching. But the highest form of pulpit instruction is that of exhortation; and through this the Church must kindle an unfailing hopefulness and stimulate the spirit of Christian enterprise. While this is done, the doctrines of the Church will fall into their proper place, being never in the air, but ballasted by a constant appeal to experience and the responsibility of immediate action [1].

And, similarly, Christian beneficence of all kinds, though its peculiar property is to be minutely personal, must be inspired by universal interests. The immediate contact with those whom we seek to benefit must be guided by wisdom and by constantly extending knowledge. Otherwise it becomes harmful. But the sense of universalism will prevent us from looking upon knowledge, such, for instance, as that of political economy, as a foreign and restrictive power. It is part of God's revelation to us, the means of guiding us to sound results. Moreover, the history of the Church shows us that out of the organisation for religious worship have issued successively all the greater organisations of society, systems of constitutional government, education, art, the festivals and jubilees of social intercourse. The system of worship begat them all, and they remained for a long time under its tutelage. And this process still continues. The leaders of public worship and teaching are often found to be the pioneers of the march of human progress, as in the case of popular education in this century. But these children of the Church grow up, and can be no longer under the tutelage of the ministers of public worship. They must then either pass on to the care of the general government, as has been the case with the Poor Law, Education, and the Reformatory system in our day, or must exist as independent institutions within the

[1] See Note XXI. A quotation from 'Ecce Homo.'

general community. This is not, as it is frequently represented, a transition from the care of the Church to that of a secular power, but from the care of the society organised for worship to that of the more general Christian community.

Moreover, when the spirit of universalism is fully accepted, the leaders of public worship will be not the most exclusive, but the most open of orders. However great is the position of leaders in such a sphere, it is at once marred by exclusiveness. The spirit of universalism demands that, so far as order and other circumstances will allow, the leaders of worship should share their functions with others. They will aim, not at making themselves indispensable and keeping their place above the rest, but at such an imparting of knowledge and right feeling to others as will progressively diminish the distance between them; and (though this is impossible in this world) they will wish that this process might be so complete that an order of ministers should no longer be necessary, but that all should, according to their varying capacities, take their share in a free and orderly worship.

2. That which in common estimation is, after the organisation for public worship, the most capable of fulfilling the functions of the Church is the family. The family is, as we may say, naturally Christian. It best enables us to trace the divine basis which, as we are pointing out, properly belongs to all spheres of social union. It may, indeed, be degraded into sensuality, or tyranny, or dulness. The Fathers of the Church in the fourth century did not scruple to abase

it, and even deride it, in contrast to the ascetic life[1]. But the love of husband and wife, of parents and children, of masters and servants, has always a window which stands wide open to heaven. When the Christian idea is fully realised, the family passes, without raising any difficulty in our thoughts, into a little kingdom of God. The love of husband and wife, which is a mutual self-giving and a mutual appropriation, becomes the exchange of Christian graces, the enjoyment of Christian confidence. The subjection of children to their parents, which at times has had so much harshness in it, becomes their training in the free obedience of Christians, and in capacity for service. The process of nourishment and maintenance becomes the means of evoking Christian care on the one side, Christian gratitude on the other. The relation of servants and masters becomes that of a union in a common vocation, in which the master leads and the servant follows with free and intelligent sympathy. The family is a school of submission and self-denial, but one in which this discipline is sweetened by Christian affection[2].

Moreover, the family is a microcosm. In it are

[1] See the writings of St. Jerome, which exercised the widest social influence in his own and the succeeding centuries. Esp. Ep. xxii. (Ed. Vallarsi): 'Ad Eustochium De Custodiâ Virginitatis;' liv.: 'Ad Furiam, De Viduitate Servandâ;' cxxiii.: 'Ad Ageruchiam, De Monogamiâ;' also the books 'Adv. Helvidium,' and 'Adv. Jovinianum.' Jerome's theory is that, though marriage is allowable, virginity is much more acceptable to God. He does not condemn marriage, but, by taking every opportunity of showing its inferiority and its inconveniences, he does all that a religious teacher can to degrade it. The other church writers of that age, when Christianity was gaining its final ascendancy, both in East and West (some exception being made for Chrysostom), were hardly behind him; and the influence of the 'age of the great fathers' endured to the Reformation and beyond.

[2] What is said here of the family is the expansion of the teaching of St. Paul in Ephes. v. and vi, and of St. Peter (1 Pet. ii. and iii.).

found the rudiments of all the social conditions: of common worship, which is nowhere more real or more precious than in the home; of knowledge, for our first lessons are learnt at our mother's knee; of art, for childhood delights in representation, and its life is made up of songs and play; of social intercourse, and of government. The family feeling, moreover, is a constant support in our public career. The nations were believed in old times to have grown out of families; and the highest ideal we can form of a nation, nay, of the human race as a whole, is that of a vast family or brotherhood.

It may be said that the family has been definitively won for Christ, so far as Christian love is self-renouncing; but, so far as Christian love is universal, it still needs the process of redemption. It is, however, quite as important in the family as in any other union of men to preserve the spirit of universalism. If in the Greek Republics there was a tendency to subject the family too much to the exigencies of the State, in Christian times there has come about too great a divorce between the family and the general community. And hence the family life is apt to grow petty, and to become dull and objectless. The Christian universalism must penetrate the family more and more. The true Christian idea of a family is that of an association in which every member has his function, some within, some without the home circle, but which affords a meeting point and a harbour of rest, where a higher life of piety or thought or art or worthy recreation can be cultivated by all in common, and where each can gain, through sympathy and prayer and affection, the support which he needs for his special work. Such an association is truly a branch of the universal Church, its intercourse Christian communion, its meals sacraments, its life a divine service; it is in itself a kingdom of God, and its aim the establishment of that kingdom everywhere.

3. Turning now to the associations which spring from the pursuit of knowledge—the school, the university, the scientific society, the literary club,—we may say that all men have a part in these; for all men may join in the cultivation of knowledge in its widest sense, by education, observation, experience, reading, and lastly by conversation; for knowledge becomes fixed in language, and thus passes from the learned to the unlearned till it becomes the universal inheritance. But we must fix our minds here upon the associations consciously designed for the increase of knowledge, and show that these are, in their true essence, branches of the Christian Church.

The objects of knowledge are in themselves divine, for all are parts of the world in which God continually works. Each perception is a perception of an object inseparable from its connection with the Infinite, the Eternal, the Holy. The aspiring learner, therefore, reaches out towards the great unity, and is from the first in some sort a worshipper. Moreover, knowledge is of universals. We never know an individual object till we have classed it; and this path of generalisation must be pursued till it reaches the highest point, the central unity, which is none other than God. Again, knowledge is personal: we never know a thing until we have some feeling about it, and until we have in some way connected it with ourselves. Thus moral feelings are necessarily evoked, whether those of simple admiration and awe, of delight, or of the sense of utility; whether it be a reflection on the harmony of the Kosmos, or on the progress of the human race, or on the development of the faculties of man in their contact with their objects. But all such feelings lead us up to the desire for the highest good for ourselves and for the race, the Christian feeling of self-renouncing, universal love. Again, knowledge is graduated. There is, as has been said [1], a scale in the mind by which we value the different portions of knowledge. We cannot but value most that which is most important to man. We look therefore upon all knowledge as subordinate to the highest knowledge, the knowledge of moral good, of that of which the Cross of Christ is the fullest expression. 'The mental unity,' says M. Comte [2], 'vainly sought before the time by the noble impulse of scholasticism, will inevitably result from the constant convergence of a science which has become philosophical and a philosophy which has become scientific. The study of man, moral and social, will obtain without resistance the just and normal ascendancy which belongs to it.'

Knowledge, therefore, is essentially moral. But it is also social and the means of social union. Knowledge, indeed, hardly exists till it is expressed. There

---

[1] Crozier, 'Religion of the Future,' p. 256-7 (Kegan Paul & Co., 1880).
[2] From 'Cours de Philosophie Positive,' vol. vi. 406 (Littré's Ed.).

is in us an irresistible tendency to impart what we know: we can, probably, only think by means of words; and when we have thought, a kind of sympathetic longing makes us desire to speak out the thought; and speech and writing make it the property of others and engender in them the same feelings which it has wrought in us. Moreover, knowledge is too vast to be pursued by one man alone. We at once feel our indebtedness to those who have preceded us, and to our fellow-workers in the same field, and to those who are treading paths of knowledge of which we know nothing but what they win for us. We are dependent on them and they on us. Thus the social spirit in its noblest form is evoked by the pursuit of knowledge. We become associates in the discovery of the will of God, in appropriating and following out His thoughts. And this is not the case only as to our own special sphere. Through conversation, and books, and social intercourse, we enter into the spheres of other learners. Language becomes the depository of each fact which is ascertained; and by the knowledge and use of language we take in some parts of every sphere of human knowledge. It is this which connects the literary and humane with the physical and non-human branches of study. Thus the pursuit of knowledge is not only a religion in itself, but also founds and maintains a branch of the universal Church. Such a Church every place of learning must become which does its work in a liberal and sympathetic spirit. Its pursuit of knowledge is a holy service rendered to God and man. Its teachers are ministers of God, leading, animating, inspiring those who learn. The longing to know becomes a prayer: the presentation of the results of knowledge becomes a Sacrament, that is, the conveying of the unseen and Eternal Truth by means of things sensible and palpable: the interchange of ideas becomes a mode of fellowship and of mutual well-doing, of which, indeed, no nobler form can be found.

4. That Art, in a similar way, is properly and essentially religious, and that its common pursuit constitutes a branch of the Christian and universal Church, is no less demonstrable. Art is the representation of objects, not as they are in themselves, but as we apprehend, or rather as we feel them. The first art is that of tone and gesture which are parts of ourselves: in all its developments art is intensely personal; and that which is personal is necessarily moral; and what is moral is religious.

But, further, the desire for expression is the soul of art. What is this longing for expression but a yearning to breathe forth towards some responsive intelligence that which we have so keenly felt, a yearning which has in it the element of sympathy and therefore of morality? Even if art be motived, as some hold, only by the sense of beauty, if it only express the pleasure we feel in an object, still pleasure is of different degrees of worth, and rises in the scale according to the culture and the spiritual condition of him who gives and him who receives it[1]. If the

[1] See, in Note XXII, a quotation from Sir F. Leighton's Lecture, entitled, 'What is the relation in which Art stands to Morals and Religion?'

pleasure which art gives is an excellence of humanity generally, it must thereby become the subject of religion which seeks to elevate the whole life of mankind. And, if one whole side of nature is the beautiful, we may rightly say that the beautiful is a part of the nature of God, and the cultivation of beauty by means of art is necessarily a kind of worship. Moreover, art is more distinctly than any other part of our nature a gift from above. It is more distinctly original and creative. If we ask why there should have been but one Homer and one Raphael, we can make no answer but that God has so willed. Even the artist himself will at times stand before his work and wonder how he created it, and mistrust his power of reproducing it. Thus we are brought very near to the original creative energy: and we have here a fruitful source of admiration, and of that longing towards what we feel to be above us, which is a true form of worship.

These remarks apply equally whether the medium of our representation be sound or words or colour or form. But we may go further, and point out that art is absolutely universal. The artistic feeling, that of pleasure in making our work beautiful and complete, is a necessary part of all true work. Till our work becomes to us a subject of delight, we have no heart in it, we can neither show any excellence in it nor commend it to others. And in this the ancient and modern senses of art are reconciled. All applications of knowledge to production are arts in the ancient sense. In their excellence and perfection they are all in the modern sense artistic. All work that is conscientiously done must aim at perfection. We seek to make our work stand out as a complete whole, and thus the sense of beauty is aroused and becomes a factor in all that we do. Every producer, every workman, shares this artistic feeling, and shares it in the proportion of his excellence and conscientiousness. Nor is art indifferent, as is sometimes asserted, to the moral sense; for in every walk of art that which is morally degrading, so soon as it is felt to be degrading, is necessarily banned as bad taste. Art is essentially moral and religious, not as confining itself to the representation of things moral and religious and taking a didactic attitude, but because it is in itself an excellence of human nature, because of its capacity to afford an ennobling pleasure, because the beauty at which it aims is a part of the divine nature, and because it contains in itself a fund of delight for the rest and refreshment of a weary world[1].

But, further, the fellowship which art begets is inseparable from its cultivation. We want to express ourselves to others and to witness their expression of themselves. Thus art becomes a form of intercourse, a form of education or self-development, a form also of instruction, we might almost say of preaching, were the idea of preaching somewhat extended. We are, moreover, most powerfully affected by the feelings which art conveys, when we feel them in common with many others. And this common feeling ministers strongly to the higher forms of sympathy. Thus art

---

[1] See, in Note XXII, the passage from Sir F. Leighton's Lecture already referred to.

becomes a binding link between men, and draws them together towards God. It forms a society which must properly be called a Church. Its yearning towards the ideal is a worship, a prayer. The sharing in artistic impressions is a genuine form of common worship. Art has its canons of taste which are its doctrinal articles; it has its ministers, its votaries, its sacraments or representations of the inner and spiritual by means of the external; its fellowship and its mutual well-doing,—a form of beneficence which even now is taking a wide and salutary extension, and is destined to occupy no mean place in the full redemption of human life.

5. The union of men for social intercourse is still more definitely a form of religion; for we meet to impart to others the best that we have and to receive the best that they can give us. The more fully, the more enthusiastically, a man throws himself into society, the more he gives himself. The more truly he cares for his companions, the more real and deep the intercourse becomes. But what is it that we thus give and receive? Ourselves. But much more than ourselves; for we are those in whom God lives. Our faculties: but much more than our faculties; for these have become spiritual gifts. So that in social intercourse in its highest forms we mutually give and receive that which is Divine.

And this is the case with social intercourse of all kinds, if only it be inspired with the Christian principle. Even in games, in sport, in the dance, the real charm is to be found in what we see of one another.

We see the spiritual being expressing itself, possibly with more reality, because with more freedom, than in more serious pursuits. But the media of intercourse, varying as they do with culture, express different parts of the man; and each of these media has a religious element in it. The friendships of school or college, begun perhaps in games and in the light interests of youth, but going deeper and deeper until the friends know each other almost without reserve; the friendships springing from common interests in the fields of knowledge, or of art, or practical work; the conversation of cultured men on literature or the events of the day; even the simple interest in each other's health and welfare which are natural to us all; all these are the means for the exchange of the higher feelings, of care and love for one another, which, where the Spirit of Christ reigns, are religious acts of the highest importance. To mix with our fellow-men, what is it but to keep up our union with the body of Christ? To give out our qualities to them, what is it but to edify the body of Christ?

And, further, the discipline of social intercourse is an important part of our religious training. It is there that self-restraint is imposed, that taste is formed, that courtesy is exercised; and there that we are brought under the criticism of our fellows, whose judgment, if it be sound, is as the judgment of God. It is also a school of liberality, for in hospitality we freely give and receive; and it is the means of smoothing away the asperities which are often engendered by direct intercourse on matters of business. In free conversation also we find points of common feeling with those whom we had thought to be wholly estranged from us. Such intercourse, further, serves many of the best interests of the larger Church of the nation and the community of nations; for in the nation it creates a general understanding among its more cultured classes; and in the still wider sphere its effects are felt, since society is largely international, and ideas and feelings are communicated at times more fully through social intercourse than through the more formal channels of business or diplomacy.

Society must, however, in order to fulfil these functions, inspire itself to the fullest extent with the universal spirit. Society must open its doors wide, to admit as large a range as possible of those who can profit by it; and those kinds of social intercourse should be most fostered which bring together men of various ranks on the footing of common and mutual interest, so that they may know each other's feelings and opinions. The social life thus becomes a branch of the Church. The leaders, if they realise their responsibility, become its ministers; the external objects, the interest in which draws men together, become Sacraments; its meetings a religious fellowship, its whole conduct a Service of God.

6. The intercourse of men in trade and professional life is also a means of religious good. The saying of Aristotle[1], that, wherever there is a field for justice, there is also a field for love, may be supplemented in the

---

[1] Eth. Nic. viii. 9. Ἔοικε δὲ περὶ ταῦτα καὶ ἐν τοῖς αὐτοῖς εἶναι ἥ τε φιλία καὶ τὸ δίκαιον· ἐν ἁπάσῃ γὰρ κοινωνίᾳ δοκεῖ τι δίκαιον εἶναι, καὶ φιλία δέ. See also c. 11.

Christian philosophy by the observation that wherever there is a field for love, there is also a field for the operation of the Divine Spirit. In business we deal with what is most obvious and necessary. In this the real man comes out. We know each other most sincerely, if not in the deepest way, through business. Moreover, business is the most necessary bond which binds men to each other. It is also the witness to the higher need of mental and spiritual intercourse. And it is most universal, since every man must take part in buying and selling. Business also is the parent of one of the greatest of virtues, that of industry, without the exertion of which it must fail; and of all the intellectual virtues which circle round inventiveness, which vastly heightens its success. Thus a necessary and permanent ground is laid for the whole system of moral and political intercourse, a home, therefore, for the religion of Christ.

Society comes together in order to live; but it really exists that men may live well[1]. This saying of Aristotle leads up to the religious view of trade. It is a great system for the relief of mankind, for the development of the earth and its reduction under man's dominion; in other words, for its transformation from a material to a spiritual state[2]. It opens the way for

[1] Politics, i. 2. 8. Πόλις ... γινομένη μὲν οὖν τοῦ ζῆν ἕνεκεν, οὖσα δὲ τοῦ εὖ ζῆν. See also B. iii. 6, especially § 4.

[2] 'The earthly material Nature, as lived in by the human race, and already relatively taken into possession by it, is the object of appropriate action; this Nature, I mean, in its close connexion with the history of man and expressly bound up with this. We may shortly express it: the Object towards which the human individual in its ethical action directs its moral functions in order to appropriate it to the human personality, this is its World.' R. Rothe, 'Theol. Ethics,' vol. ii. p. 126.

mutual benefit, a way in which honesty and enterprise, and even self-sacrifice, often succeed better than mere calculation. It gives also to human labour its true dignity; and it constantly tends to put aside fictitious claims, for there is no better test to which the pretentious talker can be subjected than to ask what character he bears in his own circle of business. Nor are the media of intercourse here merely brute and material. The material gains its value, and becomes an article of commerce, simply from the human labour and skill bestowed upon it. It is therefore, so to speak, humanised and spiritualised matter, and as such draws forth our human sympathies. We can hardly avoid thinking from time to time of those who have toiled in distant countries, or under hard conditions, to supply the common articles of our food or dress, or the staple of our industry, and feeling that something of gratitude and of sympathy associates us with them. The companies which exist for trade purposes, also, though less closely bound together (since the liability of each member, to give an extension to a commercial phrase, is limited), still form moral relations between their members, and a common life, which is susceptible of noble impulses, such as the spirit of hope and of enterprize, and ministers powerfully to the good of mankind. Lastly, trade is universal, since it brings all parts of the world together, and is the great pioneer of mutual knowledge between the nations, and the channel through which they may aid one another throughout the whole range of the needs which are supplied by Christian civilisation. Free trade, therefore, is not only an economical but a moral and a religious principle.

The great and growing society of commerce becomes, therefore, like every other form of human society, a branch of the universal Church. Its ministers are merchants and tradesmen, its prayer the constant aspiration to increase the well-being and happiness of the human race, its sacraments the commodities, through the exchange of which the inner life of mutual benevolence and of culture may be communicated, its divine service a constant activity in developing the powers of the earth according to the primæval command, and in ministering to the needs of God's children who cover its surface.

7. The Nation, or national Church, differs from all voluntary associations, even from that of public worship, in that it is more distinctly an ordinance of God. The family alone is like it in this respect. We may, as we please, enter more or less into commerce, or social intercourse, or societies for knowledge and art. We may worship alone, or in small societies, or in informal gatherings. Even of family life we may in a great measure denude ourselves. But we cannot help belonging to the nation, and that for our whole life, and with all that we have. It is sometimes assumed that the organisation for worship is divine, and the family and State, as it is said, merely human. But the contrary is the case. The organisation for worship is distinctly and demonstrably a formation of man: the family and the State are institutions of nature and of God. Further, the Nation is

most universal: every man necessarily belongs to it, and it is bound to take account of every man. It is universal also in this sense, that it contains within itself all the elements of human life. A Nationalist in religion is far more comprehensive in his religious system than one who is technically called by the name of Catholic.

The Nation is the most complete of all the societies of men now in existence. We are necessarily pledged to it with our whole existence in this world, for it has the power of directing and even of resuming all our possessions, and of life and death over our persons. Hence it calls forth a worship more complete than any other. The political life is the most absorbing of all. We may say also that the Nation is the largest organisation; for the universal Church is as yet unformed, while the Nation is highly organised, and presents a distinct field for religious action. When we consider also the immense power which the Nation has over our moral welfare by its laws and its educating power, and the influence which it exerts upon all the minor circles of moral life within it; when we think of it as becoming, as it must do more and more, the object of mental regard, of admiration, of love, even of worship (for in it pre-eminently God dwells), we shall recognise to the fullest extent its religious character and functions.

The form of national organisation to which Christian political thought has guided the Church is that of the Constitutional Monarchy, or of the Republic with a President at its head. In this alone the two great principles of a Christian Society receive a complete expression, on the one hand unity, order, and the subjection of each to the whole, on the other hand the sense of independence and responsibility. These two are united by the spirit of Christian trustfulness and brotherhood. In this spirit the Nation will aim continually at educating all its members to the full political capacity, and at including them all in the circle of political rights.

The Christian nation is in the fullest sense a Church; or rather, it alone of present organisations can claim the name of the Church; for, as we have pointed out, the universal Church has no organisation as yet. Its aim must be distinctly to impress the spirit of Christ on all its citizens. It has a right to demand the utmost devotion from them; and it must train them to help one another. It is thus a school of moral relations in the largest extent. And these moral relations must tend always not to justice only but to Christian kindness. The special direction of its policy must be to relieve and to raise the weaker classes of its citizens. It corresponds entirely in its functions with the original conception of the Christian Church. It is built upon Christ, that is, its essential idea is that of universal, whole-hearted, self-renouncing love and mutual well-doing. Its rulers alone are spoken of in the New Testament as officially the ministers of God, and they correspond more nearly than any others in their functions to the Elders and Pastors of the primitive Church. It alone has sovereign power, and can carry its will into effect[1]. It alone can embrace all the wants

[1] See Note XXIII, a quotation from Dr. Arnold's 'Fragment on the Church.'

of its members and afford them the universal instruction and elevation which they need. We must credit it, moreover, with the qualities of all the circles of life which it contains. In this way it includes the worshipping body, which is not, as sometimes supposed, itself the Church, but a circle within the Church. The nation presides over them all, establishing just relations between them, presenting a tribunal to which they can all appeal, and ensuring their free development.

There will always be in the Christian nation different orders, the governors and the governed, the ruling and the subject classes, though it cannot allow the perpetuity of a servile or pauper class. But to the relations of these classes we must especially apply the principle of election before explained. The true governor does not live for himself, but for those whom he governs. His object is to raise all to the level to which he has himself been first called, to lead the general advance. He is the man in whom the idea of the nation lives, in whom its aim is most fully represented; and, being full-charged with this himself, he endeavours to impart it to all, both individuals and classes, within the nation. This is his title to recognition as a ruler. The true ruler is a Good Shepherd, who sacrifices himself for the flock, not only by willingness to work or to suffer when need exists, but by losing his own life in the life of the people. He would impart his own soul to them, and would be willing, were it possible, that the office of ruler should pass away, provided the spirit of the national brotherhood should dwell in each member and work itself out spontaneously.

We may admit that the nation may change, or may cease to exist. It might become a minor circle within the universal Church, if the universal Church were organised. It might, on the other hand, be broken up into small fragments; or it might be a member of a confederation. We have to take things as they are; and we find the nation alone fully organised, sovereign, independent, universal, capable of giving full expression to the Christian principle. We ought, therefore, to regard the Nation as the Church, its rulers as ministers of Christ, its whole body as a Christian brotherhood, its public assemblies as amongst the highest modes of universal Christian fellowship, its dealing with material interests as Sacraments, its progressive development, especially in raising the weak, as the fullest service rendered on earth to God, the nearest thing as yet within our reach to the kingdom of heaven.

8. Yet the Church of Christ is universal, co-extensive with the race. It is true that, the universal community being as yet without organisation, all action relating to it is in a rudimentary condition. But it is also true that there is nothing of more importance, nothing, indeed, of more immediate and pressing importance than its organisation. For the present, no doubt, the nation is that which is most universal to us, since it contains all, or almost all, the elements of human life within it. But civilisation has now reached a point at which the eyes of all Christian men should be turned

distinctly in the direction of the universal Church, with a view to its definite constitution. The Church has been too long content to pray, 'Give us this day our daily bread.' It is time that it should revert to the universal prayer, 'Thy kingdom come.' No individual is complete apart from the Church or Nation; and similarly no Nation is complete without the universal Church. Moreover, each of the separate circles of union which we have enumerated reaches beyond the Nation. The organisation for worship takes its sacred readings, its prayers, its saintly examples, its books of devotion, its hymns, from many nations. The family, by intermarriages and by education, is connected with foreign countries. Knowledge passes from nation to nation, Art is cosmopolitan; trade is the unceasing reminder of the interdependence of the whole world; society is constantly refreshed by foreign intercourse; and the Nation, though in some respects complete in itself, has also its external aspects; it is a member of the greater whole of Christendom, and has its friends, its standing, its interests, its sphere of action in the great family of nations.

The organisation of the universal community must begin with Europe as the leading portion of the human race. It is as yet hardly begun. It can barely be credited with the prevention of war in a single case. Yet this is its first and indispensable function, and the demand for this, which grows louder and louder, must hasten its constitution. If this is regarded as Utopian at present, the presence of the vast subterranean forces Democracy and Socialism will certainly make it practical before long. These dread twin-giants already make the mountain shake, and will eventually upheave it. The Spirit of Christ must go before, and make their action not violent but beneficent. The idea of universality was given by Imperial Rome. Whatever its faults, and they were many, for one great merit it earned the enthusiastic gratitude of mankind, even of the Christian Fathers. The Roman peace endeared the Roman unity; and the grateful remembrance of it has never been wholly extinguished. The Empire, indeed, was a rule of force, and the Christian spirit failed to penetrate it so as to give it spiritual cohesion. Yet even the barbarians who overthrew it reverenced the fallen image, and in Charlemagne it seemed to arise once more. The Roman Church organisation attempted to create the desired spiritual unity; and for some five centuries the idea of one Church and one Empire floated before the mind of Europe. But it was an idea rather than a reality, at least as regarded the Empire; even as an idea it had the fatal fault of being dualistic, the spiritual power seeking not to penetrate but to rival and overtop the secular; and the Papal authority, never wholly supreme over the national churches, was for all practical purposes extinguished by the Reformation. The Universal Church needs to be built up on the foundation of the Christian nations, which has now been fairly laid. There has been indeed some attempt, by means of congresses and diplomacy, to recognise international obligations, and to avert the ravages of war[1]. But behind these there has been hardly any

---

[1] Bluntschli, 'Allgemeine Volkslehre,' b. i. c. 2. See Note XXIV.

spiritual conviction. The diplomatist has rarely escaped the imputation of hypocrisy, pretending to aim at the general good, but seeking always the material interests of his own nation at the expense of those of the rest. The phrase Balance of Power rings of war and rapacity rather than of spiritual brotherhood. We are oppressed by the weight of standing armies, which is fast growing intolerable. Yet the Christian spirit which might change this, though recognised by all serious writers on international law, has hardly yet gained any practical and determining power in international affairs. The Alabama Convention, and the attempts at maintaining the European concert which the last few years have witnessed, the commercial treaties, the international agreements for coinage and for posts, have shown that the spirit of universalism is rising. But the slightness of its results thus far has disheartened many of its well-wishers[1].

Yet the universal Church must stand out ever more distinctly before us as a vision and an image looming larger and nearer. Its members are the various nations of Christian Europe, which, though united, are never suppressed, but remain as living organisms. Its object is universal peace, and the carrying of Christian civilisation to its highest and most universal results. The media of its communion are the universal needs, such as commerce, correspondence, and the possessions of the various nations which it comprehends. Through

---

[1] Woolsey's 'Introduction to the Study of International Law.' See Note XXIV, in which the views of Woolsey and Fiore on International Law are given, together with the passage from Bluntschli referred to at page 326.

the regulated use or exchange of these the nations edify one another, and these therefore become the Sacraments of its life and worship. Its organs and its ministries must be established by some kind of representatives, who will exercise that portion of authority with which the nations voluntarily part. Whatever their particular functions may be, they will be, by virtue of their beneficent mission, truly ministers of God and organs of the Divine Spirit.

When Western Europe becomes one great Church, the head or leading portion of the Church of humanity will be organised. It will then have the duty of assimilating by degrees the more backward nations to itself. Colonisation, commercial and other intercourse with the barbarous and savage races, the progressive effort to raise those races by the infusion among them of the spirit of Christian civilisation, will form the functions of the Church now become fully universal; and the longed for completion of this process is that which is expressed by the religious words, the building up of the Holy City, the establishment of the kingdom of God, the universal reign of Christ.

Two things must be added. First, the various circles of human society, the churches within the Church, such as we have described them, are permanent. They aid one another, and further the life of the whole. Secondly, the chief of these circles will always be the society for public worship, the inspiring power of the spiritual life of the whole. On the principle of Election which we have maintained, the elect body is that in which the Christian spirit of universalism is most fully received and enforced, and the sources of the Christian life brought to view, in which the worship is direct, with only such sacramental media as are needed for the bare assertion of the relationship, and in which men join, not on the ground of any special qualification, but only as men related to God and to one another. If the Worshipping Body can imbue itself fully with the spirit of Christian universalism, it will be recognised as the guide and inspiring power of the whole. It will maintain its supreme position, not by any external power accorded to it, but by the influence which it legitimately wins, by the confidence which it inspires, by its power to impart and sustain the consciousness of Christ's redemption, by the enthusiasm with which it animates men, by the interpretation which it gives them of their present situation and their needs, by the inextinguishable gratitude awakened by its beneficence, and by its revelations to the universal Church of the way of the blessed life.

LECTURE VIII.

PRACTICAL STEPS TOWARDS THE IDEAL.

REVELATION xxi. 9. Come hither, and I will show thee the bride, the Lamb's wife.

IN the last Lecture the attempt was made to sketch out the fulness of the universal Church, the condition of the redeemed humanity when fully or normally constituted. I propose in the present Lecture to compare with this the state of things in which we actually live, and to show how a direction may be given to human progress in conformity with the ideal which has been thus drawn out. We must start from the foundation of things as they are, and commence to build the bridge (not quite so long perhaps as our less hopeful moods would make it appear) which leads up from our present state to the ideal at which we aim. I need not say that, in a single Lecture, all that can be done is to give an indication of the direction in which the first steps should be taken in each department of social life.

This may best be done by following the lines of the last Lecture, and applying the process successively to each of the circles or associations in which men are bound together. After this a few remarks on the actual tendencies of society, and of the conditions required to conduct these tendencies in the path by which this Christian state is actually to be reached, will bring these Lectures to a close.

1. We begin, therefore, as before, with the system of divine worship, with which instruction and beneficence are combined. It has been pointed out that in the completed state of the Church, the system of public worship will be fully inspired with the universal spirit, the spirit of the world-wide society to which it ministers, and of which it forms a part. It is from its neglect of this that it has become so largely, as it now is, a dividing and sectarian element in the community. What is needed is that Christian doctrines should be interpreted by their bearing upon life and piety. There will then be little room for division. And further, it is needed that piety should not be cultivated as an isolated thing, which brings on it the tinge of selfishness, but as the means of creating such relations to God and to one another as will issue in right conduct and just feeling in all departments of life. It will thus be kept from the excesses which at present engender division. It is needed, moreover, that the system of public worship should not claim to be the Church, but should be content with being a part of a vast whole, which is the true Church; for then the minds of its ministers, instead of turning to its more minute details, and falling into disputes about them, will see these details in their true proportion. The same thing may be said as to that which is commonly

called Church-government, but which is more truly the arrangement for the conduct of public worship, and the discipline of its ministers. As soon as it is felt that the whole system is not a separate thing, but a function of the greater whole, the exaggerated importance and false assumptions often made concerning it will cease, and it will serve its true office, that of raising into a spiritual condition the general life of mankind.

The notion that religion is primarily a cult is not a Christian but a heathen idea. If we identify religion with a peculiar cult, we may say that Christianity is not, in this sense, a religion, and that the expression Christian Religion is a misnomer. Religion was to the ancients almost synonymous with superstitious practices or usages. The writers of the New Testament rarely use it, and then usually in a bad sense, as when St. Paul speaks of his living 'according to the most straitest sect of his religion [1].' It passes, indeed, into a better sense, but by a kind of paronomasia, as when St. Paul says that the reasonable service [2] of Christians is to present themselves as an offering to God, or when St. James says that the pure religion (using the word θρησκεία [3]) is to visit the poor and to be unspotted by

---

[1] Acts xxvi. 5. θρησκεία: this word is used only in this passage, and in James i. 26, 27. The word for 'The Jews' religion' in Gal. i. 14 is Ἰουδαισμός.

[2] Rom. xii. 1. The word Λατρεία is the regular word in the LXX. and Hellenistic Greek for ritual (Ex. xi. 25, 26; Heb. ix. 1, 6). It is adopted by St. Paul for heart religion in this passage and in Phil. iii. 3.

[3] Jas. i. 26, 27. θρησκεία, usually applied to the outward observances of worship. It is used again in Col. ii. 18, 'A voluntary humility and worshipping of angel.' Other words denoting worship are used mainly in the sense of Jewish piety, which was primarily the observance of ordinances, as σέβομαι in Acts xiii. 43, 'Religious

worldliness. In this derivative sense, of doing all things in the fear of God, it has its legitimate use. Unfortunately, it is always in danger of an atavistic relapse, and reverts to its former sense of a system of worship apart from life. From that point begins its decline. Cut off from its proper aliment in real life it becomes enfeebled, and draws down with it all men's thoughts of God and of holiness.

But do not these reflections imply that the system of public worship, so commonly identified with the Church itself, is gradually and surely losing ground? And is not this decline one of the facts of our present situation, partially in England, much more on the Continent? Will not this decline continue until the system of public worship ceases? So thought Richard Rothe[1], the greatest, and certainly not the least pious, of those who have written on the subject embraced by these Lectures. He is even said to have seen without sorrow, and to have thought quite natural, the tendency, so marked in Germany, to let public worship fall into neglect; and he had the courage, speaking of the association for worship as being itself the Church, to say that the Church must dwindle and cease to be

proselytes;' προσκυνέω, as in I Cor. xiv. 25, 'Falling down on his face he will worship God;' and often in Rev.; εὐλαβής and εὐσεβής, in several places for 'devout' men according to the law; θεραπεύω in Acts xvii. 25, 'Neither is worshipped with men's hands.' But none of these are applied to the public worship of the church. The existence of church-worship is, no doubt, recognised; but the fact that only one distinct exhortation to public worship (Heb. x. 25, to which may perhaps be added Heb. xiii. 15) occurs in the New Testament shows how small a place was, in the minds of the first Christian teachers, occupied by a system which has in aftertimes been almost identified with the church in men's estimation.

[1] See, in Note XX, the opinion of Rothe.

when the other spheres of life should have become fully imbued with religion. Were that so, it would not be that the Church had ceased, but that, within the Church, the function of public worship had ceased. But it is not true that the system of public worship is likely to fall permanently into discredit. The true explanation of the phenomena which seem to men to imply the dwindling of the Church is this, that, whereas the system of public worship had in many directions overstepped its proper limit, and had undertaken what more properly belongs to the national organisations, or to the organisations for knowledge and for art, it is now losing its power over these departments, and is being thrust back from them. This has, no doubt, caused a certain mistrust of it to be felt, but the alienation, we may well believe, is only temporary. It may be in the future more honoured and more fruitful than ever in its proper sphere. Meanwhile, the functions which it had in a measure usurped are being taken over by other departments, which are, slowly but resolutely, resuming their own as branches of the Church.

Reasons have been given for believing that, in the complete state of the universal Church, the system of public worship and instruction will hold a high, and even the highest, place, as the inspirer of the whole. For this it must prepare itself. And if it be asked what is the point at which the vivifying contact may be maintained between the system of public worship and the inculcation of Christian piety on the one side and the national and universal Church on the other, the answer is, the Parochial system. Wherever a cure of souls exists, not congregational but territorial, so that the whole life of the population is brought under the influences which circle round the parish church, there a connexion is established with the Church national and universal. Amongst the members of the parish are samples of all kinds of persons, and of all the needs of humanity. The parish or commune is a little nation, which should manage its own affairs, those of public worship as well as others, on the constitutional system, which springs direct from the spirit of Christian brotherliness[1]. This process connects the clergy with the liberal influences of the Church at large, making them act less as if they were themselves the Church, or had exclusive power within it; but it gives them also a position in which they may exert their legitimate influence. A nation which, in all its territorial fractions, is subject to this influence, supposing that this influence is wisely used, in the name not of an order but of Christ and of mankind, becomes more and more capable of discharging the functions of a Church, that is, of a society caring for each of its members with Christian and brotherly love.

It is from this point of view that we may best judge of the question which is commonly called the question of Church and State. If the views which have been expressed in these Lectures are well founded, there can be no question of Church and State, since the nation is itself the truest development of the Church. And this is the actual state of things in England, since

[1] See Note XXV, on Parochial Organization.

the English nation has never recognised any Church of England but itself. It has recognised various functions within the Church; and it has established, as corporations sole or aggregate, the responsible ministers of public worship, while giving, as we have seen, full liberty of worship to all its members. But it never[1] incorporated or established as a Church a body of persons distinct from the nation. There is, therefore, within the nation a body of established clergy, but no established Church. The question which is erroneously spoken of as the question of Church and State is really the question whether the Christian community, the nation or national Church, ought by public act and recognition to maintain the system of worship, instruction, and beneficence administered by the clergy. It may justly be felt that, the more the nation accepts, according to the view taken in these Lectures, the position of a Christian Church, and opens itself to the teaching and influence of Christian ministers in all its parochial divisions, the more likely it will be to maintain and reform the existing system as a function of the national life. But, if the clergy,

---

[1] Perhaps the case of the Church of Ireland forms an exception to this. The Act under which it was set up is in form permissive; but the Corporate Body of the Church becomes by that Act a recognised and established institution with legal attributes: and the Act lays down many binding conditions as to the framework of the Church. We have therefore the paradox that in England there is no established Church, and that the only established Church existing in the British Empire is the so-called disestablished Church of Ireland; and further that, so far as it is proposed to apply the Irish precedent to England, what is aimed at is not the disestablishment of the Church (for there is no corporate body to overthrow), but the setting up or establishment of that which has never before existed, a great, and I may add clerical, corporation endowed with great powers and emoluments by the nation, yet severed from the national life.

with the tacit consent of the people, enter upon a course which narrows the sphere of their ministry and influence, and reduces the system committed to their charge to the bare functions of worship, preaching, and charity, caring almost exclusively for those who take part in these functions, and having hardly any regard for the general life; if the organization for public worship inculcates a moral system antiquated, onesided, disowned by the national conscience; if it refuses all brotherly intercourse with the voluntary societies for worship; if, in a word, it becomes clerical and congregational instead of parochial and national, a sect instead of a branch or inner circle of the Church, the national Church could not treat it otherwise than as it treats the family or those parts of human life which are best left under private management. The Church, the Christian nation, would remain; but the system of worship, thus shrunk, would be left to the conduct of private associations.

And yet it is hardly possible that this should come to pass where the provision for worship forms a vast system conterminous with the nation: for either this system is regarded as being itself the Church, or it is a function, according to our contention, of the nation which is the Church. In the former case it can hardly be left to itself; for the necessary tendency of a Church is to grow into a State, or at least to absorb the functions of the State; so that to cut off the Church from the State, were it possible, would be to construct an imperium in imperio, a source of unceasing discord. In the latter case, that is, if the nation acknowledges itself to be a Church, it can hardly do otherwise than have its own system of worship, maintaining its parochial character, and giving it such reforms as will make it minister to the national wants.

2. We turn now to the Family Life, the second of the social circles within the greater whole of humanity and of mankind.

The family life is so necessary and so Christian in its very nature, that its highest, most ideal condition does not lie out of sight of our ordinary Christian experience. We cannot doubt its continuance, nor the continuance of the sanctions and safeguards which support it. We may trace, not perhaps without some misgivings, reasons for believing that, in our own country at least, it is fulfilling its functions progressively better, and that the narrowness which is apt to cling to it will be purged away. But it is menaced by two grave dangers, each of which it must be the work of the Christian spirit to dissipate.

It is of no use to hide the fact that, both in France and in the United States of America, two branches of the Church each of which is in a different way specially advanced, there is a disposition to decline or to limit very narrowly the duty of parentage. Not to dwell upon the means by which this is effected, supposing that those means are innocent, which is exceedingly doubtful, the result cannot but be most pernicious. In the family life it destroys much of the tenderness of both the married and the parental relation. In public life it diminishes the inventiveness which is called forth by the necessity of the support of children, and limits the fresh supply of citizens. If in America the supply is made up from Europe, yet the predominance of heterogenous elements is by no means desirable ; and the moral conditions of selfishness and lack of hope, which it reveals and which it fosters, are becoming the subject of grave alarm. In France it is felt by statisticians and economists as a matter of life and death, and appearances at present point to the latter and worse alternative[1]. In reference to the more general life of the world, the evil is still more serious ; for commerce, colonisation, invention, are of the essence of its fuller life, which demands the reclamation of the waste parts of the earth and the influence of the advanced upon the backward races. These enterprises require the extension of the energies of the leading nations ; and, if these grow weak and become inadequate to the task, our best hopes for the world will be frustrated. In England it may be said that this danger is little felt : the fears conceived by Malthus eighty years ago have proved groundless ; our population is healthily

[1] The facts as to the decrease of the French population (except in the towns and in one or two of the Northern Departments) are notorious. They are well summed up in a statistical paper in the *Times* of Jan. 25, 1883. The writer speaks of the causes of this decrease as follows : ' The increasing sterility of the nation can have no other causes assigned to it but those of habit and calculation.' ' No reason can be sustained except that before mentioned, the growing indisposition of the people to have large families ; and, with the increase of wealth in the country, it is probable that this indisposition will increase instead of diminishing.' Similar testimonies are constantly borne to the decrease of the old stock in New England, and indeed of the unwillingness to have families in the native population of the United States generally, even in the flourishing states of the west. The evils connected with this (which indeed can hardly escape the notice of any one travelling in America) were described in the concluding chapter of Mr. Barham Zincke's ' Last Winter in the United States.' Murray, 1868.

increasing; and there is no reason for more than the ordinary restraint in postponing marriage according to the dictates of prudence. Yet there have not been wanting phenomena among ourselves of a contrary tendency; and that which is a recognised custom in France and America can hardly fail to affect England. It is necessary, therefore, to strengthen by religious hope, and by destroying the illusions which breed despair, the foundations of family life. The more its blessedness and sanctity as an inner circle of Christ's Church is realised, the more also the duty is felt of making our private ease give way to the benefit of mankind in the largest sense, the less disposed shall we be to place an unhealthful limit to the growth of the family.

The other danger is that social evil, the vast extent of which, whether it be or be not upon the increase, is certainly a ground for alarm and for exertion. The preaching of discipline and self-restraint to individuals, the inculcation of purity as a Christian duty, is no doubt a powerful deterrent from this evil, and so is the knowledge of the physical misery entailed by it, not on individuals merely, but on generation after generation. But the evil is still more one to be dealt with by the Church itself in its largest capacity. The healthier and fuller development of the various forms of life which we have traced out, through their recognition as branches or functions of the Church, will, we may confidently expect, have a beneficial influence: especially will this be the case when women are more fully admitted to an equality with men, and receive a similar education; for with such common knowledge comes mutual respect and an addition to the sense of responsibility and the power of self-guidance. The occupation of the mind also with worthier spheres, and the increase of hope, which is thus engendered, will, we may believe, tend to save us from the vices, which, in their most venial forms are the vices of thoughtlessness, and in their worst forms the vices of despair. But the increase of wealth which, if better distributed, will allow the poorer classes to rise to self-respect is also a necessary condition; and this again is dependent on the cessation of the vast expenditure upon war, and on the political measures by which the weaker classes are raised and the inequalities of social conditions diminished. Thus the national Church and the universal Church have directly to do with family life and private morality; and by restoring the Church idea, we may operate powerfully upon both the family and the individual.

3. Turning next to the sphere of Knowledge, what we have to aim at is a better co-ordination of its various departments. A warning as to this is needed everywhere in the present day, and, owing to the vast extension of the subjects of study, is specially needed in our University. Its need is felt by all who look upon human knowledge as a whole; but I give a description of the danger by preference from one who began with the critical side of special studies, and worked thence to the building of the general edifice, M. Auguste Comte[1]. 'The dispersive habits,' he says, 'which have

[1] 'Cours de Philosophie Positive,' vol. vi. pp. 378-9 (Littré's Edition).

been antecedently contracted have in our day pushed the preliminary régime of scientific specialism to the most disastrous exaggeration, and that at the very epoch at which it ought to give way to the definitive régime of rational generality at once mental and social. There is a revolt against the fundamental dualism, the dualism which supplements analysis by synthesis. The masons of our day will no longer suffer the architect.'

I venture here to make an appeal to the students of Physical Science. It is no longer necessary to bid those engaged in the moral and social sciences or in divinity take note of the discoveries of the students of the natural sciences. Those discoveries, and even the hypotheses founded upon them, are for the most part adequately recognised: the pursuit and the spirit of Natural Science is held in honour; and even those engaged in the engrossing work of religion and philanthropy feel increasingly bound not to contravene the proper boundaries of exact science. But the students of the exact sciences are very apt to press forward without due regard to the relative proportion and value of the various branches of knowledge. It must be the aim of the Church to re-assert the true proportion. The pursuit of Natural Science is indeed so pure and noble, so vast and so fruitful in results, that it is easy to understand how one immersed in it may fancy himself dispensed from taking notice of the moral and political world around him or of the system of public worship. Yet such an attitude is by no means a noble one. Rather it is selfish, in the sense that it ignores all but its own province. When it is felt that knowledge constitutes among those who pursue it a genuine branch of the Church, and when it is cultivated from Christian motives, it may be hoped that the votaries of the natural sciences will accept more fully the need of harmonising their own province with those of others. It may be hoped that men will arise in their own ranks capable of doing this, caring, that is, primarily for the general good of mankind, and subordinating to it their own special pursuits; men penetrated with a sense of the supreme importance of moral goodness, and seeking, in union with the heads of other departments of human knowledge, to establish on an unassailable foundation the sanctions and motives on which it rests. Then education will receive a larger expansion, being conducted in harmony with the well-known needs of the nation and the race and of all circles of life within them. When this takes place, the single cloud will have disappeared which still hangs over the triumphs of knowledge, and its pursuit will go on with mutual confidence and at an accelerated pace.

4. In reference to the Life of Art, what is needed is that it should be popular, not in the sense of being abased to the present popular taste, but rather as raising the popular taste by the presentation of the best ideals in an intelligible form. There have been artists in all departments who have, with more or less of conscious aim, asserted their own standard of excellence as a religious duty, and have succeeded, even after opposition and ridicule, in imparting it to others. There are schools of art and societies for music which

have been formed with the religious aim of being the means of refreshment to the less cultured classes, and of imparting the graces of refinement and beauty to the whole community[1]. It is this religious aim of art which the Church must seek to expand.

In this popularising of art, and especially of its musical branch, the general Church sentiment can act most powerfully. When it is felt that the mass of serious men are looking for artistic productions as a spiritual help to themselves, and are ready to impart the enjoyment of them to others, this must react upon artists of all kinds in a very favourable manner. When the various objects represented, and especially human history and the human frame, are no longer regarded as indifferent things, but as expressions of the human and divine spirit, as transfigured by their connexion with the general life of humanity and by the indwelling of God, the accession of dignity and of interest which will come to all art-work will be very great, and will be at once stimulating and ennobling. This will be seen especially in the Drama, which in England more than anywhere is in need of this stimulus and this elevation.

5. Passing on to the Life of Society, we have chiefly to lay emphasis on that which was indicated in the last Lecture. The great danger of society lies in its exclusiveness; and, to bring it to its right, its Christian state, the Church must strive with a definite

---

[1] I may refer to the Kyrle Society, which is established 'To bring beauty home to the people.' An account of the work of this Society is given in a paper by Miss Octavia Hill, entitled 'Colour, Space, and Music for the People,' reprinted from the Nineteenth Century for May, 1884 (Kegan Paul, Trench and Co.).

aim to lay society open to all the widest human interests.

Not only should all that is actually wrong be discouraged by the leaders of society, but also all that is poor and mean. Society should be a school of excellence in which each learns to give out the best that he has. This will prevent dulness, which, besides its own debasing tendency, drives men by a natural reaction into folly and immorality. For mere rules of decorum the Church should endeavour to substitute good sense and right taste which may pervade the whole society. Moreover, society should be the expression of the highest culture, and men should learn to value each other there by that standard alone, not by the standard of rank or wealth.

But further, society should acknowledge a missionary character. If this be admitted, those who lead in it will think of themselves as set for the imparting of the best and highest enjoyment to their fellows. They will treat those of their company who are less cultured than themselves as the special objects of their care, and the object proposed by the leaders will be the drawing out in those with whom they associate of the highest culture of which they are capable, and of imparting their own refinement to them. In order to bring this about, there should be as little display as possible, that every one may be at his ease. Our present society tends far too much to extravagance. There are some appliances of culture which require considerable expense, and the highest excellence in such things as instruments of music, works of art, and application of mechanical inventions, form the proper objects for the employment of wealth. But simplicity should be aimed at. The idea of ancient Roman civilisation should be reproduced in our day, 'Privatus illis sumptus erat brevis, Commune magnum.' We may be simple in our own habits although surrounded by wealth: and, by using the more costly appliances in our possession for the general enjoyment, we may realize the Christian idea of a stewardship. This is the tendency which the Church must foster in social life among all classes of its members.

6. The Expansion of Trade in the present century is probably only a prelude to its still greater expansion in the future. If only war could be done away, the extension of commerce would be immeasurable. All the greater, therefore, must be our desire to see commerce conducted on Christian principles of justice and of service, as a function of the universal Church. The frauds, the low tone of morals admitted in many branches of trades, the panics which have sprung from mistrust, the bad relations with foreign nations which have resulted from the action of traders, open to us a wide field for the Church's reformatory action[1]. On the other hand, the vast benefits which trade confers, the noble, liberal spirit in which its higher operations are often conducted, and the trustfulness engendered by commercial rectitude, must make us welcome its extension. There may be, moreover, a Christian

---

[1] See a large number of details on this subject in a paper by Mr. Herbert Spencer, entitled 'The Morals of Trade,' published with a sermon on 'Sins of Trade and Business,' by the late Canon Lyttelton (Isbister and Co., 1874).

trading, which, taking cognisance of these nobler features of commerce, will embark in it simply with a view to promote its beneficial action. Such a course, of which we see instances from time to time, is not unreasonable, though it must face the possibility of loss.

But we cannot rest satisfied with the present methods of trade, in which the interests of labour and capital are constantly at variance, and wages are rarely raised except by the brutal machinery of a strike. There is no reason why trade should be motived mainly by individual profit. We must learn to lean, in this as in all departments, upon the unselfish much more than on the selfish interests of mankind. There are already in existence companies which make trade serve the general interest rather than the profit of the individual. There are co-operative societies which make trade entirely a matter of general advantage to all their members, and in which therefore the interests of buyer and seller are reconciled[1]. This system, especially as it affects the poor, the Church must constantly seek to extend. We may look forward also, through means of this kind, to the abatement of the extreme competition now reigning in the world of trade, and which is wasteful in all respects, and productive of fraud. Co-operative production still more may be looked upon as affording scope for the bringing of trade under the dominion of the Christian

[1] See Note XXVI. An account of the Maison Leclaire in Paris, by Miss M. Hart. See also Ten Years of Co-operative Shirtmaking, by Miss E. Simcox, in the Fortnightly Review for June, 1884.

spirit; for we can hardly imagine anything more nearly fulfilling the idea of a Church than a vast co-operative guild, inspired by the Christian spirit of mutual well-doing, with rulers and a brotherhood united in the work to which their lives and interests are devoted in common, and aiming, by the labour of all together, at the supply of the wants of all its members.

Nor need it be said that competition and the desire of personal gain is necessary for the keenness and inventiveness of trade. We may look forward to a time when the unselfish motives will have a fuller development, when the wish to benefit the community will stimulate men's energies more fully than competition, and when the public recognition of service, and the gratitude of those who are benefited, may be an adequate guarantee for efficiency. Even now many things are done by municipalities which might be done by private traders: and the nation has taken over successively the Post, which is a great and flourishing trade, some branches of banking and insurance, and the holding of shares in one of the great thoroughfares of the world. Some statesmen already advocate the assumption of railways by the State. There is no reason to be jealous of this process, however far it may be carried[1], so long as the nation has real power over its own affairs, and the government is conducted for the people's benefit, and is open to

[1] The contrary opinions to this may be seen in Mr. Herbert Spencer's four articles in the Contemporary Review, April to July, 1884. For a very temperate discussion on the subject, I may refer to Mr. Goschen's address at Edinburgh on Laissez-Faire and Government Interference (Macmillan, 1883).

criticism and suggestion on all sides. Even if it be supposed that self-interest is a necessary and a perpetual factor in trade affairs, yet the honour and reward arising from good service in a public function may be as powerful a motive as that of immediate gain. But we cannot but believe that a most powerful influence in the direction of unselfishness would be exerted upon individual conduct and energy if it were the primary assumption of the whole community that it was organised for the benefit of all, that is, that it recognised the Christian principle in its action. We must, I repeat, learn to lean on the unselfish much more than on the selfish impulses in mankind. But, whether trade becomes more distinctly organised or not, the object at which the Church should aim is that it should be conducted in a Christian spirit, for public and general advantage, and so as to minister to the spiritual good of those who conduct its operations and those who are its clients.

7. In the Nation or National Church, the Church idea, as has been pointed out, attains its fullest expression. What is now required most of all is that it should be conscious of itself, and should demand that the fundamental postulate of all its public action should be that it is a Church, existing for the highest benefit of its citizens. We may accept without vanity the belief that England is the country in which the practice of political science is most advanced. And, while we admit that the universal Church needs the steadiness of the German, the intellectual capacity of the Italian, the versatility and devotedness of the

Frenchman, and that certain experiments in government have been more fully worked out in the democratic communities of America, or Switzerland, or Holland, yet in the main it must be said that England is the great political teacher of the world. Though the roots of constitutional government may be traced in ancient times and in many countries, it is in England alone that they have been gradually developed, so as to become a permanent tradition and a national inheritance. This must be acknowledged as an eminent gift of God. It is the product of the sense of Christian brotherhood. It has indeed been asked at times why men should consent to be ruled by majorities, and it has been suggested that the explanation is to be found in physical force, in the certainty that in most cases three men could get the better of two. But the true explanation is to be found in moral causes, in that sense of brotherhood and of mutual deference which is so congenial to the instincts of Christians. Suppose a society of five persons, of whom three desire one course to be pursued by the society while the other two desire another course; and suppose that they have all of them the Christian feeling of brotherly esteem for one another. Would not the two feel certainly bound to yield to the three? They would argue with themselves that there might be good reasons for the judgment of the three which they of the minority had not apprehended; that in the last resort the desire or resolution of the three was worthy of greater respect than that of the two; that, if the three were wrong, they would be convinced by experience and acknowledge their error. This simple explanation covers the whole field of constitutionalism. It enables us also to see how moral and spiritual feeling can be applied to politics; and it shows that constitutionalism, far from being, as writers like M. Comte have affirmed, an abnormal development, adapted only to the peculiar circumstances of England, is a necessary result of the acknowledgment in the political sphere of the supremacy of the moral sentiments and of Christian love.

It is evident, however, that, at the present day, the constitutional system requires readjustment from time to time in conformity with the increase and distribution of the population, and with the progress of the people in independence and intelligence. It is evident also that a process of decentralisation is required, not only for the practical conduct of business, but also for the higher spiritual object of calling forth the various gifts and capacities of individuals and of classes. This process is needed both for municipalities and for counties, and again for the conduct of the parochial system. A double process, indeed, must go on continually, guided by an accurate perception of the respective spheres of the central and the local governments, a process in which each of them yields what more properly belongs to the sphere of the other; in which, on the one hand, the central government leaves to the local perfect freedom and responsibility within its own sphere, and on the other the local looks up to the central as its guiding and protecting power. To secure this just balance in the relation of its parts must be the constant aim of the political Church.

It has been pointed out that the chief concern of a national Church must be the elevation of its weaker members. The existence of pauperism and of prevailing poverty in contrast to the progress of wealth must be made to weigh upon all men's consciences, and especially on those of the ruling classes; and no effort, no change that can be suggested, can be too great if it results in the wiping away of this reproach to our Christian state. It is not merely by dealing with pauperism and with poverty in their actual manifestations that this reproach will be wiped away, but much more by such a direction of political interests as will operate, through law and administration, for the removal of the evil; and further the framing of laws not merely so as to make men 'equal before the law,' but so as to afford the poor and the weak the uplifting help which they need. The Israelites delighted in their laws, and recognised them as the laws of the Holy One, because the laws cared for the widow, the fatherless and the stranger, the weak and the poor. There is much in the laws of our country to make us speak of them in the same strain; but much more than has hitherto been done in this direction is possible. Here is the point at which the Church may show sympathy with the socialistic spirit. Socialism is not necessarily the blind and negative impulse which it has sometimes showed itself to be. There are men like those who are called the Katheder Socialisten in Germany[1], who have worked upon the

[1] 'In requiring political equality the Progressists have in view economic equality, and this leads to so-called Socialism. They do not seek to conceal it, and I make

VIII.] *of a Christian World.* 353

principle that economic science must not be contented with merely tracing a law, but must minister to the corresponding art of social well-being, that it must show how to apply its principles according to the wants of the community, and must acknowledge the need of paternal care for the weak, and even the necessity at certain times of giving them a dead lift, to place them in a position in which they can use economical principles for their own advantages. When this is done in a truly Christian spirit, the conditions which political economy reveals may be the light by which we walk in the path of Christian benevolence, and the nation may become the channel of God's beneficence to all its members.

8. Lastly, we must glance at the universal Church, with a view to seeing what possibility there is of making towards the ideal which we have sketched out. It has been pointed out that the organisation of the universal Church, the great union first of Western Europe and through it of the world, has yet to be formed. It has been shown also that some rudiments of organisation already exist, in diplomacy, in the confession of the Treaties of Paris and Berlin that arbitra-

---

no objection to it. I belong myself to this ethico-historical economical school, which has been called the Socialists of the Chair; and for my own part, like our ancestors the "Gueux," I accept the epithet with which our adversaries have stigmatized my colleagues of German universities, invoking morals, justice, and history to raise our science above the deification of egotism, with the object of ameliorating the prospects of the working class.' 'As the oak springs from an acorn, so may Socialism be traced to Christianity. In every Christian there is a germ of Socialism, and every Socialist is unwittingly a Christian.' Emile de Laveleye, Contemp. Review for August, 1884, p. 289. M. de Laveleye refers to his recent work on 'Contemporary Socialism.' See also the chapter on 'Law in Politics' in the Duke of Argyll's 'Reign of Law.'

A a

tion should always take place before resort is had to war; in the various arbitrations which have actually taken place, such as those relating to Luxemburg and Schleswig-Holstein; in the Alabama Convention, the effect of which has been so great as to justify the largest hopes; in the concert of Europe which has of late been called into play; in the treaties of commerce and the union for postal communication. We may add that the democratic tendency of modern societies must make the causes of war progressively fewer, that the burden entailed by conscription and by keeping the nations armed to the teeth must make all countries in which the people have power shrink more and more from the military régime; and still more that European public opinion is slowly growing, and is feeling its way towards a method by which the present international anarchy may be placed under the restraint of a higher power.

There is hope that by means such as these that object may at last be attained. The Alabama Convention is in itself a first great act of universal Church policy and international religion. It is said, indeed, by some writers that the Alabama Convention was of no universal significance because it was the product of special circumstances. But the most special circumstance, the determining one, was this, that the two contracting nations felt it to be for their best interest to be at peace. It will be a great step gained towards an international tribunal when the nations who feel that their main interest is peace are willing to submit their differences to arbitration. The effort of all the scattered members of the universal Church should be that such acts should be repeated again and again. Our Peace and Arbitration Societies are the first agents in this work; but all Christian Societies which have any wide aims must join in the movement, and by prayer and effort compass the blessed result.

The two great objects of the universal Church are, as has been pointed out, first, to ensure peace and bind together the European family of nations, and, secondly, to act by a Missionary impulse upon the weaker nations, beginning with those now held under the power of the Turks. In the first of these two departments we may expect that France and Germany should lead the way, in the second our own country. At present not only is there anarchy among the European nations, but their relations with the weaker races are governed by no principle. Each seizes territory and makes war according to its own self-will, without the restraint imposed by the expression of the general judgment. 'We are Christians,' says a recent remarkable French writer[1], 'in our private life, civilised in our domestic habits. Must we then for ever in our international relations exchange nothing but an anti-Christian and barbarous policy, one of mere instinct and of ferocity, made up of diplomatic trickery and of military violence, a policy the immorality of which, if practised by the subjects of any state amongst themselves, the national law would condemn and prosecute?' A way out of such a state of things must be found, and found without delay. Nor is it difficult to see

[1] 'La Mission Actuelle des Souverains,' par l'un d'eux, p. 3.

the first steps which should be taken. If France and Germany could agree to leave the question of Alsace-Lorraine to arbitration, allowing it to be appropriated to one or the other, to be divided, or to be neutralised under an European guarantee, as might appear best to the arbitrators, the only ground of quarrel remaining in Western Europe would be removed. There would then be hardly any ground of discontent in England, France, Germany, Italy, Spain, the Low Countries, or the Scandinavian nations. In the populations federated under the Austrian monarchy there is no difficulty but a domestic one. The next step would be to solve the question of the East of Europe, reconciling the claims of Russia and Austria to the leadership of the Slavonic races, and to a commercial outlet into the Eastern Mediterranean, but above all giving effect to the claims of the subject races to develop their life in freedom. The third task will be the provision for Armenia and the other provinces of Asiatic Turkey. And beyond these lies the vast task of dealing with the barbarous and savage nations in the way of Christian education, a work nobly begun by our Missionary Societies, and also carried on with more or less success by English, Dutch, and French government in the East, and in Polynesia, but which more properly falls to the agency of the universal Church, when it shall be fully constituted. These great enterprises are partly begun, and it is therefore no Utopia at which we are aiming, but a legitimate extension and regulation which we propose for existing forces. It is also practical and extremely salutary, as is all work of a Missionary complexion: for when these great enterprises are fairly faced, and the Christian conscience set on pursuing them, men's minds throughout Europe will be drawn off from their jealousies, and will be occupied steadily with the beneficent mission of the Church of God.

Whether any system of diplomacy or of European concert, with the means now at hand, can effect these results is that which we cannot tell. It is the Christian spirit to which we must trust, and which will find its way when it is once awakened to the task to which we are calling it. That spirit, the spirit which seeks to bind the nations together not by force but by just relations and by amity, is already the primary assumption of international law [1]; and we find the great writers in that field, from Kant and Bentham onwards, feeling their way towards some central power; the greatest of them, Bluntschli, holding and defending his opinion that the establishment of such a supreme power over the States of Europe is not prevented so much by want of will or of power to form it, as by the want of a clear intellectual perception of its proper position and functions. The good thus aimed at, both temporal and spiritual, is so great that we cannot despair of attaining it. But the task is gigantic, since the war-fiend has been taken as an inmate in the household of our Christian civilisation, and has his prophets and his church-organisation where those of the Lamb should be. The prospect of reversing this state of things and of making Christendom truly the kingdom of the Prince

[1] See the opinions of International Lawyers quoted in Note XXIV.

of Peace is worthy to form the closing vista of our glance into the future.

It will be felt by many that the subject of these Lectures lies at a considerable distance from that simple practical piety, for the sake of which they have been accustomed to value Christianity. And this, no doubt, is true in one sense, but only in the sense that all teaching as to the Church or Society generally must necessarily lead us beyond the immediate interests of the individual soul. But it is by no means true if it implies that there is any separation of Christian principle or feeling between the spirit which aims at the salvation of the world and that which aims at the salvation of the individual soul. Nor is it true if it implies that the doctrine of a public Christian life has not a powerful and beneficial effect upon individual life and holiness.

It is impossible, indeed, to make a breach or draw a line between the two, nor is it material with which we begin. If we trace out the ideal of a Christian Society, we know well that it would be a hollow unreality unless it were a Society in which the Spirit of Christ reigned in individual souls. We may go further and say that the realisation of such a Society depends on the increase of practical piety; and therefore the promotion of such piety must be the constant aim of all who believe in the Saviour of the World, in all the circles of life which we have traced. If we start, on the other hand, with the individual life, we find it impossible to give it any reasonable extension apart from the life of the community to which the individual belongs.

The action also is reciprocal. If the Society be Christian, it will act both consciously and unconsciously upon every individual member in a Christian sense. If the individual be Christian, he will show it by incessant efforts to conduct, and to cause others to conduct, the social system in which he lives on Christian principles.

Moreover, there will be always those who claim more distinctly and realise more vividly the power of Christ over the individual soul, and those who embrace more fully the larger hope of His influence upon society; but no conflict could be more unreal or more unfortunate than one which should arise from an attempt on either side to limit his saving and reconciling power. It may be well, however, to point out that these Lectures have professedly been occupied with the social and universal side of the saving power of the Gospel, and that it has therefore been impossible—it would indeed have been out of place—to do more than glance at the power of Christ over individual souls.

It may be asked, further, whether there are any indications that the people generally will rally to the standard which has been here held up, and rise to the higher level to which these Lectures point. It should be noticed that in our day society is influenced more and more by great mass-movements, and that some at least of these are, amidst all their extravagances, indications of a longing for holiness. The most conspicuous of these, the Temperance movement, has laid a firm hold on the national conscience; and we may hope that the moral and Christian sense of the people having been once aroused, will attack one by one the sources of the evils by which it has been held in thrall. We may expect a movement in favour of social purity, and one in favour of peace, at least as strong as that in favour of temperance; and we may trust that all three will be successful. Moreover, those who deal with the masses know that in political questions it is the moral and religious aspect in which it is easiest to enlist their sympathy. If such a direction therefore can be given to the various social circles as has been indicated in these Lectures, if they can all be set before men as branches of the true Church, the body in which love and justice reign, we may hope that the result may no longer seem impossible. The hearts of the people will be more and more engaged in the beneficent conduct of all public affairs: they will further them with the same affection which was shown by the Israelites towards their own institutions, and, since we live in Christian and democratic times, with greater success.

But this is to be noted in all the spheres of life which we have touched upon. The Christianity we have vindicated for them is not of a stationary but of an aggressive and a missionary character. The righteousness of which both the Old and New Testament speaks, is one which goes forth beyond its possessor; not a righteousness which is even with a law, but a righteousness like that of Christ, loving, merciful, beneficent, self-sacrificing, and universal in its application. It can never rest content until it has assimilated to itself all the spheres of life with which it has to do. This alone has the promise of the Gospel attached to it. But he who dwells upon the universal love of the Eternal Father, and believes that the self-sacrifice of Christ had the salvation of the world for its object, will not find it hard to believe in the full extension of that which St. Paul called 'the mighty working whereby He is able to subdue all things unto Himself.'

What, then, are the more general and spiritual principles, underlying all the special efforts which we have described, which are needed for this consummation? What are the inner conditions of the general conscience which will help in changing the world into the kingdom of God?

1. The thing of most importance is to create the belief that this consummation, whether it be far or near, is destined, in the purpose of God, to be brought about, and that through human agency. If this belief can be created, the thing will be done, and the way to do it will be found. It may seem, indeed, that it is difficult to create such a conviction. And yet, does any convinced Christian doubt that Christ is the spiritual Lord of this world as well as of the world to come? Is there any one who does not pray, in His words, Thy kingdom come on earth? The habit of adjourning our higher hopes from this world to the next has greatly interfered with their fulfilment. But this habit is manifestly giving way, partly from the growing interest in public life and philanthropic schemes, partly through a better understanding of the Old and New Testaments. It seems clear that

the object of the life disclosed in the Scriptures is not merely to save individuals, but to train first one nation and then mankind to become the city of God: and such visions as that of the last chapters of the Apocalypse, with which the New Testament closes, are visions, not of a state beyond the world, but of a state which the seers conceived of as realiseable in this world, however much of imagination is joined with their descriptions. If it had been possible for those seers to look at Christendom even as it is at present, the contrast which it would have presented to the world around them would have seemed to them the beginning at least of the fulfilment of their hopes. A world in which slavery is abolished, in which the Spirit of Christ's life is generally acknowledged by the public conscience and is gradually moulding the institutions of men, in which almost every great need of mankind has some organisation formed for its relief, in which the sense of unity and brotherhood among men has become an admitted principle, in which Christian teaching is absolutely free, would, in contrast with the hypocrisy of Rabbinical Judaism and the hard and cruel materialism of Rome which they describe, have gleamed with the light of heaven. Why should we, who are the heirs of all the Christian ages, stand hesitating what to think or do, and not rather feel that we stand upon a vantage ground from which we may spring forward to our predestined goal?

2. A second condition of the realisation of our hopes is that Christianity is to be regarded as a life, not as the holding of a series of propositions. This does not

imply that it is without principles, for how can any good life exist without principles? But first it means that the principles which lie at the roots of the Christian life are too deep for exact definitions. As Aristotle said in reference to all moral subjects, we must make things clear according as the subject-matter admits[1]. As Augustine says, after his discussion on the Trinity in the De Doctrinâ Christianâ, 'Diximusne aliquid aut sonuimus aliquid dignum Deo? Immo vero nihil aliud me quam dicere voluisse sentio[2].' Who has attempted to define love, or life, or righteousness? Who can define God or religion? These expressions are, to quote a writer of our own day[3], 'words thrown out at a great subject;' they are no full measure of its completeness. It is, indeed, by the conscience mainly that these great things are apprehended, and the feeling of them is often genuine when the definition of them is inadequate. To think of them apart from action is almost necessarily to go wrong; and this is why we often find men of sceptical disposition grow clear and assured when they come to some act of practical service

[1] The principles of Aristotle on this point are so just, and yet so constantly ignored in theological discussion, that I venture to quote a few sentences which are (in Oxford at least) as well known as any in classical literature. 'Η μὲν οὖν μέθοδος τούτων ἐφίεται, πολιτική τις οὖσα· λέγοιτο δ' ἂν ἱκανῶς εἰ κατὰ τὴν ὑποκειμένην ὕλην διασαφηθείη· τὸ γὰρ ἀκριβὲς οὐχ ὁμοίως ἐν ἅπασι τοῖς λόγοις ἐπιζητητέον .... 'Αγαπητὸν οὖν περὶ τοιούτων καὶ ἐκ τοιούτων λέγοντας παχυλῶς καὶ τύπῳ τἀληθὲς ἐνδείκνυσθαι, καὶ περὶ τῶν ὡς ἐπὶ τὸ πολὺ καὶ ἐκ τοιούτων λέγοντας τοιαῦτα καὶ συμπεραίνεσθαι· πεπαιδευμένου γάρ ἐστιν ἐπὶ τοσοῦτον τἀκριβὲς ἐπιζητεῖν καθ' ἕκαστον γένος ἐφ' ὅσον ἡ τοῦ πράγματος φύσις ἐπιδέχεται· παραπλήσιον γὰρ φαίνεται μαθηματικοῦ τε πιθανολογοῦντος ἀποδέχεσθαι καὶ ῥητορικὸν ἀποδείξεις ἀπαιτεῖν. Ethics, I. i. 9, (3) 4. How many evils might have been avoided by attention to these simple principles!

[2] B. I, c. vi. See the quotation given more fully in Note XXVII.

[3] Matthew Arnold, 'Lit. and Dogma,' p. 41.

to their fellows. The assertion that Christianity is a life rather than a doctrine means also that it is by the life that its principles are tested, and that, constantly brought to this test, the great and simple principles of Christianity stand out most clearly, and interpret for us the doctrines in a manner which is at once rational, reconciling, and calculated to commend them to the consciences of all men.

3. But, thirdly, what is required further for the full extension of the Christian principle is the abandonment of clericalism. By clericalism I understand the system which unduly exalts the clerical office, and the function of public worship, so as to draw away the sense of divine agency and appointment from other offices and other functions. This tendency, as has before been said, is not really one which exalts the Church. It exalts the clergy alone; it dwarfs and emasculates the Church. The clergy, and those to whom the system of public worship is dear, must learn to make the great sacrifice of Christians. They must learn to 'live not for themselves,' to 'look not on their own things but also on the things of others.' The system they administer must be felt not to exist for itself but for the general community. They must efface, if need be, themselves and their system in the effort to save the world. They must be willing to be nothing that Christ may be all in all. They must desire that, if it were possible, there should be not only holy orders of bishops and presbyters, but holy orders of artists, and poets, and teachers of science, and statesmen. They should be forward to recognise good in departments

which are not theirs, and in forms very different from their own. A ministry imbued with such a spirit as this may still be the luminous and inspiring focus where light and heat are stored for diffusion through the whole mass; whereas, by almost identifying Christianity with public worship, and absorbing all ministries in the clerical function, and thinking more of correct forms of appointment and ordination than of the Divine gifts which form the true succession of spiritual leaders, we may become the greatest of all obstacles to the establishment of the kingdom of God.

4. One other thing is needed with a view to this great change; it is, that those charged with the conduct of human affairs, in whatever department, should themselves recognise their office as a Christian ministry. This does not imply merely that they should act generally upon Christian principles, nor, on the other hand, that they should be constantly speaking of Christianity in connection with their office; but that they should cherish the lofty conception of their office which the Christian ministry implies, and should not shrink from asserting it when needful. The Hebrew prophets spoke of the leaders of the people, the princes, rulers, and prophets, rather than the priests, as pastors, contrasting with the false pastors of their day the true pastor for whose advent they longed[1]: and Christ himself adopted their language, and applied it to him-

---

[1] See especially Ezek. xxxiv, compared with the language of our Lord in John x. The contrast between the blind shepherd of the people in the end of ch. ix. and the Good Shepherd of ch. x. is obscured by the division of the chapters.

self. The false shepherds, according to His description, were those who in their teaching 'strained at gnats and swallowed camels,' whose judgment, as in the case of the woman taken in adultery, or the man who had been born blind, looked at the external case, not at the inner and spiritual state, whose policy was that of Caiaphas. With these he contrasted the true Shepherd or guide who gives himself in life or death for the good of the sheep. The pastors of the present day are those who lead in all departments of human life. It is hardly possible to say how greatly their pastorate would grow in importance, were it recognised by all as a Christian ministry, and inspired with the lofty aim of bringing in the kingdom of heaven.

The object of the Bampton Lecture is to confirm and establish the Christian Faith. There are two ways in which this may be done. The one is to regard the present state of human knowledge on things divine as conclusive, to assume that terms such as The Church, the Faith, Christianity, bear a simple and definite sense, which holds good for all minds and for all ages of the world, and to defend this acquired possession against actual or possible attacks. The other method is to regard Christianity as a spiritual power which cannot be precisely defined, but which is known and felt in its effects; as the spirit of the God whose name is Love, a spirit which is not seen but blows where it lists, yet which we know to be gradually renewing the world; to trace the various institutions which have sprung up under its influence, whether consciously using the name of Christ or not; to recognise the fact that these institutions are always imperfect and liable to constant change (this, indeed, is their glory, that they can adapt themselves to the changing circumstances of the world); to point out the inexhaustible vitality of this Divine spirit and of the Church which He forms, and to make clear its aims and the grounds which assure its universal triumph. This latter is the line which has been followed in the present course of Lectures, and it is, no less than the other, a line of Christian Evidences. When the Church is seen to be the constant inspirer of human progress, there will be no sceptics but those to whom human progress is indifferent.

It is often said that the present day is specially a time of scepticism. It is very doubtful whether this is so in any sense which would not apply to many other ages of the Church, certainly to two periods, the Renaissance and the eighteenth century. But, further, the special feature of the scepticism of the present day is its earnestness, its seriousness. It is worth while, therefore, to consider whether a great part of it is not due to faults in the presentation of Christianity by its recognised exponents, just as political discontent is usually to be traced to some fault, past or present, in the system of government. We might take the French nation as a typical instance of a society in which a false presentation of Christianity has provoked, not only scepticism, but a revolt against all that is called Christian. It has been possible for a Prime Minister[1] there to say, and to say with truth, 'L'ennemi c'est le

[1] M. Gambetta.

Cléricalisme;' and for a minister of education and public worship to say, with a good array of proofs, that, the further men are from religion, the nearer they are to morality and good sense [1]. But the cause of this was patent, namely this, that the Church had narrowed itself to a clerical sect, and that the clergy, having separated religion from the common life of men, had taught superstition and folly under its name. It is very difficult for any one to hold to the Christian faith with calm and rational conviction when its authorised exponents connect it with the Papal Syllabus, which denies all liberal progress, and with pilgrimages and false miracles such as those of Lourdes or of La Salette. The true religion of France for many years to come must, except for those who are Protestants, be a religion of politics rather than of worship, and its Christianity must be mainly of the latent and unconscious sort. Is the case altogether dissimilar, when the clergy are disputing, as they have done so much of late in England, about dress and posture, and their own supposed rights of legislation and of judgment, while the spiritual interests of the nation itself as a nation, and of the great secular unions within the nation, are left almost without a thought?

The centre of all theology to a Christian lies in the character of Jesus Christ. While this is felt to be supreme, a secure basis is laid for theology and religion. That is the manifestation of the Divine, of God Himself; for no other God is conceivable henceforth than

[1] M. Paul Bert in his lecture on Education (M. Gambetta being in the chair) at the Cirque d'Hiver, in Sept. 1881.

VIII.]   *of a Christian World.*   369

God as manifested in Christ. That manifestation of the Divine is not bound up with any particular view of the Divine nature metaphysically considered, nor with any view of human nature in which our reason need find a stumbling-block, nor with miracles regarded as violations of the natural order, nor with the Resurrection of our Lord regarded as a physical phenomenon. Yet it is against one or other of these ideas that almost all the attacks of unbelievers have been made. The character of the Founder hardly any one really attacks: His Spirit almost every one, consciously or unconsciously, acknowledges. And this character and spirit are now almost universally recognised by defenders of the faith as the central and preponderant evidence of Christianity. But their arguments do not carry their full weight, chiefly because, though reasonable in themselves, they are thought to be meant to lead up to the acceptance of an untenable philosophical position, of a morality far narrower than that of Christ Himself, and of a petty clericalism instead of a genuine spiritual power. If this be so, then the best thing that Christians can do for the faith of mankind is that which has been attempted in these Lectures, namely, to exhibit the real power of Christ and of His Spirit as a redeeming influence in the whole wide field of human life. When its capacities to guide the course of the world in justice and in love are practically seen, all that is good must necessarily rally to its side. All cavillings may then be answered, like the accusations made against Scipio Africanus, by the records of its triumphs; for it will have secured, not the cold and

B b

hesitating assent, but the enthusiastic gratitude of mankind.

The view which has been opened out in these Lectures is calculated to fill us with an immense hope. It is impossible for those who take a narrower view of the aims of Christianity to be frankly hopeful. They see that the secular fields of human activity, which to them and to their highest aims appear hostile, or at least indifferent, are winning upon men more and more, while Christianity, conceived merely as a system of worship, doctrine and beneficence, is barely holding its ground: and consequently we hear from them little but expressions which imply complaint, or resistance, or a timorous waiting for what is coming. This timorous attitude of later Christianity contrasts sadly with the enthusiastic hopefulness of its first proclaimers.

We must restore the element of hope. But hope of what? Is the picture which has been drawn of a society universal, and Christian in all its departments, enough to kindle and sustain our hope? Are we to make little or nothing of the hopes of a world beyond the grave? And, if not, if we introduce that larger hope, must not the hope of heaven make all desire for a kingdom of God in this world seem vain? This has not been the experience of Christians, either in the first Christian age or in our own. The first Christians, though not excluding from their view the Resurrection and the Life to Come, yet fixed their hope primarily on a reign of Christ in this world, a hope concealed no doubt in imagery, but still distinctly recognised as a reign of righteousness on earth. It was only by degrees that they were driven through persecution to think of the heavenly state exclusively as the kingdom of God, and of this world as only a state of probation and expectancy, and of Christ as a Saviour not of the world but from the world. The more modern believers start from this later belief, making heaven their first aim, and, professedly at least, thinking this life of little value. Yet who can deny that they also have assiduously, even if inconsistently with their profession, served their own generation, and that much of the progress of modern times is to be traced to their efforts? We restore the primitive feeling under circumstances in which it is more possible for it to find its realisation. We teach men to hope for a reign of Christ in this world, that is, for the supreme influence of the Spirit of Christ in all departments of human life.

But men pass. And what, to the mass of men who will never see it, is this kingdom of the Spirit of Christ on earth? In the first place, we shall see this kingdom advancing; we partake of its hopes even now, and that is in itself a great reward. It would be a noble and a Christian thing, even if there were no world to come, to devote our span of life to the benefit of those who are to come after us. We shall at least leave our hope to our children, and they will see what many of the best men of the past have longed to see and have not seen. But, in the second place, conceive of this world as in itself the object of these hopes, and the destined field of the fulfilment of those purposes of

God on which we have dwelt, but yet as a preparation for the higher and immortal state; conceive of earthly society as the commencement of and preparation for the heavenly, of present knowledge for future, of the sense of beauty here for a fuller beauty hereafter. In that case, the more complete the organisation of the Christian life here, the better preparation will it be for that which is to come. The colonist, who has been formed by the discipline of a civilised state, is not thereby unfitted for his new country. On the contrary, there is no faculty of his which has been trained on this side the water which he does not carry with him to his home beyond the seas. He leaves the outer fabric of his former life; but he has that within him which will build up a new one wherever he lands. We may best think of the world to come as it is set before us in the New Testament, where it is often impossible to say whether this world or the next is in the mind of the seer, the one continuing and sublimating the other, the two blended together in one redeemed state. The training, not of the individual only, is to be effected here. The societies of this world will, unless man ceases to be man, be reproduced in all except their narrow conditions and unworthy features, in the world to come. Thus the completion of the earthly Church may be the preparation for the fulness of the Church above. But the earthly is that in which duty lies, and on which our whole effort must be concentrated. Let us set ourselves heartily to the work of bringing in the kingdom of God on earth, in whatever department of it our lot is cast: for in so doing we best ensure that, when these earthly conditions fail, when the walls of the flesh fall from about us, we, and those who with us form the kingdom of God on earth, shall form the kingdom of God in the new and better state, whatever it be, beyond the chasm of death.

APPENDIX.

APPENDIX.

NOTE I.

PASSAGES IN WHICH αἰών IS USED RATHER THAN κόσμος TO DESIGNATE THIS WORLD.

Rom. xii. 2. Μὴ συσχηματίζεσθε τῷ αἰῶνι τούτῳ.
Eph. ii. 2. Κατὰ τὸν αἰῶνα τοῦ κόσμου τούτου.
Matt. xiii. 22. Ἡ μέριμνα τοῦ αἰῶνος.
Luke xx. 34. Οἱ υἱοὶ τοῦ αἰῶνος τούτου.
1 Cor. ii. 8. Οὐδεὶς τῶν ἀρχόντων τοῦ αἰῶνος τούτου.
Gal. i. 4. Ἐκ τοῦ α. τοῦ ἐνεστῶτος πονηροῦ.

The normal use of κόσμος, on the other hand, is to be seen in such expressions as Ἀπὸ καταβολῆς κόσμου, Matt. xiii. 35, Eph. i. 4.

The contrast in the Parable of the Tares between κόσμος, 'the field is the world,' and αἰών, 'the end of the world or age,' that is, of the present dispensation, is specially instructive, and it is to be lamented that it was not found possible to express this contrast in the revised version.

In St. John, though κόσμος is used to express both the world as organised according to God's purpose or in a neutral sense, and also the world as organised for selfish and evil purposes, the latter sense is commonly marked by the addition of *this*, as Ἡ βασιλεία ἡ ἐμὴ οὐκ ἔστιν ἐκ τοῦ κ. τούτου.

Passages in which κόσμος is used for the world in its present evil state :—

John xvii. 16. Ἐκ τοῦ κόσμου οὐκ εἰσὶ καθὼς ἐγώ κ.τ.λ.
„ xvi. 33. Ἐγὼ νενίκηκα τὸν κόσμον.

But the sense varies in the same passage, as xiv. 30, 31, Ἔρχεται ὁ τοῦ κ. ἄρχων . . . ἀλλ' ἵνα γνῷ ὁ κόσμος : xvii. 16, Ἐγὼ ἐκ τ. κ. οὐκ εἰμί . . . ἵνα γινώσκῃ ὁ κ. ὅτι σύ με ἀπέστειλας.

NOTE II.

EXTRACTS FROM THE PAPAL ENCYCLICAL AND SYLLABUS OF ERRORS ISSUED DEC. 8TH, 1864. (Published by Bradbury and Agnew, 1875.)

Enclyclical.

P. 5. They (that is, Protestants and Liberals) do not scruple to support that erroneous opinion so fatal to the Catholic Church and the safety of souls which our predecessor of happy memory, Gregory XVI, called an insanity,—namely, that liberty of conscience and of worship is the right of every man, and that in every well-constituted State this right ought to be proclaimed and sanctioned, and that citizens have a right to put forward their opinions openly and in public whatever they may be, either by word or in print or otherwise, without limitation by ecclesiastical or civil authority.

P. 9. Amidst the perversity of depraved opinions, we—penetrated with the duty of our apostolic charge, and full of solicitude for our holy religion, for sound doctrine, for the safety of souls which have been confided to us from on high, and even for the welfare of human society—have believed it our duty to raise anew our voice. Consequently we reprobate by our Apostolic authority all and each of the evil opinions and doctrines mentioned in detail in the present letters. We proscribe them, we condemn them, and we desire and command that all the children of the Catholic Church should hold them as entirely reprobated, proscribed, and condemned. Besides all that, you know very well, Venerable Brethren, that at the present time the enemies of all truth and all justice, the bitter enemies of our holy religion (by means of pestilent books, of pamphlets, and of newspapers distributed to the four corners of the earth), deceive the people, wickedly lie, and disseminate every kind of impious doctrine.

Syllabus, presenting the principal errors of our time.

Error 12. The decrees of the Apostolic See and of the Roman Congregation prevent the free progress of science.

Section 4. *Socialism, Communism, Secret Societies, Bible Societies, Clerico-Liberal Societies.*

Pests of this description are frequently rebuked in the severest terms in the Encyclicals of November 1846, December 1849, and 1863, in the Allocutions of April 1849, December 1854.

Section 6. *Errors relating to Civil Society.*

45. The entire direction of the public schools in which the youth of Christian States is educated, except to a certain extent the episcopal seminaries, may and must appertain to the civil authority in such a manner that no other authority whatsoever shall be recognised as having the right to interfere in the discipline of the schools, the course of the studies, the taking of degrees, or the choice and approval of masters.

Section 7. *Errors concerning Natural and Christian Morality.*

57. Knowledge of philosophical things and morals, as well as civil laws, may and ought to be independent of divine and ecclesiastical authority.

Section 9. *Errors concerning the Temporal Power of the Roman Pontiff.*

76. The abolition of the temporal power of which the Holy See is possessed would conduce greatly to the liberty and happiness of the Church.

Besides these errors explicitly noted, several other errors are tacitly condemned by the doctrine which has been declared and maintained concerning the temporal sovereignty of the Roman Pontiff, and which all Catholics are bound most firmly to hold. This doctrine is distinctly taught in several Allocutions, 1849, 1850, 1861, 1862.

Section 10. *Errors having reference to Modern Liberalism.*

77. In the present day it is no longer beneficial for the Catholic Church to be considered as the only religion of the State, to the exclusion of all other forms of worship.

78. Whence it has been wisely provided by the law, in some countries called Catholic, that strangers going to reside there shall enjoy the public exercise of their own forms of worship.

79. It is false that civil liberty of all forms of worship, and the full power granted to all to manifest openly and publicly all their thoughts and their opinions, leads more easily to the corruption of the morals and minds of the people, and to the spread of the pest of indifferentism.

80. The Roman Pontiff may and ought to reconcile himself to, and to agree with, progress, liberalism, and modern civilisation.

The Vatican Decrees, July 18, 1870.—4. *Concerning Faith and Reason.*

2. If any one shall say, that human sciences should be prosecuted with such freedom, that their assertions, even when opposed to revealed doctrine, may still be held as true, and may not be proscribed by the Church; let him be accursed.

3. If any one shall say, that it is possible, that from time to time, in the course of the progress of science, an interpretation may have to be attributed to dogmas proposed by the Church other than that which has been and is understood by the Church; let him be accursed.

NOTE III.

ANALYSIS OF AUGUSTINE'S DE CIVITATE DEI, AND EXTRACTS, SHOWING THAT IT IS NOT AN ANTICIPATION OF A CHRISTIAN COMMONWEALTH.

It may be worth while to give a short account of St. Augustine's great treatise De Civitate Dei, since Christian thought and aims have been so largely coloured by it. It will be seen that the idea commonly formed of it, namely, that it gives an ideal of a Commonwealth such as is to be found in Plato's Republic or in More's Utopia, is baseless. It is said that Charlemagne delighted in having it read to him; but though he may have been stimulated by the exposition given in it of the causes of the downfall of Rome, he can have found little or nothing in it to aid in the organisation of his Empire.

It starts with a vindication of the Christians against the imputation that to them was due the destruction of Rome by Alaric in 410. Augustine shows (Bk. I) that such evils happen to all; and that actually in the sack of Rome Christianity was the means of saving many, through the respect of the Goths for the Churches. He then points out (Bk. II, III) that the Romans had constantly suffered in a similar way during the prevalence of paganism : that the true causes of their prosperity had been (Bk. IV, V) the will and providence of God and the virtues with which He had endowed them. He then shows (Bk. VI—X) the absurdities and immorality of the old Roman religion. In the Eleventh Book Augustine comes to the origin, course, and end of the two Civitates, the earthly and the heavenly. He asserts that they originated in the good and bad angels, and speaks in Books XI to XIV of the Creation and the Fall, and the effects of Adam's sin. In the next four Books he traces the progress of the two Civitates, following the account of the Old Testament as the training of men for the heavenly state, and then describing very shortly the coming of Christ, the preaching of the Gospel, and the persecutions. At length in Book XIX the subject of the future of the Church is reached. But it is not a picture of an ideal state of society under earthly conditions. The opinions of philosophers are discussed as to the summum bonum, in contrast to which the Christian ideal is given as that of Peace, which is mainly an anticipation of a heavenly state: 'Pax coelestis Civitatis, ordinatissima et concordissima societas fruendi Deo et invicem in Deo' (Ch. xiii.) The last three Books consist of an interpretation of the last chapters of the Revelation. The 1000 years' reign of Christ is the existence of the Church in its present conditions till the final judgment, when the wicked will be sent into a literal fire, the physical world will be changed by a vast conflagration, and the eternal state will begin (Bk. XX. ch. xvi). The work closes with a description of the heavenly world.

It will be seen from this that only one of the twenty-two Books, the nineteenth, deals with the prospective condition of the City of God. I subjoin two passages which most nearly approach the task of working out an ideal of the Christian Church, that is of a social state influenced by Christian principles. It will be seen that St. Augustine turns away from the task of elaborating such an ideal. It is not worth his while to do this. The Church is glad to see peace and right relations among men, but only so that it may the better pass on to the heavenly state. It has no vocation for the redemption of human society.

Bk. XIX. cap. 14. De ordine ac lege, sive coelesti sive terrenâ, per quam societati humanae etiam dominando consulitur cui et consulendo servitur.

Omnis igitur usus rerum temporalium refertur ad fructum terrenae pacis in Civitate terrenâ: in coelesti autem Civitate refertur ad fructum pacis aeternae. . . . .

Et quoniam [anima] quamdiu est in isto mortali corpore, peregrinatur a Domino; ambulat per fidem, non per speciem: ac per hoc omnem pacem vel corporis, vel animae, vel simul corporis et animae, refert ad illam pacem, quae homini mortali est cum Deo immortali; ut ei sit ordinata in fide sub aeterna lege obedientia. Iam vero quia duo praecipua praecepta, hoc est, dilectionem Dei et dilectionem proximi, docet magister Deus, in quibus tria invenit homo quae diligat, Deum, se ipsum, et proximum; atque ille in se diligendo non errat qui diligit Deum: consequens est ut etiam proximo ad diligendum Deum consulat, quem iubetur sicut se ipsum diligere. Sic uxori, sic filiis, sic domesticis, sic caeteris quibus potuerit hominibus; et ad hoc sibi a proximo, si forte indiget, consuli velit: ac per hoc erit pacatus, quantum in ipso est, omni homini, pace hominum, id est, ordinatâ concordiâ: cuius hic ordo est, primum ut nulli noceat, deinde ut etiam prosit cui potuerit. Primitus ergo inest ei suorum cura: ad eos quippe habet opportuniorem faciliorem-que aditum consulendi, vel naturae ordine, vel ipsius societatis humanae. Unde Apostolus dicit, Quisquis autem suis et maxime domesticis non providet, fidem denegat, et est infideli deterior. Hinc itaque etiam pax domestica oritur, id est, ordinata imperandi obediendique concordia cohabitantium. Imperant enim qui consulunt: sicut vir uxori, parentes filiis, domini servis. Obediunt autem quibus consulitur, sicut mulieres maritis, filii parentibus, servi dominis. Sed in domo iusti viventis ex fide, et adhuc ab illâ coelesti Civitate peregrinantis, etiam qui imperant, serviunt eis, quibus videntur imperare. Neque enim dominandi cupiditate imperant, sed officio consulendi ; nec principandi superbiâ, sed providendi misericordiâ.

Cap. 16. Quia igitur hominis domus initium sive particula debet esse civitatis, omne autem initium ad aliquem sui generis finem, et omnis pars ad universi cuius pars est, integritatem refertur ; satis apparet esse consequens, ut ad pacem civicam pax domestica referatur, id est, ut ordinata imperandi obediendique concordia cohabitantium referatur ad ordinatam imperandi obediendique concordiam civium. Ita fit, ut ex lege civitatis praecepta sumere patrem familias oporteat, quibus domum suam sic regat, ut sit paci accommodata civitatis.

Cap. 17. Sed domus hominum qui non vivunt ex fide, pacem terrenam ex huius temporalis vitae rebus commodisque sectatur, domus autem hominum ex fide viventium expectat ea quae in futurum aeterna promissa sunt, terrenisque rebus ac temporalibus tanquam peregrina utitur, non quibus capiatur et avertatur quo tendit in Deum, sed quibus sustentetur ad facilius toleranda minimeque augenda onera corporis corruptibilis, quod aggravat animam. Idcirco rerum vitae huic mortali necessariarum utrisque hominibus (fidelibus et infidelibus) et utrique domui communis est usus ; sed finis utendi cuique suus proprius multumque diversus. Ita etiam terrena Civitas, quae non vivit ex fide, terrenam pacem appetit ; in eoque defigit imperandi obediendique concordiam civium, ut sit eis de rebus ad mortalem vitam pertinentibus humanarum quaedam compositio voluntatum. Civitas autem coelestis, vel potius pars eius, quae in hac mortalitáte peregrinatur, et vivit ex fide, etiam istâ pace necesse est utatur, donec ipsa, cui talis pax necessaria est, mortalitas transeat. Ac per hoc dum apud terrenam Civitatem, velut captivam suae peregrinationis, agit, iam promissione redemptionis et dono spiritali tanquam pignore accepto, legibus terrenae Civitatis, quibus haec administrantur, quae sustentandae mortali vitae accommodata sunt, obtemperare non dubitat : ut quoniam communis est ipsa mortalitas, servetur in rebus ad eam

pertinentibus inter Civitatem utramque concordia. Verum quia
terrena Civitas habuit quosdam suos sapientes, quos divina improbat disciplina, qui vel suspicati vel decepti a daemonibus
crederent multos deos conciliandos esse rebus humanis : . . . .
factum est, ut religionis leges cum terrenâ Civitate non posset
habere communes, proque his ab ea dissentire haberet necesse, atque oneri esse diversa sentientibus, eorumque iras et odia et persecutionum impetus sustinere, nisi cum animos adversantium
aliquando terrore suae multitudinis, et semper divino adiutorio
propulsaret. Haec ergo coelestis Civitas dum peregrinatur in
terra ex omnibus gentibus cives evocat, atque in omnibus linguis
peregrinam colligit societatem ; non curans quicquid in moribus,
legibus, institutisque diversum est, quibus pax terrena vel conquiritur, vel tenetur ; nihil eorum rescindens, nec destruens, imo
etiam servans ac sequens : quod licet diversum sit in diversis
nationibus, ad unum tamen eundemque finem terrenae pacis
intenditur, si religionem quâ unus summus et verus Deus
colendus docetur non impedit. Utitur ergo etiam coelestis
Civitas in hac suâ peregrinatione pace terrenâ, et de rebus ad
mortalem hominum naturam pertinentibus, humanarum voluntatum compositionem, quantum salvâ pietate ac religione conceditur, tuetur atque appetit, eamque terrenam pacem refert ad
coelestem pacem : quae verè ita pax est, ut rationalis duntaxat
creaturae sola pax habenda atque dicenda sit, ordinatissima
scilicet et concordissima societas fruendi Deo, et invicem in
Deo ; quo cum ventum fuerit, non erit vita mortalis sed planè
(plenè) certèque vitalis ; nec corpus animale, quod dum corrumpitur, aggravat animam, sed spiritale sine ullâ indigentiâ
ex omni parte subditum voluntati. Hanc pacem, dum peregrinatur in fide, habet atque ex hac fide iustè vivit ; cum ad
illam pacem adipiscendam refert quicquid bonarum actionum
gerit erga Deum et proximum, quoniam vita civitatis utique
socialis est.

NOTE IV.

EXTRACT FROM 'LA MISSION ACTUELLE DES SOUVERAINS' SHOWING THE PROPER USE OF THE WORDS RELIGION, WORSHIP, CHURCH AND CHURCHES.

This idea of the Church as a universal polity in contrast to 'the Churches' as bodies organised only for public worship is well worked out in the remarkable work entitled 'La Mission Actuelle des Souverains' (Dentu, 1882), pp. 28, 29 :—

'La Différence entre la Religion et le Culte est facile à sentir. Le nom de religion indique le lien par excellence, celui qui réunit ou tend à réunir tous les hommes indistinctement, tous les peuples, toutes les races, toutes les Sociétés humaines, dans un même principe et dans une même fin.

'Le Culte, au contraire, indique une chose particulière, un système de culture devant se prêter aux exigences de son propre champ d'activité.

'La Religion est une dans son essence, les cultes sont et doivent demeurer différents dans leurs formes.

'L'Eglise, pour les Chrétiens, exprime dans son acception la plus générale la Religion de J. C., ou du moins la Société de tous les individus et de tous les peuples chrétiens.

'Les églises, au contraire, correspondent à la définition que nous avons donnée des cultes.'

NOTE V.

EXTRACTS FROM ARISTOTLE SHOWING THE USE IN GREEK PHILOSOPHY OF THE WORDS IMPORTING PRIORITY OF BEING.

17. Aristotle, Metaphysics, i. 3. 1 : Τετάρτην δὲ (αἰτίαν φαμὲν) τὸ οὗ ἕνεκα καὶ τἀγαθόν· τέλος γὰρ γενέσεως καὶ κινήσεως πάσης τοῦτ' ἐστίν.

4. 3. Εἴπερ τὸ τῶν ἀγαθῶν ἁπάντων αἴτιον αὐτὸ τἀγαθόν ἐστι.

8. 7. Εἰ δ' ἔστι τὸ τῇ γενέσει ὕστερον τῇ φύσει πρότερον, τὸ δὲ πεπεμμένον καὶ συγκεκριμένον ὕστερον τῇ γενέσει.

Politics, i. 2. 8. Διὸ πᾶσα πόλις φύσει ἐστίν, εἴπερ καὶ αἱ πρῶται κοινωνίαι· τέλος γὰρ αὕτη ἐκείνων, ἡ δὲ φύσις τέλος ἐστίν· οἷον γὰρ ἕκαστόν ἐστι τῆς γενέσεως τελεσθείσης, ταύτην φαμὲν τὴν φύσιν εἶναι ἑκάστου . . . . ἐκ τούτων οὖν φάνερον ὅτι τῶν φύσει ἡ πόλις ἐστί.

12. Καὶ πρότερον δὴ τῇ φύσει πόλις ἢ οἰκία καὶ ἕκαστος ἡμῶν ἐστίν.

16. Ὅτι μὲν οὖν ἡ πόλις καὶ φύσει πρότερον ἢ ἕκαστος, δῆλον.

NOTE VI.

A SHORT ACCOUNT OF M. COMTE'S ANTICIPATIONS AS TO THE FUTURE OF POLITICAL SOCIETY IN EUROPE.

There is so much in the system of M. Comte which is admirable, and its thoroughness is so captivating, that it seems worth while to give in a few words the ultimate organization of European Society which he has sketched out. If it appears almost as a jest, it was nevertheless propounded in earnest by one the negative part of whose views have widely influenced European thought, and whose ideas, if not his system, are of great use to all who look earnestly to the future. The grotesqueness of the ideal which he draws out is a warning how much more difficult it is to construct than to destroy.

Positive Catechism (Congreve's Translation, Chapman, 1858).

P. 337. Ultimately, the normal extent of the States of the Western world will be much the same as that of Tuscany, Belgium, and Holland at the present time. Sicily, Sardinia, etc. will soon follow. A population of one to three millions, at the average rate of one hundred per square mile, is the best limit for States which are really free.

P. 339. The primary condition for the attainment of this result, the harmony, viz. of society, is the separation of the spiritual and temporal powers. To secure the devotion of the strong to the weak, we must amongst the strong have a class whose social ascendancy depends entirely on their devoting themselves to the weak, as a return for the veneration freely given by the weak. Thus it is that the priesthood becomes the soul of true sociocracy. It is of course implied that the priesthood limit itself to counsel, and never exercise command.

P. 304. The doctrine and the office of the priesthood are such, that it might function of itself, with the aid of public opinion. Still, it really does require one supreme head. The supreme power is vested in the High Priest of Humanity, whose natural residence will be Paris as the metropolis of the regenerated West. His stipend is five times that of ordinary priests, 2400*l.*, and he must have besides an allowance for the expense necessarily involved by his vast labours.

He is the sole governor of the Positive clergy. He ordains its members, he changes their residence, he revokes their commission, all on his own moral responsibility. The main object of his care is to maintain the priestly character in its integrity against all temporal seductions. Every servile or seditious priest, who aims at temporal power by flattering the patriciate or the proletariate, will be absolutely banished from the priesthood. Such an one may, in certain cases, find a place amongst its pensioners, supposing him to have scientific merits to justify the exception. . . . .

To assist him in the discharge of his functions, the supreme head of Western Positivism is to have the aid of four national superiors, each of whom has a stipend of half the amount of his, 1200*l*. Under his direction, they guide their four respective Churches, the Italian, the Spanish, the English, and the German. As for France, the High Priest is the national superior, though he need not necessarily be a Frenchman, but may come from any one of the populations that are Positivist. The regular mode of replacing him is, as in the temporal order, by a successor whom he is to name himself. But in this case, such nomination must have the unanimous assent of the four national superiors. Supposing them divided in opinion, then the nomination must meet the wishes of the senior priests of the two thousand presbyteries.

P. 345. It will be as well to begin by giving you the

statistics of the patriciate when it is regularly organized throughout the West. Two thousand bankers, a hundred thousand merchants, two hundred thousand manufacturers, four hundred thousand agriculturists—such are the numbers sufficient, in my judgment, to provide industrial chiefs for the hundred and twenty millions who inhabit Western Europe. In the hands of this small number of patricians will be concentrated the capital of the West. Their task is to direct its employment. They are subject to no control, and must act on their own moral responsibility, and in the interest of a proletariate of thirty-three times their number.

In each separate republic, the government properly so called, that is to say, the supreme temporal power, will be vested exclusively in three bankers. The three will have their separate departments; they will represent commerce, manufactures, agriculture. Before these two hundred triumvirs the Western priesthood, acting under the direction of the High Priest of Humanity, will lay in proper form the legitimate claims of an immense proletariate. The exceptional class which is in the habit of habitually studying the future and the past, concentrates its care on the present. It speaks to the living in the name of those who have lived, and in the interest of those who are to live.

P. 357. The existing States will soon be broken up, and the great Western Republic will be divided into sixty independent Republics, which will have nothing in common but their spiritual organization. There never will arise within the limits of this Western Republic any temporal power with universal dominion, answering to the phantom emperor of the Middle Ages, who was for Catholicism nothing but an element of disturbance, empirically introduced from the Roman system. In the new order, all collective action will be temporary, and as such will be directed by the national triumvirates acting for the time in concert.

The High Priest of Humanity will be, more truly than any medieval Pope, the only real head of the Western world. He will have it in his power, if it be necessary, to concentrate the action of the whole priesthood so as to repress any tyrannical triumvirate. He will be able also to call on the neighbouring knights for aid, and on all neutral governments for their peaceful mediation.

P. 362. The basis for this change is already laid in the permanence of general peace, on which we may calculate for the future.

NOTE VII.

EXTRACTS FROM THE PRESIDENTIAL ADDRESS DELIVERED BEFORE THE BRITISH ASSOCIATION AT BELFAST, AUGUST 19, 1874, BY PROFESSOR TYNDALL.

'Believing as I do in the continuity of Nature, I cannot stop abruptly where our microscopes cease to be of use. Here the vision of the mind authoritatively supplements the vision of the eye. By an intellectual necessity I cross the boundary of the experimental evidence, and discern in that matter which we, in our ignorance of its latent powers, and notwithstanding our professed reverence for its Creator, have hitherto covered with opprobrium, the promise and potency of all terrestrial Life.

'In fact, the whole process of evolution is the manifestation of a Power absolutely inscrutable to the intellect of man. As little in our day as in the days of Job can man by searching find this Power out. Considered fundamentally, then, it is by the operation of an insoluble mystery that life on earth is evolved, species differentiated and mind unfolded from their prepotent elements in the immeasurable past. There is, you will observe, no very rank materialism here.

'The strength of the doctrine of evolution consists not in an experimental demonstration (for the subject is hardly accessible to this mode of proof), but in its general harmony with the method of nature as hitherto known. From contrast, moreover, it derives enormous relative strength. On the one side we have a theory (if it could with any propriety be so called) derived not from the study of nature, but from the observation of men —a theory which converts the Power whose garment is seen in the visible universe into an Artificer, fashioned after the human model, and acting by broken efforts, as man is free to act. On the other side we have the conception that all we see around us and all we feel within us—the phenomena of physical nature as well as those of the human mind—have their unsearchable roots in a cosmical life, if I dare apply the term, an infinitesimal span of which only is offered to the investigation of man.'

He adds, as flowing from the universality of evolution, the assurance that harmony will eventually be seen to exist between Religion and Science:—

'There are such things woven into the texture of man as the feelings of awe, reverence, wonder . . . the love of the beautiful, physical and moral, in nature, poetry, and art. There is also that deep-set feeling which, since the earliest dawn of history, and probably for ages prior to all history, incorporated itself into the religions of the world. You who have escaped from these religions into the high and dry light of the understanding may deride them; but in so doing you deride accidents of form merely, and fail to touch the immovable basis of the religious sentiment in the emotional nature of man. To yield this sentiment reasonable satisfaction is the problem of problems at the present hour. . . . I would set forth equally the inexorable advance of man's understanding in the path of knowledge and the unquenchable claims of his emotional nature which the understanding can never satisfy. . . . They are not opposed but supplementary, not mutually exclusive but reconcileable. And if, still unsatisfied, the human mind, with the yearning of a pilgrim to his distant home, will turn to the mystery from which it has emerged, seeking so to fashion it as to give unity to thought and faith; so long as this is done not only without intolerance and bigotry of any kind, but with the enlightened recognition that ultimate fixity of conception is here unattainable, and that each succeeding age must be held free to fashion the mystery in accordance with its own needs; then, in opposition to all the restrictions of materialism, I would affirm this to be a field for the noblest exercise of what, in contrast with the *knowing* faculties, may be called the creative faculties of man.'

NOTE VIII.

FROM 'MAN'S PLACE IN NATURE,' by PROFESSOR HUXLEY (Williams and Norgate, 1864), pp. 111-2.

I have endeavoured to show that no absolute structural line of demarcation, wider than that between the animals which immediately succeed us in the scale, can be drawn between the animal world and ourselves; and I may add the expression of my belief that the attempt to draw a psychical distinction is equally futile, and that even the highest faculties of feeling and of intellect begin to germinate in lower forms of life. At the same time, no one is more strongly convinced than I am of the vastness of the gulf between civilised man and the brutes; or is more certain that, whether from them or not, he is assuredly not of them. No one is less disposed to think lightly of the present dignity, or despairingly of the future hopes, of the only consciously intelligent denizen of this world. Thoughtful men, once escaped from the blinding influences of traditional prejudice, will find in the lowly stock whence man has sprung the best evidence of the splendour of his capacities; and will discern in his long progress through the Past, a reasonable ground of faith in his attainment of a nobler Future. Due reflection on the teachings of the geologists instead of diminishing our reverence and our wonder, adds all the force of intellectual sublimity to the mere aesthetic intuition of the uninstructed beholder.

And after passion and prejudice have died away, the same result will attend the teachings of the naturalist respecting that great Alps and Andes of the living world—Man. Our reverence for the nobility of manhood will not be lessened by the knowledge that man is, in substance and in structure, one with the brutes; for he alone possesses the marvellous endowment of intelligible and rational speech, whereby in the secular period of his existence he has slowly accumulated and organised the experience which is almost wholly lost with the cessation of every individual life in other animals; so that now he stands raised upon it as on a mountain top, far above the level of his humble fellows, and transfigured from his grosser nature by reflecting, here and there, a ray from the infinite source of truth.

NOTE IX.

The relation of the Doctrine of Evolution to that of Free-will.

The doctrine of evolution is often charged with the reproach of fatalism. Yet its fundamental postulate is variation. Each individual animal or plant is different, in a greater or less degree, from the rest: and in this difference lies the origin of species. Darwin endeavours to account for the original variation by causes such as the excess of nutriment in the parents and altered conditions. But the character once impressed, by whatever means, goes on developing, and gains an energy of its own, which is discernible first in vegetables, then more markedly in animals, to whom a certain character and power of choice must be conceded, and lastly in man, in whom it attains the faculties of reflexion, judgment, will. It may be that the tendency of evolutionists is to dwell on the *circumstances* which determine the tendency. But it is not denied that the main circumstance is the individual character; and when to character is added consciousness and the sense of responsibility, there is no fear of the introduction of an element which Christian faith would count immoral, such as compulsion by physical causes ab extra.

Darwin says (Variation of Animals and Plants under Domestication, i. 252–3): 'When we reflect on the individual differences between organic beings in a state of nature, as shown by any wild animal knowing its mate; and when we reflect on the infinite diversity of the many varieties of our domesticated productions, we may well be inclined to exclaim, though falsely as I believe, that variability must be looked at as an ultimate fact, necessarily contingent on reproduction.'

Darwin indeed believed that the individual differences here alluded to were all the result of circumstances, which in many cases could be ascertained. But, however originating, it is certain that these individual differences are the indispensable condition of development. And when we read in 'The Origin of Species' of the sudden appearance of new forms of vegetable life like the teasel (32), of individual difference in plants (43), of prejudices and dislikes among birds (102), of divergence of character among animals (157-8), and of the great varieties of instincts (258), we have the ground laid for all that any sober assertor of Free-will in the human individual would claim.

'I saw,' says Mill (Autobiography) in speaking of his recovery from the dejection caused by the incubus of fatalism, 'that, though our character is formed by circumstances, our own desires can do much to shape these circumstances, and that what is really inspiring and ennobling in the doctrine of Free-will is the conviction that we have real power over the formation of our own character; that our will, by influencing some of our circumstances, can modify our future habits or capabilities of willing.'

NOTE X.

ILLUSTRATIONS OF THE CONTRAST BETWEEN THE EASTERN AND WESTERN CHURCH-TEACHERS IN THEIR VIEW OF THE VIRTUES OF THE HEATHEN.

Clement of Alexandria, who may be taken as the representative of the Eastern Fathers, in his Λόγος προτρεπτικὸς πρὸς "Ελληνας, while denouncing the immorality of heathen mythology, appeals to men, as bearing God's image, to rise to a nobler life. He represents Christ as saying (p. 92), Μὴ μόνον τῶν ἀλόγων ζῴων πλεονεκτεῖτε τῷ λόγῳ, ἐκ δὲ τῶν θνητῶν ἁπάντων ὑμῖν ἀθανασίαν μόνοις καρπώσασθαι δίδωμι .. καὶ Λόγον χαρίζομαι ὑμῖν, τὴν γνῶσιν τοῦ Θεοῦ, ... ὧν πολλαὶ μὲν εἰκόνες, οὐ πᾶσαι δὲ ἐμφερεῖς· διορθώσασθαι ὑμᾶς πρὸς τὸ ἀρχέτυπον βούλομαι, ἵνα μοι καὶ ὅμοιοι γενῆσθε.

In Strom. i. 20 (p. 377) he says, Καίτοι καὶ καθ᾽ ἑαυτὴν ἐδικαίου ποτὲ καὶ ἡ φιλοσοφία τοὺς "Ελληνας, οὐκ εἰς τὴν καθολοῦ δὲ δικαιοσύνην εἰς ἣν εὑρίσκεται συνεργός, καθάπερ καὶ ὁ πρῶτος καὶ ὁ δεύτερος βαθμὸς τῷ εἰς ὑπερῷον ἀνιόντι. The philosophers, he says, have taken some of the truths of Revelation (he believed that Plato had borrowed from the Old Testament). But they had only perceived them through a mist of conjectural reasoning. When converted they see these same truths clearly.

Contrast this with the estimate of heathenism and the fate of heathens in the passage from Tertullian, de Spectaculis, c. 30, quoted by Gibbon, ch. xv (vol. ii. 91), and with the assertion of Jerome to Marcella that the excellent Vettius Agorius Praetextatus was in Tartarus [Ep. xxiii, Ad Marcellam, De Exitu Leae]. 'I tell you this,' he says, 'ut designatum Consulem de suis socculis (saeculis) detrahentem esse doceamus in Tartaro.'

NOTE XI.

EXPRESSIONS OF ARISTOTLE CONFESSING THE PRACTICAL IMPOTENCE OF HIS MORAL PHILOSOPHY.

The last chapter of Aristotle's Ethics describes this impotence (x. 10):—

2. Οὐδὲ δὴ περὶ ἀρετῆς ἱκανὸν τὸ εἰδέναι, ἀλλ' ἔχειν καὶ χρῆσθαι πειρατέον, ἢ εἴ πως ἄλλως ἀγαθοὶ γινόμεθα.

3, 4. Νῦν δὲ φαίνονται οἱ λόγοι ... τοὺς πολλοὺς ἀδυνατεῖν πρὸς καλοκἀγαθίαν προτρέψασθαι· οὐ γὰρ πεφύκασιν αἰδοῖ πειθαρχεῖν ἀλλὰ φόβῳ.

22. Παραλιπόντων οὖν τῶν προτέρων ἀνερεύνητον τὸ περὶ τῆς νομοθεσίας.

Compare with this the words put by Thucydides (iii. 45) into the mouth of Diodotus: Τῷ χρόνῳ ἐς τὸν Θάνατον αἱ πολλαὶ (ζημίαι) ἀνήκουσι· καὶ τοῦτο ὅμως παραβαίνεται.

NOTE XII.

EXTRACTS FROM LEADERS OF MODERN THOUGHT ON THE RELATION OF KNOWLEDGE TO MORALITY AND RELIGION.

Carlyle on Moral Relations as a condition of knowledge.
'Heroes and Hero Worship,' pp. 167–168.

Without hands a man might have feet, and could still walk:

NOTE XII.] *Carlyle on Knowledge and Morality.* 395

but, consider it, without morality, intellect were impossible for him, he could not know anything at all! To know a thing, what we can call knowing, a man must first *love* the thing, sympathize with it, that is, be *virtuously* related to it. If he have not the justice to put down his own selfishness at every turn, the courage to stand by the dangerous-true at every turn, how shall he know? His virtues, all of them, will lie recorded in his knowledge. Nature with her truth remains to the bad, the selfish and the pusillanimous, for ever a sealed book: what such can know of Nature is mean, superficial, small; for the uses of the day merely.

> Sir J. Lubbock on the connexion of Intellectual and Spiritual Progress. 'Pre-Historic Times,' pp. 488-491.

Thus, then, with the increasing influence of science, we may confidently look to a great improvement in the condition of man. But it may be said that our present sufferings and sorrows arise principally from sin, and that any moral improvement must be due to religion, not to science. This separation of the two mighty agents of improvement is the great misfortune of humanity, and has done more than anything else to retard the progress of civilisation. But even if for the moment we admit that science will not render us more virtuous, it must certainly make us more innocent. Out of 129,000 persons committed to prison in England and Wales during the year 1863, only 4829 could read and write well. In fact, our criminal population are mere savages, and most of their crimes are but injudicious and desperate attempts to act as savages in the midst, and at the expense, of a civilised community....

Thus, then, the most sanguine hopes for the future are justified by the whole experience of the past. It is surely unreasonable to suppose that a process which has been going on for so many thousand years should have now suddenly ceased; and he must be blind indeed who imagines that our civilisation is unsusceptible of improvement, or that we ourselves are in the highest state attainable by man. If we turn from experience to theory, the same conclusion forces itself upon us.

The great principle of natural selection, which in animals affects the body and seems to have little influence on the mind, in man affects the mind and has little influence on the body. In the first it tends mainly to the preservation of life; in the second to the improvement of the mind and consequently to the increase of happiness. It ensures, in the words of Mr. Herbert Spencer, 'a constant progress towards a higher degree of skill, intelligence, and self-regulation—a better co-ordination of actions—a more complete life.' Even those, however, who are dissatisfied with the reasoning of Mr. Darwin, who believe that neither our mental and material organisation are susceptible of any considerable change, may still look forward to the future with hope. The tendency of recent improvements and discoveries is less to effect any rapid change in man himself, than to bring him into harmony with nature; less to confer upon him new powers, than to teach him how to apply the old.

It will, I think, be admitted that of the evils under which we suffer nearly all may be attributed to ignorance or sin. That ignorance will be diminished by the progress of science is of course self-evident; that the same will be the case with sin, seems little less so. Thus, then, both theory and experience point to the same conclusion. The future happiness of our race, which prophets hardly ventured to hope for, science boldly predicts.

The manner in which a needless conflict grows up between Science and Religion is well illustrated by the following curious letter of Darwin, in which Science is taken in a far narrower sense than that in which it would be applied to the works of the great biologist, and Revelation is taken as implying some direct communication from Heaven of a different kind from that contained in the life of Christ.

A letter sent by Katharina Macmillan to the 'Pall Mall Gazette' of Saturday, Sept. 23, 1882, and reprinted in the 'Guardian' of Sept. 27, from Charles Darwin to a student at Jena.

Sir,—I am very busy, and am an old man in delicate health, and have not the time to answer your questions fully, even assuming that they are capable of being answered at all. Science and Christ have nothing to do with each other except in so far as the habit of scientific investigation makes a man cautious about accepting any proof. As far as I am concerned, I do not believe that any revelation has ever been made. With regard to a future life, every one must draw his own conclusions from vague and contradictory probabilities.

Wishing you well, I remain, your obedient servant,

CHARLES DARWIN.

DOWN,
June 5, 1879.

NOTE XIII.

THE INFLUENCE OF GREEK PHILOSOPHY AND ROMAN LAW ON CHRISTIAN THEOLOGY, FROM SIR H. MAYNE'S 'ANCIENT LAW,' p. 257.

'Why is it that on the two sides of the line which divides the Greek-speaking from the Latin-speaking provinces there lie two classes of theological problems so strikingly different from one another? . . . I affirm without hesitation that the difference between the two theological systems is accounted for by the fact that, in passing from the East to the West, theological speculation had passed from a climate of Greek metaphysics to a climate of Roman law. . . . Almost everybody who has knowledge enough of Roman law to appreciate the Roman penal system, the Roman theory of its obligations established by Contract or Delict, the Roman view of Debts and of the modes of incurring, extinguishing and transmitting them, the Roman notion of the continuance of individual existence by Universal Succession, may be trusted to say whence arose the frame of mind to which the problems of Western theology proved so congenial, whence came the phraseology in which those problems are stated, and whence the description of reasoning employed in their solution.'

NOTE XIV.

KESHUB CHUNDER SEN ON CHRISTIANITY FOR EUROPE AND ASIA.

From ' Lectures and Tracts of the Brahmo-Somaj,' pp. 33, 34.

'If, however, our Christian friends persist in traducing our nationality and national character, and in distrusting and hating Orientalism, let me assure them that I do not in the least feel dishonoured by such imputations. On the contrary, I rejoice, yea, I am proud that I am an Asiatic. And was not Jesus Christ an Asiatic? Yes, and his disciples were Asiatics, and all the agencies primarily employed for the propagation of the Gospel were Asiatic. In fact, Christianity was founded and developed by Asiatics, and in Asia. When I reflect on this, my love for Jesus becomes a hundredfold intensified; I feel him nearer my heart, and deeper in my national sympathies. Why should I then feel ashamed to acknowledge that nationality which He acknowledged? shall I not rather say, He is more congenial and akin to my Oriental nature, more agreeable to my Oriental habits of thought and feeling? and is it not true that an Asiatic can read the imageries and allegories of the Gospel, and its descriptions of natural sceneries, of customs and manners, with greater interest, and a fuller perception of their force and beauty, than Europeans? In Christ we see not only the exaltedness of humanity, but also the grandeur of which Asiatic nature is susceptible. To us Asiatics, therefore, Christ is doubly interesting, and his religion is entitled to our peculiar regard as an altogether Oriental affair. The more this great fact is pondered, the less I hope will be the antipathy and hatred of European Christians against Oriental nationalities, and the greater the interest of the

Asiatics in the teachings of Christ. And thus in Christ, Europe and Asia, the East and the West, may learn to find harmony and unity.'

NOTE XV.

AN EXTRACT FROM MILL'S LOGIC (VOL. II. PP. 16-18) ON THE USE OF HYPOTHESIS IN SCIENTIFIC INVESTIGATION.

'The function of hypothesis is one which must be reckoned absolutely indispensable in science. When Newton said, " Hypotheses non fingo," he did not mean that he deprived himself of the facilities of investigation afforded by assuming in the first instance what he hoped afterwards to be able to prove. Without such assumptions science could never have attained its present state : they are necessary steps in the progress to something more certain ; and nearly everything which is now theory was once hypothesis. Even in purely experimental science, some inducement is necessary for trying one experiment rather than another.

'Neither induction nor deduction would enable us to understand even the simplest phenomena "if we did not often commence by anticipating on the results; by making a provisional supposition, at first essentially conjectural, as to some of the very notions which constitute the final object of the inquiry " (Comte's Philosophie Positive, ii. 434, 437). Let any one watch the manner in which he unravels a complicated mass of evidence ; let him observe how, for instance, he elicits the true history of any occurrence from the involved statements of one or of many witnesses: he will find that he does not take all the items of evidence into his mind at once and attempt to weave them together: he extemporises, from a few of the particulars, a first rude theory of the mode in which the facts took place, and then looks at the other statements one by one, to try whether they can be reconciled with that provisional theory, or what alterations and additions it requires to make it square with them. In this way, which has been justly compared to the Methods of

Approximation of mathematicians, we arrive, by means of hypotheses, at conclusions not hypothetical.'

NOTE XVI.

An Excursus on the Books of the Old Testament as a basis for History.

It is unsatisfactory to make any statements such as those contained in the Second Lecture on the Hebrew Commonwealth and Laws without forming a clear estimate of the sources whence our information is drawn. Putting aside the slight intimations which are found in Egyptian writings, especially those of Manetho which are not without value for the history of the Exodus, we have to consider solely the books of the Old Testament. Are we justified in basing history upon them? The answer to this question is that, though many things remain uncertain, the ground is sufficiently secure. It becomes more possible every year to fix the historical value of the books.

In the first place, the writings of the prophets, with the exception of Daniel, the later part of Isaiah, and the later part of Zachariah, are unchallenged. We have thus a mass of literature of the highest importance from the eighth to the sixth century B.C., blended in the most intimate way with the history of the contemporary period—a period when Greek and Latin history is still fabulous, when Greek literature only existed in the shape of the songs of the rhapsodists or of Hesiod, a period mostly before Buddha or Confucius. The Psalms, also, which make us understand the national life, though they are of various dates, are genuine productions, and the dates of the majority of them are not hard to fix. The historical books, again, from Judges on to Nehemiah, with the exception of the Books of Chronicles, form one uninterrupted narrative, embodying the writings of various prophets, in many cases on the events of their own times. We are thus on firm ground in the chief part of the Old Testament, and can accept the framework which it presents for our historical conceptions.

NOTE XVI.] *as a Basis for History.* 401

It is unnecessary for the purposes of the second of these Lectures to enter upon the questions raised as to the second part of the book of Isaiah, or the book of Daniel and the second part of Zechariah. By whomsoever written and at whatever date, the second part of Isaiah evidently relates to the Babylonian exile, while the book of Daniel and the second part of Zechariah are written in view of the Maccabæan era: and neither of them furnish anything of great importance for our present purpose.

Neither need we enter into questions relating to the books called by the Jews Hagiographa. Of the Psalms I have already spoken : the book of Job is a speculative poem, and, though its date and origin are matters of religious and literary interest, it has little bearing on the history or laws of Israel. Of the book of Proverbs, a book of universal rather than Judaic morality, the same may be said. As to Ecclesiastes, it is evidently the production of a late age, probably the same time as Malachi, and, though of a high and peculiar religious value, is only a witness to the mode of thought among the Jews of a certain class at a particular epoch, probably that of the last Persian kings. The Song of Songs has no assignable date, and, though it is an idyll in praise of chaste married love as opposed to licentiousness, and thus touches one of the springs of the later Jewish greatness, may have had as little to do with the peasants of Shunem as the bucolics of Theocritus and Virgil had to do with the real life of the peasants of Sicily and North Italy. The book of Esther is evidently of much later date, and not to be depended on for historical purposes. The books of Chronicles, which were reckoned by the Jews among the Hagiographa and formed the last book of their Canon, are now recognised as belonging to the time of Ezra or his immediate successors, and as representing a Levitical rehandling of the history of the kings of Judah, though drawing partly from different sources than those used by the compilers of the earlier histories.

Of the three great divisions of the Old Testament, namely, the Law, the Prophets, and the Hagiographa, we have spoken of two. It remains to speak of the most difficult part, the Pentateuch

D d

and the book of Joshua, or, as it has been called, the Hexateuch, on which the battle of criticism has raged, and is not yet finally decided.

The critical questions relating to the Pentateuch have been needlessly complicated by doctrinal controversy. It has been assumed that the Mosaic authorship and the exact accuracy of the books are involved in the acknowledgment of their religious value as parts of the Bible. But, since they make no statements as to their authorship, and the common appellation of them as Books of Moses and the allusions in the New Testament to 'Moses' writings' need imply no more than allusions to David's Psalms or Solomon's Proverbs, we may put aside this difficulty, while recognising inspiration, according to the true meaning of the term, in the spirit which breathes through the books. That this spirit is in the main that which as Christians we acknowledge to be divine, though expressed according to the capacities of a backward age, and only tending by progressive increase towards the perfect holiness of Christ, may easily be discerned. The religious value of the Hebrew law has been fully vindicated in the Lecture.

When we once admit into our minds the possibility that parts of the Pentateuch may have been written subsequently to the time of Moses, we can hardly fail to assign a much later date to the book of Deuteronomy. Not only is its style eminently prophetic, recalling the manner of Jeremiah more than that of any other Scriptural writer, but some of its provisions are such as it seems impossible to believe could have been known during the earlier history. The chief of these is the prohibition in Deuteronomy of sacrifice at any but the one central sanctuary. It is evident that no such law was acknowledged in earlier times. Not only did men like Samuel and Elijah sacrifice on special occasions at other places than the central sanctuary, but in the life of Samuel we find that on all solemn occasions when there was a 'sacrifice of the people,' he came in to bless it in the city where he dwelt (1 Sam. ix. 13); he inaugurates the choice of David by a sacrifice (1 Sam. xvi. 2, 5); David's family had a yearly sacrifice at Bethlehem

(1 Sam. xx. 6); Absalom, during David's reign, sacrifices at Hebron (2 Sam. xv. 12). Joshua makes a pillar at Shechem (xxiv. 26); God appears to Solomon when he worships and sacrifices at the great high place in Gibeon (1 Kings iii. 4); Isaiah declares that there shall one day be a pillar to Jehovah in the border of Egypt (xix. 19), whereas the Deuteronomic legislation requires that all pillars, groves (asheras or poles), and high places should be destroyed. This is precisely what was attempted by Hezekiah and accomplished by Josiah. It is therefore natural to place the writing of Deuteronomy at some time in the age from Hezekiah to Josiah.

But the contrast is not only between the ideas of worship in Deuteronomy and in the historical books, but between Deuteronomy and all the Pentateuch from Exodus xxv. to the end of the book of Numbers. In Deuteronomy the Priests and Levites are one, in Leviticus xviii. the distinction is drawn between them in the strongest manner. In Deuteronomy, the Levites who come in to Jerusalem are nourished by the same offerings as those given to the Priests; in Numbers xviii. the Levites have a different support assigned them, that of the tithes: in Numbers xviii. again, the tithes are assigned to the support of the Levites, in Deuteronomy xiv. 22–29 they are to provide a family feast, of which the Levite partakes only on the same terms as the stranger, the fatherless, and the widow. The general tenor of the Deuteronomic legislation is also quite different from that of those parts of the Hexateuch with which we are contrasting it; for in those parts the idea of the service of God is almost wholly sacrificial and ceremonial; in Deuteronomy it is almost wholly moral and political.

Turning to the historical and prophetical books, we find that in the time of Josiah the priests of the high places were brought in from the cities of Judah into Jerusalem (2 Kings xxiii. 8, 9), when the high places were defiled and broken down, though some of these priests did not come up to the altar of Jehovah at Jerusalem, but ate of the unleavened bread among their brethren. This seems to correspond with the provisions of Deuteronomy xviii. 6–8, that the Levites who should elect to come to Jerusalem should serve with the Levitical priests and have their portion there like them. On the other hand, this is in contrast with what we read in Ezekiel xliv. 10, that the Levites because they had gone astray should be merely keepers of the door and assistants, and these are evidently the general body of the Levites as contrasted with the priestly family of Levites who were descended from Zadok. This representation of Ezekiel agrees with the representation of the books of Numbers and Leviticus, and also with that of Ezra, when the Levites are comparatively insignificant in numbers and office (ii. 36-40; ix. 1; Nehem. viii. 9).

The historical theory which appears best supported by these facts is as follows:—The law of Israel grew up by gradual development. The first sketch of the law in Exodus xx-xxiii. may be believed to have come from the earliest times, and from this probably grew up the body of customary law by which the people were governed in the days of the judges and the early kings. This law, as also the constitution of the nation, was in many points vague and elastic. To pious and orderly minds it was held together by the consciousness of the indwelling of Jehovah as their king, which is the true theocracy. But there was much lawlessness, as indicated by the expression of the book of Judges (xix. 1; xxi. 25): 'In those days there was no king . . . every man did that which was right in his own eyes.' The law was more fully enforced by kings, such as David and Jehoshaphat; but the worship of Jehovah was still very generally of a debased character, notwithstanding the protests of individual prophets like Elijah; and the law partook of the character of the worship. Then came the great prophetic outburst of the eighth century B.C., which purified both the worship and the law, and which synchronises with the reforms of Hezekiah. These in their turn give rise to the legislation of Deuteronomy, to the more stringent reforms of Josiah, and to the directly spiritual teaching of Jeremiah and Ezekiel. But now in the prophets of the exile and the return a new sacerdotal and sacrificial element appears. Even in the second part of Isaiah we read of the doom entailed by ceremonial impurity (Is. lxvi. 17): the test of the strangers who join themselves to Jehovah is that they should keep the Sabbaths, and the promise to them is that they should offer acceptable burnt sacrifices (lv. 6, 7); and the ideal for those who return from exile is that of them some shall be taken for priests and Levites (lxvi. 19–21). In Ezekiel, who was himself a priest, we find an elaborate system of sacrificial worship drawn out, which appears to have been the model followed by the restored community. It may well be that the sense of the need of atonement was so great at that time that it could only be satisfied by the intensifying of this element. That this element existed from the first is not denied, and that some kind of a priestly Torah was formed of customs and decisions relating to sacrifices and ceremonies. (See the allusions to ceremonial customs in 1 Sam. xiv. 33, xx. 26, 29; 2 Kings iv. 23.) But when we consider that the passover was never celebrated as a national feast from the time of Solomon to that of Hezekiah (2 Chron. xxx. 26), nor the feast of tabernacles from the time of Joshua to that of Ezra (Nehem. viii. 17), we may believe that little attention was paid to the details of the sacrificial system, and that the offerings, however numerous, were spontaneous and irregular. The best evidence of the change from this irregularity to the subsequent precision is to be found by comparing the earlier prophets with those after the exile. Especially we may compare the teaching of Jeremiah who declares that no law had been given to the fathers as to offering and sacrifice (vii. 22) with Malachi whose expostulations with the people are all connected with the sacrificial system. 'Cursed be the deceiver who hath in his flock a male and voweth and sacrificeth unto the Lord a corrupt thing' (Mal. i. 14). Such a sentence as this could not have occurred in the earlier prophets; nor again the sentiment of iii. 9, 10, where the removal of the curse upon the nation is made dependent on the payment of tithes.

It is natural to infer from these facts that the sacrificial system became much more stringent after the return from Babylon. The saying that 'post-exilian Judaism was rabbinical and not sacrificial' is true only of the later times. It may be that the sacrificial system did not last long after it was reduced to a stringent system. It is not uncommon for a practice to be pursued with an extreme fervour at the moment when it is about to pass away, as was the case with the Roman temple-architecture under Antoninus Pius just before its complete debasement under Caracalla, or of the building of vast towers to churches and monasteries just before the Reformation. But the men of the age from Ezra to Malachi, during which, according to the Jewish tradition, the whole of the older documents were revised and re-edited, must have set about their task with minds deeply imbued with the importance of the sacrificial system and the priestly office. This appears distinctly in the books of Chronicles, which were unquestionably written at this time. It is most natural to believe that the book of Leviticus also was compiled or reduced to its present state at the same time. The same tendency, it is believed, is to be traced in the rehandling of the other books of the Pentateuch, especially the later part of Exodus and the book of Numbers. The book of Deuteronomy, being a connected whole, is not susceptible of such treatment; but the book of Joshua is coloured by it.

We have, then, three periods of Jewish literature and legislation. First, the simpler period, to which belongs the underlying substance of the books of Genesis, Exodus, Numbers, and Joshua, and the whole of the earlier histories; secondly, the Deuteronomic period, to which belong the book of Deuteronomy, the prophets except the prophets of the exile and return, and the later part of the history; and thirdly, the Levitical period, to which belong the prophets of the exile and return, the books of Leviticus and the Chronicles, and the general rehandling of the Pentateuch except Deuteronomy and the book of Joshua. The Psalms belong to all the periods : and the Hagiographa bear only incidentally upon the history.

In the views now expressed Kuenen, Colenso, and Robertson Smith substantially agree, and, though with some differences, Wellhausen. It is obvious that they are of great importance for a correct estimate of the Hebrew history, and make it more harmonious with what we know of history generally, though in the case of Israel the seminal point is different from that to be found in other nations, being nothing else than a conscious relation to the Supreme Unity and Holiness.

NOTE XVII.

ON CUSTOMARY LAW AS DESCRIBED BY SIR H. MAYNE.

Sir H. Mayne, in his 'Ancient Law,' pp. 11-13, distinguishes two epochs antecedent to the reduction of Laws to Codes; the first that of almost arbitrary commands, or 'Themistes,' the second that of Customary Law. Of the first he says:—
'It is certain that, in the infancy of mankind, no sort of legislature, not even a distinct author of law, is contemplated or conceived of. Law has scarcely reached the footing of a custom, it is rather a habit. It is, to use a French phrase, "in the air." The only authoritative statement of right and wrong is a judicial sentence after the facts, not one presupposing a law which has been violated, but one which has been breathed for the first time by a higher power into the judge's mind at the moment of adjudication.... An Englishman should be better able than a foreigner to appreciate the historical fact that the Themistes preceded any conception of law, because, amid the many inconsistent theories which prevail concerning the character of English jurisprudence, the most popular, or at all events the one which most affects practice, is certainly a theory which assumes that adjudged cases and precedents exist antecedently to rules, principles and distinctions.'

Of the second, the customary period, he says that it coincides with a period in which aristocracies were formed and became the depositaries of the law:—

'Customs or Observances now exist as a substantive aggregate, and are assumed to be precisely known to the aristocratic order or caste.... Before the invention of writing, and during the infancy of the art, an aristocracy invested with judicial privileges formed the only expedient by which accurate preservation of the customs of the race or tribe could be at all approximated to.

Their genuineness was, so far as possible, ensured by confiding them to the recollection of a limited portion of the community. The epoch of Customary Law, and of its custody by a privileged order, is a very remarkable one. The condition of jurisprudence which it implies has left traces which may still be detected in legal and popular phraseology. The law thus known exclusively to a privileged minority, whether a caste, an aristocracy, a priestly tribe or a sacerdotal college, is true unwritten law. Except this, there is no such thing as unwritten law in the world.'

He adds: 'There was once a period at which English common law might reasonably have been termed unwritten. The older English judges did really pretend to knowledge of rules, principles and distinctions which were not entirely revealed to the bar and to the lay-public.'

It is evident that we have traces of both these periods, as well as of the stage of codified law, in the history of Israel, though these periods are not quite mutually exclusive. It is generally believed that the 'Book of the Covenant' (Exod. xx–xxiii) dates from the earliest times. But such judgments as that of David on the supposititious case brought before him by Nathan (2 Sam. xii. 5, 6) or the famous judgment of Solomon are instances of Themistes, immediate judgments upon the facts held to proceed from divine inspiration. On the other hand, the position ascribed to the tribe of Levi (Deut. xxxiii. 9, 10, xxi. 5) and the connexion of judgment with the sanctuary, as seen in the use of the word Elohim for judges in Exod. xxi. 6, xxii. 8, 9, indicates the second stage when the knowledge of law belonged to the priestly tribe. Deuteronomy and Leviticus show the process of codification in two different stages and forms.

NOTE XVIII.

1. EXTRACTS FROM THE LIFE OF BARON BUNSEN, SHOWING THE WORKING OF ABSOLUTISM IN THE CHURCH IN GERMANY.

Vol. i. p. 198. He [the King of Prussia, Frederick William III] was intensely anxious to heal the wounds of his own ravaged and dissevered dominions, by effectually securing the advancement of Christianity, as the best means of renewing well-being in every direction; and he had a strong impression of the peculiar duty inherited by the House of Brandenburgh, to create peace and unity between the observances of the Reformed (or Calvinistic) Churches and those of the Lutheran Confession. Could the King have had his wish, it would probably have taken the form of an absolute merging of variations into a solid and uniform establishment like that of the Church of England, which he knew to have originated in a compound of the maxims of the two Reformers, to be modified according to German peculiarities. This is not the place to note in detail the course of serious study and the manifold difficulties undertaken and worked through by the conscientious King and his favourite aide-de-camp, Witzleben, during many years. The King's researches after modes of conciliation had encountered much opposition, and only in the military deference of this much-respected officer, and his honest appreciation of the object in view, did he find assistance in the construction of a form of prayer for his own private chapel, put together from various liturgical fragments, which he proceeded, after the mode of the long established paternal (i.e. absolute) government, by degrees to introduce throughout the kingdom. The King's 'Agenda' became the authorised form of public worship in the 'United Evangelic Church of Prussia,' in the years following the tercentenary festival of the Reformation in 1817, when the King, although a Calvinist, had for the first time partaken of the Lord's Supper in a Lutheran Church.

P. 259. The Government of the Prussian dominions had

always been a system of royal orders and decrees, constituted with exemplary regard to positive and actual law, and obeyed with military precision. When the King's will was once known, there was no question of remonstrance or of opposition:—for instance, when King Frederick William (father of Frederick the Great) resolved to maintain the cause of his Protestant brethren in Heidelberg (persecuted and driven out of their own Church by the Roman Catholic Elector), and therefore declared that, as long as they were not restored to their hereditary possessions, he would retaliate on the Church of Rome, by withholding from his Catholic subjects in Magdeburgh their immunities and the use of their church, he was only considered as doing 'what he would with his own,' and never accused of a breach of vested rights. When therefore the Prussian dominions received the large accession of territory consisting of the ancient dioceses of Cologne, Trêves, and Paderborn, the Prussian ordinances were alone reckoned upon for the regulation of the new countries as well as of the old. The Prussian troops were, as such, to march into the Protestant church after parade, whether recruited among the Catholic or the Protestant population; and if a marriage was to take place between persons of different persuasions (a so-called 'mixed marriage'), the law of Prussia vested in the father the sole right over the religious education of his children, and forbade his entering into stipulations on the subject before marriage. This was law, and the monarch's will—and how should it be interfered with?

P. 309. The King of Bavaria has commanded the Protestant soldiers to fall down before the Host. Those at Regensburg have refused; and the King allows the alternative of quitting the service or complying. A letter has been published (to Count Senfft, the Austrian Ambassador Extraordinary in London for the Belgian question) signifying that the Pope will never allow Roman Catholics (those of Limburg and Luxemburg) to be transferred to Protestant Sovereigns. Of both these things due use will be made here.

NOTE XVIII.] *Prussian Church Reform.* 411

2. EXTRACTS (TRANSLATED) FROM THE INTRODUCTION TO 'DIE KIRCHENGEMEINDE-ORDNUNG FÜR DIE EVANGELISCHE LANDES-KIRCHEN PREUSSENS .... ERLÄUTERT VON F. RICHTER,' 1882. (Berlin, Fr. Kortkampf.)

All the laws of the National Church issue from the king in virtue of his right as the person charged with the ecclesiastical government. The king calls together, closes, or adjourns the general synod; his commissioner has the right of speaking and making proposals at any time. The king nominates thirty members in the general synod, and a sixth part of the number of members in each of the provincial synods. All members of the body of church officials, that is, of the parochial councils and of the consistories, and the superintendents are nominated by the king; the complete identification of the whole body of church officials with the synod, whether as offshoots from it, or as boards selected from the synods, and consequently the attribution to them of an exclusively ecclesiastical character with regard to hierarchical position and discipline, has been decisively renounced. The difference from earlier times consists in this, that the sovereign conducts the ecclesiastical government in a constitutional, not an absolute manner.

Lastly, we must also examine the question of superintendence by the state. We can best describe the oversight which the state officials will exercise over the action of the ecclesiastical organisations when they shall have been disconnected from the control of church affairs, in the words of the state-government itself which are added to the project of law for the regulation of the general synod : ' The object of the state-superintendence over the management of the property of a corporation existing by public right (for it is in this character that church communities present themselves in the regulation of the law of the state) is, to prevent that anything contrary to law or anything hurtful to the public weal should be committed, and to take care that the property which belongs to the perpetual corporation, but which does not stand at the free disposal of the actual members at any given time, should be maintained from generation to generation. By this the limit of the state-oversight is prescribed. Where nothing contrary to law or hurtful to the common weal appears, where a property is managed in such a way as not to endanger the future of the corporation, the state does not need to interfere, nor to encroach upon the Church power through pretext (so-called) of prescribing a policy, whether in the way of command or of prevention. In such a case the prescribed organs must retain freedom and independence of movement as to the power of managing their property. Starting from this principle, the system of universal oversight by the state which laid its hands on everything is abandoned in the law of June 20th, 1875, and the system is adopted of a special statement of those acts of administration which require the superintendence and the ratification of the state authorities, so that, with the exception of these special cases, the administration of property may be carried on freely and independently by the ecclesiastical organs, under the superintendence of the Church authorities. It is of course understood that henceforward the same system must be brought to bear on the Evangelical Church, and for this reason also article 23 of the project of law appears as a copy of § 50 of the law of June 20th, 1875. The project of law regulates the rights of superintendence by the state in express terms.

Thus all the rights of management hitherto exercised by the state authorities which do not remain in article 23, and those rights of superintendence which are not mentioned in article 24, are abolished. On the other hand, the state has not withdrawn from ecclesiastical legislation, though it no longer takes part in the decision of special cases, or in the application of ecclesiastical laws.

NOTE XIX.

EXTRACT FROM HOOKER'S ECCLESIASTICAL POLITY ON THE MAKING OF ECCLESIASTICAL LAWS AND THE ROYAL SUPREMACY.

Bk. VIII. c. vi. § 11. The most natural and religious course in making of laws is, that the matter of them be taken from the judgment of the wisest in those things which they are to concern. In matters of God, to set down a form of public prayer,

NOTE XIX.] *Hooker on the making of Church Law.* 413

a solemn confession of the articles of Christian faith, rites and ceremonies meet for the exercise of religion; it were unnatural not to think the pastors and bishops of our souls a great deal more fit, than men of secular trades and callings : howbeit, when all which the wisdom of all sorts can do is done for devising of laws in the Church, it is the general consent of all that giveth them the form and vigour of laws, without which they could be no more unto us than the counsels of physicians to the sick: well might they seem as wholesome admonitions and instructions, but laws could they never be without consent of the whole Church, which is the only thing that bindeth each member of the Church, to be guided by them. Whereunto both nature and the practice of the Church of God set down in Scripture, is found every way so fully consonant, that God Himself would not impose, no not His own laws upon His people by the hand of Moses, without their free and open consent. Wherefore to define and determine even of the Church's affairs by way of assent and approbation, as laws are defined of in that right of power, which doth give them the force of laws; thus to define of our own Church's regiment, the parliament of England hath competent authority.

Touching the supremacy of power which our kings have in this case of making laws, it resteth principally in the strength of a negative voice; which not to give them, were to deny them that without which they were but kings by mere title and not in exercise of dominion. Be it in states of regiment popular, aristocratical, or regal, principality resteth in that person, or those persons unto whom is given the right of excluding any kind of law whatsoever it be before establishment. This doth belong unto kings, as kings; pagan emperors, even Nero himself had not less but much more than this in the laws of his own empire. That he challenged not any interest in giving voice in the laws of the Church, I hope no man will so construe, as if the cause were conscience, and fear to encroach upon the Apostles' right.

If then it be demanded by what right from Constantine downward, the Christian emperors did so far intermeddle with the Church's affairs, either one must herein condemn them utterly, as being over presumptuously bold, or else judge that by a law which is termed Regia, that is to say royal, the people having derived into the emperor their whole power for making of laws, and by that means his edicts being made laws, what matter soever they did concern, as imperial dignity endowed them with competent authority and power to make laws for religion, so they were taught by Christianity to use their power, being Christians, unto the benefit of the Church of Christ. Was there any Christian bishop in the world which did then judge this repugnant unto the dutiful subjection which Christians do owe to the pastors of their souls? To whom in respect of their sacred order, it is not by us, neither may be denied, that kings and princes are, as much as the very meanest that liveth under them, bound in conscience to show themselves gladly and willingly obedient, receiving the seals of salvation, the blessed sacraments, at their hands, as at the hands of our Lord Jesus Christ, with all reverence, not disdaining to be taught and admonished by them, not withholding from them as much as the least part of their due and decent honour. All which for any thing that hath been alleged, may stand very well without resignation of supremacy of power in making laws, even laws concerning the most spiritual affairs of the Church.

Which laws being made amongst us, are not by any of us so taken or interpreted, as if they did receive the force from power which the prince doth communicate unto the parliament, or to any other court under him, but from power which the whole body of this realm being naturally possessed with hath by free and deliberate assent derived unto him that ruleth over them, so far forth as hath been declared. So that our laws made concerning religion do take originally their essence from the power of the whole realm and Church of England, than which nothing can be more consonant unto the law of nature and the will of our Lord Jesus Christ.

NOTE XX.

RICHARD ROTHE ON THE CHURCH.

In his great work on Theological Ethics, which, written in 1826, still continues to be reprinted in Germany, and has never been surpassed, Rothe takes the Church as meaning the Society which is concerned with spiritual relations pure and simple, as contrasted with Societies which exist for the general moral purposes of human life. He appropriates the word Church to that which I have in these Lectures called the Association for worship. He points out that religion must work itself out to moral and political results; that, as a corporate brotherhood, the Church necessarily gives birth to political life, and similarly that it is the parent of all the great forms of moral association. But he contends (1) that the Church only uses these Associations for its own purely spiritual purposes, and (2) that when these Associations have been fully inspired with the moral and religious spirit, the Society occupied with purely spiritual objects will have no further ratio essendi, and, according to his use of the term, the Church will vanish away. I subjoin a translation of the passage in which he expresses this remarkable opinion. I have given my reasons in the Lecture for not agreeing with it; but it is important as the judgment of a deeply thoughtful and far-seeing Christian teacher. The passage is from the Theologische Ethik, vol. ii. pp. 247-9 :—

'The community which exists for the purposes of piety *purely and exclusively as such* is the Church. The Church is accordingly, until the full termination of the moral development of humanity, the highest unity: in it the multiplicity of special circles of fellowship, into which the community of moral relations unfolds itself, passes again into absolute unity; and in it by this very fact the Society which exists for the religious-moral purposes of the individual, and which is confined in itself and limited, widens out into an universalism which has no limits and advances to the measure which our moral being demands, and thereby also gains true purity and enlightenment. It is, therefore, an unconditional demand of morality on every individual that he should take part in the Church, and this in all the substantial departments of his moral being (the whole moral person); and the participation of the individual in the other special modes of moral fellowship reaches its morally normal state only so far as it is united with a proportionate participation in the Church, and is held together by it in its several special departments.

'From this conception of the Church, however, it at once follows that, with the completion of the moral development of humanity (since with it the Society which combines religion with morality will in its action have reached an absolutely complete universality, and thus have been expanded into a bond which embraces all men without exception), the Church entirely falls away; for then the sphere of the Society in which religion is combined with morality (that is, the whole made up of the several circles of this religious-moral fellowship), now in its actual circumference (both extensive and intensive) completely occupies the sphere of the fellowship formed for purely religious purposes. The existing contrast between the two communities is entirely grounded on the fact that their circumferences are not the same. In proportion, therefore, as the normal moral development advances, and the moral fellowship approaches its consummation, the contrast between the two communities disappears; that is to say, in that same proportion the Church, the exclusively religious society, more and more retires before the advance of the religious-moral society.

'According to the proper conception of the Church, the business for which it forms a community is that of religion purely and exclusively. The occupation of the Church is, according to its very conception, not that of religion combined with morality, but a religious-moral occupation from which the moral element is completely withdrawn. It is consequently, to come more close to the matter, on one side a knowledge which is entirely, exclusively religious, and with this a piety, a yearning after God which is not at the same time a moral yearning or a yearning which has the world for its object, accompanied by a contemplation which is not at the same time a moral contemplation or a contemplation of the world; it is, further, a theosophy, but one which is not at the same time a moral knowledge and a process of thought, or a knowledge which has the world for the object of its thought, accompanied by a system of prophesying which is not at the same time a moral representation, a representation of the world; and on the other side a culture entirely, exclusively religious, and with this a system of devotion which is not at the same time a moral appropriation, an appropriation of the world, accompanied by a hope of blessedness which is not at the same time a moral enjoyment, and a consecration of life (a making of sacraments) which is not at the same time a framing of things moral, and therefore earthly, accompanied by a religious service which is not at the same time a moral acquirement, an acquirement of a personal possession in this world. Within the sphere of the Church, the normal occupation is that which is purely and exclusively religious. It is, however, inherent in the very conception of it that it is, in its pure and morally normal state, a merely transitory thing, as is the Church itself, that is, that it falls more and more completely into the background, in the same proportion in which the moral fellowship develops itself progressively as one which combines religion with its moral life and grows nearer to its completion.

NOTE XXI.

FROM ECCE HOMO. THE LAW OF EDIFICATION.

' A flourishing Church requires a vast and complicated organisation, which should afford a place for every one who is ready to work in the service of humanity. The enthusiasm should not be suffered to die out in any one for want of the occupation best calculated to keep it alive. Those who meet within the church walls on Sunday should not meet as strangers who find themselves together in the same lecture-hall, but as co-operators in a public work the object of which all understand and to his own department of which each man habitually applies his mind and contriving power. Thus meeting, with the *esprit de corps* strong among them, and with a clear perception of the purpose of their union and their meeting, they would not desire that the exhortation of the preacher should be, what in the nature of things it seldom can be, eloquent. It might cease then to be either a despairing and overwrought appeal to feelings which grow more callous the oftener they are thus excited to no definite purpose, or a childish discussion of some deep point in morality or divinity better left to philosophers. It might then become weighty with business, and impressive as an officer's address to his troops before a battle. For it would be addressed by a soldier to soldiers in the presence of an enemy whose character they understood and in the war with whom they had given and received telling blows. It would be addressed to an ardent and hopeful association who had united for the purpose of contending within a given district against disease and distress, of diminishing by every contrivance of kindly sympathy the rudeness, coarseness, ignorance, and improvidence of the poor and the heartlessness and hardness of the rich; for the purpose of securing to all that moderate happiness which gives leisure for virtue, and that moderate occupation which removes the temptations of vice; for the purpose of providing a large and wise education for the young; lastly, for the purpose of handing on the tradition of Christ's life, death, and resurrection, maintaining the Enthusiasm of Humanity in all the baptised, and preserving, in opposition to all temptations to superstition or fanaticism, the filial freedom of their worship of God.'

NOTE XXII.

RELIGION AND ART. EXTRACT FROM AN ADDRESS TO THE STUDENTS OF THE ROYAL ACADEMY SCHOOLS, ON SATURDAY, DECEMBER 10, 1881, BY THE PRESIDENT, SIR F. LEIGHTON.

After showing that Art must be emancipated from the supposed duty of directly inculcating moral and religious truth the President proceeded to point out the true connexion of Art and of the character of the artist with morals and religion:—

'There is a field in which art has no rival. We have within us the faculty for a range of emotions of vast compass, of exquisite subtlety, and of irresistible force, to which art and art alone among human forms of expression has a key. These, then, and no others, are the chords which it is her appointed duty to strike; and form, colour, and the contrasts of light and shade are the agents through which it is given to her to set them in motion. Her duty is, therefore, to awaken those sensations, directly emotional and indirectly intellectual, which can be communicated only through the sense of sight, to the delight of which she has primarily to minister. And the dignity of these sensations lies in this, that they are inseparably connected by association of ideas with a range of perceptions and feelings of infinite variety and scope. They come fraught with dim, complex memories of all the ever-shifting spectacle of inanimate creation and of the more deeply stirring phenomena of life, of the storm and the lull, the splendour and the darkness of the outer world, of the changeful and transitory lives of men. Nay, so closely overlaid is the simple æsthetic sensation with elements of ethic or intellectual emotion by these constant and manifold accretions of associated ideas that it is difficult to conceive of it independently of this precious overgrowth. I cannot here enter at any length on this most interesting subject, but a moment's reflection will furnish you with illustrations of it. You will find, for instance, that, through this operation of association, lines and forms and combinations of lines and forms, colours and combinations of colours, have acquired a distinct expressional significance, and, so to speak, an *ethos* of their own, and will convey, in the one province, notions of strength, of repose, of solidity, of flowing motion, and of life; in the other, sensations of joy or of sadness, of heat or of cold, of langour or of health. It is this intensification of the simple æsthetic sensation through ethic and intellectual suggestiveness that gives to the arts of architecture, sculpture, and painting so powerful, so deep, and so mysterious a hold on the imagination. And, here, also we find the answer to the second of those fallacies to which I just now alluded—to wit, that moral edification can attach only to direct moral teaching. The most sensitively religious mind may indeed rest satisfied in the consciousness that it is not on the wings of abstract thought alone that we rise to the highest moods of contemplation or to the most chastened moral temper, and assuredly arts which have for their chief task to reveal the inmost springs of beauty in the created world, to unfold all the pomp of the teeming earth, and all the pageant of those heavens of which we are told that they declare the glory of God, are not the least eloquent witnesses to the might and to the majesty of the mysterious and eternal Fountain of all good things. We should thus find ourselves abundantly armed, were it needful to be so armed, to meet those who affirm that to convey moral edification can alone give the highest *status* to an intellectual pursuit. But we have no need of defence against a fallacy so palpable, a fallacy of which the adoption contains the disparagement of every form of pure science with all its marvellous achievements, achievements more marvellous than the dreams of fancy, and in their results unspeakably beneficent. On the absurdity of such an attitude it is needless to dwell. In fact, the nature of man is a complex organism in which are many and various germs of growth, and only in the full and balanced development of these several elements can that organism achieve in this world its perfect maturity. To art belongs the development of one group of these rich and fruitful germs, a sufficient, and, surely, no ignoble task.

'Let me recapitulate the points on which, in this rapid and too summary glance at the bearing of ethics on art, we seem to have established our position. We have laid down as an unassailable axiom that the special function of a mode of expression is to convey those ideas, emotions, or impressions of which it is the fittest vehicle, and we have recognised that the proper vehicle of purely ethical ideas is speech. Art, on the other hand, we said, being the proper and only channel for impressions of another order—namely, æsthetical impressions, cannot have for its highest duty the conveying of ethic truths. We saw, further, that though the impressions which it is the exclusive privilege, and therefore the proper function of art to convey are primarily æsthetic, they are very complex in their nature, and receive an incalculable accession of strength through the operation of associated ideas; and again, we saw that these complex impressions, in which intellectual and ethical elements are thus added to the fundamental æsthetic sensation, having, like those stirred in us by music, the power to raise us to the highest regions of poetic emotion, deserve to rank among the noblest delights of men. And, lastly, we have seen that, while the inculcation of moral and religious truths must be admitted not to be the object of art, as such, nor moral edification its appointed task, it is not therefore true, as some would have us believe, that the artist's work is uninfluenced by his moral tone, but rather that the influence of that tone is, in fact, upon it, and controls it from the first touch of the brush or chisel to the last. And once again, I say I would fain stamp this vital fact deeply in your minds. Believe me, whatever of dignity, whatever of strength we have within us will dignify and will make strong the labours of our hands; whatever littleness degrades our spirit will lessen them and drag them down. Whatever noble fire is in our hearts will burn also in our work, whatever purity is ours will chasten and exalt it; for as we are, so our work is, and what we sow in our lives, that, beyond a doubt, we shall reap for good or for ill in the strengthening or defacing of whatever gifts have fallen to our lot.

NOTE XXIII.

EXTRACTS FROM 'A FRAGMENT ON THE CHURCH,' BY DR. ARNOLD (Fellowes, 1844), pp. 6–13.

By the Christian Church, I mean that provision for the communicating, maintaining and enforcing of Christian knowledge by which it was to be made influential, not on individuals, but on masses of men. This provision consisted in the formation of a society, which by its constitution should be capable of acting both within itself and without; having, so to speak, a twofold movement, the one for its outward advance, the other for its inward life and purification; so that Christianity should be at once spread widely, and preserved the while in its proper truth and vigour, till Christian knowledge should be not only communicated to the whole world, but be embraced also in its original purity, and bring forth its practical fruit. Thus, Christian religion and the Christian Church being two distinct things, the one acting upon individuals, the other upon masses; it is very possible for the former to continue to do its work, although the latter be perverted or disabled.

. . . .

The co-operative principle, founded on the great dissimilarity which prevails amongst men, was by Christianity to be applied to moral purposes, as it had long been to physical; each man was to regard his intellectual and moral gifts as a means of advancing the intellectual and moral good of society; what he himself wanted was to be supplied out of the abundance of his neighbour; and thus the moral no less than the physical weaknesses of each individual were to be strengthened and remedied till they should vanish as to their enfeebling effects both with respect to himself and to the community.

Nothing could be more general than such a system of co-operation. It extended to every part of life; not only going far beyond that co-operation for ritual purposes, which was the social part of the old religions, but, so far as men's physical well-being had been the sole object of existing civil societies, it went far beyond them also. For though it is possible, and unhappily too easy, to exclude moral considerations from our notions of physical good, and from our notions of ritual religion, yet it is not easy, in looking to the moral good of man, to exclude considerations of his physical well-being. Every outward thing having a tendency to affect his moral character, either for the better or for the worse, and this especially holding good with respect to riches or poverty, economical questions, in all their wide extent, fall directly under the cognizance of those whose object is to promote man's moral welfare.

But while thus general, the object of Christian co-operation was not to be vague. When men combined to offer sacrifice, or to keep festival, there was a definite object of their union;

but the promotion of man's moral welfare might seem indistinct and lost in distance. Something nearer and more personal was therefore to be mixed up with that which was indistinct from its very vastness. The direct object of Christian co-operation was to bring Christ into every part of common life, in scriptural language, to make human society one living body, closely joined in communion with Christ, its head. And for this purpose, one of the very simplest acts of natural necessity was connected with the very deepest things of religion—the meal of an assembly of Christians was made the sacrament of the body and blood of Christ. And the early Church well entered into the spirit of this ordinance, when it began every day by a partaking of the holy communion. For when Christ was thus brought into one of the commonest acts of nature and of common society, it was a lively lesson, that in every other act through the day he should be made present also; if Christians at their very social meal could enter into the highest spiritual communion, it taught them that in all matters of life, even when separated from one another bodily, that same communion should be preserved inviolate; that in all things they were working for and with one another, with and to Christ and God.

Such appears, even from the meagre account of a stranger, to have been the manner of living of the Christians of Bithynia, about a hundred years after the birth of our Lord, and about seventy therefore from the first preaching of Christianity. They met before day, and sang together a hymn to Christ: then they bound themselves to one another by oath—according to Pliny's expression, 'sacramento,' but in reality, we may be sure, by their joint partaking of the communion of Christ's body and blood—that they would neither steal, nor rob, nor commit adultery, nor break faith, nor refuse to restore what had been entrusted to them. Then they went to their day's work, and met again to partake their meal together, which they probably hallowed, either by making it a direct communion, or by some prayers or hymns, which reminded them of their Christian fellowship.

Now, in this account, short as it is, we see the two great principles of the Christian Church: first, co-operation for general moral improvement, for doing the duties of life better; and secondly, the bringing Christ as it were into their communion, by beginning the day with Him and deriving their principle of virtuous living directly from His sacrament. The Church of Bithynia existed on a small scale, in a remote province; but here are precisely those leading principles of the Christian Church exemplified, which were fitted for all circumstances and all places, and which contain in them that essential virtue which the Church was to embody and to diffuse.

It is obvious, also, that the object of Christian society being thus extensive, and relating not to ritual observances, but to the improvement of the whole of our life, the natural and fit state of the Church is that it should be a sovereign society or commonwealth; as long as it is subordinate and municipal, it cannot fully carry its purposes into effect. This will be evident, if we consider that law and government are the sovereign influences on human society; that they in the last resort shape and control it at their pleasure; that institutions depend on them, and are by them formed and modified; that what they sanction will ever be generally considered innocent; that what they condemn is thereby made a crime, and if persisted in becomes rebellion; and that those who hold in their hands the power of life and death must be able greatly to obstruct the progress of whatever they disapprove of, and those who dispose of all the honours and rewards of society must, in the same way, be greatly able to advance whatever they think excellent. So long, then, as the sovereign society is not Christian, and the Church is not sovereign, we have two powers alike designed to act upon the whole of our being, but acting often in opposition to one another. Of these powers, the one has wisdom, the other external force and influence; and from the division of these things, which ought ever to go together, the wisdom of the Church cannot carry into effect the truths which it sees and loves; whilst the power of government, not being guided by wisdom, influences society for evil rather than for good.

NOTE XXIII.] *as a Sovereign Society.* 425

The natural and true state of things then is, that this power and this wisdom should be united; that human life should not be pulled to pieces between two claimants, each pretending to exercise control over it, not in some particular portion, but universally; that wisdom should be armed with power, power guided by wisdom; that the Christian Church should have no external force to thwart its beneficent purposes; that government should not be poisoned by its external ignorance or wickedness, and thus advance the cause of God's enemy rather than perform the part of God's vicegerent.

This is the perfect notion of a Christian Church, that it should be a sovereign society, operating therefore with full power for raising its condition, first morally, and then physically; operating through the fullest development of the varied faculties and qualities of its several members, and keeping up continually, as the bond of its union, the fellowship of all its people with one another through Christ, and their communion with Him as their common head.

With this notion of a perfect Church two things are utterly inconsistent; first, the destroying of the principle of co-operation through the varied talents and habits of the several members of the society, and substituting in the place of it a system in which a very few should be active and the great mass passive; a system in which vital heat was to be maintained, not by the even circulation of the blood through every limb, through the healthy co-operation of the arteries and veins of every part, but by external rubbing and chafing, when the limbs, from a suspension of their inward activity, had become cold and paralyzed.

Secondly, the taking of any part or parts of human life out of its control, by a pretended distinction between spiritual things and secular; a distinction utterly without foundation, for in one sense all things are secular, for they are done in time and on earth; in another, all things are spiritual, for they affect us morally either for the better or the worse, and so tend to make our spirits fitter for the society of God or of His enemies. The division rests entirely on principles of heathenism, and tends to make Christianity like the religions of the old world, not a sovereign discipline for every part and act of life, but a system for communicating certain abstract truths, and for the performance of certain visible rules and ceremonies.

These two notions, both utterly inconsistent with the idea of a true Christian Church, have been prevalent alternately or conjointly almost from the beginning of Christianity. To the first we owe Popery in all its shapes, Romanist or Protestant; the second is the more open form of Antichrist, which by its utter dissoluteness has gone far to reduce countries nominally Christian to a state of lawlessness and want of principle worse than the worst heathenism.

But these two Antichrists have ever prepared the way for each other; and the falsehood of the one has led directly to the falsehood of its apparent opposite, but really ally and co-operator.

NOTE XXIV.

The Views of International Jurists as to a Tribunal of Arbitration as a substitute for War.

The efforts of international jurists have in recent years turned with hope and earnestness towards the establishment of some power which may obviate war.

Woolsey in his 'Introduction to the Study of International Law' points out that the Roman Imperial Power originally fulfilled this function, and that this was feebly perpetuated in the dispensing authority of the Mediæval Popes, which was held to override the national laws. He shows that International Law exists only for those countries which have the tradition of the Roman law, and in which, through the acknowledgment of Christianity, there is a community of moral principles. The great defect of International Law is the want of an authoritative exponent of its principles. Another defect is that the principles are not equally acknowledged by all; and a third, that the Law only binds the Christian nations among themselves, not in their dealings with the other races; and further, that there is no umpire.

Many attempts, he shows, have been made to correct these evils. Henry IV. of France formed a design of this kind, with a view to prevent the recurrence of the wars of religion, to unite Europe against Turkish aggression and to repress the tyrannical action of Spain and Austria. The efforts in the seventeenth and eighteenth centuries to maintain the balance of power recognised a common interest and a kind of authority above the individual states. In 1789 Bentham proposed a scheme for a general congress of arbitration. Each state was to agree to fix the amount of its armaments, and to give a contingent for enforcing the decrees of the central tribunal. Kant a few years afterwards (1795) wrote his treatise 'Zum ewigen Friede,' in which he advocated a homogeneous constitution for the several States, who would unite in a confederation, and thus form a common code of laws and a citizenship of the world.

In more recent times there has been a disposition to attempt to give practical effect to views of a similar tendency. The declaration of the Treaty of Paris (1856) is as follows: 'The Plenipotentiaries do not hesitate to express in the name of their Governments the wish that States between which a serious disagreement should arise would, before appealing to arms, have recourse, so far as circumstances admit, to the good offices of friendly powers.' A similar declaration was made by the Treaty of Berlin (1878). The success of the Alabama Convention has shed a fresh ray of hope on such efforts. The Société de Droit International and the Arbitration and Peace Society hold their congresses to promote these views. Bluntschli, as will be seen by the subjoined extract, went further, and believed in the possibility of a 'World-State' supreme over the various nations. Fiore (Trattato di diritto internazionale publico, vol. i. p. 95), while considering Bluntschli's idea Utopian, yet expresses the strongest hopes for the establishment of an authoritative system of arbitration.

It may be well to recall the efforts of the present English Government to promote the European concert. I may quote the declaration of Mr. Gladstone in his speech on the Vote of Credit for the Expedition to Egypt (July 24, 1882): 'I believe that it is the just opinion of reflecting men that there is nothing more important for the future of civilisation than to make free resort, wherever it can be done, to that authority of united Europe, which, when it does speak, does really speak with weight, and which possesses a real title to be heard.'

I subjoin a translation of a passage in Bluntschli's 'Allgemeine Volkslehre,' Bk. i. c. 2 :—

'The mind of Europe already casts its looks over the whole globe, and the Aryan race feels itself called upon to regulate the world.

'That point has not yet been reached. But at present it is not so much the will and the power as the intellectual maturity which is wanting. The final result will only then be possible, when the enlightening word of knowledge has been spoken concerning this, and concerning the essential state of mankind, and when the nations are ready to hear it.

'Until then the one Universal Kingdom will be an idea towards which many will aspire, which none will be in a position to realise. But as an idea in the future the science of international law may not overlook it. Only in the one Universal Kingdom will the real state of man be made manifest; in it the law of nations will find its perfection, and an assured existence in a higher form. The separate States hold the same relation to the universal kingdom as the different nations hold to mankind in general.'

Bluntschli adds, that most men in the present day will think this idea a dream; 'but,' he says, 'I must speak my conviction; posterity will decide.'

NOTE XXV.

The Parish as a Church.

I venture to give, as an illustration of the liberal and national aspect of the Parochial system, a portion of a Pastoral Address sent out to the Parishioners of St. Mary's, Bryanston Square, in London, for the year 1879. I may be allowed, I hope, without seeming egotistical or trivial, to show that what is said in the text of these Lectures is not a mere theory, and that Christian nationalism is a spiritual and a practical system :—

NOTE XXV.] *The Parish as a Church.* 429

'The Church is not the body of Christians simply when met for worship and instruction, but it is the unity of Christians in the whole circle of their lives. We should consider that Christians are meant to live together and to help each other in their common life : and that a common life lived in faith and love is the truest sacrifice, the most reasonable service, which we can render to God. We should consider also that the principle of Neighbourhood is not merely fortuitous but providential; and that God has placed us in contiguous dwellings in order that our neighbourly relations may be cemented by Christian love, and that we may by living together help each other to be true Christians. In short, the body of persons living within the bounds of a parish should be looked upon as forming a Christian Church ; and the Pastor's effort should be to induce each individual to realise his membership in this parochial church, first by believing and acting as a Christian himself, and then by helping others to do the same. It must be admitted that there are special difficulties thrown in the way of this by the fact that in London the parish forms but a fraction of a vast metropolitan whole. But it would be quite a mistake to suppose that it has not, on that account, a very practical meaning to us. It means that the parish clergyman tries to influence in some way every soul living in the district assigned to him by law. It means that systems of charitable relief, of district visiting by both paid and unpaid agents, of schools, mothers' meetings, clubs, provident funds, maternity charities, and similar things, are set on foot, in which every one to whom they apply is invited to join simply because he lives in the district. It means, further, that by the support of such institutions the richer parishioners are invited to aid their poorer brethren. And it means also that it affords a channel and a stimulus by which all who have any talent or willingness to work for their less favoured brethren may have their gifts drawn out.

'The Parish Church is the natural centre of all these Christian works, and the worship there carried on should be made to issue in such a system of mutual well-doing as has been described, and in general to promote a high tone of morals in the conduct of life. The worshippers in the Parish Church form a kind of nucleus and first-fruits of the whole parochial brotherhood. We might wish, indeed, that all parishioners could be in some way united with us in worship; but this is manifestly impossible in a London Parish. It is, however, by no means the case that those who do not worship in the Parish Church are necessarily separated from the church system such as I have described it. On the contrary; experience proves that the parochial church regarded as a system of mutual well-doing is often a reality to persons to whom the worship is, for whatever reason, less acceptable. In our own parish some of our largest subscribers and some of our most earnest workers are not members of the congregation. It was my misfortune some years ago, through a proposal which I made for holding lectures in the church on the bearing of religion on secular life, to incur the suspicion of some valued members of the congregation. They ceased to worship with us, but by no means separated themselves from the work of the church. On the contrary, they very generously took every opportunity of showing their union with us in our work, and have never ceased to fulfil actively the duties they had kindly undertaken in the administration of our charities. And least of all do we find that the fact of other worshipping bodies existing in our neighbourhood hinders this more general Christian union of which I am speaking. We have Nonconformists in our Church Council; I have never failed to receive a hearty welcome at the Nonconformist chapels, and on the last occasion in which I was present at Paddington Chapel one of the speakers kindly alluded to me as "our Rector," after I had propounded the very views I am now expressing. I may add that we have among our subscribers many Jewish gentlemen and ladies, and a gentleman belonging to a Jewish family gives us great assistance in the work of Poor Relief. Let me add one other instance. A few weeks ago a deserving couple belonging to the Primitive Methodists had suffered through the performance of a public duty. Some members of their little community were desirous of bringing their case before the public, with a view to some compensation for their losses; but they felt that their own society had hardly the requisite influence; and they did not

NOTE XXV.] *The Parish as a Church.* 431

scruple to ask me as head of the more general Christian society of the parish, to bring the matter before our neighbours: to which our neighbours very willingly responded. I call such acts as these acts of the Church as much as public worship or preaching. I am persuaded also that if the conception I am here putting before you of the national Church (and its subdivision the parochial Church), as a great comprehensive brotherhood existing for the sake of mutual well-doing, were generally recognised by its administrators, this conception would exercise the most salutary, conciliating and quickening influence over the whole Christianity of our country. I must repeat, that I say this not by any means to prejudge the discussion of any proposed changes, but to produce if I can the conviction that in any such changes regard should be had to the preservation of this most important object, the binding together of those who in God's Providence live side by side in the brotherhood of a common Christian life.

'I admit, of course, that this is only an aim, not a thing realised. But we do aim at it constantly, and in some degree accomplish it. Our visitors (including in this term the lady visitors and the Mission-women) visit every poor family. The aim of the assistant clergy is first to make acquaintance with every poor family and then to pay special visits when illness or any other cause calls for it. I endeavour myself to keep up some personal relation with all the families residing in the larger streets and squares, as may be seen by the fact that we have contributions to our charities from some two hundred and twenty of these wealthier families. The tradesmen, of whom I regret to say we see least, are yet very ready in many cases to aid us; and there is none of our Social Gatherings in the autumn more fully attended than that from * * * * Street, the special abode of tradesmen. Our Magazine, of which nearly one thousand copies are bought every month, spreads the intelligence of our various institutions to all parts of the Parish. Our Almanack finds its way to the home of every poor family, and it is also welcomed by the servants in our larger houses, among whom I have personally taken part each year in its distribution. Thus we endeavour to realise as far as circumstances will permit the object of the parochial ministry as described in the Ordination Service of our Church, "to use public and private monitions and exhortations, as well to the sick as to the whole, within our cure, to maintain and set forward, as much as in us lies, quietness, peace, and love among all Christian people, especially among them that are committed to our charge."

'I have confessed in previous addresses how impossible it is to be satisfied with the comparatively little we are able to accomplish, and the yearning, which I suppose every Christian pastor feels, which Dr. Chalmers expressed in the words, "O that I could bring myself fairly alongside of the souls of my parishioners." But as I look down any of the streets in which I know most of the families, I am not altogether without a pastor's satisfaction. There is a considerable number of families who worship with us or who take part in our work, and whose members I can feel to be directly under the influence of our ministry. There are others whom, though in no way connected with our organisation, I know to be under the influence of other ministries, or interested in other good works in which I have no reason to doubt they are receiving and doing good. There are, no doubt, some who are living a vain and worldly life; but I trust and believe they are quite the smaller number. There are few whom I cannot hopefully recognise as belonging to the Christian brotherhood of which I have spoken, wishing to live the Christian life and to grow in goodness and usefulness. And if there are some whom the sceptical spirit of the age has caused to feel some mistrust of Christian teaching and ordinances, I am often able in such cases still to feel that the heart and intention is sound and that there is a readiness to take pains for the good of others which is one of the best marks of true discipleship.

'I feel, therefore, that what is called the theory of a national church, and of the parochial system, is by no means unreal with us. We wish to include every one who resides within our boundaries, leaving out none, and to treat them as members of a Christian brotherhood, to help them to rise to this position themselves and to call upon them to help others. We wish that the natural relations which exist between neighbours should be cemented and sanctified by the Spirit of Christ, and that thus the process should go continually on amongst us by which the kingdom of the world will at last become the kingdom of God.

'I ask all who read this to keep this high object in view, as I hope to keep it in view myself; and in their individual life, in the family, and in all their social and public relations, to remember that they belong to Christ and to his mystical body, "which is the blessed company of all faithful people."'

NOTE XXVI.

THE MAISON LECLAIRE AT PARIS, AN EXAMPLE OF SUCCESSFUL CO-OPERATIVE INDUSTRY IN A FIRM OF DECORATORS; FROM A PAMPHLET BY MISS HART, GIVING A FULL ACCOUNT OF THE SCHEME. (Decorative Co-operators' Association, 405 Oxford-street.)

The final scheme proposed by Leclaire, which was based upon the recommendations of a committee, received the approval of the workmen assembled in general meeting, and on January 6th, 1869, became the binding Charter of the firm. The working capital was now fixed at £16,000, of which Leclaire contributed £4,000, M. Defournaux £4,000, and the Mutual Aid Society, representing the workmen's interest, £8,000.

There was also a Reserve Fund of £4,000, which could be drawn upon in case of emergency. The firm became by this Charter a 'Société en Comandite,' i.e. a partnership in which the acting partners are responsible without limitation, and the dormant ones to the extent of their capital only. From this date Leclaire ceased to appropriate any part of the profits—only 5 per cent. interest on his invested capital.

At the present time the two managing partners draw a salary of £240 each for superintendence. Interest at 5 per cent. is paid to them and to the Mutual Aid Society on their respective capital. Of the net profits, one quarter goes to the two managing partners jointly, the senior partner taking two-thirds, the junior one-third; one quarter goes to the Mutual Aid Society: the remaining half is divided among the workmen and others employed by the firm in exact proportion to wages earned. During the last five years these bonuses have averaged 18 per cent.

The Mutual Aid Society confers the following advantages, besides performing all the functions of an ordinary benefit club:—it bestows a retiring life pension of £48 per annum on every member who has attained the age of fifty, and has worked twenty years for the firm, and it continues the payment of half this annuity to the widow of such pensioner during her life. Previous to 1875 these life pensions were £32 per annum, they were then raised to £40, and again in 1880 increased to £48 per annum.

It insures the life of every member for the sum of £40, to be handed over to his family at his death: and further, if a worker, though he be neither a member of the society or on the list of those permanently employed by the firm, meet, whilst engaged in its service, with a disabling accident, he becomes at once entitled to the full retiring life pension of £48, and if the accident terminate fatally, the widow retains half the pension.

But the principle of 'participation' with Leclaire had for its end a great deal more than 'sharing profits;' it meant likewise 'sharing responsibilities;' it meant, besides material welfare, the moral and social 'uplifting' of the wage-earning class, and he brought the principle into operation in such a manner as to constitute the education of all who came into contact with it.

To attain this end, Leclaire instituted a governing body, which he called the 'Noyau,' i.e. the nucleus or kernel, which has now become the moving spirit of the whole body. To be eligible for admission, a workman must be in the prime of life, between the age of twenty-five and forty, of unblemished moral character, and a skilled workman.

Applications for admission are addressed to the 'Court of Conciliation,' and reported on by this committee to the general assembly of the 'Noyau.'

The 'Court of Conciliation' is elected by the general assembly of the 'Noyau.' It consists of five workmen and three clerks, under the presidency of one of the managing partners. This

NOTE XXVI.] *The Maison Leclaire at Paris.* 435

committee constitutes a moral tribunal; before it are brought cases of misconduct or insubordination; the offenders receive advice and warning in the first instance, and if these are neglected, the committee is empowered to sentence them to suspension from employment by the firm for one, two or three months, or even dismissal.

At the Annual Meeting of the General Assembly of the 'Noyau,' the foremen are elected, and to show the complete confidence Leclaire reposed in the good sense of the men, on the death or resignation of a partner his successor is elected by this body of workmen.

The Members of the Firm who constitute the 'Noyau' now number nearly 300.

In reply to inquiries which I made of M. Robert concerning the number of unworthy appearances in the course of a year before the 'Court of Conciliation,' I was furnished with the following facts:—From the 21st February, 1879, to July 23rd, 1880, there were but *six* cases of delinquency; two grave offences were punished with dismissal, and of the remaining four cases, one received a warning, two were suspended respectively for five and fifteen days, and the fourth for eighteen months. Appended to the report is the following note:—'*We have had no cases of drunkenness for several years.*' This, be it borne in mind, in a firm which employs over 1100 workers.

These are the chief points of the Charter signed by Leclaire, Defournaux, and M. Chas. Robert, as president of the Mutual Aid Society, in the presence of the assembled workmen, January 6th, 1869. On this occasion Leclaire recalled the advice he had given—the desires and hopes that had animated him in 1864: adding—'To-day, I may say, on all sides there is agitation; everywhere people are busy with social improvements. Turn a deaf ear—let us occupy ourselves with activity and perseverance in perfecting our organisation: it has received the baptism of time; it rests upon a sure foundation. The growth and development of our work has become an object of public attention both at home and abroad; it has received the approbation of illustrious personages. This approbation imposes on all of us heavier duties.

'It is not enough that antagonism between employer and employed has died out between us; it is not enough that the *cause* of strikes has disappeared amongst us. The sentiments of brotherhood must be more and more manifest; our courtesy and *savoir vivre*, even in our most intimate relations, ought to express those feelings; we must on every occasion so conduct ourselves as to raise our moral level to the proportion of the grand work that we are doing.'

Leclaire died at Herblay, July 13, 1872, aged 71, happy in the consciousness of having carried out all the dreams of his youth, and the assurance that bread was secured to those who had grown old with him. The last pleasure of his life was to know that the sum of £2,000 had, the week before, been paid over and above wages to 600 of his men, and that the conduct of all was exemplary.

NOTE XXVII.

St. Augustine's Confession of Agnosticism.

De Doctrinâ Christianâ, Book I. ch. vi. After a passage in which he speaks of the Trinity in words comparable to those of the Athanasian Creed, Augustine continues :—

'Diximusne aliquid et sonuimus aliquid dignum Deo? Imo vero nihil me aliud quam dicere voluisse sentio. Si autem dixi, non est hoc quod dicere volui. Hoc unde scio, nisi quia Deus ineffabilis est? Quod autem a me dictum est, si ineffabile esset, dictum non esset. Ac per hoc ne ineffabilis quidem dicendus est Deus, quia et hoc quum dicitur, aliquid dicitur. Et fit nescio quæ pugna verborum, quoniam si illud est ineffabile, quod dici non potest, non est ineffabile, quod vel ineffabile dici potest. Quae pugna verborum silentio cavenda potius quam voce pacanda est. Et tamen Deus, quum de illo nihil digne dici possit, admisit humanae vocis obsequium, et verbis nostris in laude suâ gaudere nos voluit. Nam inde est et quod dicitur Deus. Non enim re vera in strepitu istarum duarum syllabarum ipse cognoscitur : sed tamen omnes Latinae linguae scios quum aures eorum sonus iste tetigerit, movet ad cogitandam excellentissimam quamdam immortalemque naturam.'

INDEX.

Abbey and Overton on 18th Century, p. 278 n.
Abelard, 201.
Adalbert, 185.
Agnostic philosophy, 22 n., 336, 416.
Agriculture, the normal pursuit of Israelites, 57.
Alabama Convention, 327, 354, 427.
Alexander the Great, 40.
Alfred, King, 180.
Ambrose, 167, 168, 170.
America, Discovery of, 190; Puritan settlements in, 227; religion in, 235; liberty in, 275; tendencies adverse to family life in, 338.
American and Hebrew slavery contrasted, 60.
Anne Boleyn, 252.
Apologetics, 3, 369.
Apostolate, 129.
Appeals to Rome abolished, 243, 244; to the Crown in all ecclesiastical causes, 244.
Aquinas de Regimine Principum, 177.
Arbitration between nations, 354.
Argyll, Duke of, 353 n.
Aristotle, on priority of being, 15, 385; complains of lack of moral power, 30, 396; influence on Christian theology, 43; Politics, 54 n.; connects justice and love, 317; gives the moral aim of common life, 318; on definition in morals, 363.
Arnold of Brescia, 201.
Arnold, Dr., on the Church, 112 n., 161 n., 322; extract from, 421-6.
Arnold, Matthew, 96 n., 363 n.
Art, its connexion with religion, 36, 280, 292, 293; elevates life, 313; keeps alive the ideal, 314; and forms a Church, ib.; must be popularised, 344; and become a function of the Church, 344.
Articles of Religion, 266, 273.
Asceticism, 167.
Atonement, Doctrine of, 296.
Augustine, De Civitate Dei, 8 n., 169, 380-4; De Doct. Christ., 363; his Confession of Agnosticism, 336.

Babylonians, contrasted with Israel, 57.
Bacon, Leonard, Genesis of New England Churches, 227 n.; quotation from, 236.
Balde, the poet, 216.
Bampton Lectures, their object, 2, 366; summary of, for 1883, 45, 46; for 1880, 160.
Bancroft, 268 n., 270 n.
Baptism: its effects, 288; its significance, 302.
Barbarossa, 178.
Barzillai, 57.
Basle, Council of, 190.
Battle Abbey, 240.
Becket, 153, 173, 239, 273.
Beneficence, a constant factor in the Church, 154; needs to be inspired by universal interests, 305; its place in politics, 323, 360.
Bentham, 185, 357, 427.
Bernard of Morlaix, 170.
Bert, M. Paul, 368.
Bible, its power in the 16th century, 269.
Bilney, 240.
Bingham, on Church Discipline, 160 n.
Bishops, origin of the title, 125; its various meanings, 129.
Bluntschli, 357, 427.
Böhmen, Jacob, 215.
Bollandists, 215.
Bolton Abbey, 187.
Boniface, Bp. (Winfried), 186.
Boniface VIII, 182.
Bonner, Bp., 246 n.
Borgia (Alexander VI), 187, 203, 207.
Bouvier, Professor, 212 n.
Brace, C. Loring, Gesta Christi, 33 n., 185 n.
Brahmanic and Christian ideas of God, 24.
Brahmo-Somaj of India, 398.
Brodrick, Hon. G., 41 n.
Brotherhood, fostered by Hebrew polity, 58.
Bryce's Holy Roman Empire, 176 n., 178 n., 179, 186 n.

Buddhistic and Christian morality, 24; Buddhism gives peace in despair, 31; is unpolitical, 54.
Bungener's life of Calvin, 209 n.
Bunsen, God in History, 24 n.; on Absolutism in German Churches, 409.
Burke, love for English constitution, 54, 275; his religion, 279.
Burnet's History of the Reformation, 246 n.
Burns, 226.

Calvin, 209.
Canon Law, 173, 181 n., 244.
Canons of 1604 and 1639, 271.
Cardwell, 261 n., 271 n.
Casimir, John, King of Poland, 216.
Central authority in Israel, 64.
Ceremonial system of Israel, 69.
Chalmers, Dr., Commercial Discourses, 146.
Charles the Great, 151, 152, 178; his government, 179, 200.
Charles I, 272, 273.
Charles II, 275.
Chatham, 278.
Chillingworth, 276.
CHRIST, Divinity of, 21, 25; The Word, 27; effect of His manifestation, 29; His social power, 31; His aims, 98; belongs to the East, 43, 398; change in His teaching, 103; His Kingship misunderstood, 108; gives the type of true relations, 114; His decisions on divorce and quarrels, 117; His coming, 136; His self-sacrifice compared with that of the Decii, 148; His character the centre of theology, 368.
Christendom, 362.
Christian ideal of life, 34, 362.
Chrysostom, 167.
Church, its functions, 1, 121, 125, 159, 281; its origin, 98; its definition, 9, 32, 140, 299; its changes, 11; its universality, 23, 44, 291, 297; works by election, 31, 289; its authority, 105; not a *merely* spiritual society, 110, 161, 286; its requirements, 115; its laws, 117, 172; organized for practical needs, 119, 128, 133; various offices in, 128-134, 365; idealized by St. Paul and St. John, 133; its government, 158; is a sovereign society, 163, 421; acquired the habits of a sect, 165; its relations to the State, 175, 336, 337; enfolds many like organisms, 295.
Church of England, 238; in Saxon times, 239; identical with the nation, 242, 248, 263; the King head of, 265; its practical unity, 276.
Clarendon, Constitutions of, 239.
Clement of Alexandria, 146, 393.
Clement of Rome, 172.
Clergy, inclined to mistrust, 253; not the sole ministers of religion, 256; discipline of, 260; ought to be the most open of orders, 305; may by narrowness ruin their system, 336.
Clerical power, often tyrannical, 258; gradual emancipation from, 139; its result in Charles I's reign, 273; and in the present day, 277.
Clericalism, 162, 170, 173, 187, 253, 367, 369; must be abandoned, 364, 425.
Coleridge, Aids to Reflexion, 147.
Colet, 190, 250.
Collier, 249 n.
Commerce. See TRADE.
Commons, House of, opposes clericalism, 271; ill-treated by Charles I, 272; its supremacy acknowledged, 276.
Commonwealth, identified with the Church, 248, 281.
Comte, on future of European society, 20, 386; on the two powers, 173.
Confucius; the golden rule, 24; moral maxims, 30.
Congreve, Dr., 41 n.
Constance, Council of, 190.
Constantine, 162, 164, 165; his laws, 166.
Constitutional government, 280; is a Christian idea, 321; its rationale, 350; its need of readjustment, 351.
Contemporary Review, article on Genevan Church, 212 n.; on the Man and the State, 348 n.
Convocations of Clergy, restrained, 245; revived claims of, 271; their influence, 276; cease to be taxing bodies, 280.
Co-operative industry, 347, 433.
Courts of High Commission, 246, 271; abolition of, 280.
Covenant, National, in Scotland, 223.
Cranmer's Commission as Archbishop, 246 n.; draws up Reformatio Legum, 265.
Creighton's History of the Papacy, 178 n.
Cromwell, Oliver, 274.
Cromwell, Thomas, 197.
Culture, not to be opposed to Christianity, 39; its expansiveness, 39; in reign of Elizabeth, 266, 279.
Cyprian, 161, 171.
Cyrus, 40.

Index. 439

Daniel, 86.
Dante, De Monarchiâ, 177.
Darwin, Evolution and Free Will, 22, 392; doctrine of Pangenesis, 296; on Science and Revelation, 397.
Davenport, founder of Newhaven in Connecticut, 232.
Davies, Rev. J. Llewelyn, on Ambrose, 168; on Erastus, 218 n.
Deacons, 128.
Decretals, the False, 172, 181 n., 183 n.; others, 171, 172.
Democracy, 325, 357.
Design, mechanical conception of, 22.
Diman's Religion in America, 235 n.
Diplomacy, 325, 359.
Dissenting societies not separate churches, 254, 277, 430.
Divorce, forbidden by Malachi, 60; Christ's decision about, 117.
Dixon's History of the Church of England, 246.
Dotation of Constantine, 181.

"Ecce Homo," 116; extract from, 417.
Ecclesia, synonymous with synagogue, 125.
Ecclesiastical Courts, 181, 185, 243, 245.
Ecclesiastical Legislation in England, 245; only by Parliament, 261; Hooker on, 412.
Education, 305.
Edward VI supports Reformation Settlement, 264.
Edwards, Jonathan, 234.
Egyptians contrasted with Israel, 57.
Eighteenth Century, not so irreligious as often assumed, 277.
Election, 31, 290.
Eliot, Sir J., 274.
Elizabeth, Queen, restores Reformation Settlement, 265; tries to keep ecclesiastical affairs in her own hands, 266.
Elliott's New England History, 227 n.; quotation from, 237.
Encomium Moriae, 195.
England. Its development in the 17th and 18th centuries, 280-281; its faults, 283; its political eminence, 349. See CHURCH OF ENGLAND.
Enlightenment brought about by the Reformation, 195, 199, 266.
Ephesians, Epistle to, 15.
Erasmus, 195.
Erastus' system of church-government, 218.

Europe, present state of, 356.
Eusebius on the martyrs of Vienne, 127.
Evangelical Revival, 278.
Evidences of Christianity, 3, 369.
Evolution, doctrine of, 20, 22, 392.
Ewald, Antiquities, 55.
Excommunication, 161.

Faith, its various phases, 153.
Faiths of the world, 24 n.
Falkland, 274.
Family, becomes a church, 137, 288, 340; is naturally Christian, 307; is a microcosm, 308; the highest idea of, ib.; its present state and dangers, 338.
Fathers, Western and Eastern, on the virtuous heathen, 25.
Feasts of Israel, 65.
Ferdinand, Emperor, 216.
Fiore on international law, 427.
Florence under Savonarola, 205.
Fox, Charles, 275, 279.
France, decrease of population in, 339; a branch of the Church, 338; its position in Europe, 355; religion in, 368.
Francis I, his Concordat with Rome, 201.
Frankfort, Council of, 179.
Frederick the Second, 178, 182.
Freewill and evolution, 22, 392.

Gambetta, 367.
Genesis, patriarchal system in, 84.
Geneva under Calvin, 209.
Genevan model of church government, 268, 270.
Germany, autocratic church government in, 221, 409.
Gerson, 151.
Gesta Christi, 33 n.
Gibbon, his statement of the causes of the spread of Christianity, 155; on the laws of the Roman Empire, 166.
Gladstone, Mr., on European concert, 427.
GOD, immanent and transcendant, 17; Brahmanic idea of, 24; metaphysical notions of, 42; Hebrew conceptions of, 74; purpose of, 16, 19, 286, 361; undefinable, 363, 436.
Goethe, his ideal of life, 26.
Goschen, Mr., on Laissez faire, 348 n.
Gratian, 173.
Greek Empire, 40.
Green's History of the English People, 49 n., 269 n.

Guizot's European Civilization, 19, 20, 161, 185, 197; inadequate view of the Reformation, 198, 199; view of the English Reformation, 238.

Hadrian I, 179.
Hallam, 275.
Hampden, 274.
Hatch, Dr., Bampton Lectures, 160 n.
Hebrew history a revelation, 50; polity contrasted with those of Greece and Rome, 67; art, 88; ideal of life, 96.
Henotheism, 298.
Henry II of England, 178 n.; assertion of his divine authority, 239.
Henry IV of England, 240.
Henry IV of France, 427.
Henry IV of Germany, 184.
Henry VIII of England, his divorce, 243; his attitude towards the clerical system, 263.
Henry of Luxemburg, 177.
Herder; ideal of society, 20.
Hermann of Metz, 177 n., 183.
Hilarion, 152.
Hildebrand, 153, 184; his excommunication of the Emperor, 161, 177 n.; destroyed the family life of the clergy, 164; his views on government, 177, 200; claims power over kings, 183.
Hincmar of Rheims, 161.
History, philosophy of, 18-20.
Hobbes, 274.
Hooker, defends ecclesiastical legislation by Parliament, 261; on Church government, 267; criticism of his work, 266-9; extract from, on Royal supremacy, 412-4.
Hope, want of, in the Church, 8; must be restored, 370.
Horace on the faith of the just, 24.
Humane progress in the middle ages, 185.
Humanity, Universal Society of, 39, 44, 300.
Hume, 226.
Huss, 190, 201.
Hutchinson, Mrs., 232.
Huxley, on Man's place in Nature, 21, 391.
Hypothesis, use of, in scientific theology, 47, 399.

Ignatius Loyola, 213.
Immortality, doctrine of, 145.
Independent systems of morality, 27.
Individual Christianity, 296, 358.
Innocent III, 154, 184.
Innocent IV, 182.

International law, 357, 426.
International relations and religion, 38, 325, 354.
Ireland, Church of, 336 n.
Ishmael, contrasted with Israel, 56.
Israelites, their conquests, 80.

James II, 275.
Jehovah, debased worship of, 75.
Jerome, 146, 154, 156 n., 169; his depreciation of family life, 307; his belief in the perdition of heathen, 394.
Jesuits, their attempt to renew the world on mediaeval system, 213.
John, St., opening of his Gospel, 13, 287.
Jouffroy; reign of peace, 20.
Judges in Israel, 62.
Justification by faith, doctrine of, 195.
Justinian, 166.

Kant, on peace, 20, 357, 427.
Ken, Bp., 278.
Keshub Chunder Sen, 43 n., 398.
Kings of Israel, their duties, 65, 79.
Knowledge, its connexion with religion, 36, 292, 293, 309; centres in that of man, 310; begets a social union, ib.; its votaries form a church, 311; co-ordination of, needed, 341.
Knox, John, his attempt to make Scotland a kingdom of Christ, 222.
Kyrle Society, 344 n.

Laud, 254, 268, 273.
Laveleye, M. de, 353 n.
Law, William, 278.
Law, limits of, 258.
Laws of Israel, successive casts of, 52; their care for the poor and weak, 53, 59. Land laws, 56; enactments for just dealing, 58; for family life, ib.; on retaliation, 60; war, 61; aliens, ib.; the centre of constitution, 62; of theology, 67; of history, 77; of literature, 83. Source of prosperity, 77; not exclusive, 88.
Laws of the Church, 117, 133. See ECCLESIASTICAL LEGISLATION.
Lay power, uprising of, at Reformation, 196; supreme in England, 247; resisted by Laud, 271.
Lecky's History of Rationalism, 259; European Morals, 167; History of 18th Century, 278.
Leclaire, Maison, 347 n., 433.
Lee, Dr. R., of Edinburgh, 218 n.
Leighton, Sir F., 312 n.; extract from address by, 418.

Leo III, Pope, 178.
Leopardi, 86.
Lightfoot, Bp., on St. Paul and Seneca, 149.
Lollardism, 240.
Lord's Supper, 303.
Lorenzo de Medici, his ideal of life, 26; his relations with Savonarola, 204.
Louis of Bavaria, 178 n.
Louis, St., 180, 201.
Love, self-renouncing, the true principle of social life, 33; its various forms, 153.
Luther, 195, 199; his appeal to the German nobility, 197 n.; his difficulties, 214.

Macarius, 152.
Macaulay, 226.
Maccabees, 68, 83.
Mahomet; ideal of life, 26; iconoclasm, 31.
Malachi, forbids divorce and polygamy, 60; peculiar relation to Levitical law, 82, 403.
Malthus, 339.
Marcus Aurelius, Soliloquies, 25; ideal of life, 26; humility, 147; resignation, 30; ideas in common with those of Christians, 148.
Marsiglio's Defensor Pacis, 178 n.
Mary, Queen, 265.
Mather, Cotton, 227 n., 232.
Max Müller, 298 n.
Maximilian of Bavaria, 216.
Mayne, ancient law, 43 n., 52 n.; on theological terms, 397; customary law, 407.
Mediaeval attempt to save the world, 185; its failure, 186, 193; its benefits, 189, 193.
Mediaeval theory of government, 176, 179.
Medicine, progress in, 280.
Merivale's Conversion of the Roman Empire, 149.
Mill, J. S., 47, 393, 399.
Milman's Latin Christianity, 178 n., 181 n., 166 n., 201.
Milton, 272.
Miraculous powers in the Church, 157.
Mission Actuelle des Souverains, 9 n., 355, 385.
Molini, 215.
Montesquieu, 51 n.
Moral ideal, the centre of Christianity, 144; its changes, 151.
Moral ideas, how they spread, 148.
More, 190, 251.

Nation, the, God's ordinance, 320; the only complete society, 321; is in the fullest sense a church, 322; its rulers are pastors, 323; its organization as a church, 324, 349; its chief duty, 352.
National life asserted in the Reformation, 197.
'Natural religion,' 84 n., 97 n.
Neander; Life of Christ, 103; Memorials of Christian Life, 185.
Nebuchadnezzar, 40.
Neoplatonism, 147.
New England, settlements in, 227.
Newton, 280.
Nicaea, Council of, 165, 171.
Nicodemus, Gospel of, 109.

Old Testament, as basis for history, 51, 400–7; importance of, 91.
Optatus, on Church and Empire, 177.
Origen, 146.

Paleario, 196.
Palfrey's History of New England, 227.
Papal Encyclical and Syllabus, 6, 368, 378.
Papal system, 41; its rise, 171; relation to Empire, 176; vast claims, 183, 188; aimed not at liberty but dominion, 257.
Paraguay, 216.
Parish, the, is a little nation, 335; and a section of the National Church, 428.
Parliament, its position in the Church system, 262, 266, 267, 412; the Long, 275; in the reign of Charles II, ib.; its action in the 17th century, ib.
Paul of Samosata, 160 n.
Pericles on Athenian character, 54.
Perry's History of the Church of England, 270.
Persian Empire, 40.
Peter Martyr, 221, 265.
Phoenicians contrasted with Israel, 56.
Pilate, Acts of, 109.
Pippin, 180.
Plato; the death of the just man, 24; ideal of life, 26; influence on Christian theology, 43; protest against false conceptions of God, 156.
Pliny's letter to Trajan, 134, 145, 423.
Plutarch, 148.
Politics properly religious, 38, 241, 256.
Polygamy in Israel, 59.
Praemunire and Provisors, 240.

Prayer, 302; freely exercised at first, 131.
Prayer Book, 263; Second, of Edward VI, 261; defended by Hooker, 268.
Preaching, 304; freely exercised at first, 131; 'Ecce Homo' on, 417.
Presbyterianism, its religious value, 225; influence on education, 226.
Presbyters in early Church, 128.
Priesthood of all believers, 294.
Priscillianists, 168.
Prophets, 28; their policy, 80; their individuality, 85; in the Church, 120.
Prussia, alteration of Church Law in, 411.
Psalms, expressing the national life, 53, 86.
Public worship, system of, 255; not identical with the Church, 300; the parent of other organizations, ib.; its needs, 331.
Publicans, 283.
Puritan emigrants, 227; their aims, 228; their laws, 230; difficulties in their theory of life, 232; benefits conferred by their action, 235.
Puritans, 267; criticism of, 270; not dominant at first, 272; their political ideal, 273; their ruin, 274; and survival, 275.
Pym, 272, 274, 276.

Raymond Lully, 185.
Redemption, universal need of, 28; connected with sense of sin, 281.
Reform Act, 275.
Reformatio Legum Eccles., 265.
Reformation, the result of mediaeval Church life, 191; a fresh attempt to Christianize society, 193; not negative but positive, 194; conducive to freedom, 199.
Reformation in England, political, 241; settlement of, 228; phases of, 263.
Reforms, resisted by representatives of the Church, 6.
Religion, the ideal of life, 42; etymology of, 48; concerned with human relations, 49, 95.
Religious worship, Christian idea of, 332. See PUBLIC WORSHIP.
Renaissance, 190.
Renan, on synagogues, 126 n.
Revolution, The English, 275, 276.
Richardson, Dr., on Mosaic Law, 70.
Ridley, Bishop, 261.
Rienzi, 202.
Roman Empire, 40, 41; The Holy, 176, 178.

Roman Law, its influence on theology, 43; did not inspire affection, 54; its study in Middle Ages, 182.
Rome, its state in the 12th Century, 202.
Rothe, Richard, 318 n.; his opinion about the Church, 333; extract from, 415.
Rousseau, 209.
Royal Society, 280.
Ruling, the chief function in the early churches, 130, 160.
Ruling elders, 268.

Sacramental idea, 293, 302.
Sakyamouni, his ideal of life, 26.
Sanctuaries in Israel, local, 62, 68; central, 65.
Sanhedrin, 126 n.
Saul, 57.
Savonarola, 203.
Scepticism, past and present, 367.
Scholasticism, 190.
Science, Natural, its discoveries, 280; its greatness and purity, 342; must be co-ordinated with other departments, 341-2.
Scotland, under Knox, 223.
Scripture, its use in system of public worship, 304.
Servetus, 209.
Service, Divine, 294. See PUBLIC WORSHIP.
Sesostris, 40.
Slavery in Israel, 59; in America, 60; in Rome, ib.
Smith, Adam, 226.
Smith, Goldwin, on Hebrew laws, 60; on American colonies, 227 n.
Snow, Rev. G. D'Oyly, Theologico-Political Treatise, 21.
Social evil, 340.
Social intercourse, its connexion with religion, 315; is a religious training, 316; and a form of Church life, 317; its right direction, 345.
Socialism, 325; relation of the Church to, 352; Papal view of, 379.
Socrates, 113; ironical strength of, 30; protests against false conceptions of God, 156.
Spain, 183. 185.
Sparta, Laws of, 54.
Spencer, Herbert, on Religion, 22 n.; on Trade, 346; on The Man and The State, 348.
Spirituality, 297.
Stanley, on Zoroastrianism, 24 n.; on Synagogues, 126 n.; Lectures on Scottish Church, 223.

State, divine sanction of, 139.
Stephen, St., 124.
Stoics, Roman, 40, 41.
Struggle for life, and survival of the fittest, 23.
Stubbs, Constitutional History, 239 n.; Hist. Appendix on Eccles. Courts, 245 n.
Submission of the clergy, 245.
Supremacy of the Crown, 245; its real significance, 246; approved by men of progress, 249; and of piety, 250, 253; vindication of, 253; devolves on Prime Minister, 262; perversion of, 271.
Switzerland, attempts at reformed Christian life in, 213.
Synagogues, their constitution, 119; their functions, 126, 126 n.; prototypes of churches, 126, 131.
Synods, not the organs of liberty of conscience, 257.

Tauler, 201.
'Teaching of the Twelve Apostles,' 119 n.
Temporal and spiritual power, theory of, discussed, 173, 180, 183.
Tenterden Steeple, 188.
Tertullian, 146, 156, 177, 394.
Thaddeus of Suessa, 178.
Theocracy in Israel, 67, 95; in Christendom, 96.
Theodosius, 168.
Theology, Catholic and Protestant, 7–9.
Thomas à Kempis, 154.
Thucydides' distrust of Athenian laws, 54.
Tilly, 216.
Toleration Act, 276.
Trade, its bearing on religion, 37, 314, 318; ministers to knowledge and love, 319; business life becomes Church life, 320; Christian and co-operative, 347, 349; competition not essential to, 348; Government action in, ib.
Treaties of Paris and Berlin, 352, 427.
Tribunals in Israel, 72.
Tunstal, Bp., 251.
Tyndale, William, 186, 188; awakes a thirst for knowledge, 195, 199; his teaching the underlying force of the Reformation, 240; approves royal supremacy, 250; his life and views, 251.
Tyndall, Address at Belfast, 21, 389.

Ulrich von Hutten, 197.
Ultramontanism, 173.
Universal Church, not yet organized, 324, 353; should prevent war, 325, 355; previous efforts to form it, 326; is the object of hope, 327; its chief objects, 355

Valdes, 196.
Van Eyk's picture of the Immaculate Lamb, 10 n.
Virtues of early Christians, 157.

Wesley, 278.
Wilberforce, 279.
William the Conqueror, 183, 239.
William of Ockham, 178 n.
Williams, Roger, 232, 234.
Witanagemot, 239.
Wolfgang Musculus, 218.
Wolsey, 252.
Woolsey's International Law, 327 n., 426.
World, senses of the word, 5; transformed by the Christian spirit, 44, 112; uses of Greek words for, 378.
World to come, 167.
Worship, public, Society for, not the Church, 300; capable of universality, 302; will maintain its supremacy, 329; must not separate itself from other parts of life, 332; is mistrusted, 334; may be ruined, 337.
Wycliff, 190.

Xavier, 215.

Yahweh, or Jehovah, 74.

Zeal of early Christians, 156.
Zend Avesta on truth and immortality, 24.
Zincke, Rev. Barham, 339 n.
Zoroastrianism and Judaism, 24.
Zunz on Sanhedrin and Synagogues, 126 n.
Zwingli, 217.

NEW BOOKS AND NEW EDITIONS

IN COURSE OF PUBLICATION BY

MESSRS. RIVINGTON

WATERLOO PLACE, LONDON

NOVEMBER, 1884.

Letters of the Rev. J. B. Mozley, D.D.,
late Canon of Christ Church, and Regius Professor of Divinity in the University of Oxford.
Edited by his Sister.
      8vo.   12*s.*

The World as the Subject of Redemption.
Being an attempt to set forth the Functions of the Church as designed to embrace the Whole Race of Mankind.
Eight Lectures delivered before the University of Oxford in the year 1883 on the Foundation of the late Rev. John Bampton, M.A., Canon of Salisbury.
By the Hon. and Rev. W. H. Fremantle, M.A., Canon of Canterbury, and Fellow of Balliol College, Oxford.
     8vo.   [*In the Press.*

Footprints of the Son of Man, as traced
by S. Mark. Being Eighty Portions for Private Study, Family Reading, and Instruction in Church.
By Herbert Mortimer Luckock, D.D., Canon of Ely; Examining Chaplain to the Bishop of Ely; and Principal of the Theological College.
   Two Vols.   *Crown 8vo.*   [*Nearly ready.*

3, WATERLOO PLACE, LONDON.

Life of S. Francis of Assisi.
By H L. Sidney Lear, Author of "Life of Lacordaire," &c.
Crown 8vo. [*In preparation.*

Monte Carlo and Public Opinion.
Edited by **A Visitor to the Riviera**. With Illustrations.
Crown 8vo. 3s. 6d.

Maxims and Gleanings from the
Writings of the Rev. **T. T. Carter**, M.A. Selected and arranged for daily use.
By **C. M. S.**, Compiler of "Daily Gleanings of the Saintly Life," "Under the Cross," etc. With an Introduction by the Rev. **M. F. Sadler**, Rector of Honiton, Devon.
Crown 16mo. 2s.

Modern Doubt and Unbelief: Its Extent,
Causes and Tendencies.
By **Edward Bickersteth Ottley**, M.A., Minister of Quebec Chapel.
Crown 8vo. [*In preparation.*

A Treatise on the Church of Christ.
By **William Palmer**, M.A., of Worcester College, Oxford.
New and Revised Edition. Two Vols. 8vo. [*In preparation.*

The Four Holy Gospels according to the
Authorized Version.
With variations of type in the use of Capital letters, and with Marginal Notes, containing selections from various Readings of the Earlier English Translators, of the Authorized Version, of the Revisers of 1881, and others.
By the Rev. **Edwd. Thos. Cardale**, late Rector of Uckfield.
Crown 8vo. 5s.

De Vitâ Pastorali.
The Office and Work of a Priest in the Church of GOD.
By the **Lord Bishop of Lichfield**.
Crown 8vo. [*In preparation.*

3, WATERLOO PLACE, LONDON.

A Life of Edward Bouverie Pusey, D.D.,

Regius Professor of Hebrew, and Canon of Christ Church, Oxford.
By H. P. Liddon, D.D., Canon Residentiary of S. Paul's.
                                                8vo.   [*In preparation*

The Apostolic Fathers.

The Epistles of S. Clement, S. Ignatius, S. Barnabas, S. Polycarp, together with the Martyrdom of S. Ignatius and S. Polycarp. Translated into English, with an Introductory Notice.
    By Charles H. Hoole, M.A., Student of Christ Church, Oxford.
             Second Edition. Crown 8vo.   [*Nearly ready.*

The Gospel according to S. Matthew,

With Explanatory Notes for the Use of Teachers.
    By **Henry Herbert Wyatt**, M.A., Principal of Brighton Training College, and Vicar of Bolney, Sussex; Author of "Principal Heresies relating to Our Lord's Incarnation."
    With Commendatory Preface by the Archbishops' Inspector of Training Colleges.
                    Crown 8vo. 2s. 6d.

From Morn to Eve.

A Companion Poem to "Yesterday, To-day, and For Ever."
By the Rev. **E. H. Bickersteth**, M.A., Vicar of Christ Church, Hampstead, and Rural Dean.
                  18mo.   [*In preparation*

The Profitableness of the Old Testament

Scriptures.
A Treatise founded on 2 Timothy, iii., 16, 17.
By **W. A. Bartlett**, M.A., Vicar of Wisborough, Sussex.
                Crown 8vo. 7s. 6d.

Good Friday.

Being Addresses on the Seven Last Words delivered at St. Paul's Cathedral, on Good Friday, 1884.
By the Rev. **H. S. Holland**, M.A., Canon Residentiary of St. Paul's, and Senior Student of Christ Church, Oxford.
                  Small 8vo. 2s.

3, WATERLOO PLACE, LONDON.

The Missioner's Hymnal.
Edited by the Rev. A. G. Jackson, Resident Chaplain of the Farm School, Redhill, Surrey.
Royal 32mo. Sewed, 1d.; cloth boards, 3d.
With Music, Small 4to. 2s. 6d.

The One Mediator.
The Operation of the Son of God in Nature and in Grace. Eight Lectures delivered before the University of Oxford in the year 1882, on the Foundation of the late Rev. John Bampton, M.A., Canon of Salisbury.
By **Peter Goldsmith Medd**, M.A., Rector of North Cerney; Hon. Canon of S. Albans, and Examining Chaplain to the Bishop; late Rector of Barnes; formerly Fellow and Tutor of University College, Oxford.
8vo. 16s.

Selections from the Writings of H. P.
Liddon, D.D., Canon Residentiary of S. Paul's.
Second Edition. Crown 8vo. 3s. 6d.

Selections from the Writings of John
Keble, M.A., Author of "The Christian Year."
Crown 8vo. 3s. 6d.

Selections from the Writings of Edward
Bouverie Pusey, D.D., late Regius Professor of Hebrew, and Canon of Christ Church, Oxford.
Crown 8vo. 3s. 6d.

Selections from the Writing of John
Mason Neale, D.D., late Warden of Sackville College.
Crown 8vo. 3s. 6d.

The Hymn "Te Deum Laudamus."
Observations upon its composition and structure, with special regard to the use, Liturgical and Choral, of this and other Canticles and Psalms, and to the true character of the Chant. Together with the Canticles carefully printed, pointed, and accented in accordance with their poetical structure for antiphonal chanting.
By the **Rev. Francis Pott**, B.A., Rector of Northill, Bedfordshire.
8vo. 3s.

---

3. WATERLOO PLACE, LONDON.

The Three Hours' Agony of our Blessed

Redeemer. Being Addresses in the form of Meditations delivered in S. Alban's Church, Manchester, on Good Friday, 1877.
By the Rev. W. J. Knox Little, M.A., Canon Residentiary of Worcester, and Rector of S. Alban's, Manchester.
New Edition. Small 8vo. 2s. ; or in Paper Cover, 1s.

Letters and Sermons of the Rev. Lewis

M. Hogg, M.A., sometime Rector of Cranford, Northamptonshire.
8vo. 4s.

Maigre Cookery.

Edited by H. L. Sidney Lear.
16mo. 2s.

Practical Reflections on every Verse of

the New Testament.
By A Clergyman. With a Preface by H. P. Liddon, D.D., Canon Residentiary of S. Paul's.
Crown 8vo.
Vol. I. THE HOLY GOSPELS. *Third Edition. 4s. 6d.*
Vol. II. ACTS TO REVELATION. 6s.

Of the Five Wounds of the Holy Church.

By Antonio Rosmini. Edited, with an Introduction by H. P. Liddon, D.D., Canon Residentiary of S. Paul's.
Crown 8vo. 7s. 6d.

Second Series of Sermons preached be-

fore the University of Oxford, 1868-1882.
By H. P. Liddon, D.D., Canon Residentiary of S. Paul's.
Third Edition. Crown 8vo. 5s.

Lectures and other Theological Papers.

By J. B. Mozley, D.D., late Canon of Christ Church, and Regius Professor of Divinity in the University of Oxford.
8vo. 10s. 6d.

A Lent with Jesus.

A Plain Guide for Churchmen.
Third Edition. 32mo. 1s., or in Paper Cover, 9d.

3, WATERLOO PLACE, LONDON.

Logic and Life, with other Sermons.
By H. S. Holland, M.A., Canon Residentiary of S. Paul's.
Second Edition. Crown 8vo. 7s. 6d.

A Review of the Baptismal Controversy.
By J. B. Mozley, D.D., late Canon of Christ Church, and Regius Professor of Divinity in the University of Oxford.
Second Edition. Crown 8vo. 7s. 6d.

The Reformation of the Church of
England ; its History, Principles, and Results.
By John Henry Blunt, D.D., F.S.A., Editor of "The Annotated Book of Common Prayer," etc., etc.
Two Vols. 8vo. Sold separately.
Vol. I. A.D. 1514-1547. Its progress during the reign of Henry VIII.
Fifth Edition. 16s.
Vol. II. A.D. 1547-1662. From the Death of Henry VIII. to the Restoration of the Church after the Commonwealth. 18s.

A Companion to the New Testament;
being a Plain Commentary on Scripture History from the Birth of our Lord to the End of the Apostolic Age.
By John Henry Blunt, D.D., F.S.A., Editor of "The Annotated Book of Common Prayer," etc., etc.
With Maps. Small 8vo. 3s. 6d.

Studies in the History of the Book of
Common Prayer. The Anglican Reform—The Puritan Innovations—The Elizabethan Reaction—The Caroline Settlement. With Appendices.
By Herbert Mortimer Luckock, D.D., Canon of Ely, etc.
Second Edition. Crown 8vo. 6s.

Counsels of Faith and Practice.
Being Sermons Preached on Various Occasions.
By the Rev. W. C. E. Newbolt, M.A., Vicar of S. Matthias, Malvern Link.
8vo. 7s. 6d.

Sunrise. Noon. Sunset.
A selection from various Authors.
By H. L. Sidney Lear, Editor of "For Days and Years," "Precious Stones,' etc., etc.
Three Vols., with red borders, 48mo, 1s. each.
Also a superior Edition, printed on Hand-made Paper, 2s. each ; or Bound in Parchment, 3s. each.

3, WATERLOO PLACE, LONDON.

Plain Sermons on the Catechism.
By the Rev. Isaac Williams, B.D., late Fellow of Trinity College, Oxford; Author of a "Devotional Commentary on the Gospel Narrative." Two Vols. *New Edition.* Crown 8vo. 5s. each. *Sold separately.*

Sermons preached for the most part in Manchester.
By the Rev. W. J. Knox Little, M.A., Canon Residentiary of Worcester, and Rector of S. Alban's, Manchester.
Second Edition. Crown 8vo. 7s. 6d.

Manuals of Religious Instruction.
Edited by John Pilkington Norris, D.D., Archdeacon of Bristol, and Canon Residentiary of Bristol Cathedral.
I. THE CATECHISM AND PRAYER BOOK.
II. THE OLD TESTAMENT.
III. THE NEW TESTAMENT.
New and Revised Editions. Small 8vo. 3s. 6d. each. *Sold separately.*

Sermons, Parochial and Occasional.
By J. B. Mozley, D.D., late Canon of Christ Church, and Regius Professor of Divinity in the University of Oxford.
Second Edition. Crown 8vo. 7s. 6d.

Thoughts on Personal Religion.
Being a Treatise on the Christian Life in its Two Chief Elements, Devotion and Practice.
By Edward Meyrick Goulburn, D.D., D.C.L., Dean of Norwich.
New Presentation Edition, elegantly printed on Toned Paper.
Two Vols. Small 8vo. 10s. 6d.
An Edition in one Vol., 6s. 6d. ; *also a Cheap Edition*, 3s. 6d.

A Plain Exposition of the Thirty-nine
Articles of the Church of England, for the Use of Schools.
By William Baker, D.D., Head Master of Merchant Taylors' School, and Prebendary of S. Paul's.
16mo. 2s. 6d.

Lyra Apostolica.
[Poems by J. W. BOWDEN, R. H. FROUDE, J. KEBLE, J. H. NEWMAN, R. I. WILBERFORCE, and I. WILLIAMS ; with a New Preface by CARDINAL NEWMAN.]
New Edition. With red borders. 16mo. 2s. 6d.

3, WATERLOO PLACE, LONDON.

Prayers for a Young Schoolboy.
By the Rev. E. B. Pusey, D.D. Edited, with a Preface, by H. P. Liddon, D.D., Canon Residentiary of S. Paul's.
Large type. Second Edition. 24mo. 1s.

Maxims and Gleanings from the
Writings of **Edward Bouverie Pusey, D.D.** Selected and arranged for daily use.
By C. M. S., Compiler of "Daily Gleanings of the Saintly Life," "Under the Cross," etc. With an Introduction by the Rev. M. F. Sadler, Rector of Honiton, Devon.
Second Edition. Crown 16mo. 2s.

Under the Cross.
Readings, Consolations, Hymns, etc., for the Sick; original and selected. Compiled by C. M. S. Edited by the Rev. M. F. Sadler, Prebendary of Wells, and Rector of Honiton, Devon.
Crown 8vo. 5s.

Lovest thou Me?
Thoughts on the Epistles for Holy Week.
By L. C. Skey, Author of "Comforted of God," "All your Care," etc. With an Introduction by the Rev. W. H. Hutchings, M.A., Rector of Kirkby Misperton, Yorkshire.
Crown 16mo. 2s.

Voices of Comfort.
Edited by the Rev. Thomas Vincent Fosbery, M.A., sometime Vicar of S. Giles's, Reading.
Sixth Edition. Crown 8vo. 7s. 6d.

The Beginnings of the Christian Church.
Lectures delivered in the Chapter-room of Winchester Cathedral.
By **William Henry Simcox**, M.A., Rector of Weyhill, Hants; late Fellow of Queen's College, Oxford.
Crown 8vo. 7s. 6d.

The Life of Christ.
By S. Bonaventure. Translated and edited by the Rev. W. H. Hutchings, M.A., Rector of Kirkby Misperton, Yorkshire.
Crown 8vo. 7s. 6d.

Life of Robert Gray, Bishop of Cape
Town, and Metropolitan of Africa.
Edited by his Son, the Rev. Charles N. Gray, M.A., Vicar of Helmsley, York.
With Frontispiece. New Edition, abridged. Crown 8vo. 7s. 6d.

3, WATERLOO PLACE, LONDON.

The Litany and the Commination Service.
From the Book of Common Prayer.
With Rubrics in red. Royal 8vo. 4s. 6d.

A Commentary on the Office for the
Ministration of Holy Baptism. Illustrated from Holy Scripture, Ancient Liturgies, and the Writings of Catholic Fathers, Doctors and Divines. By the Rev. H. W. Pereira, M.A., M.R.I.A., formerly Scholar of Trinity College, Dublin.
8vo. 14s.

The Mystery of the Passion of our Most
Holy Redeemer.
By the Rev. W. J. Knox Little, M.A., Canon Residentiary of Worcester, and Rector of S. Alban's, Manchester.
Second Edition. Crown 8vo. 3s. 6d.

The Lord's Table; or, Meditations on
the Holy Communion Office in the Book of Common Prayer. By the Rev. E. H. Bickersteth, M.A., Vicar of Christ Church, Hampstead, and Rural Dean.
16mo. 1s.; or Cloth extra, 2s.

Five Minutes.
Daily Readings of Poetry.
Selected by H. L. Sidney Lear, Editor of "For Days and Years," "Christian Biographies," etc.
Second Edition. 16mo. 3s. 6d

The Children's Saviour.
Instructions to Children on the Life of our Lord and Saviour Jesus Christ. By Edward Osborne (of the Society of S. John Evangelist), Assistant Minister of the Church of the Advent, Boston, Mass.
With Outline Illustrations. 16mo. 3s. 6d.

Precious Stones.
Collected by H. L. Sidney Lear. PEARLS—Grace. RUBIES—Nature. DIAMONDS—Art.
Three Vols. 32mo. 1s. each; or in Paper Cover, 6d. each.
Also a superior Edition, printed on Dutch Hand-made Paper, with red borders, Crown 16mo. 2s. each.
Also an Edition in One Volume, with red borders, 16mo. 3s. 6d.

3, WATERLOO PLACE, LONDON.

The Collects of the Day.

An Exposition, Critical and Devotional, of the Collects appointed at the Communion. With Preliminary Essays on their Structure, Sources, and General Character; and Appendices containing Expositions of the Discarded Collects of the First Prayer Book of 1549, and of the Collects of Morning and Evening Prayer.

By **Edward Meyrick Goulburn**, D.D., D.C.L., Dean of Norwich.

Two Vols. Third Edition. Crown 8vo. 8s. each. Sold separately.

Thoughts upon the Liturgical Gospels

for the Sundays, one for each day in the year. With an introduction on their origin, history, the modifications made in them by the Reformers and by the Revisers of the Prayer Book, the honour always paid to them in the Church, and the proportions in which they are drawn from the Writings of the Four Evangelists.

By **Edward Meyrick Goulburn**, D.D., D.C.L., Dean of Norwich.

Two Vols. Crown 8vo. 16s.

Yesterday, To-Day, and For Ever.

A Poem in Twelve Books.

By **Edward Henry Bickersteth**, M.A., Vicar of Christ Church, Hampstead, and Rural Dean.

One Shilling Edition, 18mo; With red borders, 16mo, 2s. 6d. The Small 8vo. Edition may still be had, 3s. 6d.

Weariness.

A Book for the Languid and Lonely.

By **H. L. Sidney Lear**, Editor of "For Days and Years," "Christian Biographies," etc.

Large Type. Third Edition. Small 8vo. 5s.

The Apostolic Liturgy and the Epistle

to the Hebrews: Being a Commentary on the Epistle in its Relation to the Holy Eucharist, with Appendices on the Liturgy of the Primitive Church.

By **John Edward Field**, M.A., Vicar of Benson.

Crown 8vo. 12s.

After Death.

An Examination of the testimony of Primitive Times respecting the State of the Faithful Dead, and the Relationship to the Living.

By **Herbert Mortimer Luckock**, D.D, Canon of Ely, &c.

Fourth Edition. Crown 8vo. 6s.

3, WATERLOO PLACE, LONDON.

The Organization of the Early Christian Churches.
Eight Lectures delivered before the University of Oxford in the year 1880. On the Foundation of the late Rev. John Bampton, M.A., Canon of Salisbury.
By **Edwin Hatch**, M.A., D.D., Vice-Principal of S. Mary Hall, Grinfield, Lecturer on the Septuagint, Oxford, and Rector of Purleigh.
Second Edition. 8vo. 10s. 6d.

A Narrative of Events connected with
the Publication of the "Tracts for the Times." With an Introduction and Supplement extending to the Present Time.
By **William Palmer**, Author of "Origines Liturgicæ," etc.
Crown 8vo. 7s. 6d.

Corpus Christi.
A Manual of Devotion for the Blessed Sacrament.
With a Preface by the Rev. **H. Montagu Villiers**, Vicar of S. Paul's, Wilton Place.
With red borders. Royal 32mo. 2s.

All your Care.
By **L. C. Skey**, Author of "Comforted of God: Thoughts for Mourners."
With a Preface by the Rev. R. W. Randall, M.A., Vicar of All Saints, Clifton.
32mo. 1s.

Maxims and Gleanings from the
Writings of **John Keble**, M.A. Selected and arranged for daily use.
By **C. M. S.**, Compiler of "Daily Gleanings of the Saintly Life," "Under the Cross," etc. With an Introduction by the Rev. M. F. Sadler, Rector of Honiton, Devon.
Crown 16mo. 2s.

Guides and Goads,
An English Translation of ETHICA et SPIRITUALIA. Being short Sayings from the Fathers and other Ancient Authors.
By **Chr. Wordsworth**, D.D., Bishop of Lincoln.
Crown 16mo. 1s. 6d.

Here and There.
Quaint Quotations. A Book of Wit.
Selected by **H. L. Sidney Lear**, Editor of "For Days and Years," "The Life of S. Francis de Sales," etc., etc.
Crown 8vo. 5s.

3, WATERLOO PLACE, LONDON.

The Children's Hymn Book.

For use in Children's Services, Sunday Schools, and Families, arranged in order of the Church's Year.
Published under the revision of the Right Rev. W. Walsham How, Bishop Suffragan for East London; the Right Rev. Ashton Oxenden, late Bishop of Montreal and Metropolitan of Canada; and the Rev. John Ellerton, Rector of Barnes.

   A. *Royal 32mo, Sewed*, 1d.; *Cloth limp*, 2d.
   B. *Royal 32mo, Cloth*, 1s.; *Cloth extra*, 1s. 6d.
   C. *With Music, Crown 8vo, Cloth*, 3s.; *Cloth extra*, 3s. 6d.

The Vision of the Holy Child.

An Allegory.
By **Edith S. Jacob**, Author of "The Gate of Paradise."
With Illustration. Square 16mo. 1s. 6d.

Characteristics and Motives of the Christian Life.

Ten Sermons preached in Manchester Cathedral in Lent and Advent, 1877.
By the Rev. **W. J. Knox Little**, M.A., Canon Residentiary of Worcester, and Rector of S. Alban's, Manchester.
Third Edition. Crown 8vo. 3s. 6d.

The Annotated Bible.

Being a Household Commentary upon the Holy Scriptures, comprehending the Results of Modern Discovery and Criticism.
By **John Henry Blunt**, D.D., F.S.A., Editor of "The Annotated Book of Common Prayer," etc.
Three Vols. With Maps, etc. Demy 4to. Sold separately.
   Vol. I. (668 pages.) Containing the GENERAL INTRODUCTION, with Text and Annotations on the Books from GENESIS to ESTHER. 31s. 6d.
   Vol. II. (720 pages.) Completing the OLD TESTAMENT and APOCRYPHA. 31s. 6d.
   Vol. III. (826 pages.) Containing the NEW TESTAMENT and GENERAL INDEX. 21s.

Henri Dominique Lacordaire.

A Biographical Sketch.
By **H. L. Sidney Lear**, Author of "Christian Biographies," etc.
With Frontispiece. Second Edition. Crown 8vo. 7s. 6d.

3, WATERLOO PLACE, LONDON.

The Witness of the Passion of our Most
Holy Redeemer.
By the Rev. W. J. Knox Little, M.A., Canon Residentiary of Worcester, and Rector of S. Alban's, Manchester.
Crown 8vo. 3s. 6d.

Thoughts for Holy Days and Vigils.
Original and Selected.
With a Preface by the Lord Bishop of Derry.
16mo. 2s. 6d.

The Confessions of S. Augustine.
In Ten Books.
Translated and Edited by the Rev. W. H. Hutchings, M.A., Rector of Kirkby Misperton, Yorkshire.
Cheap Edition. 16mo. 2s. 6d.
Also with red borders. Small 8vo. 5s.

The Life of Justification:
A Series of Lectures delivered in Substance at All Saints', Margaret Street.
By the Rev. George Body, M.A., Canon of Durham.
Sixth Edition. Crown 8vo. 4s. 6d.

The Life of Temptation:
A Course of Lectures delivered in Substance at S. Peter's, Eaton Square; also at All Saints', Margaret Street.
By the Rev. George Body, M.A., Canon of Durham.
Fifth Edition. Crown 8vo. 4s. 6d.

Christian Womanhood and Christian
Sovereignty.
By Chr. Wordsworth, D.D., Bishop of Lincoln.
Crown 16mo. 1s.

A Church History.
By Chr. Wordsworth, D.D., Bishop of Lincoln.
Four Vols. Crown 8vo. Sold separately.
Vol. I. To the Council of Nicæa, A.D. 325. *Third Edition.* 8s. 6d
Vol. II. To the Council of Constantinople, A.D. 381. *Second Edition.* 6s.
Vols. III. & IV.—From the Council of Constantinople, A.D. 381, to the Council of Chalcedon, A.D. 451; with Index to the Whole Work. 6s. *each Volume.*

3, WATERLOO PLACE, LONDON.

Thoughts on the prescribed use of Bread

and Wine in the Lord's Supper. By a Communicant. Edited by the Rev. R. W. Johnson, M.A., Vicar of S. Giles', Packwood, Warwickshire.

8vo. *Paper Cover*, 1s.

Edward Bouverie Pusey.

A Sermon preached in St. Margaret's Church, Prince's Road, Liverpool, in Aid of the Pusey Memorial Fund, on Sunday, January 20, 1884. By H. P. Liddon, D.D., D.C.L., Canon Residentiary of S. Paul's.

8vo. *Paper Cover.* 6d.

The S.P.C.K. and the Creed of Saint

Athanasius. Remarks upon some recent action of the Christian Knowledge Society, together with a digest of evidence proving the Creed to be earlier than the Ninth Century.

By G. D. W. Ommanney, M.A., Vicar of Draycot, Somerset; Author of "The Athanasian Creed: an Examination of Recent Theories respecting its Date and Origin," and of "Early History of the Athanasian Creed."

8vo. *Paper Cover*, 1s.

Solitude and Sympathy in the presence of

Death. A Sermon preached in Quebec Chapel on Sunday, March 30, 1884, with reference to the Death of H.R.H. Prince Leopold, Duke of Albany. By the Rev. Edward Bickersteth Ottley, M.A., Minister of Quebec Chapel.

8vo. *Paper Cover.* 6d.

What says the Bible as to Marrying a

Deceased Wife's Sister.
By the Rev. Daniel A. Beaufort, M.A., formerly Rector of Lymn-with-Warburton, Cheshire.

Crown 8vo. *Sewed.* 3d.

True Temperance, as taught by the Bible.

By M. A. Austen Leigh.

Crown 8vo. *Sewed.* 3d.

Sobriety.

Teachings of Holy Scripture on this subject applied to recent developments of the Temperance Movement.
By the Rev. C. Lambert Coghlan, M.A., Vicar of Marchwood, Hants.

Crown 8vo. *Sewed.* 3d.

3, WATERLOO PLACE, LONDON.

The Fiftieth Year of the Reformation of

the Nineteenth Century. A Sermon, in three parts, preached in the Church of All Saints', Margaret Street, on the first three Sundays of November, 1883. By **Berdmore Compton**, Vicar.

8vo. Paper Cover, 1s.

Marriage, as affected by the Proposed

Change in the Marriage Laws. A Letter addressed to English Wives. By **Edith Mary Shaw**.

8vo. Paper Cover. 1s.

A Charge.

Delivered at his third Triennial Visitation to the Clergy of the Diocese of St. David's, October 17-24, 1883. By **William Basil Jones**, D.D., Lord Bishop of St. David's.

8vo. Paper Cover, 1s.

The Church in Wales.

A Retrospect and a Defence. By **John Morgan**, Rector of Llanilid and Llanharan, Glamorganshire.

8vo. Paper Cover, 1s.

The Foreign Church Chronicle and

Review. Published Quarterly.

8vo. 1s. 6d. each Number.

The Church Builder.

A Quarterly Record of the work of the Incorporated Church Building Society, and of other works of Church extension.

8vo. 3d. each Number.

The Question of Incest relatively to

Marriage with Sisters in Succession. By **Henry H. Duke**, Rector of Brixton Deverill, Wilts.

Second Edition. 8vo. Paper Cover, 6d.

3, WATERLOO PLACE, LONDON.

The Annotated Book of Common Prayer.

Being an Historical, Ritual, and Theological Commentary on the Devotional System of the Church of England.
Edited by the Rev. **John Henry Blunt**, D.D., F.S.A., Author of "The History of the Reformation," "The Annotated Bible," etc., etc.
Revised and Enlarged Edition. 4to. £1 1s.;
or, Half-bound in Morocco, £1 11s. 6d.

Private Prayers.

By the Rev. **E. B. Pusey**, D.D. Edited, with a Preface, by **H. P. Liddon**, D.D., Canon Residentiary of S. Paul's.
Second Edition. Royal 32mo. 2s. 6d.

Conjectural Emendations of Passages in

Ancient Authors, and other Papers.
By **Chr. Wordsworth**, D.D., Bishop of Lincoln.
8vo. 4s.

Lectures on the Industrial Revolution in

England. Popular Addresses, Notes, and other Fragments.
By the late **Arnold Toynbee**, Tutor of Balliol College, Oxford.
Together with a Short Memoir by **B. Jowett**, Master of Balliol College, Oxford.
8vo. 10s. 6d.

The Limits of Individual Liberty.

An Essay.
By **Francis C. Montague**, M.A., Fellow of Oriel College, Oxford.
8vo. [*In the Press.*

Sophocles.

Translated into English Verse.
By **Robert Whitelaw**, Assistant Master in Rugby School; late Fellow of Trinity College, Cambridge.
Crown 8vo. 8s. 6d.

The Annual Register.

A Review of Public Events at Home and Abroad, for the Year 1883.
8vo. 18s.

3, WATERLOO PLACE, LONDON.

www.ingramcontent.com/pod-product-compliance
Lightning Source LLC
Chambersburg PA
CBHW051851300426
44117CB00006B/347